THIEVES OF BAGHDAD

Praise for *Thieves of Baghdad*

"Bogdanos is a remarkable blend of warrior, academic, and communicator, and he cuts through politics and hyperbole to tell an engrossing story abundant with history, colored by stories of brave Iraqis and Americans, and shaded with hope for the future."   —*Publishers Weekly*

"Fascinating."   —*Oregonian* (Editor's Pick)

"Warrior and prosecutor, classicist and amateur boxer, Marine Col. Matthew Bogdanos faced one of the great legal and investigative challenges . . . getting to the bottom of the plunder of the National Museum of Iraq."   —*Chicago Tribune*

"Bogdanos . . . has pursued the missing Iraqi antiquities with the same relentless fervor that earned him the nickname 'Pit Bull' from the New York tabloids for his dogged prosecution of high-profile defendants like hip-hop impresario Sean Combs."   —*Art News*

"When the history of the Iraq war is written, Col. Matthew Bogdanos will undoubtedly be owed a debt beyond reckoning by scholars."

—*Palm Beach Post*

"Admits us to a world as only the greatest novelists, the Tolstoys and Flauberts, are able to do."   —*Seattle Weekly*

"Bogdanos writes with swagger and a sense of humor coated with searing wit."   —*Canadian Broadcasting Corporation*

"It is certain to get your undivided attention and keep it. *Thieves of Baghdad* . . . is one of those rare books that will keep you guessing as to what lies ahead on the next page (or even paragraph). It is a book that will inform, entertain, and make you think."   —*Armchair General*

"The book offers a fast-paced and insightful accounting of the marine's experience and code of behavior, as well as a riveting chapter on how he raced to rescue his wife and children from their apartment building near the World Trade Center."   —*Montreal Gazette*

"Stolen priceless artifacts, cobwebbed hidden tunnels, an irresistible mystery, and an unstoppable hero. Best of all? It really happened. An incisive, penetrating look at what it truly takes to catch a thief. From war-torn Baghdad to the beauty of Babylon, Bogdanos doesn't just investigate—he attacks, dissects, and reassembles like an obsessive master puzzlemaker."   —*New York Times* bestselling author Brad Meltzer

"*Thieves of Baghdad* is a riveting adventure, packed with wartime intrigue, the unique insights of a brave combatant, and the candor and humor of someone quite comfortable on the front lines, at home and abroad . . . Bogdanos is a real-life hero, a scholar, and a natural-born storyteller, and he proves it all in this gripping new book."

—*New York Times* bestselling author Linda Fairstein

"A hybrid of Indiana Jones, T. E. Lawrence, and Zorba the Greek, Colonel Bogdanos narrates the story of his youth with poignant humor and tragedy . . . His chapter on 9/11 . . . is a vivid, gripping first-person account of tragedy and survival . . . and his Sherlock Holmes-like investigator's maxims have the ring of authenticity . . . His experiences are interesting, his dance of life lively, and his perspective on honor and the warrior's code commendable."

—*U.S. Navy Institute Proceedings*

"Col. Matthew Bogdanos—infantryman, scholar, amateur boxer, and one-time waiter at his father's Greek restaurant . . . makes his way through postwar Baghdad quoting everyone from Cicero to samurais. He seems to operate at twice the speed of the world around him."

—*Associated Press*

"Matthew Bogdanos . . . has been described, with only a minimum of hyperbole, as a real-life Indiana Jones."   —*Independent* (UK)

"When thousands of antiquities were looted from Baghdad's Iraq Museum, US Marine Matthew Bogdanos pledged to get them back. After two years of sleuthing he has become a national hero."

—*Guardian* (UK)

"Bogdanos writes *Thieves of Baghdad* with the character . . . of a great Agatha Christie mystery novel . . . His candor and humility in relaying this story make *Thieves of Baghdad* an intimate portrait of the Marine efforts in Iraq."   —*Navy Leaguer*

"A riveting, dramatically paced tale . . . With refreshing candor, Bogdanos appraises the difficulties of diplomacy, intelligence gathering, and dealing with the media in a combat zone, and assesses formidable obstacles to international prosecution of illicit cross-border trafficking."

—*School Library Journal*

"A Hollywood writer could not have created a better plot."

—*Marine Times*

THIEVES OF BAGHDAD

*One Marine's Passion to Recover
the World's Greatest Stolen Treasures*

MATTHEW BOGDANOS
WITH WILLIAM PATRICK

BLOOMSBURY

Photo credits: Plates 1, 2, 5, 8, 11–14, 16–18, 29, 30, 32–36, 38: Matthew Bogdanos.
Plates 3, 4, 6, 9, 10, 15, 19, 21–23: Roberto Pineiro.
Plate 37: Richard Confalone. Plates 7, 20, 26: © Scala/Art Resource, NY.
Plate 24: © D. G. Youkhana. Plate 25: photo by Bill Lyons, www.billlyons.com. Plates
27, 28: © Lynn Abercrombie. Plate 31: photo by Helene C. Stikkel.

Maps and diagrams by James Sinclair

Published by Bloomsbury USA, New York
Distributed to the trade by Holtzbrinck Publishers

All papers used by Bloomsbury USA are natural, recyclable products made
from wood grown in well-managed forests. The manufacturing processes
conform to the environmental regulations of the country of origin.

The Library of Congress has cataloged the hardcover edition of this book as follows:

Bogdanos, Matthew.
Thieves of Baghdad : one marine's passion to recover the world's greatest stolen
treasures / Matthew Bogdanos with William Patrick.—1st U.S. ed.
p. cm.
Includes index.
ISBN-13: 978-1-58234-645-8 (hardcover)
ISBN-10: 1-58234-645-3 (hardcover)
1. Iraq War, 2003—Destruction and pillage. 2. Iraq War, 2003—Personal narratives,
American. 3. Archaeological thefts—Iraq. 4. Iraq—Antiquities.
5. Matòhaf al-'Iråaqåi. 6. Thieves—Iraq. I. Patrick, William Dennis, 1948–
II. Title.

DS79.76.B635 2005
956.7044'31—dc22
2005027652

Paperback ISBN-10: 1-59691-146-8
ISBN-13: 978-1-59691-146-8

First published in the United States by Bloomsbury in 2005
This paperback edition published in 2006

1 3 5 7 9 10 8 6 4 2

Typeset by Westchester Book Group
Printed in the United States of America by Quebecor World Fairfield

This book is dedicated to the four proofs of God's existence: Michael, Diana, Jason, and Nicole. There may be other such proofs, but these are mine. And to Claudia, who makes everything possible.

All translations from Greek and Latin are by Matthew Bogdanos.

CONTENTS

Color plates, maps, and diagrams
follow page 134.

Author's Note

The Marine Corps doesn't like people who go to war and write books about themselves. Neither do I. To a Marine, one of the finest words in the English language is *team*. "MacArthur" took the Philippines, "Patton" raced across the French countryside, and "Nimitz" won the Battle of Midway. But "Marines" raised the flag on Iwo Jima, "Marines" fought and froze at the Choisin Reservoir, and "Marines" held Khe Sanh against all odds.

These may be my memories, then, but this book is *not* about me. It *is* about an Iraqi people whose warmth and hospitality in inviting me into their homes and hearts will stay with me always, about Afghan women discarding their bhurkas and Afghan children singing verses from the Koran, and about why a bunch of old rocks with funny writing matter so damn much.

Although some of our actions in Iraq and Afghanistan remain classified, I do my best in the pages that follow to present what I saw and heard as completely as possible—*with* candor and *without* bias or agenda. But in a part of the world where the few official records were often destroyed or falsified, and where people have lived under terror for so long, it is difficult to elicit and confirm truth. Some of my findings, therefore, are incomplete. As time passes and more facts come to light, others may prove inaccurate. These are, after all, memories and impressions. But however history judges the investigation into the looting of the Iraq Museum, the successes belong to the remarkable people who appear on these pages. I am merely the vehicle through which their extraordinary actions are made public.

There is courage to celebrate here. It is the courage of soldiers, sailors, airmen, and Marines; of Iraqis and Afghans; of customs agents and archaeologists; of cops and journalists.

Only the errors are mine. The story is theirs.

New York, New York
October 2005

1

IN MEDIAS RES

Men never know the good that was in their
hands until they've lost it.—Sophocles

O N MAY 2, 2003, I was working my way through Iraq's national museum in the heart of Baghdad, investigating the rampage and the looting that had taken place during the war. With me
were other members of the multiservice, multiagency unit that I led,
military trigger-pullers and analysts teamed up with law enforcement
officers from a dozen other agencies.

As we passed through the museum's long, central corridor—the
musty, poorly lit room that had just been on the cover of *Newsweek*—
our guide was Dr. Nawala al-Mutwali, the museum's director. We
stepped over rubble and shattered glass, cracked sarcophagi, and the
broken heads of ancient statues. The large objects that had fared better
were surrounded by sandbags or wrapped in foam-rubber padding.

While most people found Nawala to be dour and difficult, we had
become friends. In fact, our affection for each other was so obvious
that the team joked relentlessly about my carrying on some mad affair
with this imposing and somewhat older woman.

After two weeks of laborious, room-by-room inspections, we were
ready to examine the underground storage area, the first portion of the
museum that was virgin territory, completely undisturbed since the
looting. That meant our first clean crime scene and the possibility of a

significant investigative breakthrough. We might even get something we had seen little of so far: evidence. On that day, we had a BBC film crew tagging along. They wanted the story, and I wanted to be able to use their footage to document our findings. Like everything else in a war zone, their presence was a quid pro quo, a horse trade.

The list of missing objects already read like a compilation of Mesopotamia's "greatest hits." There was the Sacred Vase of Warka, the world's oldest carved stone ritual vessel. There was the Mask of Warka, the first naturalistic sculpture of the human face. There was the gold bull's head that had adorned Queen Shub-Ad's Golden Harp of Ur, discovered in 1929 by a team that included Sir Leonard Woolley, Sir Max Mallowan, and Mallowan's future wife, Agatha Christie. There was the Bassetki Statue, one of the earliest known examples of the lost-wax technique of casting copper, as well as the Lioness-attacking-a-Nubian ivory, and the twin copper Ninhursag bulls. These pieces alone were a year's course in art history. They were all in one museum. And they were all gone.

We had repeatedly tried to open the heavy, steel doors that would lead us down into the basement. So had the looters—some of the doors bore sledgehammer marks. Others were covered over by heavy grates wrapped with the kind of cable locks we use in Manhattan so that motorcycles stay put. Much later, watching the BBC footage while back home, I noted how one of Nawala's AK-47-toting assistants showed up behind me with a set of keys. The museum had this curious arrangement of separate, but overlapping, circles of security, born out of their even more curious system of centralized authority and palpable interdepartmental animosities. Not only did staff from one department have no idea about the inventories or practices of other departments, no one person had the keys to every sector. None of the keys were ever marked, and this set was no exception. Nawala had to try every single one, and even then she could not find the key that would get us into the sanctum sanctorum of the underground storage room.

We took the difficulty as cause for optimism. Actually, given that this area held some of the museum's most highly valuable and most easily transportable objects, it was closer to elation. If we couldn't get in, chances are the bad guys hadn't either.

As we would later determine, there were four underground rooms in an L-shaped configuration, plus a fifth that had to be accessed through a different route. In the deepest, darkest corner were two rows of ordinary, unmarked lockers that would have fit right in at the gym in New York City where I'd learned to box. Only instead of sweaty workout clothes, these held the world's greatest collection of ancient gold and silver coins. In these same brown and beat-up lockers, in the same dark corner, was also the world's greatest collection of ancient cylinder seals, highly prized by collectors and, accordingly, highly prized by thieves. About the size of a piece of chalk, these intricately carved pieces of lapis lazuli, carnelian, or other stone had once been worn on a string around the neck by upscale citizens of ancient Mesopotamia. These were the people who'd invented writing, scratching wedge-shaped (*cuneus forma* in Latin; hence, *cuneiform*) symbols into soft clay with a stylus beginning about 5,500 years ago. As the final touch to any correspondence, they would use the seal the way my grandmother used a rolling pin to smooth out phyllo. The impression left in the soft clay by the inscribed seal was the distinctive "signature" of that individual.

Nawala, a descendant of these ancient and inventive people, was one tough lady—I had watched her break her toe just a few days earlier and not utter a sound. On that day, we had also been trying to open a locked door, one that was ten inches thick. When it finally gave, she could have jumped back out of the way, but in doing so she would have touched me—a violation of *sharia*, the religious law. So she stayed put, the heavy steel door raked across her toe, and she silently crumbled into herself, biting one of her thumbs.

In the hot glare of the BBC's cameras, Nawala was frustrated by the endless number of unmarked keys. I heard her mutter to herself in Arabic. Then, in English, she said, "There is the other way."

I glanced at my guys from ICE, the Bureau of Immigration and Customs Enforcement.

"It has been sealed off with bricks," she said. "So there is no way anyone could enter." I didn't know if it was the custom in Iraq, but my thought was, "knock on wood when you say that."

This back door Nawala told us about was at the bottom of a narrow stairwell, accessed from a landing just off a room displaying Roman antiquities from Hatra. Those are the ruins of an ancient commercial crossroads that you see in the opening scene from *The Exorcist* when a Mesopotamian demon escapes from an archaeological dig.

We went through the Assyrian and Babylonian galleries and entered the Hatran Gallery. All we noticed at first were some three-foot-high partitions in front of a doorway in the corner. After walking closer, we moved the partitions. The lower portion of the locked glass door was smashed, and behind that, down about knee level, the steel grate across the door had been bent with a crowbar.

Nawala threw up her hands, gasping out the Arabic equivalent of "Oh my God!" The small area beyond the glass door was like a broom closet beneath a stairway. In fact, the underside of the museum's main stairs passed overhead, ascending from right to left. But immediately inside the small alcove, to the right, was another, extremely narrow stairway going down to the basement. At the bottom of this narrow stairs, the metal door was wide-open, but—as we had come to expect by now—there were no signs that it had been forced open. We could see the cinder blocks that had been mortared into place behind this door to seal the actual opening itself. We could also see that two cinder blocks from the top row, and two from the second row had been pried loose and removed. At this point, we asked the BBC crew to stay behind and politely appropriated their equipment.

Steve Mocsary, the senior ICE agent on my team, picked up the big Ampex camera and started filming. His most immediate purpose, though, was to direct the TV lights into the cavernous area beyond the doorway, as Bud Rogers and I prepared to go over the wall.

Bud was also ICE, as well as former Army Special Forces. He had been on a classified operation in Romania when we'd first entered Iraq, but as soon as we decided to undertake the museum investigation, Steve told me Bud was the best in the business and requested permission to bring him in country. One phone call later, Bud was getting off a Blackhawk, and I learned quickly that Steve had not been exaggerating.

For his own part, Steve may have been a bit long in the tooth—this was certainly his last shot in the field before a desk job and then retirement—but he was no slouch. A former Navy SEAL and veteran of UDT, the Navy's elite underwater demolition team, he was tough and seasoned, utterly unflappable, and he knew explosives.

The hole in the cinder blocks was big enough for only one of us to go through at a time. On the other side of the wall, the stairway continued on down. I went first, like a diver—head foremost, arms extended. I'd like to say that I landed in a perfect combat roll with catlike reflexes, peering into the unknown darkness, my 9 mm poised and ready to fell any evildoer with a double tap to center mass. In fact, I landed in a clump and scratched both elbows—but at least my pistol was ready.

Then Bud Rogers dropped down beside me.

In Iraq, every place at every moment is hotter than hell, but underground it was hotter than the hinges of hell, specifically, the hinges of Dante's eighth circle, the one he reserved for thieves and hypocrites to suffer together for eternity. The room was airless and, aside from the BBC camera's light shining over my head, pitch-dark. Steve maneuvered the beam so we could assess the situation before we moved. We could not be 100 percent certain that we were alone down here, and holding a flashlight in front of your body is like wearing a nice big target pinned to your chest.

I looked ahead and tried not to blink as the salty sweat trickled down, burning my eyes. Then I saw footprints in the dust making a beeline across the floor. These thieves had a clear idea of where they were going and, presumably, what they were after: the coins and the cylinder seals, some of which were worth $250,000 a pop. Given their size, anyone could carry off a million dollars' worth in a single fanny pack.

What I didn't know was whether they had reached their objective. But of more immediate concern, had they left any surprises for us? We had found rocket-propelled grenades, hand grenades, Iraqi uniforms, and assorted small arms scattered throughout the museum. This last corner of the basement would have been an excellent place to leave a parting gift wired with explosives.

As an investigator, I was thinking about that straight line in the dust. As a Marine, I was thinking about rods, cones, and night vision—in the dark you're supposed to look slightly off-center—and trigger pull. As a classical-history buff, passing sarcophagi and amphorae I was thinking, "Wow, this is like the catacombs."

Slowly, and with great care, we crept down the few remaining steps and followed the path of the footprints. The smell of damp clay was overpowering. We stayed just astride the beam of Steve's camera light, which showed the way ahead, but only directly ahead. We went as far as we could in that one direction, dust motes swirling above us like snowflakes. Then we turned around and retraced our steps.

I had dispatched a couple of other ICE guys—Claude Davenport, our computer whiz, and Bud Adada, one of three fluent Arabic speakers on the team—to wire up the basement to our generator outside. We needed to get the lights back on before we started exploring more broadly. Unfortunately, air-conditioning was not an option.

Once we were back to the sealed doorway on the stairs, Steve extended a meter-long pry bar through the small opening. It would have been much easier to break down the wall from the outside, but the steel bar was too long to maneuver in the narrow space. The guys who last passed this way had been better prepared. Somehow, they knew to bring a hammer and chisel.

Doing the best we could from the inside out, Bud and I took turns chipping away at the mortar holding those big, gray cinder blocks. It took us over an hour to loosen another seven or eight rows, removing enough blocks for the rest of the team, including Nawala to make it through. We generated buckets of sweat, as well as buckets of dust and rubble, sucking down water and struggling to breathe.

When the wall was about knee-high, Nawala climbed over. Her two assistants with the AK-47s seemed eager to tag along. One of them raced forward, but I put my hand on his chest and he stopped. He looked at me, I looked at him, and he backed down. But not out of fear. He was acknowledging the obvious: that I was in charge—for now. He was also letting me know that my authority did not extend beyond this moment. In that one look, we understood each other perfectly. In other circumstances, we would each go for the trigger, and I made a mental note never to turn my back on him.

"I had no idea," Nawala muttered to herself in Arabic as she followed on my heels. "No idea," she repeated in English, ostensibly for me.

We were doing it my way. In single file, stepping in the footprints already made. Even before we had passed through the first room, she had begun to hyperventilate. Her face was flushed, but not just from the heat. It was as if she had a child trapped down here, and she had to know if that child were dead or alive. It did not help that she was covered from head to toe, including the *khimar* that swathed her head.

The overhead lights were on now, and we could easily make out the footprints leading into the next room. We could also see that while everything in this storage area was filthy, dusty, dank, and cram-packed with pots and statuettes, it was also totally, and incongruously, undisturbed. Clearly, the people who had entered before us were not impulse shoppers. They knew exactly where they were going.

We continued following the footprints, turned a corner, and then it was as if we had crossed paths with a tornado. The entire floor was strewn with what were, essentially, plastic fishing-tackle boxes. Some were upside down, some had been flung aside, and others had been smashed into the walls. It looked as if the intruders had simply thrown a fit. Remnants of burned foam-rubber padding lay on the floor everywhere, still giving off an acrid smell. And behind all this, standing silently, were the thirty brown storage cabinets containing the coins and the seals.

The first of these cabinets stood open and empty.

Nawala went down on one knee. She had hoped against hope that the looters had failed, but now that hope seemed dashed.

Bud Rogers pulled over a chair for her and she sat down. Then her head listed to one side and she hit the floor.

I motioned to Steve to turn off the camera. I also noticed that a couple of the BBC guys were following us now at a distance. "Clear the room!" I yelled. Then I sent for Claude, our computer whiz, who was also an EMT, an emergency medical technician.

I knelt down and touched Nawala's face. She was out cold. Her skin felt clammy, and she had only the faintest suggestion of a pulse. She was in shock—acute circulatory failure, with barely enough blood pressure to transport oxygen to the brain. And it doesn't take much of this before brain cells start dying from hypoxia.

We elevated her feet and fanned her face, but she gave no response. Claude came running and knelt down beside her. He was around Steve's age and I could see the sweat soaking his graying goatee. He looked her over. Then he turned to me and said, "Colonel, she might go out of the picture."

Now I was the one feeling light-headed. Nawala and I had become close. But it was also true that if she died, we were in deep trouble. I could see the headlines now: FAMED IRAQI EXPERT DIES IN U.S. CUSTODY.

"We've got to get her headgear off," Claude said.

That much was obvious. But I also knew that Nawala was no "Ash Wednesday, Palm Sunday" sort of Muslim. I thought back to the way she had broken her toe to avoid touching me. For all the hours we'd worked together and the friendship we'd struck—and my team's nonstop "girlfriend" jokes notwithstanding—she and I had never so much as shaken hands. My team's mission in Baghdad was delicate enough without scandalizing Muslim sensibilities.

"We've got to get some women down here," I said.

Bud Rogers took off, running back up to the main floor, looking for some of the girls who were conducting the inventory of what was left of the museum's collection.

Trying to carry Nawala up to the first floor would be a sure way to kill her. In fact, given the absurdly narrow stairs, we were not at all sure that we *could* carry her back up to the first floor. We had no choice but to revive her where she was. But for that, we had to get her out from under all that fabric so she could breathe. If the female assistants had already left, we were screwed. Given the chaos that still reigned on the streets, their male relatives usually came to pick them up in the early afternoon so that they could make it home well before dusk.

Bud came back with two young women who spoke no English but still understood what we were asking them to do. They too were covered head to toe. One of them, in addition to the *khimar* covering her head, wore a scarf as a veil over her face.

Looking down at Nawala, they shook their heads, and I could see that their hands were trembling. Even as women they could not do this—uncover another Muslim woman's head in the presence of men, especially non-Muslim men.

I told all the guys except for Claude to turn their backs. While one of the women unbuttoned Nawala's jacket, it fell to me to remove her *khimar*. For whatever damage it would do to U.S.-Iraq relations, I also held her hand.

I remember wishing in that moment that I had learned enough Arabic to coax Nawala back to consciousness. Meanwhile, the other side of my brain was stressing over what was happening to my evidence. Rumors of Nawala's demise had brought museum staffers and even journalists creeping downstairs until there must have been forty people in the basement.

"Steve, crime scene," I yelled. It was all he needed to hear. Pro that he was, he got everyone to back out slowly, and in the same footprints that they had made when they'd entered.

I turned my focus back to Nawala, and waited.

Half an hour later, her eyes began to flutter. We let her take her time. She was still woozy, but she was going to recover. She wasn't ready to stand, but we helped her into a chair, positioning it so that she was not facing the cabinets. She kept turning around to look at them. So I came back to her several times to redirect her gaze, and each time I'd shift the chair. Then each time she would simply crane her neck still farther to look back at the lockers. By the time we were done, I had rotated her chair beyond the 180-degree mark, so that now she was looking back over her *other* shoulder.

It was another hour before Nawala was able to stand up and go home. This day's discoveries had come to an end. We would have to wait until she was in better shape to see what was or was not inside those cabinets.

I was desperate to know what was behind the rest of those cabinet doors, but we had to maintain discipline in assessing the only undisturbed crime scene in the entire museum. A rookie would have gone straight to the lockers the very next day, but then I would have put that rookie on a C-130 aircraft heading home before nightfall. We needed to bring in a proper forensic unit and have them with us the next time we went down there. A crime-scene analysis is like losing your virginity—you only get to do it once—because as you examine the evidence, you disturb the evidence. So we sealed up the entrance to the basement with crime-scene tape and went back upstairs.

This was a war zone halfway around the world, not the Manhattan District Attorney's Office, where I'd worked before September 11, and I had no idea what resources were available to me. At the very least, I needed a fingerprint unit and a forensic videographer. But I also wanted the ability to collect and analyze whatever else I might find: blood, fibers, skin, footprints—all the stuff you see on *CSI*—and I needed them all at the same place, i.e., the Iraq Museum, at the same time, i.e., as soon as possible. But I had no idea when that would be.

Given that some of the experts I needed might be in Frankfurt, some might be in London, and, for all I knew, some might be in Fort Hood, Texas, I knew that this could take a while to line up. And I didn't even know which agency had which of the necessary specialists available. And if they were coming to Iraq, they'd need anthrax shots. Were they up-to-date on their other vaccinations? And what if I needed a locksmith? Or luminol testing as a preliminary to blood analysis? Once you've picked up a piece of paper off the floor, you can't ask the rest of the team to stand like statues while you go find someone to check out the dried brown droplets underneath.

Practicalities aside, even the idea of requesting a crime-scene investigation team in a combat zone was highly unusual. So over the next several days, I received several calls on my satellite phone from perplexed officers. "Sorry, Colonel, but can you explain to me exactly what the hell you need, and why?"

And so the days passed and we did our job examining other rooms in the museum, all the while wanting to examine *that* room. For Nawala, life was governed by *Insha' Allah*. God's will. Where we tolerated the suspense through immersion in our work, she did so by resignation to Allah's plan.

Ten days later, on the morning of the twelfth, the assembled crime-scene technicians arrived, and we went back into the underground storage rooms to begin a methodical forensic investigation. Almost immediately, we recovered several readable sets of fingerprints from the doors of the lockers themselves. Two ICE agents later hand-delivered those prints to the FBI's lab in Quantico, Virginia, for comparison against all U.S. databases of known criminals, federal employees, and U.S. military personnel.

Meanwhile, we continued to play it by the book, assessing every square meter, one millimeter at a time, on our hands and knees with feather dusters.

On top of the lockers were small cardboard cartons stacked six feet high. A few had been knocked to the floor, but seemingly by accident. The rest were untouched, in sharp contrast to the 103 "tackle boxes" that had been thrown around and left on the floor.

More of these cardboard cartons rested atop a row of combination safes standing directly across from the lockers. Steel gray, manufactured in Germany, and evidently procured at great expense, they had never been used. In fact, they were still partially covered with clear plastic, like a new washer and dryer delivered from Sears. It would appear that they had been acquired to provide a more secure storage place for the goods that were in the lockers. So why had the coins and the cylinder seals never been transferred? And while we were at it, why had the thieves ransacked the tackle boxes but left the more numerous cardboard cartons undisturbed? Not until we took down the cartons and examined them did we discover that they were all empty. How could the looters have known that in advance? Judging from the evidence in front of us, they had not even bothered to check.

I was just beginning the mental calculation, trying to add up these random thoughts, when another ICE agent, Kevin Power, said, "Look what I found."

He pointed to a set of keys on a string, jumbled inside one of the plastic boxes.

We brought Nawala over to identify them. Slowly, hesitantly, she said, "They were hidden."

I said, "Show me where."

She took me to a dusty shelf in a remote corner of the room and pulled out a long drawer. She then showed me the place where the keys had been stuffed behind a fat collection of index cards. The cards were where they had always been. Neither they nor anything else in the drawer had been disturbed.

At this point, within the pinball machine inside my DA's head, the quarter finally dropped. The subterranean rampage that had left all this debris had already come into focus for me, and from the moment we discovered the breached wall I had no doubt we were dealing with an inside job. We had, however, just significantly narrowed the number of applicants for the position of suspect. Probably many dozens of people in the world knew what was in those cabinets but did not have enough knowledge to lay their hands on the keys. "Eliminate the impossible and whatever remains, however improbable, must be the truth," Sherlock Holmes had told Dr. Watson. Seeing the hiding place for the keys, we had eliminated an entire universe of archivists, archaeologists, and stock clerks as impossible, leaving—however improbable it might be—a small and select group of managers as possible suspects.

The scenario I had worked out so far went like this. There was no electricity while the thieves had been down here. After years of embargo, batteries were scarce in Iraq. So forget about flashlights. The bad guys had improvised. They had gone back up to the galleries where the staff had prepared for the invasion by sandbagging all the friezes and wrapping large pieces of foam rubber around the statues. The bad guys then brought some of these hunks of foam back downstairs, set fire to them, and tried to use them as torches. The fumes in that sealed basement must have been awful, not to mention the singed fingers. Maybe they got dizzy or even sick. But one thing we know for sure—one of them dropped the keys. Not only that—he dropped the keys into one of the 103 plastic tackle boxes that had been on the floor in front of the lockers. We found over four hundred cylinder seals left behind in those boxes, so very likely more had been taken. (Later, we would determine just how many.) But only inches away from one of the world's great treasures, some genius had screwed the pooch, and the rest of the gang had gone nuts in frustration, looking for that string of keys.

For the first time I allowed myself to feel a glimmer of hope. I nodded to the lockers, then asked Nawala, "Are you strong enough?"

She took a deep breath and said, "Yes, but we do it together."

"As you wish," I said.

I had made a little joke. *As you wish* was an expression she used again and again during our time together at the museum. You would have needed a shutter speed of about 1/800th of a second to capture it, but I believe Nawala smiled.

As we stood side by side, I inserted the key into the first lock, turned it, and opened the metal door. Nawala let out a shriek. Her knees buckled, but she held her ground.

All the gold and all the silver—more than one hundred thousand pieces—were exactly where they were supposed to be. As were the rows upon rows of exquisite cylinder seals, each revealing its delicately carved scene of ancient myths, ritual dances, and moments from ordinary life five thousand years ago.

My mouth dry and pulse thumping, I went down the line, opening each locker in turn. All thirty were untouched. Every last piece of treasure under lock and key was in its proper place.

Nawala began to sob, her chest heaving with relief. Setting aside, at least for a moment, more than thirteen hundred years of Islamic tradition, she also gave me a hug that I thought would break my neck.

2

PATTERN RECOGNITION

It is a sin to believe evil of others,
but it is seldom a mistake—H. L. Mencken

CRIME SCENES CAN tell you a lot about what happened during any outburst of greed or violence. But only if you listen.

When we'd arrived two weeks earlier, and I'd seen the infamous hole in the façade of the Children's Museum—the result of a single round fired from the 120 mm main gun of a U.S. M1A1 Abrams tank—I began to understand the world-wide condemnation. Then I saw the evidence. The tank gunner said that he fired only after someone had fired an RPG, rocket-propelled grenade, at him from that building. On the roof, we found a stash of RPGs and, inside, blood splatter whose pattern suggested that at least two Iraqis had been on the third floor when the round hit its mark(s).

In the aboveground storage area of the main museum, the damage near a window presented a similar pattern. One round from a Bradley fighting vehicle's 25 mm chain gun had penetrated the exterior wall and, according to our later reenactment, missed the sniper who had been set up at that spot by about eighteen inches at mid-thigh height.

In a career spent in law enforcement, I have learned that the art of investigation is largely about pattern recognition. The process is a pyramid with experience, intelligence (leavened by street smarts), and hard study (legal, forensic, and psychological) at its base. The next layer up is where you organize and analyze the raw data to narrow the universe of possibilities. At the top is the gut sense that lets you screen out the white noise and recognize the pattern. The gut, or intuition, is what lets you see the dots that others don't see. It also lets you connect those dots faster than the bad guys.

Using intuition, however, should never be confused with making assumptions. The former is essential; the latter is nothing more than intellectual laziness. Any time you assume, you close off avenues of possibility. Or you open up so many possibilities that your investigation swirls into chaos.

That said, intuition will not convict, and inference plays a role only when it is linking up empirical data to create a convincing "theory of the case." That's why investigators must proceed from hard evidence, following Holmes's rational process of eliminating possibilities. You begin with the entire universe, and eventually you narrow your focus to specific actions carried out by a specific suspect or team of suspects. Value judgments can freeze you, and politics can throw you off the mark. Nothing hinders a good investigation more than trying to affix moral labels such as *good* or *bad*, *right* or *wrong*, to the actions or actors in the mystery you are trying to solve.

Investigators do live in a binary universe, but we use a different calculus: Either you are lying or you are telling the truth. Either you did the act or you didn't. Either I can prove it or I can't. The "why" you did it is interesting only to the extent that it leads me to you in the first place, provides me with a hook to get you to confess, or allows me to prove at trial that you did it. The "why," as in you did it because of the emotional scars from a painful childhood, is an important consideration . . . to your therapist. To a good investigator, it is as irrelevant as skin color, religion, gender, sexual orientation, or political party.

In April 2003, when we arrived to assess the looting of antiquities from the Iraq Museum, assumptions were rampant. Everyone from Baghdad to Bristol had a theory, and moreover, everyone was pissed off. In the polarized atmosphere of the invasion, most of what my team of investigators had to go on was misinformation, exaggeration, and spin. The looting was an "inside job." It was American soldiers. It was the fifty thousand street criminals that Saddam Hussein had released from prison to greet the invaders. And then the theories got really sinister, even paranoid: It was the resident diplomats. It was a worldwide conspiracy of Bond Street and Madison Avenue art dealers who had been preparing for a decade, just waiting for another American assault.

The most fundamental distortion about the looting, however, was the scope of what had occurred. Launching reporters off into the ozone was an initial report that 170,000 items had been stolen—an estimate, we quickly determined, that overshot the mark by a factor of more than ten.

But even if the initial press reports had not been so wildly exaggerated, our first task would have remained the same: going from room to room, shelf by shelf, trying to determine exactly what had been taken and what remained, all the while searching for evidence. This museum for antiquities had an inventory system that was itself an antique, exacerbated by a complex system for assigning catalogue numbers that left tens of thousands of recently discovered pieces, essentially, "uncounted."

It was also true that, fearful of anticipated bombing and artillery fire, and with the experiences of the Iran-Iraq War and Desert Storm fresh in their memory, the staff had moved certain prized objects to many other locations.

So what was missing, and what was simply someplace else? This city was about as culturally different from my home turf of New York as a place could be, and getting a direct answer has proven remarkably difficult.

In civilian life, as an assistant district attorney in Manhattan, I have made it a habit to show up at crime scenes at all hours to sit, and watch, and think. At the museum, I would start every morning with my first canteen cup of coffee in hand, by walking around the compound for the same purpose. I finished every walk with an equally slow stroll in the galleries, picking a different room each time, but always asking a non-English-speaking-member of the museum staff to accompany me inside the building. I never wanted to be in the museum unescorted, but I didn't want to have any obligation to carry on a conversation either. "We live as we dream—alone," Conrad noted, and I wanted the space to think.

The other guys took their strolls as well, and on one of them, came upon a fire smoldering in the courtyard. Later, when we sorted through the unburned fragments, we found Ba'ath Party files and identification cards. Founded by a Syrian Christian, Michel Aflaq, in 1944, Ba'athism proclaimed the unity of all Arab speakers. Ba'athists are largely secular, but since 1958, when they overthrew Iraq's British-sponsored monarchy and seized power, they have shown a willingness to use Islam as a source of solidarity. In Iraq, being—or not being—a party member came to have the same implications as being—or not being—a member of the Nazi Party in 1930s Germany, or a member of the Communist Party in the 1950s Soviet Union. Saddam Hussein was there at the beginning of Ba'athist rule, but only as a twenty-one-year-old thug and murderer. By 1968, he had worked (killed) his way to power, after which he modeled his style of governance on that of his two avowed heroes—Hitler and Stalin.

The fact was that the Iraq Museum was an official agency of the Iraqi government—until two weeks before, synonymous with the "Ba'ath Party"—and everyone who worked at the museum had served at the pleasure of Saddam Hussein.

Since May 2003, I have watched my copy of the evidence tape the BBC shot for us that day in the basement with Nawala dozens of times, always trying to see a pattern that I may have missed before, always trying to dig a little deeper. One thing that stands out is the presence of Nawala's shadowy guardians, the two young Iraqi men with AK-47s darting in and out of the frame. Another is her characteristic posture, walking slightly hunched over, wearing her *khimar*, the Muslim head scarf, and clutching her bag as if someone were going to steal it from her.

Drinking tea every day with museum officials and extending every courtesy might earn their trust, but it was never going to sort out the question of each staff member's fundamental loyalty and perhaps shadowy, bloodstained past. The museum staff, in truth, were a complex bunch.

Moreover, we had a certain history to overcome. When the Iraqis invaded Kuwait in 1990, Saddam's army looted the Kuwait National Museum, packed up almost the entire collection, and trucked it off to Baghdad. After the war, the UN arranged for the looted antiquities to be returned; but Kuwaiti officials insist that 20 to 30 percent of their collection missed the bus for the trip back home. Moreover, at least one senior museum official in Baghdad was convinced the Americans were now going to confiscate the entire Iraq collection and give it either to Kuwait or, just for spite, to Israel.

But looming above all, as the most delicate aspect of this complex investigation, was the fact that it had never "officially" been sanctioned through normal channels. It was, in fact, my own improvisation, and a good many people—some in positions of authority—had said that it was a harebrained stunt that was going to end my career.

I was in Iraq as the deputy director of the Joint Interagency Coordination Group (JIACG), a counterterrorism investigative team—combining the military, FBI, CIA, Bureau of Immigration and Customs Enforcement, Treasury and other agencies in a single unit—reporting to U.S. Central Command. Our primary task was to find evidence of terrorist cells, illegal weapons, terrorist financing, and other violations of UN Security Council resolutions directed at reining in Saddam Hussein. I had been assigned that role as an officer of Marines, with all the standard infantry skills, as well as some counterterrorism experience picked up on prior assignments all over the world.

Of course, I also had almost seventeen years as a prosecutor, specializing in homicides and serial violent crimes—what we call patterns. As a result, I had the "flesh under the fingernails" routines you see on *NYPD Blue* down pretty cold. Steam rising from corpses on a winter night and blood-streaked bedrooms in the summer no longer faze me. It was actually quite a surprise, then, when I realized just how naïve I could be. It wasn't until I came to Baghdad that I got to see the real knife work.

Baghdad is a city of six million people, with the Tigris meandering across the map from top left to bottom right. The Iraq Museum is very much in the heart of things on the western bank of the Tigris, lying on the main road between the nearby central train station to the west, the old souq (market) and financial districts (including the Central Bank) across al-Ahrar Bridge to the east, and the "main" presidential palace to the south along a bend in the river.

Part of a complex that sits within an eleven-acre walled compound, the museum and its parent organization, the State Board of Antiquities and Heritage, consists of three buildings designed in a U-shape and opening south toward the main street (see maps following page 138). On the left, facing the compound from the street, is the two-story building that houses the public galleries (constructed around two central courtyards) and the storage rooms. There are eight storage rooms on three floors: one on the first, two on the second, and five in the basement—the latter "for keeping antiquities [safe] in the event of wars and emergencies." Straight ahead, at the bottom of the U is a one-story building with the administrative offices and technical sections. To the right are the library and auditorium. The Children's Museum, a replica of a Neo-Assyrian gate, is a detached three-story building, the one closest to the main street in front with the infamous hole.

Within the compound at the rear of the museum are a garage and a police station that had been turned into a command post, complete with tactically prepared military maps for tracking the battle. Scratched onto one of the exterior walls in the back we found crude outlines of human forms that Iraqi forces had used for target practice. There are also several residential buildings in this rear area.

In front of the museum, across an open courtyard, is the front gate. And across the street from the gate is what was left of a Special Republican Guard compound—previously housing Hussein's elite of the elite. The guard shack next to the museum's main gate was, by the time we arrived, manned by the U.S. Army Third Infantry Division's Task Force 1-64.

When we took up residence in the museum's library, we came with buckets and mops, ammonia and Clorox. Aware of the Marine Corps' penchant for hygiene—we shave in battle, largely because of the discipline it represents and reinforces—Eleanor Roosevelt once observed, "The Marines I have seen around the world have the cleanest bodies, the filthiest minds, the highest morale, and the lowest morals of any group of animals I have ever seen. Thank God for the United States Marine Corps!"

We had spent the preceding month in the southern Iraqi cities of Umm Qasr and Basra, and had a good idea of what to expect in Baghdad. Along with a certain amount of rubble and plumbing and electrical problems, every image of the former president of Iraq would have been pissed on. We were not disappointed. Accordingly, this Marine joined other middle-aged investigators in swabbing the decks.

After we hauled in our gear, we pushed the display cases perpendicular to the wall to create living space for all fifteen men currently in the unit. Senior—known to the Air Force as Senior Master Sergeant Roberto Piñeiro, my right-hand man—had a small rug to put his feet on beside his rack. Claude, our EMT and computer whiz, had all his electronic toys set up around his. Steve and Bud had an array of weapons within arm's reach that would have withstood Armageddon. Me—I had a good light for reading.

We parked our electrical generator in front of our door as a barricade. One of our SUVs was always backed up in front of it as well, nose pointing out, ready to roll. But more to the point, the engine block provided an extra shield against suicide bombers who might drop by. On more routine days, it would also stop bullets.

From the library, the back courtyard was accessible through a covered walkway that did not expose us to snipers or to the street. The library's location near the front gate was also favorable because I wanted us to be available when some informant at the gate said, "*Psst! Psst!* Over here." It was not as if we would be like professors holding office hours. I had other reasons for wanting to be closer to the gate than the staff was. I didn't really know them yet, and where this regime change would end up was, at this point, still anybody's guess.

The library was also a good location for us because, to the best of our knowledge, it was free of bad juju. During violent regime change, moving into governmental buildings is usually the best choice in terms of force protection. Such buildings have thick walls, the best wiring, and good "standoff" distance—meaning that they are *relatively* safe from direct-fire, shoulder-launched weapons and improvised explosive devices. They also tend to be empty after invasions. But that safety often comes at a price in terms of public perception about the old regime and the new order, bad guys and good guys. ORHA (the Office of Reconstruction and Humanitarian Assistance), soon to be rechristened CPA (the Coalition Provisional Authority), had taken up residence at Saddam Hussein's main palace—derisively called "Four-Head" Palace for the four mammoth heads of Hussein that sat atop its roof. It may have been a fine location, but it was not necessarily a great symbol in the battle for the hearts and minds of the people.

Just inside the museum compound gate there was a garden hose where we took our showers. Of course, *shower* is a grand term for standing in your cammies (camouflage utility uniforms) and your boots with your shirt off, rinsing your head and splashing water under your arms for forty-five seconds. News photographers loved it, but we were concerned that we might in some way be offending local sensibilities. So, in time, we relocated our *toilette* to the rear courtyard where there was also a hose. Some of the guys later set up two water bladders to add a couple of gallons of sun-heated water to our list of amenities—but as the boss I always used the cooler water from the hose.

Out of respect for the museum staff, I did not wear body armor inside the compound. I never went anywhere, however—not even just leaving the bunk area in the library—without my 9 mm Beretta, concealed if possible. It is "not always easy to put abstractions before necessities," as F. Scott Fitzgerald said.

We began our assessment immediately, and there was plenty of damage to assess. Every one of the 120 administrative offices in the museum compound had been completely trashed. Files, photographic slides, books, and papers were used to make bonfires on the floors. Air conditioners, teapots, computers, telephones, desks, and chairs were either stolen or, more interestingly, wantonly destroyed. To the extent that the break-in could be seen as rage against the old regime, this is where it was most eloquent. Here, and at the dozens of ransacked presidential palaces we had seen throughout the country.

But amid the raging masses there were also some professional crooks. As the insiders had done in the underground storage area, time and again the professionals in the galleries had gone straight for the more valuable items, leaving behind copies and the less rare originals. In the public galleries, where the premier items were on display, it was as if they were working from a shopping list, filling orders placed in advance from well-heeled dealers and collectors in New York or London or Tokyo. There were 451 display cases in the public galleries—of which 450 had been cleaned out. But only 28 had their glass smashed. In the only display case where something had been left behind, that something was a complete Neanderthal skeleton, dating back forty-five thousand years. Incongruously, even though the grave goods that had once surrounded the skeleton in the display were gone, the glass case was intact. If we were to believe what we were told by the staff, the looters had lifted the glass, slid it to the side, taken what they wanted, and then put the glass back in place. And yet, even more curiously, the glass had no fingerprints or even smudges where prints might have been rubbed clean. Who would have gone to such pains when one whack with a hammer would have done the trick?

Here again, the most problematic and pervasive question bubbled up where the complexity of the crime and the complexity of the museum staff intersected: Were we getting the straight story? Who was lying to us? And who might be working against us from within?

I quickly realized that my initial estimate—three to five days for an assessment of the looting—was ridiculous. Sorting this out was going to take more like three to five years.

Shortly after our arrival, I called my boss, Air Force major general Victor E. "Gene" Renuart Jr., head of the Operations Directorate at

U.S. Central Command. I went up to a protected place on the roof, just above the archway between the library and the rear courtyard, where my satellite phone got the best reception. The only catch was that, while speaking, I had to lie down flat on my back to avoid presenting a target for snipers.

"Sir, I need more time," I explained. "I propose using the museum as a staging area while we continue to carry out our other counterterrorism missions."

I went on to spell out the advantages. Controlling the traffic in illicit weapons was one of our primary objectives, and we had quickly picked up that the people smuggling weapons were the same people smuggling antiquities. Thus, I could make the case that by staying on to track down the antiquities, we would be killing two birds with one stone.

He said, "Fine. Do your thing. But keep producing. Don't forget that you're in country to pursue weapons and terrorist financing. It's called the global war on *terrorism*, Matthew."

"Roger that, sir. I won't let you down." Once again, my boss had put his ass on the line for me and this mission. I hung up and lay there for a moment. Herodotus had said, "Great things are won by great risks." Well, we were sure as hell taking the risks.

With that informal authorization to conduct a real investigation, I then faced my next most pressing issue, the news media. Reporters were lined up ten deep, and I was being asked for a dozen interviews every day. It seemed to me that one standard for journalism had already been set by Baghdad Bob, aka Comical Ali, the crazed Iraqi minister of information who broadcast daily assurances that no U.S. forces had entered Baghdad, even as tanks could be heard rumbling in the background. When we walked into the museum, we had walked into a storm of hyperbole and competitive misinformation.

The *Independent* ran a story about how "not a single pot or display case remained intact," and along with it they ran a photograph showing a forlorn-looking museum guard staring at an empty display case. The caption read, "An armed guard surveys the museum's empty shelves." Thereafter, virtually every major newspaper in the world ran the same photograph. We later learned that every one of the shelves in the photograph had, in fact, been emptied by museum staff, and the artifacts moved *before* the invasion.

In the *Guardian*, Eleanor Robson, an Oxford don and a council member of the British School of Archaeology in Iraq, said, "This is a tragedy with echoes of past catastrophes: the Mongol sack of Baghdad, and the fifth-century destruction of the library of Alexandria." Elsewhere, she brought it closer to home, saying, "The looting of the Iraq Museum is on a par with blowing up Stonehenge or ransacking the Bodleian Library."

But she was subdued compared to University of Michigan professor Piotr Michalowski. He told the History News Network, "The pillaging of the Baghdad Museum is a tragedy that has no parallel in world history. It is as if the Uffizi, the Louvre, or all the museums of Washington, D.C., had been wiped out in one fell swoop."

"Ten thousand years of human history has been erased at a moment" was how Professor John Russell, of the Massachusetts College of Art, summed it up on the *NewsHour*.

But the story became more pointed, and more of a specific black eye for U.S. forces, when the *Guardian* ran the headline MUSEUM'S TREASURES LEFT TO THE MERCY OF LOOTERS, with the subheading "U.S. generals reject plea to protect priceless artifacts from vandals."

When we arrived in Baghdad, I could tell an Akkadian from a Babylonian from a Sumerian piece—but probably not much more than that. As an undergraduate, I had focused on classical literature and philosophy—Greek as well as Latin. Later, my interests expanded to include archaeology, especially Roman, Greek, and Mesopotamian. I also studied the transmission of texts from brick, papyri, and parchment, whether written in hieroglyphics, cuneiform, or Greek. This was all a big deal at Columbia, where I did my graduate work while pursuing my law degree.

But my first opportunity to go on a real archaeological dig did not come, in fact, until after I had been involved with the museum investigation for more than a year. In the summer of 2004, I was invited to a dig on Yeronisos, a small island off the coast of Cyprus. I felt completely at home in that Mediterranean landscape, and in that specific setting, virtually unchanged since the time of Christ.

That's also how I felt during the many months I lived at the Iraq Museum. I loved every minute of it there. It did, however, take a few days to appreciate fully where I was, and to grasp that the objects I was seeing were not images in an oversized art book, but the real thing. One of the first eureka moments was when I came across a black basalt stela from Uruk depicting the king as lion hunter—I vaguely remembered that it was the oldest stone carving of its size ever recovered in Iraq and the first known attempt at indicating perspective in bas-relief. Another such moment was my first time in the Assyrian galleries—walking past intricate, sometimes narrative friezes that were a literal monument to two of ancient Mesopotamia's greatest pastimes: massacring their enemies and glorifying the massacres in larger-than-life-size relief.

Maybe fifty meters beyond the wall of the compound was a minaret, and the *muezzin* up there had a great voice. He would lull us to sleep every night, calling the faithful to prayers. This was, of course, after we'd had our MREs (meals ready to eat) for dinner, then burned the day's excrement in a steel drum out in the courtyard.

The director of research at the Iraq Museum, Dr. Adonia George Youkhanna (known to the world as Donny George, but to me as Brother Donny), once told an Australian film crew how he loved to come to the galleries and absorb the antiquities. I know precisely what he means. Even when the politics seem brutal or the underlying theology xenophobic and misogynistic, these ancient peoples got it right with their artifacts.

In this collection of their handiwork, as perhaps nowhere else, you can trace early human civilization in one unbroken stream. It runs from Ur of the Chaldees (the Mesopotamian city where Abraham—patriarch of Judaism, Christianity, *and* Islam—was called away "to a land I will show you") through the Sumerians, to the Akkadians, the Assyrians, the Persians, the Greeks, and on into modern times. The timelessness and perfection of this human expression, written in clay and in gold and on carnelian and lapis lazuli, was surely what Keats had on his mind when he appealed to that "still unravish'd bride of quietness" on his famous Grecian urn.

I have to confess that being surrounded by such magnificence made me feel about the size of a medium shrimp. Even if I manage to live a good four score, I know that shrimp-sized is how big my life will be compared to this ocean of history. But it was my identification with that history, and with the expansive sensation it affords, that accounts, in part, for why I came to the museum in the first place.

3

HECTOR'S GHOST

Never give a sword to a man
who can't dance.—Celtic proverb

WHEN I WAS twelve years old, my mother—a waitress—gave
me a copy of the *Iliad*.

My parents had a stormy relationship, loud and sometimes publicly
so. Having four boys within three years—all of whom shared a single
bedroom until I was thirteen—probably didn't help. I'd sometimes go
into the closet and read to tune out the shouting, leaving the door
slightly ajar for light. (I always wanted a flashlight, which is why to this
day I give each of my kids a flashlight at bedtime.) For me, reading the
Iliad and inhabiting Homer's world of heroes, duty, honor, and glorious
deaths was the only thing that could turn down the volume on domestic discord.

Reading about that world, but most especially about Hector and
Achilles challenging each other so valiantly before the walls of Troy,
pretty much set the course for, and in many cases validated, everything
else I've done since. (At fifteen, for instance, I was overjoyed to read that
Alexander The Great had also slept with the *Iliad* under his pillow.) In
many respects, getting a master's degree in classical studies was just
another excuse to read more. It was identification with the Bronze
Age Greeks and their values that led me to take up boxing, to join the
Marines, to become a prosecutor. And it was my fascination with history

and my appreciation of the Greek concepts of *themis* (what's right) and *arête* (excellence for its own sake) that made me want to track down, reclaim, and protect some of the world's oldest and most precious antiquities.

There is also the obvious influence of my heritage: Bogdanos is a Greek name. At the age of six, my father's father had left his home on the Greek island of Lemnos, in the northeastern Aegean, to become an indentured apprentice in Egypt. He worked as a baker in Alexandria, completed his required service, then returned to Lemnos to get my grandmother. Earlier, during one of the many Turkish pogroms against the Greeks, her family had been hidden by a neighboring Turkish family. Together, these two came to the States. A world-class wrestler, my grandfather put aside his athletic dreams to raise four children, and he took the only job he could get: short-order cook at the YMCA. We lived with my father's parents for many years in their two-bedroom apartment on Seventieth Street in Manhattan, while each of my parents held down two jobs.

When my parents met, my father was a salesman in a music store. He was a huge fan of jazz and blues and loved Miles Davis, Louis Armstrong, and the big bands. He had also done a stint in the Marines during the Korean War, but never told his mother and father until he had returned to the States. He had a seventh-grade education, but he read two books a week. And like his father before him, he could cook Greek and Italian food that made you think you were in the elysian fields. After a string of jobs, including disc jockey, dishwasher, bartender, and chef, he eventually opened up his own restaurant, and then two more.

The driving force in the family, though, was my mother. An American of French descent, she was a high school graduate, an Anglophile, and also a bookaholic. When she wasn't working—which wasn't often— she was always taking classes in French, drafting, dance, and art history. Ultimately, my parents divorced when I was nineteen, but before that they had separated half a dozen times—often for six months at a clip. They should probably have split up when I was two, but like many of their generation, they stayed together for the kids.

"The kids" included my twin brother, Mark, and my younger brothers, Konstantine (Deno) and David. None of them went to college, but they can quote Shakespeare at length, make a three-course dinner for six on two hours' notice, and bluff you out of the game with nothing more than a pair of deuces. I also strongly recommend not getting into a fight with any one of them.

"Home" was a fifty-seat place on Twenty-sixth Street and Third Avenue in Manhattan called Deno's. My father's name is Konstantine, pronounced *kostandenos* in Greek; hence *Deno*. Dad cooked, Mom waited tables, and from the time we were seven, each of us worked in a succession of jobs from drying silverware and busing tables to washing dishes and peeling shrimp—I still remember with pride the day my dad told me that, at eleven, I was now big enough to peel shrimp. (If you peeled it wrong, you ruined the shrimp and we couldn't afford that.) All of our meals were eaten in the restaurant. Dinner was usually the mistakes: if a customer changed his mind and didn't want the moussaka, no problem: one of us would eat it. But no more than two of us could ever eat at the same time. Even so, no matter how busy we were or how packed the restaurant, table #1 was for homework. Anyone willing to help us with our spelling or arithmetic could get a free glass of wine or a piece of baklava. More than twenty years later, during a trial, Shirley Levitan, the four-foot-something former French Resistance partisan and legendary New York judge, took obvious pleasure in saying to me—in front of the jury, of course—"I taught you math when you were eight. You were a precocious brat then, and you're a precocious brat now. Objection overruled!"

Whatever lessons I didn't learn from the *Iliad*, I learned from my mom and dad in the restaurant. All were the kind that would serve me well in Afghanistan and Iraq. Keep your eyes open: Who's ready to order, who needs deciding? Pay attention to body language: Who is ready for dessert, who is in a hurry and needs the check? Anticipate future actions based on past experience: Who had the souvlaki last time and wanted extra peppers, who likes the feta on the side? Particularly applicable to my handling of the museum investigation, they insisted that each of the four boys know how to do every job in the restaurant—from dishwasher to chef—not only to be able to fill in when someone called in sick, but to show everyone that the boss's kids, and by extension the boss, got his hands dirty right alongside the guy who mops the floor.

I learned other lessons in between rush hours. Once when I was interviewing a police officer who looked familiar, he started to laugh. He had just remembered that I was the kid whose dad—in kitchen whites—used to teach him how to play stickball in front of the restaurant between the lunch and dinner shifts. No matter how busy we were or how tired he was, my father always found the hours in the day to spend time with us. The restaurant is also where I learned that mission comes first: one busy Friday night I had just finished checking the order against the dupe (the duplicate, white part of the check the kitchen uses to make the order). Hurrying to place the dupe on the spindle, I slammed down my palm and saw the steel spike protruding from the back of my hand. From the kitchen, my dad reached over the counter, pulled out the spindle, and, moving my wrist away from the food, poured Clorox into the hole. Before the pain could even register, he kissed my hand and said, "Table thirteen is waiting for their dinner." Picking up the plates with my other hand, I turned to my mother for sympathy. She kissed me on the forehead, then said, "Table thirteen also needs water."

The music in the restaurant was 100 percent Greek, but the music in our apartment was 100 percent Broadway show tunes. As kids, we could recite the lyrics to every song from *My Fair Lady*, *Guys and Dolls*, and *The Music Man*. And once the customers left, we would waltz with my mother to "Shall We Dance" from *The King and I*. I've continued the tradition. *A Chorus Line*, *Camelot*, *1776*, *Pippin*, and *City of Angels* are playing in my apartment all the time. My oldest daughter (aged five) can sing "I Could Have Danced All Night"; my oldest son (aged six) loves "Hi-Lili Hi-Lo" and "They're Playing My Song."

Exasperated with four boys who were fighting all the time—and not just among ourselves, but down the street and at school—my parents sent us to Don Bosco, a parochial high school over the George Washington Bridge in New Jersey. They sent us there for the structure and the discipline. They also sent us there to learn, but only for the sake of learning itself, never as a means to an end. Books were precious and beautiful, but it never occurred to us that they were a way to get into a good college and become a big deal in life.

When my twin brother and I graduated from Don Bosco—as usual, Mark beat me out, I think he was fourth in the class and I was fifth or sixth—we were the only kids who didn't go to college. When the college recruiters had come to the campus, we didn't even meet with them. What for? To us, education was reading, and reading was personal, something you did every moment of every day, all your life, and not just for four years in some youth ghetto cordoned off by pizza joints.

For my first two years out of high school, I continued to work in the restaurant—but now, like my mom and dad, pulling double shifts. I had a fifth-floor walk-up on Thirtieth and Third, and my father set out to show me that I didn't really want to be in the business. He didn't want me to be his age and working over a grill eighteen hours a day just to stay afloat. At that time he had three restaurants side by side. He gave the Greek place to me to run, and he gave Mark the Italian one. Sure enough, I was sleeping on the tables after closing because there was no point walking the four blocks to my apartment only to turn around and come back. My father wanted something "better" for me. He didn't have a concrete plan—to him, anything was better than this.

I wanted better things too. I wanted to tend bar, meet more girls, and become a boxer—the best.

The first time I walked into Gleason's Gym at Thirtieth Street and Eighth Avenue I was seventeen. Inside the doorway was a sign that read:

Let him who has courage and a strong and collected spirit in his breast, step forward, lace on the gloves, and put up his hands.

Virgil in a boxing gym? I knew I was in the right place. But five seconds later, I began to have my doubts.

Sammy Morgan had to have been in his seventies by this time. His nose moved as he walked, and he couldn't bend any of his fingers because of boxing arthritis. The first thing he said to me was, "Ah, you're no good, kid, you're a friggin' white kid, look at your nose, it ain't never been broke, you never done any boxin'." But then he relented and said, "Okay, okay . . . be here tomorrow at five o'clock."

Sammy was the cliché old broken-down fighter out of Damon Runyon—newsboy cap and everything. He lived alone in the Bronx with his ten dogs, and he closed up the gym every night. Whatever he once was, when I met him, he was the janitor. He cleaned up in the late afternoon, when I would go in between the lunch and dinner shifts.

When he started training me, he put me in the far corner of the gym away from the other fighters and made me shadowbox from one end of that gym to the other, throwing nothing but left jabs. Thousands of them. I was working days and nights, but from five o'clock to seven o'clock, six days a week, I was at Gleason's, going up and down the gym floor with the left. After a few weeks, Sammy let me use the right hand. But some serious fighters, even world champions, worked out at Gleason's—Roberto Duran and Wilfredo Benitez, among others. One time I saw Benitez do this little bob of the head. So I tried it and Sammy came running over out of nowhere. "You no good son of a bitch, what did you just do? I told you to stick with the jab, the jab. Don't ever do that again. I'll tell you when to do that!"

He stood back, shaking his head in disgust.

"You got a halfway decent jab, kid, but how the hell'm I gonna do anything with you if you don't listen. Don't do nothin' fancy. You're killin' me with that fancy garbage."

Then he started in on my footwork.

"Go dance with them fairies, kid. They got good footwork."

So I did—to become a better boxer, I started taking ballet. Truth be told, I loved it.

In all the years we were together, spanning about a decade, I don't think I ever heard Sammy say a kind word to me. This includes the times I came back to train with him while in law school in New York and again later when home on leave from the Marines. It just wasn't his style. But the first time I ever knocked anyone down in the ring with a left hook, I was so excited I didn't know what to do. Jumping up and down, I looked over to my corner and there was Sammy, smiling so hard that you could see every cracked tooth. Later that week, I heard Sammy tell another trainer how "*my* kid done all right in his fight."

I wasn't there the day Sammy died. I don't think anyone was. And it's been more than two decades since he last chewed me out. But to this day, I can still hear his voice whenever I try to be too fancy.

I've had twenty-six fights in my career—and I still fight once a year for the New York City Police Department Widows and Orphans Fund. I have zero talent for boxing, but thanks to Sammy I've got the fundamentals down cold, and somehow I've managed a 23-3 record as a 160-pound middleweight—including 4-1 since my fortieth birthday. The three losses? They weren't even close. In one of them, I was knocked down five times in three rounds, but got up every time and finished the fight, albeit with a broken nose, swollen-shut eye, and a concussion. I finished the fight on my feet. I've finished every fight I've ever had on my feet. Things like that matter to a pug like me.

But boxing has always been more than a way to let off steam, or to channel youthful, somewhat chaotic ambitions. After years of boxing, the strategic and instinctive aspects of warfare come naturally to me. Once I got into a combat zone, I did not have to relearn innate skills.

During my late teens, I still had no intention of going to college, but I did take an accounting course at a community college as a way of saving money at the restaurant. After all, why pay an accountant if you can do the books yourself?

Then one Friday night in January 1976, after I'd been out of high school for about two years, I was out drinking in an Irish pub on Third Avenue with some old football buddies from high school.

After a while, one of the guys—he had been a pretty good lineman, but clearly he wasn't going anywhere based on brains—stroked the side of his beer and said, "You know, I'm thinking of joining the Marines."

This from a guy who could barely remember his jockstrap, but suddenly, everyone was looking at him with respect. From all around the table, I heard a slightly drunken "Wow."

I looked at my buddies, appalled. All he said was that he was *thinking* about it. So I said, "I could do the Marines." Everybody instantly looked over at me, but just with their eyes. Nobody moved his head. I added, "My dad was a Marine." Then they all gave me the eye roll that said, "Yeah, sure." I was a boxer and a defensive back, but I was five foot seven, not likely to be up for the John Wayne part in *Sands of Iwo Jima*.

"Please, we're talking the *Marines* here," somebody said. So the next morning, for reasons I don't entirely remember, I showed up at the recruiter's office. I've seen those forms. I was still so hammered that my signature missed the line. I took all the standardized tests. Then I came back a week later to talk about my results.

"I'm not taking you," the recruiter said. I was devastated. "I'm not signing you up because you're going to college." I stared at him, not really understanding what he was saying. "You should be an officer. Officers have to go to college. So, go get accepted to college and I'll take you in the officer program."

I had never thought about going to college. It wasn't that we did or didn't have enough money, the question was simply never asked in my family; it simply wasn't in our frame of reference. We didn't know anything about doctors or lawyers or judges. To us, a lawyer was a guy who came in wearing a suit and ordered the most expensive thing on the menu (at the Greek restaurant, that would've been the shish kebab and the lamb chops; at the Italian restaurant, setting aside the question of why anyone would order steak at an Italian restaurant, it was the sliced steak). These kinds of careers didn't mean anything to me. I had no idea what these people did.

Smart kids in hard-luck places often view college as a way out, but I didn't want out. My life was the restaurant, boxing, reading, and girls, and that was just fine with me. But I did want to join the Marines, and this was the only way the recruiter would take me. I went to the bookstore and I picked up the *Barron's Profiles of American Colleges*. When we were kids, my mother would get us the Sears catalogue each year so that we could go through it and then write Santa Claus about what we wanted for Christmas. That's the way I felt looking at *Barron's*. I stayed up all night and made a list of the things I wanted in a school.

I did not know about majors, certainly nothing about the concept of a Classics Department. But I knew I wanted to study Alexander and Aristotle. I also wanted to be close to my family, three hours' drive at the most. I once knew a girl who lived 180 miles away, and the three-hour drive wasn't so bad. So I took out a map and a compass and I drew a circle with a 180-mile radius around the New York metro area. And it had to have an enrollment between three thousand and five thousand. I have no idea why, it just felt right—one thousand a class, plus or minus. And I wanted them to have a football team. It should not be in a city, and it had to have average SAT scores above 1200. The only school that met all those criteria was Bucknell.

The reason I wanted a smaller town was not so much an attempt to escape New York but an attempt to replicate Don Bosco. I wanted to read and play sports the way I'd done there. Don Bosco had been a fantasy world for me, and I often learned more after school than I did in the classroom. The brothers would give me books to read outside class. For detention, which I suffered often, and always for fighting, one of the Salesians, Brother Paul, used memorization as punishment. Before you could leave, you had to memorize and declaim a poem or literary passage. I started challenging him to find longer and longer pieces, and soon I was stopping by his classroom after school even when I wasn't on detention. He favored Kipling, Browning, Whitman, and Shakespeare, and I can still recite most of those. The Salesians also taught me how to study and made me realize that I did well in a highly structured environment.

I spent the rest of that weekend completing my college application. The only problem was that this was six weeks after the deadline. Ultimately, I got in because I wrote a letter to the president of the college. I don't really remember much about it, except pontificating about the artificiality of deadlines and quoting Homer and Alexander. I got a letter back a week later saying, "You win."

I entered Bucknell in September of 1976. As promised, I was allowed to enter the officer program a few months later, on January 15, 1977.

Bucknell, of course, is a private school, expensive, and my family ran a couple of mom-and-pop restaurants. Fortunately, my father had for years hosted a Friday-night poker game, frequented primarily by members of the city's finest, some of whom love to gamble.

We were in the Thirteenth Precinct, and the place was cop-friendly. (Once when I was a kid, a certain now-well-known police official was a rookie cop and broke the sink in our restroom with a female officer.) No one in uniform ever got a check, but no cop ever hurt us by ordering shrimp, steak, or lamb. A rookie might have, but then his partner would have explained. And, unlike lawyers, cops were great tippers, even when they came in off-duty and got a full check.

My dad would close up around midnight, and the game would start as soon as the last customer left. This was a friendly, but serious, card game. No one ever got skinned, but you could win $500. Everyone was good. No turkeys, no chickens for plucking.

I used to serve them coffee, sandwiches, and baklava throughout the night. I got a cut out of every pot—a dollar for the house. In the course of a night, three hundred hands, that's $300—say $150 goes for food and coffee (nobody ever drank at that table) and the rest was a tip for me. By the time I was in my early teens, they were dealing me in. More important still, I learned to count cards. And at eighteen, my brother Mark and I started going to Atlantic City every couple of weeks. Going to the casinos was a cold-blooded business proposition. We would pool our money, taking $500 to $1,000 apiece. We would always sit at the $25 table, and we would play for a specified number of hours. Sometimes we lost, but more often we won, and Mark and I split everything, fifty-fifty.

We played blackjack. We had a simple plus/minus system of card counting, and I would memorize all the probabilities. One night, we won $16,000.

At that time, tuition was $5,000 a semester, which meant I didn't have to work while I was at Bucknell. Still, holidays and every summer I waited tables in the restaurant.

I boxed, I played football (I was a walk-on defensive back), and I studied classics and philosophy. I also joined Sigma Chi with the rest of the football team and learned that the thick-necked jocks were also among the smartest, hardest working, and most compassionate members of the student body. But not all of them. Freshman year, some guys with too much testosterone and not enough maturity started pushing me around on the basketball court. One of the bigger guys shoved me pretty hard, and I used the clean left hook that Sammy had taught me, leaving my feet to reach his jaw. I broke it just below his ear, and after that, I never had a problem. This was fortunate, because not long afterwards, a lady came into the weight room and said, "How many of you muscle-bound young men would like to spend an hour a day lifting up beautiful young women?" I looked around sheepishly, then said, "Sure, I'll do it."

"It" was ballet class and she needed male dancers for her pas de deux. After the first class, she pulled me aside and said, "You've done this before, haven't you?" I said, "Yes, ma'am." Thanks to Sammy Morgan, I had taken ballet classes to improve my footwork.

She said, "Don't worry, I won't tell anybody."

Only Nixon could go to China, and I guess only a boxer could do ballet.

But, in fact, I enjoyed dancing so much that I gave up playing football. I mean, there really are only so many hours in the day, and "playing" in my case should be understood as being the tackling dummy in practice and sitting on the bench during games. While I got a kick out of football, boxing was my passion. So my last two years of college were all about boxing and classics and dance.

After graduation, I was commissioned an officer in the Marines and, at the insistence of my commanding officer, went to law school and graduate school (both at Columbia University) while on active duty. Then I did a three-year tour as a judge advocate, popularly known as a JAG, before being appointed a Special Assistant United States Attorney for my last year.

Growing up as I did, where I did, just about all you were allowed to talk about among the guys were sports and girls. So I always felt a little out of it that I was also interested in things like dance and theater and good books. The split or contrast perplexed me, until I read *The Birth of Tragedy*, Nietzsche's exploration of the interplay between the Dionysian and the Apollonian. He showed me that two seemingly irreconcilable forces can actually form a more coherent whole. It was confirmation that I wasn't crazy. You can actually do all these different things and they merge and form a synthesis. They might even leverage one another. As Nietzsche sees it, balance is not striving to achieve the Aristotelian Golden Mean. In fact, like Alexander before him, he despised the middle road as mediocrity, and in many ways I share his dislike of moderation. For me, anything worth doing is worth overdoing, and balance means overdoing everything equally. "A man's reach," I can still hear Brother Paul quoting Browning, "should exceed his grasp, or what's a heaven for?"

The place where all these influences came together was at the restaurant. Every Friday night from the time I was fourteen, my father and my brothers and I did a whole set of Greek dances for each sitting—roughly at eight, at ten, and at twelve. I was the waiter, and Mark and my father were in two different kitchens. So they would have to coordinate to make sure that all the orders got out.

We would start out together, the three of us, dancing a slow, arm-in-arm sailors' dance, a Syrtaki or a Hasapiko. Then we would each do a Zeimbekiko, a solo dance with echoes in Greek warrior culture. Always my father, Mark, and then I—in order of age. Then we would do the fast Zorba's dance, which I would finish off up on the table. I did this until the time that I was in the DA's office, often going to the restaurant after a particularly tough case and teaching my fellow prosecutors how to dance.

In *Zorba the Greek*, Kazantzakis wrote, "Every minute death was dying and being reborn, just like life. For thousands of years young girls and boys have danced beneath the tender foliage of the trees in spring—beneath the poplars, firs, oaks, planes, and slender palms—and they will go on dancing for thousands more years, their faces consumed with desire. Faces change, crumble, return to earth; but others rise to take their place. There is only one dancer, but he has a thousand masks. He is always twenty. He is immortal."

So dancing is kind of a Greek way of saying what Keats was saying in his "Ode on a Grecian Urn." It's that same appreciation for timelessness that you get walking through the Iraq Museum or the British Museum or the Oriental Institute at the University of Chicago. That life is short, but art is long. Understanding that begins to explain why I went to Baghdad to recover the lost antiquities. But there are other, far more immediate reasons why I was in a war zone in the first place.

4

A VISIT TO THE UNDERWORLD

When sorrows come, they come not single spies,
but in battalions.—Hamlet

I HAD JUST bent down to kiss my kids good-bye for the day when
the sound of the explosion blew through our apartment. As a native
New Yorker, and having spent the past ten years living a block from the
World Trade Center, I assumed this roar was just one more precon-
struction demolition. Then again, I was a bit preoccupied.

I was scheduled to start a murder trial, and I was worried about the
latest in a long line of witnesses who had decided the defendant was
just too dangerous to go up against in open court. It was also the day of
the annual Artie Johnson Memorial softball game. This series between
the DA's Office and detectives from the elite Manhattan Robbery
Squad was a grudge match like the Red Sox and the Yankees, and the
lawyers had won three in a row. As captain of the DA's team, I had lined
up the best field down at Grand Street Park just off the FDR Drive on
the East River. As usual, my brother Mark had all the hot dogs, ham-
burgers, and steaks ready for the much attended after-game picnic. Detective Michael Kennedy, with whom I had worked more than one
hundred cases in thirteen years, was one of my best friends and a phe-
nomenal detective. But on this day he was the enemy, the captain of the
opposing team. The first pitch was scheduled for five thirty, but Judge
Charles Solomon, himself a ballplayer and former DA, would adjourn

by four if need be. Most judges knew about this game; the good ones made sure any detective or DA in their courtroom got there on time.

It was the morning of September 11. At eighteen months, my daughter Diana seemed to accept my assurance that the loud noise was probably just another building being knocked down in the name of progress. But my son Michael, being three, ran to the window to see for himself. "Daddy, look at the big fire!" he yelled back. I took the three steps from the kitchen to the living room to see what he was seeing. About twenty floors from the top of the North Tower, flames and smoke spewed from an enormous hole. Michael was mesmerized by the close-up view—the World Trade Center was, after all, not a couple hundred yards from our apartment. We stood in front of the window in silence. "How could the pilot have been so incompetent," my wife muttered as she came over.

Seventeen minutes later, at exactly 9:02 A.M., the second plane crashed into the South Tower, and we caught on. Claudia was seven months pregnant, and both kids were running low-grade fevers, but she was perfectly calm. There would be no playground today, and this was as good a place to be as any. Terrorist attacks are traumatic and discrete events, I assured her, but then they are over. "Just stay away from the windows," I said. "I'll call when I get to the office." Then I kissed everyone good-bye again and went downstairs.

In my mind, the fact that two airplanes had just flown into the World Trade Center did not mean that everything else had stopped. I was living in the same neighborhood as I had been on February 26, 1993, when an earlier terrorist attack on the towers had killed six civilians and injured more than one thousand. I still had a job to do then. I still had a job to do now. Being at your appointed place of duty at the appointed time is one of the General Orders drilled into every member of the U.S. Marines. It is bedrock, part of the warrior code, and personal preference does not enter into it.

In retrospect, my behavior seems a little nuts, but on September 11, 2001, the Criminal Courts Building, 111 Centre Street, four blocks north of City Hall, was my appointed place of duty. I wanted to stay home. My duty was in court. I went to court.

At the last minute, I decided to take my car. I was afraid it would get blocked in at the apartment by emergency services vehicles as it had in 1993. So I drove to the DA's Office, just across from the Courts Building at One Hogan Place. Given all the pandemonium north of me, I headed south, planning to drive down around the Battery, and over to the FDR Drive. The cops had already shut off the West Side Highway in both directions, so I had to show my badge to get on. But after I "tinned" them, I made it to the East Side in minutes, because every inch of the roadway was empty.

Driving along the southern tip of Manhattan, I thought about what we call consequence management, and all the work NYPD was going to have to do. I was also worried about all the guys I knew who were first responders. At that point, I still had no specific fear for my family.

By the time I exited the FDR, however, the level of hysteria had ramped up. I slowed to a crawl along Worth Street and saw people running and shrieking and looking over their shoulders. I jumped the curb and parked on the sidewalk in front of my office. As soon as I turned off the ignition, I felt the ground shake. I looked behind me and watched the South Tower disappear in a cloud of smoke. It was 10:05 A.M.

This was the point at which it hit me: "What the hell have I done?" The only thing separating my wife and kids from falling buildings was a couple lanes of traffic. And now, separating me from them is what was soon to become known as Ground Zero.

I knew my cell phone would be dead, so I ran up the seven flights of stairs to the DA's Office and picked up the first phone I could reach.

Dead.

I ran back downstairs, hit the street, and started to sprint.

Immediately I was bouncing off people, leaping over the hoods of cars, going the wrong way against traffic. This was not just a mile run—it was a steeplechase—and I had to remind myself to breathe.

Everyone else was running the other way. Panic-stricken, covered in grime, they looked like extras fleeing Godzilla through the streets of Tokyo.

I went straight down Worth Street from the DA's Office—a two-way street, nice and wide—but at Broadway, it became impassable. I turned left and then right on Thomas Street, immediately thinking bad idea— it's too narrow, and buildings have already fallen down. So then I turned left and ran down Church, right on Duane, then made the left onto Greenwich. By this time, the people coming toward me were thoroughly covered with ash, pale gray like the shades drifting through Hades. I took off my shirt and wrapped it around my face.

I had to get as far west as possible while still working my way south, but then I ran right into the crash site. I could not see the rubble of the

South Tower because the view was obstructed by the North Tower. Office workers where jumping out of windows holding their briefcases. Groups were jumping to their deaths holding hands. I heard, but could not see, several bodies hit the ground. I was trying to judge the distance and determine how wide a berth I needed to steer to avoid the other jumpers I knew would follow.

I cut across the West Side Highway by Stuyvesant High School, which is when I spotted my old platoon sergeant, James McEniry, now with the NYPD's Emergency Services Unit. He was on top of his truck suiting up. Nearby, a police officer I didn't know was setting up a barricade and telling me to stop. McEniry saw me and yelled down, "Sir, what are you doing? You're going the wrong way."

"My family's in there."

The other officer held up his hands, determined to stop me.

"That's my old CO," Mac yelled to him. "He knows what he's doing. Let him in." Within the year, Marine master sergeant McEniry would be in the thick of it as General Tommy Franks's bodyguard.

After another block, I faced off with a white shirt, a lieutenant. I didn't know him and I didn't recognize his insignia because he wasn't from Manhattan. He certainly didn't know me and was in no mood to talk. So I said, "Okay, we'll do it by the book, Lieu, here it is . . ." My shirt was already off. And—boom, I dropped my trousers. "I'm a DA. Not carrying any bombs . . . just trying to get to my family." And then I kept going. He would have had to shoot me to make me stop.

I was at the World Financial Center at 10:28, not a hundred yards from the World Trade Center, when the North Tower fell. The bodies and the smoke and the hysteria and the death had become white noise to me. All I cared about was getting to Claudia and the kids and it seemed to be taking forever.

When I reached our building, there was no doorman, no one else in sight. I ran up nine flights of stairs to the apartment. When I opened the door, I felt the blast of air in my face, immediately thinking all of the windows had been blown in. Everything was covered in ash, two or three inches thick. I looked for blood, but there wasn't any. I prayed as I ran back down the stairs. Please, God, they've got to be okay.

I hit the lobby and I saw the doorman. "Peter, where's my family?" I shouted. He pointed to the room where the doormen take their breaks.

There were no lights, but I could see her sitting on the floor with Michael and Diana beside her. She looked calm, but the kids looked scared to death, huddled under her wing. Then she saw me and she sort of fell apart. She had held it together that long for the kids, but now she let it out. We were all safe. I held her for a moment. She told me they were all okay, but that she'd decided to let Cordelia, our black Lab, manage on her own. The dog was too smart to wander far, and probably running free was best. Sometimes they let horses out of their stalls to outrun tornadoes.

My initial assessment was that the streets were not safe because of the debris, falling bodies, and panicked civilians. I saw one woman who had made it to safety, then panicked at the sight of U.S. fighter jets overhead. She began to climb over a railing. I screamed out that the planes were ours. She jumped anyway, but not into the river. She went headfirst to her death onto a recessed walkway ten feet below. Under these conditions, I thought it best for us to stay put. But then the cops came in telling everyone that it was time to go. They had an evacuation route laid out. They had boats on the Hudson ready to take us to Ellis Island or Liberty Island or New Jersey.

I recognized one of the cops and I went up to him and said, "I'm good here."

He said, "Oh, yeah. I know you. You're the DA who's a Marine. Do what you have to do."

But to everyone else, he said, "Out. Let's go. Move."

There was no advantage to staying in the lobby, and we needed food, milk, and diapers anyway. So we went upstairs.

The moment we got inside the door, Claudia's first comment was, "How are we ever going to get this place clean?"

I started prepping the apartment. Unplugging the appliances, putting wet towels under the doors, filling bottles with water before it was turned off. Claudia put the kids in the double stroller and began pushing them up and down the hallway, trying to get them to sleep.

My plan was to stay through the night and reassess in the morning. I could control the environment in the apartment, but I could not control what was going on with crazed people, falling buildings, or secondary explosions. To stay the night, however, we would need more milk and water and ice.

I put on my combat boots and an NYPD baseball cap. I got my .45 out of the gun safe, took off my shirt, hung my DA's shield around my neck, put on my ALICE pack (all-purpose, lightweight, individual carrying equipment), then went downstairs.

DA's and detectives carry the same gold shield, and I wore it for IFF: identification—friend or foe. I was going to be moving at speed and didn't want to be stopped every five steps. That's also why I went without my shirt. I wanted it clear at a glance that I did not have a bomb strapped to my chest. The .45 was concealed, but only barely.

On the way downstairs, I saw our neighbor Angelique with her daughter and carried her stroller down for her. At that point I could hear people screaming on each floor. I realized that there must be a great many more people in this building with kids in strollers.

In the lobby there were two dozen people, some hysterical. They saw me—the shield, the weapon—and asked what to do. Days later, when I replayed the scene in my mind, it struck me that some had been the kind no prosecuter would ever want on a jury: well-educated Manhattan types who appear to maintain a fashionable suspicion of, if not outright contempt for, the police and the military. But in a crisis, they were looking to me for help. Kipling saw the same thing more than one hundred years ago in England's treatment of her ordinary soldiers, nicknamed Tommys:

> While it's Tommy this, an' Tommy that, an' "Tommy, fall be'ind,"
> But it's "Please to walk in front, sir", when there's trouble in the wind.

At that moment—like those Tommys before me—my duty was to ease their fears. And I did my best. Keep your heads. Find a police officer. But they kept asking me again and again, "Are they going to come back?" There is no way anyone can launch a concerted military attack against us, I told them. So it has to be terrorist activity. They've done what they wanted to do. Now, with the heightened security, there most likely won't be another attack: high risk, low payoff. Another place, another time perhaps. But not today and not here. Nonetheless, with structural damage you need to leave. They listened and seemed reassured. We were like GIs in a World War II movie, overcoming our differences in the face of a common enemy.

My advice to them was not so inconsistent with what I was doing. I knew that staying in the apartment was a calculated risk, but the most logical way for residents from this location to get out of the danger zone was by boat. I did not want to go with my family on a boat. Overcrowded ferries are notorious for sinking. I had an eighteen-

month-old and a three-year-old—they weren't going to survive a cap-
sizing, or even a panicked crowd.

Then I carried more strollers. I went up to eight, opened the door,
and said, "Is everyone okay? Does anyone need help?" It was pitch-
black in the stairs. "Come to my voice." Some people were too flus-
tered to answer.

I went to seven and did the same thing. Others were doing likewise.
We all should have been exhausted, but there was something extraordinarily invigorating about running up and down flights of stairs with
strangers.

Then a neighbor told me there were people in the next building who
needed help, so I went into the lobby next door, opened the door to the
stairway, and out jumped Cordelia and scared the hell out of me. I took
her back to our own lobby and told her to stay. And then I started running. I kept trying to go east, but I had to keep going farther south because too many streets were blocked off. I went all the way down to
Battery Park, then all the way to Gold Street near Beekman Hospital
before I could find a deli that was open and had some milk. This was
just south of Police Plaza, so I had pretty much run all the way back to
the DA's Office.

I tried a different way home to find a route we could take if we decided to leave. I was wearing a bandanna over my face—a camouflage
bandanna—which I realized later made me look like a looter. I reached
the Battery Tunnel but I couldn't get across, so I had to go down south
again all the way to Battery Park and across the West Side Highway.
Huge hunks of steel and smashed cars were on the pavement. I ran past
the landing gear from one of the planes.

But overall, the situation on the street seemed to have improved. It
was much calmer now, almost deserted. And in terms of infrastructure,
I believed—mistakenly—that whatever was going to fall had already
fallen.

I knew that I would be fine in the apartment overnight, but I wasn't
sure how well my family would do. Without running water, we
couldn't even flush the toilet, and pregnant Claudia and my two little
kids were not Marines. I couldn't expect them to get by in conditions
that were worse than expeditionary. My biggest concern, of course, was
what this ash in the air might be doing to Claudia and our unborn baby.
What about the asbestos and the fumes? It seemed to me that the smoke

and stress alone might induce premature labor. Fortunately, my wife is a runner—in great shape—and a cool customer in times of crisis.

We packed up and carried the two-seater stroller—front and back— with my little boy and my little girl inside. I told Claudia, "Make a mental list of everything you disagree with, everything that I do or say that bothers you, and I promise you there will come a time when we will talk about it in excruciating detail. But not today. Today, we do what I say, when I say it, without question or hesitation." Shockingly— and no one who knows my wife can believe it—she nodded her head and said nothing more than, "Just get us out of this."

As we opened the door and stepped out onto the street, I was already back in uniform in my mind. After my release from active duty in 1988, I immediately transferred to the Marine reserves. In the intervening thirteen years, I had averaged sixty to seventy-five days a year on military duty maintaining old skills and learning new ones as I increased in rank. I had also recently served in Kazakhstan and Uzbekistan, conducting what are officially called multinational "peacekeeping and engagement exercises." The only question was how long it would be before I was back in the "Stans," tracking down the people responsible for this attack.

As I glanced down at the kids, I thought about Hector in the *Iliad*, and how he leaned down to kiss his infant son before going into battle. The baby burst into tears, terrified. Realizing little Astynax was frightened by his plumed helmet, the "loving father" Hector took it off and gently kissed his son. Hector and his wife both knew that he was going to his death, but for a Greek in Homer's time, trying to avoid *moira*, your fate, was unthinkable. Also unforgivable. I was in Manhattan, of course, not Bronze Age Greece, and I had a mortgage, two kids, and a third on the way. Was leaving my family at a time like this *arête*—excellence and duty—or was it *hubris*—the overweening pride that leads to doom? The only answer I could come up with was that Hector would not be Hector unless he went out to face Achilles. I had signed on a long time ago as an officer of Marines, and my appointed place of duty had just shifted.

We put one of those clear plastic covers over the stroller and tied it to the bottom to make it as windproof as possible. To make it all a game, we dressed the kids in their Halloween costumes, the masks placed over their faces to protect them from falling ash and debris. We told them that the wet towels wrapped around our heads were so the Lion King's hyenas couldn't get us.

At roughly five P.M. we picked up Cordelia in the lobby, leashed her to the stroller, then started off going right, left, right, left—zigging and zagging south and east. We were trying to get to the DA's Office where my car was parked.

Except for a very few looters and people with cameras, the streets were completely deserted. You could go for blocks and not see a single human being. But the pavement was littered with high-heel shoes. Michael was obsessed with how messy the streets were, wondering out loud why all these women's shoes were all over the place.

While we were walking, a guy came running up to us with a huge camera and press credentials on a chain around his neck. He stuck the camera under the plastic covering and into the stroller and started firing off pictures, scaring the kids. I grabbed the camera out of his hands and said, "What the hell are you doing!"

He started shouting about "freedom of the press." In law school, we'd learned that every freedom has limits—my kids were those limits. Some cops were passing by, covered in ash, and he ran over to them screaming that I'd taken his camera.

I told my wife to keep walking and I ran back to the cops, telling them what had happened. They looked at me and one of them said, "You're not going to hurt him, right?" I gave them my word and then, like every other cop that day, they ran to the buildings.

I turned to the guy and said, "I'm not going to break your damn camera and I gave my word I wouldn't break you. I'm going to put the camera down on the corner, and you can pick it up when I get a block away."

And then I ran and caught up with Claudia and the kids.

Minutes later, a police van came screeching up, and another white shirt—a lieutenant—yelled, "Get off! Get off! This isn't safe! Another building just went down." It was 5:20 P.M. Number 7 World Trade Center had just collapsed.

We kept making detours, and then we came to another street that had been clear earlier but now was completed blocked. So we just kept making detours, trying to get as far east as we could. But the Battery Tunnel, the Brooklyn Bridge, the Stock Exchange—these were all obvious targets, "minefields" waiting to explode.

Around six, we got to the DA's Office, and miraculously, my car was where I had left it on the sidewalk.

We put the stroller in the trunk, the kids and the dog in the backseat, and took off, driving up Center to Lafayette to Third Avenue. It was slow going at first, with no streetlights as we kept heading uptown, toward my in-laws' place on Seventy-ninth.

North of Thirty-fourth, I could still smell the fire and ash, but life began to look increasingly normal. With each additional block we were that much farther removed from the reality of what had just happened. I saw people drinking and laughing and I couldn't understand. I thought, "How can you laugh? Don't you get it? This is Pearl Harbor." We began to pass restaurants, and I was struck by the fact that people were eating dinner. I said to myself, "Why are they eating dinner?" My own survivor's guilt had reared its ugly head, and I was projecting it onto other people. "How dare you eat dinner? How dare you go on with your lives? How dare you be alive?"

By the time we got to Seventy-ninth Street, it was early evening. My wife's parents had been calling all day, panicked, worried about us all. They told me they had been glued to the TV, but they still didn't have a sense of how truly bad it was. But here we were, all together, all of us safe.

When my father-in-law took Michael over to the window, my son said, "Look, Grandpa, they've cleaned the streets." Then Claudia and her mother started working over the stroller in the hallway. Covered with soot and grime, it seemed totally out of place in the pristine East Seventies.

That night Diana slept in a Pack 'n Play, and we borrowed an air bag from a neighbor for Michael. Claudia and I started out on the foldout couch, but it was so uncomfortable that we wound up sleeping on blankets and sofa cushions on the floor of the room that had been hers growing up.

Claudia noticed that I was bleeding. I had a decent gash but I had no clue how I'd got hurt. I did a quick body search to see if anything else was wrong. But mostly, my mind was fixated on "Are my kids going to have nightmares about all this? How is it going to affect their view of the world?" Writing from the trenches in World War I, the British poet Siegfried Sassoon described how an officer feels about his men, how you never really have the time or energy to feel tired or hungry or even scared yourself because you are so focused on those in your charge for whom you are responsible and who depend on you. I tried hard not to think how Sassoon finished his meditation: that if he couldn't save them, at least he could share the dangers and discomforts they endured.

I was also thinking about the separation to come. At that moment, on Tuesday night, September 11, I was still a DA, but my current assignment in the Marine reserves was as an IMA—individual mobilization augmentee—one of two thousand Marine reservists who are recalled to active duty not as units but as individuals based on their experience and background, their "mission essential" skill sets. I was attached to the Operations Directorate (called J3) at U.S. Central Command, headquartered at MacDill Air Force Base, Tampa, Florida. My essential skill set was counterterrorism operations. And my region was the Stans.

Before we went to bed, I phoned my operational sponsor, Master Sergeant J. J. Girgos, whose job it was to get all of U.S. Central Command's individual reservists to the right place at the right time. I left a message: "I just lost my apartment, and my cell phone doesn't work, but here's a number where you can reach me. And, oh, by the way, *they do this in my house?* Give me some time to get settled, give me some time to move my family into a safe place, and I want in. Big-time."

The next morning when he called back, he laughed and said, "Sir, thanks for volunteering, but your name's already on the list making its way to the president." In other words, you don't really have a choice in the matter.

But then he said, "How much time do you need? This one may be for the long haul, so you better take as much as you need." I was, of course, thinking in terms of months on active duty, not years, and naïvely, I was also assuming that sooner started, sooner done.

I said, "Can you give me a few weeks?"

He said, "I can give you until November."

I said, "Not necessary. Just give me enough time to put my family in a new apartment."

I spent much of the next day on the phone, just checking in. Is everybody okay? Have you heard from so-and-so? The idea of people missing—first responders, i.e., my friends in the NYPD—had started to weigh on me. Tommy Jurgens, a twenty-six-year-old court officer from Judge Solomon's court, had run all the way to Ground Zero to help out. He had been married only three months earlier, had been a combat medic in the Army, and when I'd been prosecuting Puff Daddy and had needed a laugh, he would lean over and tell me a joke that invariably began, "Have you heard the one about the Marine . . ." After being told to evacuate, Tommy's last radio transmission was, "There are people here who need our help." He never came back.

Then I remembered Gunsite, the weekend shooting trip I'd planned with Jerome, my shooting partner. Located in Arizona, Gunsite is the foremost shooting school in the country. Jerome and I had rounded up ten guys, mostly detectives, and found a fleabag motel where we could all stay cheap. Gunsite would set up a mock-up combat town full of bad guys (steel pop-ups) waiting to be captured or shot by the good guys (us). Jerome and I had designed the course for three weapons: pistol, shotgun, and rifle. We had included quick-reaction pistol shooting, house-clearing and other shotgun drills, and sniper shooting—Jerome's favorite—to be followed by a run-through-the-mud, take-no-prisoners final exam in which we killed every pop-up and saved the women and children. We had sat in my office for hours, eating sushi and planning each aspect with military precision.

Jerome and I had become friends in the early nineties. While on mototcycle patrol, he'd discovered a body that led to his and my first homicide case. We had a few more together after that one and always laughed when we thought back to the idea of two rookies on the same homicide. A few years later, he had made the NYPD Emergency Services Unit, New York's version of SWAT. These are the guys who talk you off the ledge. They also pick you off at a distance if you've taken hostages. But mostly they do rescues. Which made Jerome very much a "first responder." I had no doubt that he was at Ground Zero and would be there around the clock for days if not weeks.

But now I was in a quandary, because it had taken us a year to put this shooting trip together. Jerome, who was engaged to fellow cop Jessica Ferenczy, had been looking forward to this weekend with the guys for a long time. He would not give it up without a fight.

On Wednesday night, I left a message on his home phone: "Hey, Jerome, I know you must be swamped—probably in there pulling out the bodies. I really think we need to reschedule this weekend. I mean, obviously, we're not doing it. But don't be pissed at me: We're not canceling the course, we're rescheduling. Just be careful."

Meanwhile, at Ground Zero, NYPD had set up a command center in the schoolyard where Michael was signed up for preschool. There were still police details at barricades. The fires were still not out, and there was concern about looting. There were also questions about whether any more buildings might collapse.

By Thursday I had "clearance" to go back down. There was nothing official about this. It was more a matter of my saying, "Guys, I'm going in," and their saying, "Sure . . . you want us to come with you?"

Every room in our apartment, every single surface—beds, clothes, furniture, kitchen counter, everything—was still white with ash. Luckily, none of the damage was structural, but I wasn't there to assess. I was there to get stuff for the kids and leave.

At about this time, I called and left a second message for Jerome. He was number sixteen on my speed dial, but my cell phone still wasn't working. I was also still procrastinating about canceling, because I knew he would be so pissed. He'd call me a "weenie." He'd say, "Bullshit! We're going. Now more than ever, this is when you really need your shooting skills." On the second message I said, "I know you have no way to get hold of me, so I'll track you down."

On Thursday, the city opened the tunnels and bridges, and that evening we went out to our place in New Jersey. Before we left, I called again. "Hey, Jerome, I haven't heard from you. I'm probably going to head out to the cabin. Here's the number."

Our weekend place is a couple of hours out of the city, and definitely nothing fancy, but the backyard slopes down to a lake. Basically, it's one big room with a huge fireplace, surrounded by four bedrooms, a big kitchen, a small office, and two baths. I have a workout room—heavy bag, speed bag, and double-end bag. Dumbbells and a pull-up bar.

Out here in the country, a kind of cognitive dissonance set in. Claudia kept thinking about the people who'd worked in the basement of the World Trade Center. That was a little underground village where she did her shopping. She was fixated on a woman named Allison, who worked at the Kelly Film place there. I assured her they would have gotten out right away—it wasn't like the people trapped one hundred stories up at Windows on the World. These were not Claudia's close friends, but she saw them every day. How could such a big part of the world disappear? How can so many human beings just go up in smoke? And how can any group of men be so insane that they would willingly create this kind of devastation and loss of life?

I had already begun getting the kids ready for my mobilization, describing how I was going to have to go fight the bad guys. Michael would chide me if I skipped any part of my exercise routine. He'd say, "Daddy, you have to do more push-ups. You have to be strong to fight the bad guys." But then he'd add in a small voice, "Daddy, are you really stronger than all the bad guys?" I assured him that I was.

But mostly we tried to provide happier images to replace those that Michael and Diana had been exposed to. At the cabin in New Jersey, we played with the kids all day and watched movies at night. Diana sat on my stomach during crunches. Michael kept saying, "Daddy, you're hugging me too much." He put me on a kissing quota. "Daddy, you can have sixteen kisses." Sixteen was the biggest number he knew.

That feeling of unreality intensified on Saturday when I drove to the nearest convenience store to pick up the *Times*. All those pictures of flame and rubble and death, firefighters who took their last rites *before* running into the building. And as I flipped the pages, there was Jerome's picture. Officer Jerome Dominguez . . . blah, blah, blah.

My first thought was self-deception. Okay, what heroic thing has he done now? But then I started to shake. It was the wrong kind of picture. It was the formal portrait in the dress blue uniform that they always use when cops and Marines have been killed.

I thought I was going to be sick. I went back into the store and bought the *Daily News* and the *Post*. Already the images were flowing into my head, such as the time years earlier when Jerome sat with me at the courthouse on a Friday, waiting for the jury to make up its mind in a case I was prosecuting. I had to be in Garden City to catch a plane for one of my active-duty assignments, and I had cut it a bit too close. I had my Marine seabag packed and with me, and we hung out eating sushi and waiting. The moment the verdict was rendered, Jerome drove me with lights and sirens to my muster station while I changed in the patrol car. I made the plane.

I heard later that he had not even been on duty on the day he'd died. He and his partners had known that the tower might collapse, so they turned off their radios. They did not want to be called out so long as there were people they might be able to rescue. His whole team had just ceased to exist.

Of the twenty-three police officers who died that day, twelve of them were friends. Some of them had been in my office the week before. Some I knew pretty well, but no one as well as I knew Jerome.

They never found his remains. I was deployed before they gave up the search. They held the memorial service without a body. One day in Afghanistan I got an e-mail from NYPD lieutenant, Robert Dovekin, a mutual friend, saying what a great service it was.

That first weekend at the cabin, I spent a lot of time cooking with Claudia and the kids. For me—as for most Greeks—cooking is not work. It's therapy. We also watched a lot of videos. It reminded me of when I was not much older than Michael and my dad would come home from the restaurant and want to watch the late movie on TV. We would have left the restaurant earlier in the evening and gone to bed, but he would "accidentally" wake us up, and after about five minutes of begging, Mom would relent and we would all pile blankets on the floor and watch old movies. By the time I was fifteen, I'd probably seen *It's a Wonderful Life* five times; the same for *The Maltese Falcon, High Noon, The Magnificent Seven*, and *The Prisoner of Zenda*. If my mom got to the channel first, it would be *Singing in the Rain, Easter Parade*, or anything with Fred Astaire and Ginger Rogers. It might be during the week with school the next day, but whenever Dad felt like it, it became a special night.

I wanted to give my kids that same feeling of comfort and connection, figuring we could all use a break from what we had been through. But what we watched first and foremost, piled under the blankets in the big room with the fireplace, was my favorite of all time, *Casablanca*. The dialogue, the story, the acting—it's a work of art. And after the number of times I've seen it, I feel as if Rick and Louie and Ilsa are friends of mine. I know what they're going through. I admire them for who they are. Rick, especially, was good at what he did, and he followed the code. He had run guns in the Spanish Civil War, he ran a great gin joint, and when push came to shove, he did not take the letters of transit for himself. But the reason that *Casablanca* is the greatest movie ever made is that Ilsa gets on that plane with Victor Laszlo, and Rick stays behind in the fog on the tarmac with Louie. If Rick had put "the concerns of three little people" ahead of the cause he believed in, if he had kept Ilsa for himself and tried to live happily ever after, *Casablanca* would have been just another B movie with one memorable song and some really snappy dialogue.

5

MOBILIZATION

*Man should share the passion and action
of his time at peril of being judged not
to have lived.*—Oliver Wendell Holmes, Jr.

THREE DAYS AFTER the 9/11 attacks, Tropical Storm Gabrielle swept along the west coast of Florida with 68 mph winds and eleven inches of rain, but at MacDill Air Force Base in Tampa, U.S. Central Command continued operating around the clock. The usual workforce of a thousand or so would hit three thousand before the end of the year. To absorb the overflow, staffers "hot-racked" the desks and computers, meaning that one guy would occupy the space for twelve hours and then another guy would come in and work at that same desk, phone, and computer for the next twelve hours.

On September 21, 2001, President Bush gave an ultimatum to Taliban leader Mullah Mohammed Omar, the de facto head of state in Afghanistan: Close down the al-Qaeda training camps and either turn over the terrorist leaders who had just murdered 2,973 innocent men, women, and children from seventy countries, or be on the receiving end of U.S. retaliation. NATO had already voted to support a U.S. counterstrike, with French, Italian, and British forces soon deployed off Pakistan.

Back in New York, Claudia, the kids, and I were returning to our apartment, steam-cleaned by the Little Elves Cleaning Company. Our building has a washer and dryer on almost every floor, and Claudia and her mother had filled every one of those machines with sheets and towels and all the children's clothing, as well as their washable toys. There were five loads of stuffed animals alone.

The counterstrike, known as Operation Enduring Freedom, began on October 7, 2001, as B-2 and B-52 heavy bombers, Tomahawk missiles, and Air Force F-15 Eagles and F-16 Falcons streaked to their targets inside Afghanistan. At the same time, we sent in parachute drops of food and other humanitarian relief. Over one million Afghans had fled the country, so we were also setting up refugee camps in Pakistan, Uzbekistan, and Tajikistan.

Ten days later, on October 17, U.S. Army four-star general Tommy Franks, commander of U.S. Central Command, launched a revolution in U.S. efforts against terrorism. He requested permission from Secretary of Defense Donald Rumsfeld to stand up a new unit to coordinate military operations, military intelligence, civilian intelligence, and law enforcement. This was the team that I would lead into Baghdad a year and a half later.

That same day, October 17, 2001, I closed the door to my office and walked to my going-away party at a bar a few blocks away from the courthouse in lower Manhattan.

I had joined the New York County District Attorney's Office on February 22, 1988, four days after leaving active duty in the Marines. During thirteen and a half years on the job, I had kept every card and letter that every witness or victim had ever sent me. There were many hundreds, and before I left that day I reread every one of them, wishing I could tell each of these people how profoundly *they* had affected and enriched *my* life. Instead, I simply left an outgoing message on my voice mail saying, "I have been recalled to active duty with the United States Marine Corps and will be out of the office from October 17, 2001, for an undetermined period of time."

Any U.S. military action in the "central" part of the globe, from the Horn of Africa, across the Middle East to the Hindu Kush and Pakistan, is owned and operated by U.S. Central Command (CENTCOM). The concept of regional commands for war fighting—CENTCOM is one of five—was put into law by the Goldwater-Nichols Act of 1986. Before that time, the various branches of the U.S. military maintained their own discrete command structures, coordinated only in the most remote and Olympian fashion by the Joints Chiefs of Staff, themselves established by the National Security Act of 1947.

But having the various chains of command isolated within organizational silos or stovepipes had shown its fatal limitations in 1980. Five months into the Iran hostage crisis, President Jimmy Carter sent in a strike force to rescue American citizens being held at the U.S. embassy in Tehran. This hoped-for extraction required precise coordination among different units from different branches of the service. But once on the ground, they discovered that they could not even speak to each other on the same radio frequencies. The whole operation was a fiasco, finally aborted when U.S. choppers crashed and were stranded in a desert sandstorm, killing eight American servicemen.

Diversity among doctrines is good: It multiplies the perspectives brought to bear on each mission or problem set and it adds depth to the planning process. Competition among the armed services—of which the U.S. military has always had plenty—is also good. When healthy, rivalry helps develop esprit de corps, enabling each of the services to develop its own unique culture, as well as its own highly refined combat expertise.

The Marines are a "lean and mean" mobile strike force that can launch almost anywhere in the world within six hours from receipt of mission. The words "Send in the Marines" have been uttered at one time or another by every U.S. president for over a century. We kick open the door, but then we need the Army's numbers, heavy armor, and logistical support system to keep that door open. The Navy gets us where we need to be, but it also holds the shoreline and maintains vital lines of communication and points of access. Naturally, each of these forces has its own air capability. The Air Force, however, fights the "deep" or distance air battle, reducing the enemy's strength before the ground assault finishes the job.

Goldwater-Nichols put all these distinct arrows in the same quiver, requiring compatible communications and establishing a clear line of centralized authority. After 1986, the Marines, Navy, Army, and Air Force would continue to function independently in terms of doctrine, training, and recruiting, but there would be a new, unified command for actual engagement. As a result, the services now buy the weapons and train the people, but then, when action is imminent, they "source"— meaning that they supply equipment and personnel—to one of these unified commands. Depending on the location of the hot spot, this would be either Central, headquartered in Tampa; European, headquartered in Stuttgart, Germany; Pacific, headquartered in Hawaii; Southern (for South America), headquartered in Miami; or Northern (for North America), headquartered in Colorado. (There are also four "functional" commands. Two—Special Operations and Transportation—integrate with whichever regional command needs their services, and two—Joint Forces and Strategic—function more as think tanks, analyzing actions and trends and publishing papers, regulations, and lessons learned on current and future operations.)

In 2001, al-Qaeda was operational in sixty countries, but their nerve center was in Afghanistan, squarely within CENTCOM's AOR, or area of responsibility. As in the early nineties with Desert Storm, the on-air briefings for Enduring Freedom would come from Tampa, with CENT-COM commander Tommy Franks in the leading role once played by former CENTCOM commander Stormin' Norman Schwarzkopf.

The first response to 9/11 was for Marine lieutenant general Michael Delong, General Franks's number two, to call my boss, Air Force major general Gene Renuart, head of the CENTCOM Operations Directorate, and tell him to stand up his CAT, the crisis action team, which is essentially the basic staff running on steroids, around the clock, 24/7. Renuart locked down all bases overseas, including CENTCOM forward headquarters in Qatar, on the Persian Gulf.

To root out the Taliban, al-Qaeda's hosts and protectors who controlled 80 percent of Afghanistan, General Franks decided to rely on anti-Taliban Afghans as "force multipliers" for our own investment in men and matériel. Asymmetric warfare, relying on indigenous fighters enhanced by U.S. advisors, training, and hardware, built squarely on the kind of training I had been involved in for the preceding three years. Since 1998, I had been sent as a reservist on temporary active duty in an advisory capacity (in twenty-five- to sixty-day increments) to South Korea, Lithuania, Guyana, Kosovo, Kazakhstan, and Uzbekistan.

On each deployment, the mission was always the same—to train and equip foreign soldiers to do their job better, both in terms of combating terrorism and of keeping things under wraps once the immediate crisis had cooled down, what we call peacekeeping and stability operations. As advisors, once we'd demonstrated credibility in combat expertise, we also got in a word or two about the virtues of respect for the rule of law and of civilian control of the military.

And each time I was placed on active duty, I would begin the process of being gone. First, I would coordinate with all detectives, defense attorneys, and judges with whom I had open cases to identify those cases that could be adjourned until my return and those that could not and had to be reassigned. Such was the consummate professionalism of my colleagues and adversaries, that my cases were almost always adjourned without incident or demur until my return. Second, I would update my medical records, ensure that my will and other legal matters were in order, and file the necessary notices with my credit card companies, etc. After thirteen and a half years as a reservist and assistant district attorney, I had the whole process down to a science and could do it all in a day or two. Finally, I said my good-byes—a simple "See you in a few weeks (or months)," and then I got a haircut, hung up my suit, put on my uniform, and got on a plane.

These new ad-hoc, short-notice, "advisor-type" assignments once I joined CENTCOM represented the third phase of my development as an officer of Marines. The first phase was as a JAG on active duty, learning critical investigative, forensic, and fundamental military skills. Phase two was the ten years I spent as a reservist in a Marine infantry battalion—during the first two years of which I was simultaneously working to persuade Headquarters Marine Corps to permit me to change my specialty from law to infantry. I practiced small-unit tactics until they became second nature, I refined my terrain-appreciation and map-reading skills, and I learned how to call in mortar, artillery, and air strikes. The Marines also taught me how to survive in the hottest deserts (Death Valley), the coldest mountains (California's Sierra Nevada range), and the wettest jungles (Panama). The deeper lessons were in what it meant to be a leader, how it was far more effective to influence the actions of others by example, will, and shared vision than it was to rely on force, threats, or position. But it was only after 9/11—phase four—that I was called upon to incorporate into my military toolkit the skills I had developed as a criminal investigator and prosecuting attorney.

One of the indirect consequences of the 9/11 attacks was that it brought to light the multiple levels of inadequacy and incongruity that still existed within our national defense establishment. But while it was incompatible radio frequencies and procurement programs that underlay the failures of the late seventies, it was incompatible computers, databases, and organizational cultures that characterized pre-9/11 governmental bureaucracy. *The Report of the President's Commission on 9/11* went on at length about the absence of cross-referencing among the State Department's TIPOFF program, the Federal Aviation Administration's "No-Fly" list, and the CIA's, FBI's, and U.S. Customs Service's individual watch lists. The FAA's list even included the names of three of the 9/11 hijackers—information that was never put to use to thwart the attack. While Goldwater-Nichols had repaired interservice incompatibility by forcing the services to work together, it had done nothing to fix (or even address) interagency incompatibility. The real challenge was to work as a single team despite the diverse cultures, competing interests, and differing priorities of the dozens of different governmental organizations that had a role in national security.

According to U.S. policy in effect on September 11, 2001, any counterterrorism investigation overseas had to stop at "the water's edge," where U.S. territory began. There might well be a parallel investigation of the same threat being carried out on the criminal side by a domestic law-enforcement agency, but there was to be no communication among agencies, or even among units within agencies. Each section had a different piece of the puzzle. They even attended the same meetings—but took care to follow regulations and not share information. There are, of course, perfectly good reasons for keeping the military and intelligence services out of domestic law enforcement. Unfortunately, abuses of investigative powers during the civil unrest of the sixties, and more especially during Watergate, inflamed opinion to the extent that policy makers turned what had been a reasonable and even advisable separation into a barrier as rigid and impermeable as the Great Wall of China. At the same time that our enemies were evolving beyond traditional forms, shifting into ever more amorphous shapes, the law-enforcement and counterterrorism functions of the U.S. government were trapped in a completely regulated and ruthlessly monitored separation.

In hindsight, the failure to coordinate seemed about as clearheaded as former U.S. Secretary of State Henry Stimson's objections to forming an espionage service before World War II—"Gentlemen do not read other gentlemen's mail."

But the 1993 World Trade Center bombing notwithstanding, policy makers maintained a convenient though false dichotomy: international terrorists operated overseas, homegrown extremists set bombs at home. Islamic extremists had blown up the USS *Cole* in Yemen and the embassies in Kenya and Tanzania. Timothy McVeigh, a former U.S. soldier with a grudge against the FBI, blew up the Alfred P. Murrah Federal Building in Oklahoma City.

On 9/11, al-Qaeda shattered the illusion of our security against foreign attackers. Belatedly, policy makers saw that we needed to get our cops and our war fighters on the same page. We were to become that page.

On October 25, 2001, General Myers, Chairman of the Joint Chiefs of Staff, and Mr. Rumsfeld approved a new interagency concept for all regional commands. At CENTCOM, we immediately began coordinating with the National Security Council, but this was still a world of finite resources. The FBI had few agents it could spare. The same was true with the CIA, DEA, and Customs, soon to become the Bureau of Immigration and Customs Enforcement, or ICE. But because the presumptive center of action—the Middle East and Central Asia—was within CENTCOM's area, we got first dibs on whatever players were available.

General Franks told Brigadier General Gary Harrell to put a team on the ground in Afghanistan as soon as possible, and Gary Harrell is not one to waste time, or sentiment. On Harrell's body, you will find scar tissue from top to bottom. On his résumé, you will find Airborne, Ranger, Delta Force, Bronze Star with a V for valor and two oak-leaf clusters (meaning he has three Bronze Stars), and another couple dozen medals. But you won't always be able to determine the mission for which he received them—because that's classified. In 1993, during the raid in Mogadishu portrayed in *Black Hawk Down*, it was Brigadier General—then Lieutenant Colonel—Gary Harrell who was the Delta commander. After the Blackhawk crashed, two Delta snipers specifically requested permission to descend into a sea of heavily armed Somali fighters in an attempt to protect the downed helicopter crew. So long as there was the slightest chance to save the crew, it was the right thing to do. But everyone had to know that it was essentially a suicide mission. "Every decision should be made within the space of seven breaths," wrote the seventeenth-century samurai Yamamoto Tsunotomo. Gary Harrell took one breath and gave them permission to try. Both men were later awarded posthumous Congressional Medals of Honor, but they did their job and saved the life of the one crewman who survived the initial crash. There was only one Gary Harrell and, unfortunately for al-Qaeda, he was assigned to CENTCOM.

General Harrell began tapping people for this new unit that—for operational security reasons—was code-named Task Force Bowie while in Afghanistan. He quickly brought in officers from the New York City Police Department. New York had already partnered FBI agents with cops from the NYPD, combining the broader authority of the Feds with the street smarts of NYC detectives in its Joint Terrorism Task Force. And that unit had the corporate knowledge and the open indictments on Usama bin Laden. General Harrell also coordinated with foreign government agencies such as the British MI5 (Security Service), MI6 (Intelligence Service) and SAS (Special Air Service).

On the U.S. military side, General Harrell swept through the halls at CENTCOM, selecting only those he or someone close to him had worked with in the past. Only Marines, Army Special Forces, Navy SEALs, or Delta need apply. No rookies either, rookies being defined as anyone with fewer than fifteen years of experience in their craft. In fact, many selectees, such as Marine lieutenant colonel Scott Duke and Army sergeant major Vince Perez had already retired—gold watch and everything—until they got a phone call from Gary Harrell telling them to get on the next plane to Tampa. The paperwork could be filled out and the legalities worked out later, he told them.

Since General Harrell and I had never met, my interview was a little unorthodox and not terribly complicated. One day in Tampa, Lieutenant Colonel Terry Sopher, a superb officer I had gotten to know during my work with Kazakh, Kyrgyz, and Uzbek military forces, approached me and said, "Matthew, would you like to join an experimental multiagency counterterrorism unit General Harrell is forming?"

"What is it?" I replied.

"I can't tell you. It's focal point" (meaning a security clearance above top secret, and—like 99.99 percent of the people—I didn't have that clearance).

"What will it do?"

"I can't tell you that either."

"You can't tell me where it'll operate either, can you?"

"Nope."

"Sounds good. I'm in."

Once "in," I learned that we (and at that point the inclusive pronoun was nothing more than determination on my part) would hit Afghanistan with approximately one hundred investigators and operatives from military units and a dozen different federal law-enforcement organizations including CIA, Customs, National Security Agency, FBI, Diplomatic Security Service, Justice, Treasury, and the Drug Enforcement Administration.

We were institutionalizing a vital function that had, for generations, been entirely dependent on which people liked to hang out together after work, and whether back home they played squash or hunted squirrels. Before the task force came along, any instance of interagency coordination was entirely driven by the personalities involved. If the regional security officer at the embassy and the CIA station chief were buddies, then they would have some idea of what was on the other's agenda. Otherwise, it was that old Chinese Wall.

We were already well supplied with trigger-pullers, so from the CIA we recruited analysts, translators, and techies. If you kick down a door and recover fifty computers, you damn well better have a computer forensic-examination capability to see what's on those hard drives. You also better have people able to speak and read Dari or Pashto. It took the general twenty-five days—from October 25 to November 20—to track down the right people, who immediately went to work developing and compiling the intelligence necessary to create "targeting folders," dossiers on the bad guys that would lead to specific strategies for "direct action." The goal was to develop the targeting folders, then immediately carry out the action as well—one-stop shopping. But we had to put our ducks in a row. To obtain the requisite legal authorities for this type of operation, we needed to write a clear mission statement and a detailed concept of operations and get both approved.

To get everything ready in time, we set up cots beside our desks and worked around the clock.

CENTCOM is housed on MacDill Air Force Base and sits on a spit of land that juts south from the city of Tampa into Tampa Bay. The facility is located at "standoff distance," meaning that it is far enough away to be protected from direct-fire weapons from the nearest unsecured location, as in direct fire from a building across the street or from a highway overpass. There is the perimeter fencing of the base itself, and then within that, the perimeter fencing around CENTCOM.

The building—a ten-sided, sand-colored stucco with window slits on six sides, that has two floors aboveground and one floor below—sits directly on the water, where it is protected by patrol boats around the clock, as well as by multiple concentric circles of security that include passwords, swipe cards, and lots of heavily armed guards. It also has a satellite dish that's only a little smaller than Yankee Stadium.

The center of the CENTCOM universe is the JOC (Joint Operations Center) floor, yet another perimeter, requiring yet another swipe and yet another password. The walls of this rectangular open space, about half the size of a basketball court, are covered with enormous flat-screen monitors that display maps and video feeds from Predator drones (small, unmanned reconnaissance planes) anywhere in the world. On the floor are about fifty desks, each of which has two or three different computers, as well as a red phone, a black phone, and a white phone, representing different security levels.

On November 20, General Franks approved the plan for Task Force Bowie. This would be the U.S. government's first fully functioning, all-source interagency task force ever deployed by a combatant commander to a combat zone.

The first members of the advance team began moving out the day after Thanksgiving, flying commercial—and definitely coach. Anyone associated with Task Force Bowie was a high-value target, so the team deployed separately under a strict protocol—two people on this plane, one person on that one, three people through Frankfurt, four people through Ankara. If the team traveled on a single plane, then hundreds of years of counterterrorism expertise could disappear in a single blip. No one wore or even carried military uniforms. Civilian clothes were "sanitized" by ripping out the labels. Beards and longer hair were the order of the day.

For the last leg into Afghanistan, each of us came in on a C-130 Hercules transport flying under combat conditions.

Virtually all of the sixty nonmilitary personnel in Task Force Bowie had been recruited specifically to go to Afghanistan, but among the thirty-five military people, about ten were going to stay behind in Tampa to mind the store. I knew that most of the military guys boarding those C-130s were going to be Special Forces who had served with General Harrell in Somalia or Kosovo or some other hot spot. The people who stayed in the rear with the gear would be the NFGs—the new guys—and I was determined not to be among them for long.

When I hit Tampa, I took the twelve-hour midnight shift, then stayed on for much of the day as well. "You can rest when you're dead," my drill instructor at Officer Candidate School had told us, and I was determined to make myself indispensable. Then one day we had a staff meeting to discuss the variety of escape routes ("rat lines") the bad guys could use to leave Afghanistan. Anytime they chose, they could exfiltrate on pack animals over the mountains, on small planes, or on a 737 out of Kabul's completely unregulated airport. During this meeting, one of my fellow officers pitched a new, analytical methodology for targeting high-value individuals—law enforcement procedures integrated with both military operations and border security.

Back in 1996, during one of my temporary active-duty assignments,

I had commanded a joint task force along the Mexico-Arizona border, so I had some credibility with these issues. Mostly, I saw border security as my ticket to Afghanistan. So I didn't ask anyone. I simply went back to my room, packed, and brought my seabags into our SCIF (secure, compartmented information facility) for my normal midnight shift. Throughout the next day, I framed any and all subsequent conversations as if it were a done deal: "When I get there, this is what I want to do first." "When I get there, this is the way I want to handle this."

I was overdue for a deployment physical, so I went to the hospital on base. The doctor gave me the standard battery of tests. When we were done, he casually and without comment handed me a piece of paper and said, "You're not deployable."

There was no sign of awareness that he had just shattered my world. He just as easily could have been saying, "Wrong office. It's down the hall."

I intentionally did not react. I did not ask the usual questions: How bad is it? What can I do? (And with a thought to future deployments, I will likewise spare you the specifics of this minor ailment.) I wanted to spend as little time with him as I could. I wanted to minimize the chances that he would ever remember me.

"I'll walk the records down the hall for you, Doc," I told him.

Fortunately, he was just as indifferent about procedure as he was about me.

"Sure," he said. He probably had some forms to fill out. He was the kind of doctor who, I think, enjoyed filling out forms.

Then I walked down the hall to another medical guy I knew. I figured I had to give it a shot.

I said, "Look, I'm going to Afghanistan." I did not tell him that neither my deployment nor the mission as a whole for that matter had even been approved yet. I needed to create a sense of urgency. I also did not let him read the papers I had in my hand, because I wanted to give him plausible deniability. He knew that I had lost my apartment on 9/11. He knew that I had buddies from the NYPD who were killed that day.

"There's a chance that these papers might indicate that I am nondeployable," I said. "But I need to do this."

We stepped into his office, he signed his name on another piece of paper, and he said, "You're deployable."

When I got back to our SCIF, I shredded the original documents.

There is no doubt a regulation somewhere that says I shouldn't have done that, and I'll bet the first doc could quote it.

Back in the office, I approached Marine lieutenant colonel Jim Sweeney, the senior Task Force Bowie officer still in Tampa, and gave him my proposal for initiating border security in Afghanistan. I told him my bags were packed and that I was medically cleared. Given the austere environment in Afghanistan and the experimental nature of Task Force Bowie, we had a strict limit on head count, and every seat on those C-130s going into Kabul was highly prized. Sweeney knew that if I went, it was that much less likely that he would get his chance. But team player that he was, he also saw the value in the mission. He looked at me, nodded slowly, and said, "I'll be right back." Then he went into his office and called General Harrell on the satellite phone. He came out a few minutes later and said, "Get on the next plane."

Fewer than forty-eight hours after first hearing about the border-security mission, then, I was lifting off from Tampa, en route to Afghanistan.

Six months later, on the way back, I brought the doc who had cleared me some kind of present—I can't remember what it was. We stepped into an office, and that's when I noticed the picture of Jerome on the wall. Aside from being in the NYPD's Emergency Services Unit, Jerome had been an Air Force reservist. It turns out that he had been sent down to Tampa to help train CENTCOM guys in emergency procedures. One of the trainees was this doc who had bent the rules to allow me to get to the show. Just as when he had driven me with lights and sirens years earlier, Jerome was still getting me where I needed to be. I fully expect him to remind me of that one day.

I deployed to CENTCOM in mid-October and my son Jason was born on November 29. I missed out on one of the great experiences of my life. Had I stayed in Tampa, I would have been able to fly home for any emergency and, perhaps, the odd weekend every month. I certainly *could have* stayed in Tampa. Military planning is valuable work, and all those down there were away from home and making the kind of sacrifice they had committed to when they signed up. So why was I so insistent on getting to the center of the action, 6,736 miles away from safety and security and comfort, my wife and my kids and my dog?

For one thing, this is what I had been trained to do. I had spent twenty-one years (active and reserve) talking the talk—now it was time to walk the walk. Which is another way of saying that I firmly believed it was my duty. Kant says the concept of duty has no meaning when it coincides with what you would otherwise be inclined to do. Duty only takes on meaning to the extent that it is contrary to what you would otherwise wish. In the fall of 2001, my sense of duty required me to be wherever the Marine Corps and CENTCOM needed me, but it wasn't because I didn't want to be home with my family. It wasn't because I didn't have a good civilian job that I enjoyed. And it wasn't because I wanted the extra paycheck. ("Imminent danger pay," as it is officially called, was $150 a month extra—raised to $225 in April 2003.)

It also struck me that it was my fate. Here was a new kind of enemy, and defeating them would not be limited to military actions like storming across beachheads in Normandy or in the South Pacific. This battle was just as likely to be carried out in an apartment in Hamburg or a police raid in Marseilles as on the Afghan plains. We needed to integrate the investigative skills of law enforcement with military tactical know-how, which sounded like a smarter version of me. The bad guys were even operating out of a region where I had experience—me again. *Amor fati*, Nietzsche had called it. Love of fate.

Moreover, my study of history had imbued me with an overwhelming admiration for "those that have gone before," for those men and women who had made incredible sacrifices for their beliefs, their families, and their country. I had read their stories and wept when their widows were handed a folded flag at the grave site. I had once handed over the flag myself. I considered it an honor to serve in the tradition they had established.

On a more personal level, it was also vitally important to me to do whatever I could to ensure that my children never have to put Halloween costumes on *their* kids and breathe through wet handkerchiefs and say it's because they're playing a game. No guarantees, of course, but I wanted to be able to say, "Not on my watch," or at least, "Over my dead body."

There were other, more selfish reasons as well. I love the action and the challenges I experience in the military—I make no bones about that. As Churchill said, "Nothing in life is so exhilarating as to be shot at without result." I had been called, but had seen no action in the last shooting war (Desert Storm), and I wanted to see how I would measure up. You don't train for twenty years and then sit out the race. Perhaps second only to the security of my children, though, the reason I had to get to Afghanistan was because, like Henry V, "if it be a sin to covet honor, I am the most offending soul alive."

Was Hector being heroic or selfish when he went off to do battle with Achilles, knowing full well that he would be killed? It all depends on your perspective. Certainly his wife might have thought it selfish— had she not been a creature of the Homeric world. But Andromache knew that if Hector had not gone to his death, he would not have been Hector. We are all stuck, in varying degrees, with what the Greeks call our *moira*, our fate. My fate is to march to the guns. And maybe it's my wife's fate to be married to me.

A year and a half earlier, when Diana was born, Claudia had been in labor fewer than two hours, and knowing that I would not be around for the birth of our third child, I wanted to make sure that my wife got to the hospital with time to spare. More for my peace of mind than hers, I picked half a dozen of the best NYPD detectives I knew, men that I would trust (and have trusted) with my life, and asked them if they would be on call. Mike Kennedy, Joe Sweeney, John White, Rob Mooney, Kevin Flanagan, and Arty Caddigan were all over it. I knew which ones worked nights or weekends, so with each of them taking turns, I could ensure 24/7 coverage. On Monday it was Kevin Flanagan, Tuesday was Mike Kennedy . . . They had their baby chart, just like the chart for a homicide investigation.

As it turned out, when Claudia went into serious labor, she was having dinner at a restaurant on Thirty-fourth Street, between Second and Third avenues, and she simply walked the four blocks and gave birth in the hallway of the hospital. I was pained that her friend Karyn was there instead of me, but at least Claudia wasn't alone.

At three, my son Michael was just old enough to fully experience my absence, so I set up the situation for him in terms of *The Lion King*. I told him, "You remember Mufasa could still see Simba from the sky even after he was gone?" (*Gone* was the only participle I was prepared to use. I've never had the strength to use the D-word.)

"Never forget that I'm just as strong as Mufasa and I'll always be there with you no matter what happens." Later, when I would call from Afghanistan, I would ask Claudia what Michael was wearing. When Michael got on the phone, I would describe what he had on as if I were watching him at that very moment. Then I'd say, "Look up in the sky, Michael, can you see me behind the clouds?"

"Which cloud, Daddy?"

"Count them," I'd say. "I'm behind the fourth one."

"One, two, three . . . that one? But I can't see you."

I'd say, "Of course you can't see me. I'm behind it. I wouldn't be a good hider if you could see me." Then he'd laugh and giggle, asking if I had fought any hyenas today. I think it made all the difference in the world to him.

Approval for my deployment had come on Thursday, and my flight out on Friday was commercial, and typical for the military, the cheapest possible itinerary, which means the worst possible route. The woman arranging the travel hit me with a curve. She said she had to schedule me for an eight-hour layover at JFK airport in Queens—about an hour from my apartment. Would I mind?

Obviously, I called home. Claudia came and picked me up at the airport and we were all able to spend a few hours together, and I got to see the kids, including Jason, our newborn. What I didn't anticipate was what we call the second- and third-order effects of my fortuitous layover. As she told me later, Claudia became convinced that this bizarre gap in the flight schedule was some kind of divine intervention, which was actually God's way of letting me say good-bye. As in, capital-G *good-bye*. I had actually had the same feeling as I boarded the plane leaving JFK.

But then I remembered Albert Einstein's famous lines about randomness and order in the universe. He was expressing his dissatisfaction with the Heisenberg Uncertainty Principle, and everyone remembers the first part of what he said, but not the second sentence, which I hoped applied to my situation. What Einstein said was "God does not play dice with the world." But then he added, "He is subtle, but he is not malicious."

6

THE IRRATIONAL TENTH

To be alive is to undo your belt
and look for trouble.—Zorba the Greek

I CAME IN on a C-130 in the middle of the night to Bagram Air-field, twenty-five miles outside of Kabul. Slightly high on fumes from the aviation fuel, I was strapped to the cargo netting in the un-heated cargo hold, freezing my ass off and reading T. E. Lawrence's (Lawrence of Arabia) *Seven Pillars of Wisdom*. I was the only passenger, but conversation would not have been an option anyway. The drone of the heavy turboprops was way too loud.

I had flown from New York through Heathrow, then on to Adana in Turkey—commercial flights all the way. My .45 had been in the checked baggage and declared. Once in Adana, I took a short military hop and then boarded the C-130 Hercules cargo plane, wondering whether Lock-heed Martin knew that the original Hercules had actually murdered his wife and children in a fit of madness.

Afghanistan is one-half hour out of sync with the rest of the world, and I had not yet changed my watch, but I knew we must have been getting close when all the lights went out. I turned off the reading flashlight that hung around my neck. I would have to wait another day to learn whether Lawrence had taken Damascus. Then I heard the engines change pitch and felt the nose of the plane drop. This was not, however, the comforting "be there soon" feeling of a commercial flight beginning its descent. The plane pitched to the left and then to the right. The nose went back up, then dropped like an elevator cut loose from its cables. Suddenly, it was as if we were flying into the worst storm imaginable, with a pilot who had lost his mind—all SOP, standing operating procedure, for a hot LZ, a landing zone that could expect to take enemy fire.

Military pilots want their planes to be within the weapons envelope as briefly as possible, so they stay above the range of shoulder-launched, surface-to-air missiles, then do a combat roll and drop like a rock. Our plane began to shake as the pilot zigged and zagged. For all he knew, half a dozen jihadists had us bobbing in and out of their sights all the way down.

We slammed onto the tarmac, the engines roared, and the plane shuddered along the pockmarked runway. The loadmaster stepped back into the cargo area and signaled for me to get ready. The engines stayed on and the crew stayed in the cockpit, monitoring their instruments for the heat sources or tracer rounds that might signal hostile action. They had no intention of spending any more time on the ground than necessary. I'm not even sure the plane ever came to a complete stop.

The loadmaster lowered the hatch and let in a blast of frigid air. He slid two pallets full of supplies down the tail door onto the tarmac and I followed. He shoved my bags down after me, gave me a wave, then hit the button to raise the rear hatch.

I looked up at the ice blue stars and felt the cold grip my chest as the big cargo plane taxied away from me. The constellations were so intense that they seemed to swirl, and my mind, deprived of sleep, began to swirl with them. Behind me, the C-130 roared down the runway and climbed back into the sky. And then it was completely still. Not a sound. No crickets chirping. No birds singing. No wolves howling. Nothing.

It was roughly two o'clock in the morning, with no artificial light, and my first thought was that there were eleven million land mines in Afghanistan left over from the Soviet invasion. I stood still, looking up at that van Gogh sky, until I heard a pickup truck crawling along the edge of the tarmac. I realized that I didn't know the day's challenge and password. Five seconds on the ground and I'd already made my first mistake. "Nice going, rookie," I thought.

I picked up my rucksack and my parachute bag and took a few steps toward the truck. My skin stung from the cold, and I could hear the gravel loud under my feet as I moved forward.

The truck pulled to a stop in front of me and a man got out of the passenger side. It was a friendly face, Don Beam, a Navy SEAL whom I had come to admire in the few months I had known him. He came forward but neither of us spoke. He put a hand on my shoulder, and I nodded. That was greeting enough. Then he leaned over and said quietly, "Mines. Walk in my steps."

He grabbed my parachute bag and threw it into the bed of the truck. He handed me an M4, the lighter version of the standard M16 assault rifle. Then I rolled over the tailgate and leaned back on my rucksack against the cab, covering the rear.

In just a few minutes we came to a perimeter of concertina wire, huge rolls four feet high. Within it, a couple of Afghan guards stood outside an ugly poured-concrete structure, the Soviets' most significant contribution to twentieth-century architecture. U.S. forces had fallen in on several of these bombed-out hellholes at the airport complex. One was now the command operations center. From the outside, it appeared vacant, but even at this hour of the morning it was fully manned. We stepped inside several sets of doors, waiting for one to close until opening the next one to maintain light and noise discipline. A dozen guys sat in front of video and computer screens wearing headsets, monitoring satellite feeds streaming in from all over the war zone. Another dozen stood in front of laminated maps with grease pencils planning operations and plotting recent enemy activity. No one even looked up.

When we got to the rear of the same building, Don pointed to a small room that looked as if it belonged in the Alamo. With the penlight around my neck, I could see shell holes in the walls covered over with plywood and duct tape. There were three guys crashed out and one empty cot. I dropped my stuff, took off my boots, and passed out.

The Soviets had fought for a decade trying to subdue Afghanistan, but they failed because they wound up fighting everyone. They didn't distinguish among Hazaras in the west, Uzbeks or Tajiks in the north, or the Pashtuns in the south. Their view that an Afghan was an Afghan became self-fulfilling. All these very different ethnic groups rallied together in only one respect—their desire to get rid of the Soviets. The enemy of my enemy, as Golda Meir once noted.

After the Soviets withdrew in 1989, the Taliban filled the vacuum, allowing their rugged, isolated country to become a training ground for Islamic terrorists. Fortunately, the warlords of the Northern Alliance were no more receptive to domination from Kabul than they were to domination from Moscow.

By contrast, we chose to rely on those Afghan warlords as force multipliers. One of many reasons is that in the Hindu Kush running north-south along the border between Afghanistan and Pakistan, *the floors* of the mountain passes are at fifteen thousand feet—higher than the peak of California's Mount Whitney, the highest point in the continental United States. Given the icing conditions and the lack of air density at that altitude, neither our helicopters nor our C-130s could operate there with any meaningful payload. We needed to make the most of resources already in that region, not deplete our energies transporting resources along a supply line that is almost seven thousand miles long.

On October 20, 2001, Army Special Forces had linked up with the Northern Alliance to begin the ground campaign. These army irregulars wore beards and Afghan headdresses, if only to avoid being picked off by snipers. They also wore panty hose. Fighting Afghan-style meant horseback, which meant saddle sores. At first our guys tried Vaseline as a remedy. Bad idea—it picks up dust and sand. The answer? Panty hose.

Critics of our strategy of using Afghans never seemed to grasp that there was simply no way we could have put enough of our own boots on the ground to do the job. Aside from having to maintain a logistical tail running halfway around the globe, we would have suffered thousands of casualties, half of them to frostbite, high-altitude mountain sickness, and exposure. But to bring order to a country, you need to establish a credible military presence at some point. So, in December, the U.S. Army's Tenth Mountain Division came on board to do just that.

Kabul is on the central plateau, a plains city with mountains in the distance, like Denver. When I woke up that first morning and looked out, I remembered a bit of Kipling I'd memorized for Brother Paul:

> *When you're wounded and left on Afghanistan's plains,*
> *And the women come out to cut up what remains,*
> *Jest roll to your rifle and blow out your brains*
> *An' go to your Gawd like a soldier.*

I chose not to share that passage with anyone else that first morning. Looking out toward the mountains, this part of the world looked prehistoric, with no major structural changes since the introduction of the camel. Inside our camp at Bagram, however, the aesthetic was pure Stalinist realist. I looked around to see who was in the room with me. There were four of us together, all lieutenant colonels, a psychologist, a lawyer, and a logistics expert, and it turned out I already knew one of them. They all nodded and said, "Good to have you." The psychologist was not there to make sure we were "okay." He was there to advise in the interrogations of HVDs, high-value detainees.

I checked my .45 in my shoulder holster and looked for the rest of my stuff.

Very much aware that I was the new guy, the NFG, I didn't run around asking, "What should I do? How do we do that?" Instead, as Yogi Berra noted, you can observe a lot by watching. You watch some guy grab a bottle of water and a small pan the size of a baking dish and go outside to "bathe" and you do the same. It's like the three-second delay on live TV.

That first morning, just before the daily TAC—tactical—meeting I met General Harrell. He was in his fifties and a grandfather, but I wouldn't suggest trying to take him down. He would crush you like a bug, and he might even enjoy it. I walked up to him, and after he shook my hand, he held it just a little longer than necessary and his eyes met mine. His voice said, "I've heard about you. Good to have you here." His eyes said, "Let's see what you've got, NFG." That was it. No speech. No "How was your flight? Did you sleep well?" I hadn't earned it yet.

A few minutes later, Terry Sopher, the lieutenant colonel who had recruited me, announced to the group, "Matt's here. Some of you know him, he'll start working border security," which was followed by a nod or two. That was it. My welcome. Not unfriendly, not overly friendly and no surprise either. I had yet to earn any more than that. To look at them, this was a pretty ragtag bunch, most having gone native with beards and headcloths. All were battle-hardened, the youngest was maybe thirty-five, and each was the best at what he or she had to contribute or he or she wouldn't have been there.

For those first couple of days, I was wondering if maybe I had made a mistake in crashing this party. Letting your reach exceed your grasp is all well and good, but overreach in this group and they'll cut your arm off at the elbow. I wasn't having a crisis of confidence. It was more a recognition that these guys were the real deal: stone-cold professionals at the top of their game. Guys like Special Forces master sergeant Bob Lonegan and Major Ashton Naylor had already seen their share of action, but they were back in the mix, answering the call one more time. Marine lieutenant colonel Mike Grogan had more advanced degrees than anyone I knew, but here he was freezing his ass off as Task Force

Bowie's chief of intelligence. And I was the forty-something NFG. Having read a lot of books, knocked a couple dozen guys out in the ring, and sent some very bad guys to prison did not mean a damn thing. I needed to establish some credibility. Fast.

This was the first time that the United States had operatives from so many different agencies in the field together and able to compare notes. I might have electronic intercepts from a cell phone or the bad guy's canceled checks, and you might have satellite photographs or his mistress's phone number or the name of his landlady's cat. With Task Force Bowie, we would be able to put the pieces all together to find the target and develop the plan. We were taking in information from the National Security Agency (NSA), from the CIA and other agencies, and it was all coming in to this one location, with NYPD sitting next to the FBI, sitting next to the CIA. With our reach-back capability, our FBI guys on the ground in Afghanistan could communicate with our FBI guys back in Tampa, and likewise CIA, NSA, and all the rest.

In such rugged territory, it doesn't do you any good to have a border-security checkpoint if seventy-five miles on either side of that checkpoint is open wilderness. Part of the strategy, then, was to determine the most likely crossing points, both historically and geographically. If the bad guys need "rat lines" to get out of the country, what routes are they going to use? Perhaps the smugglers' routes that have been used for maybe two-thousand years? It was the DEA agents who had been in Pakistan awhile who knew those routes cold.

In developing targeting folders, once you get a location, then you determine the delivery mechanism. Throughout the entire process, you have to think nontraditionally, nonlinearly, in both kinetic and nonkinetic terms. Sometimes the answer is a bomb, but sometimes it is a snatch team. Sometimes the delivery mechanism is an informant, whom you begin to exploit, or whom you insinuate into the target's daily life. Maybe it's as simple as a monitoring device. If you know a guy who's delivering money to bin Laden, you are going to do everything you can to keep that guy alive and functioning as a source of continuing information. So you become his guardian angel.

Operating in Afghanistan, there was also the question of getting a feel for the space, understanding choke points, danger areas, and terrain. Where are the potential ambush sites? In a combat zone, you can't just say, "Hey, guys, I'm going to run down to the corner for a quart of milk." Every time you leave a secure site (whether that site is a forward operating base or a safe house), you have to develop a tactical plan for force protection. How many vehicles? Usually two to four. How many men in each vehicle? Usually three to four. What are the radio frequencies? They change daily. How many weapons? Usually one long gun (rifle) and one short gun (pistol) per person. Is there enough water, fuel, and food in the vehicle? At least two days' worth. What's the rendezvous plan, what's the "no comm" plan, meaning, what happens if there's no communications? Fall back on the objective rally point—usually the last place you were all together. At what point do we send out a search and rescue? Eight hours? Twelve? Twenty-four? It depends on the mission. All of this is, in principle, SOP (standing operating procedure), but each of us from different agencies had to learn the specific SOP for this specific operation.

And then there was the local culture. Along with an infrastructure that did not include light switches or toilets, much less DSL, we faced rivalries among the Uzbeks, Tajiks, Hazaras, and Pashtuns that had been going strong when Alexander passed through in 328 B.C.

A young Afghan who worked with us told me this story: In one particular province there is a ten-o'clock curfew—the purpose of which is to keep strangers or outsiders off the streets—and two Afghan sentries are on watch. They see a man walking across the street. One of the sentries looks at his watch and it's nine forty-five. His partner does the same, then lifts his AK-47 to his shoulder and shoots the guy dead. The first sentry looks at the shooter and says, "What did you do? The curfew is ten o'clock. It's only nine forty-five and you killed him!" His partner turns to him and says, "Yeah, but I knew this guy. He would never have made it home by ten o'clock."

This young man must have told me that story a dozen times, but not just because it made us all laugh. It also explains a lot about Afghan culture, where there is a deep, systemic knowledge of and respect for ancient rivalries. Nothing is merely what it seems to be on the surface. Always woven in somewhere is, "His grandfather stole a goat from my grandfather," maybe going back to the tenth generation.

The first few days were exclusively "What do you need?" and "What can I do for you?" I had to get smart on everyone else's programs, and I also had to get the lay of the land. At every morning's meeting, someone would say, "I need a body to ride shotgun today," and I'd say, "I got it." Then I'd saddle up and go for a ride.

In a moving vehicle in a combat zone, nobody gasses on about the weather or last night's Yankees game. Not much gets said that's not directly related to "I've got a ravine a thousand meters up . . . speed up, slow down . . . good ambush site coming up." The attitude is, "I'm sure you've got a great personal life—and if you want to get back to it, then shut up and pay attention."

When there is downtime, you're usually doing something like cleaning your weapon, fixing your gear, or catching up on intelligence reports and interrogation results. Often that activity is done in informal, rotating groups of three and four. A lot of what gets said is details of past missions, hypotheticals for the next, and revisiting an interrogation to decide where it should go next—finally something on which I could make a contribution. But I did so slowly and in small gulps.

At times, though, when we'd be sitting around having a portion of our MRE (meals ready to eat), we might shoot the breeze a little. You take turns telling stories. Preferably, nonwar stories. Like Homer's, these accounts were formulaic and exaggerated, but only slightly.

Often these stories were about how stupid you had been as a lieutenant—a subject about which I could speak with authority—or about the time in the Philippines when the bar girl turned out to be a man, but nothing graphic. And rank always goes first. The general, if he has stopped by for a few minutes, tells a story, and then the other officers fill in the void, taking turns at random. This could go on for maybe thirty minutes. Maybe there would be six or seven guys, and by the end, each of them would have told one story.

But not when the subject turned to kids. When somebody brought up his kids, maybe one or two would follow suit, but then somebody would change the subject. Fast. It was just too painful, particularly around Christmas and birthdays.

Because of satellite phones—and tactical situation permitting (the enemy can locate you by tracking the signal)—we could have called home every day, but most of us chose not to do that. For one, you proceeded in abject fear of losing the signal and being cut off at just the wrong moment. My wife might understand the suddenly dead line, but there was no way my kids would. On one occasion, Claudia told me that Michael had cried after we had been cut off a few days earlier.

But it's also true that your family has to get on with their lives. You can't be Banquo's ghost, hanging around as some disembodied presence that keeps everyone in a state of worry and longing. There's a measure of self-protection involved too. You could always tell when someone on the team had called and talked to his kids because he had the "thousand-yard stare" that is not reserved only for post-combat.

Many times, I would call Claudia and not talk to the kids. I would ask, "Are you okay, are the kids okay, is there anything you need?" I even took to calling Claudia when the kids were sleeping so I wouldn't be tempted to talk to them.

On February 14, Valentine's Day, three thousand people came to wait at Kabul's antiquated airport terminal, even though no planes had shown up for more than forty-eight hours.

Border security (which included airport security) had been my hook to get there. But Marine lieutenant colonel Vinnie Coglianese—a brilliant logistician who knew biometrics and border security cold—had already taken the lead. He showed me the ropes for a few weeks. Then he was reassigned to something else, leaving airport security to become a loose ball that I picked up.

This was the season of the *hajj*, the obligatory pilgrimage to Mecca, and the first time since the Taliban had come to power that ordinary individuals could travel. Unfortunately, those most inclined to go on the hajj are the old and frail—who knows if this will be their last chance?

Five of the task force had shown up that morning, along with five hundred would-be passengers left over from the day before. Then another five hundred Afghans showed up, expecting to go out on the fourteenth. Another two thousand people, mostly family members, were waiting in the holding area at the mosque across the street.

The Afghans crowded against the fences and tensions rose as, again and again, flights were delayed without explanation. There was, of course, no PA system for announcing changes, and there was no airport security, because there was no airport authority. The few airline employees did little more than act as lightning rods for the angry crowds.

Even though we were dressed in civilian clothes, we were Americans and looked sufficiently "official" to become targets for questions and pleas for assistance. But there was nothing we could do. As the crowd became more agitated and tensions mounted, President Karzai came out to speak to everyone and to ask for their understanding. He had charisma and presence, but even his calming effect was limited. Shortly after he left, the would-be passengers stoned and beat the president of Ariana Airlines, the Afghan national carrier.

At this point, Vinnie—the senior officer on the scene—correctly decided it was better to be absent than to be hopelessly outnumbered and ultimately forced into impossible and potentially fatal choices.

Less than an hour later, Vinnie's decision proved prescient: two 747s arrived, but by that time three elderly *hajjis* had died of crowding and exposure. Evidently, this was the final straw. The crowd rose up, pulled the aviation minister off one of the planes, and stabbed him to death. Then again, an enraged crowd can make a plausible cover for premeditated assassination.

Returning the next day, we began to provide food and blankets to the people still waiting. But our real job remained the same—to try to create long-term order out of Central Asian chaos. To achieve this, we needed to stop bad people from coming in and going out, to create a database of all travelers, and to develop a professional border control service.

On March 12, most, if not all, of the seven thousand people who had left through the airport between February 13 and 19 would start coming back. We had no idea how many of these were really *hajjis* and how many had gone to London or Los Angeles to check in with their al-Qaeda cells. To have access to that kind of information, we had to have our systems in place before they returned. It was going to be tight—if we made it at all.

One of the guys who had been out on the tarmac when things got lively was Senior Master Sergeant Roberto Piñeiro, an Air National Guard reservist who, in civilian life, had logged twenty-seven years at United Airlines. His being a part of Task Force Bowie had nothing to do with his airport experience though—he was an intelligence analyst. That he knew passenger operations inside and out was sheer coincidence. Or maybe it was manna from heaven. So was our meeting. From the moment he introduced himself to me in the mountains of Afghanistan, this fifty-two-year-old newlywed—the first thing he did after being notified he was going to Afghanistan was to marry his girlfriend—fit effortlessly into his new role as the voice of reason to leaven some of my more impulsive ideas.

Learning the ropes in Afghanistan, Senior and I would go out and watch the planes take off and land every day. We watched from five hundred meters or so, driving around, sufficiently distant to not present a threat. After the crowds had dispersed, I would ask questions—what about this, what about that? He would point out things that were wrong and things that were reasonably okay. There were few of the latter.

But sometimes for hours on end we would simply sit and watch the planes land and be met by the standard, machine-gun-mounted-in-the-back pickup trucks called technicals. (In Somalia in the nineties, relief agencies had hired warlords to put serious weapons in their pickups and serve as security. The only budget line they could find for this service was "technical assistance," and the name stuck.) People would get on the planes, or off the planes, and then the planes would fly away.

To understand whatever murky truths lay beneath this simple procedure, I had to crack one of the most complex organizational charts in the annals of dysfunctional government. The fundamental question was who owned the airport: the minister of public security, the minister of the interior, or the military? And if it was the military, which military? Which local commander? Getting answers took a long time, because meetings in Afghanistan do not get right down to business. With each new encounter, before we talked about border security, we had to drink tea and eat almonds and raisins.

As the weeks wore on, there were several claimants, but in fact, power on the ground ebbed and flowed depending on which local commander, aka warlord, was feeling confrontational that day. Afghan warlords see turf battles in terms of entrepreneurial opportunities won or lost. Border real estate under one's control improves one's portfolio in the heroin trade. Why shouldn't control of a database or authority over hiring an airport security service be viewed the same way? If the government imposes screening on those who travel, it follows, does it not, that those who travel will be willing to pay a fee to avoid such a meddlesome procedure? Everything was viewed in terms of power and income stream.

When we began training security workers, for example, the head of Public Security—who had, by the way, just been released from prison for the murder of the aviation minister—sent over his twelve-year-old son. The boy was obviously sent as a spy, but he had the best English, not to mention computer skills, of any of the trainees. And for my program to have any hope of success I needed his father's support. I welcomed this young prodigy with open arms.

Early in March, a half dozen of us at the airport were surrounded by a group of armed Afghan soldiers and told to stop what we were doing. My interpreter, a nineteen-year-old Tajik named Nasrullah, said I should go with the soldiers to see their commander, Colonel Katra. When I refused, not wanting to give this colonel any legitimacy, "Nash" turned to me ashen-faced and said, "Sir, they are not *asking*." I told the head of my security detail, Army major Bill Bailey, that I would be going with just Nash. Bill is a damn good officer and tried to talk me out of it, but I pulled rank and said, "Follow at a distance if you can. If I'm not back in an hour, then send for the cavalry." He smiled and said, "Sir, I thought we *were* the cavalry."

The ride through back streets and alleys lasted for about half an hour, and I gave up trying to memorize the route. Still, I conspicuously checked the chambers of my rifle and my pistol during the ride to make sure there was a round ready to fire in each. Neither of the "escorts" in the backseat spoke any English, and both of them smiled at my forced bravado. I suddenly realized that between them they had probably killed more Soviets than they could count. They must have found me amusing. Frankly, *I* found me a little amusing, and we all chuckled nervously—except Nash. He had not stopped talking from the time I'd met him (despite my repeated requests to the contrary). But now he had not said a word since the airport.

We pulled up to an old government building, and Nash and I were taken to a smoke-stained office. Forty bearded warriors with that scratchy, John the Baptist look sat in a circle on filthy sofas. Colonel Katra asked me to sit next to him and, of course, cordially served tea, raisins, and almonds, while he explained how happy he was to have the Americans. Then he warned me, however, that we were making enemies by insisting on checking everyone who passed through the airport. I sipped my tea and told him he looked more like a warrior than a politician. I took another sip and asked if he had made enemies while fighting the Soviets. With a laugh, he said, "I like you, Colonel." He proceeded to tell some very good stories, virtually every one of which ended with the phrase "and then we killed the Soviet dogs." We were driven back to the airport without further incident.

In his *Seven Pillars*, T. E. Lawrence wrote, "Nine tenths of tactics were certain enough to be teachable in schools, but the irrational tenth was like the Kingfisher flashing across the pool. And in it lay the test of generals. It could be *pursued* only by instinct, sharpened by thought practicing the stroke, until at the crisis it came naturally, a reflex."

My irrational tenth consisted not just of a charm offensive with warlords and government officials. It also included going down to this one particular neighborhood almost every day to play with the kids, which was irrational to the point of being unsafe. This was only for half an hour or so every afternoon, but following any predictable pattern in a war zone is potentially life-threatening.

Senior would say, "Sir, we're not going to go see the kids again, are we?"

And I'd say, "What do you think?"

Always the voice of reason, Senior still never required more than a look from me to be on board. So he would stand on one street corner, while another guy, Vinnie's younger brother, Marine major John Coglianese, an intelligence officer, stood on the other, both armed and dangerous, so that I could have time with the kids.

The children were always excited to see us, and they would rush over in a little mob to say hello, practicing their English. They knew how to say "Hey, Joe!" "How are you?" "Got any gum?" And they taught us bits of Dari and Pashto. These were kids for whom toys and kites had been banned by the religious zealots. One little girl had been whipped in the face for learning to read, even though her only book was the Koran.

One afternoon, a black armored SUV came speeding down the street showing no intention of stopping for any children in its way. I grabbed one of the little girls with one arm and—New Yorker that I am—slammed the side of the car with my hand. It was a stupid thing to do. The car screeched to a stop and four well-dressed, heavily armed men jumped out. They were not Afghan. John, as good with weapons as he was at intelligence, moved to the sidewalk to get a better shot. I put the girl down to free my shooting hand. No words were spoken, but there were six fingers on six triggers. After a few moments the men got back in their car and sped away. John walked up to me shaking his head. "Sir, I know you can handle a weapon, but there were four of them. I also recognized them. They were Iranian intelligence."

Even after school was opened in March 2002 (for the first time since the Taliban had come to power), many parents were afraid to allow their children—especially the girls—to attend for fear that Taliban spies were taking notes and just waiting until the Americans left to punish them. We went family to family, promising them it wouldn't happen. At the end of the first day of school, I brought a case full of candy as a treat. But I was the one who got the best treat that day: Fifteen or twenty of the students—including the girl who had been whipped—serenaded me with verses from the Koran they had learned in school.

When I got back to the States in April 2002, I came across an e-mail

I'd sent out to family and friends earlier that winter, trying to convey what Afghanistan was like. I remember writing it in the middle of night, with a flashlight, strapped to my head, working against the clock because each of us had only a certain amount of computer time allotted:

. . . Though people surround you, the overwhelming feeling is loneliness or, better, isolation. The other emotions are fear and . . . the constant flow of adrenaline. Each of us is convinced, quite regardless of probabilities, that the next mortar round or bullet or RPG is coming directly at him personally. It does not matter that you can tell by the sound that the mortars are well beyond range. Somehow, through some freak atmospheric occurrence, it is going to hit you (and only you).

. . . What really keeps you going is the guy next to you. The one counting on you to do your job, just as you are counting on him to do his. You have his "6" (his six o'clock, his back) and he has yours. It is a refusal to let your buddies down. In writing of his experiences as a Marine on Okinawa, William Manchester observed that any man in combat who lacks comrades who will die for him, or for whom he is willing to die, is not a man at all. He is truly damned. And that guy's race, skin color, religion, gender, or sexual orientation are not even close to being relevant . . . we (that is, those with the rifles in our hands) do not care.

. . . Nor does it matter that you met a week ago or that you will never see each other again back in the world. (In a classic case of life imitating art, the "world" is what we call you guys. We also imagine that you eat eggs benedict and pommes frites for breakfast every morning, poached salmon with a light dill sauce for lunch, and a thick prime rib—end cut, of course—with a good bottle of Montepulciano every night for dinner. You do, right?)

So, what is it like? On a good day, you get a hot meal—of course, calling it a "meal" is somewhat misleading. In a good week, you get a hot shower—hot water is decidedly not overrated. And a good month? When you still have all your body parts. I have lost count of how many good kids have not had a good month. Every one of them is a hero. Me? Just another guy

doing the best I can and praying that no one ever dies because I
failed to do my job. Those details that I can give you are mundane: you wake up in the morning with a sore throat and one of
a dozen, albeit minor, eye or ear infections. You get dressed
quickly before the warmth of the sleeping bag wears off, pack
everything up, and then dump out your piss bottle. I know that
is more information than you might want, but it gives you an
idea of the conditions: you do not go around in the dark looking
for a place to relieve yourself. Not if you want to have a good
month. See above re: body parts. So, you carry a bottle and
empty it in the daylight.

I will give you another example. About a week ago, we got a box
of pears for breakfast. I have no idea where they came from.
When we opened the box, the pears were all brown and black and
covered with small holes where some member of the insect or
(and?) animal kingdom had nibbled. Definitely not the kind of
pear you would pick at the corner bodega. If it were the last one
left, you would go to the peaches. If you saw it in your refrigera-
tor, you would throw it away. I ate it. It was the best pear I have
ever had.

Now up, you do what you must to get through the day. Every
bend in the road is a potential ambush site. Every shadow hides
an Arab or Chechen fighter. Every person you meet is suspect
until proven otherwise. Competing against this necessary
paranoia . . . is the overwhelming affection you feel for the
Afghan people. They are all (Pashtun, Tajik, Hazara, and Uzbek)
warm and (when not trying to kill you) very friendly people . . .
Nor does it matter if the tea is being served in the only room
with a roof, where the remainder of the mud-brick house is
bombed-out rubble. Most of the houses I have seen outside of
Kabul are mud-brick, but every one has a guestroom with their
best carpet and, sometimes, pillows.

It is during tea you hear about the real horrors, things done by the
Taliban and al-Qaeda you find impossible to believe—until you
walk outside and see how many people are missing body parts. You
also see the despair, the hunger, and the poverty, and you know they

are telling you the truth without embellishment or exaggeration. You feel uncontrollable rage, softened by the children laughing and playing; even if they are playing across the road from a minefield. That is my favorite part—the children, not the minefield. They love chocolate. So I always make sure to carry around enough in my pockets. I show them the chocolate first and then make them eat the delicious MREs before I give them the chocolate.

As I said, you do what you must to get through the day . . . There is a lot of death. Everywhere. And it takes a little more out of you every day. I think the psychologists call it "accommodation." You hope these accommodations are temporary and that you will become "normal" again when you are back home. You hope all these things will fade from your memory. Of course, you are never sure.

I told you already about a good day. There have also been some bad ones. Michael's first day of pre-school in January. I was supposed to be the one to pack his Clifford lunch box. It was supposed to be my hand he squeezed extra hard when we walked into class. That was a bad day. Another was the day Jason was born in November. I wish I had been there. I'll miss Diana's 2nd birthday next week too. I know she wants Cinderella pajamas—I hope someone gets them for her. But whenever I start to feel sorry for myself, I think of all those children whose mothers and fathers did not come home on September 11 . . .

Time is up. This is where I belong for now, but I cannot wait to be done and come home. It has been five months; and every second is one second too long. And you never get them back. I do not know our schedule, but we will return to U.S. Central Command Headquarters before redeploying to the next country. I do not know where that will be, but I can guess as well as anyone. I am guessing hot with a lot of sand. I hope to get some leave and come home while stateside before the next deployment. Insha'Allah (God willing). Semper Fi.

One week after my meeting with Colonel Katra, a flight arrived from Dubai. I had just ordered two well-dressed Afghans to produce their passports when we were surrounded by twenty to twenty-five ragtag but heavily armed soldiers I had never seen before. They began to question my presence with an AK-47 jabbed into my chest. I remember thinking how big the muzzle looked and how bad the kid holding it smelled. And I remember his eyes—small, nervous, the kind that make mistakes. I held the muzzle with my right hand and muscled it to the ground as I slowly placed my left hand on my .45. Although my Afghan airport trainees spoke English, I told Nash to repeat in Dari, so everyone would hear, "Put your hands on your weapons but do not draw them." While we were thus engaged, the two well-dressed Afghans passed on by, unscreened. About ten minutes later, the face-off ended when the soldiers simply walked away. Mission accomplished. Message to the Americans delivered.

To catch a passenger who is up to no good, you have to be able to punch in a passport number and see who that person is. But first you have to have reliable information on the other end—a name or a photograph or a fingerprint. And Afghanistan was a world largely without documentation. In fact, the only people authorized to travel under the prior regime were players in the Taliban or in al-Qaeda. This is where one of Vinnie Coglianese's provocative ideas arose.

Early on, he had picked up rumors of what came to be called the Taliban Book, a couple of ledgers that listed everyone approved to travel, complete with vital addresses and other information, including passport photographs. While most of the intelligence community discounted this as being too good to be true, for me it became the Holy Grail, the motive force behind one of the most "irrational" things I've ever done.

In earlier days at various governmental offices, various employees had taken various ledgers as insurance. Some of these civil servants were now returning to offices where they had worked before and after the Taliban took over in 1996. So we began seeking out these people— meaning more tea and almonds and raisins—in cafés, in parking lots, and in offices.

Obviously, we were armed everywhere we went—even (especially) when moving through governmental buildings. But the more sensitive the building, the more likely that I was going to be searched. On the other hand, the more likely I was to be searched, the more likely it was going to be a good building. I'd been burned a few times—they found every weapon—so I started getting better at hiding them, eventually secreting a pistol where no Muslim would look for it, as well as a decoy in "concealed-weapon hiding place number one," where my two-year-old, Diana, could find it in about two seconds. When the guy found the decoy, I would always laugh and tell him how good he was.

Over time I had developed a certain patter with guys doing screening at these official doorways. "I have an appointment with so-and-so. He's not here? Oh, did I say so-and-so, I meant such and such." These guys had big weapons, but they were not rocket scientists, and I usually got through the gate.

Once inside, the objective was to stay inside as long as possible, for no other reason than to see what might develop. To do this, I needed to become familiar and nonthreatening. I would sit and wait for hours for my "important meeting," while in reality I was just hanging out in the hallways, observing by watching. I was simply continuing a practice I had started back in the DA's Office. Because people are creatures of habit, whenever I picked up a new case, I would go back to the scene of the crime at the time of the crime and sit. That's it—just sit. Looking for patterns, habits, lighting, anything. Unfortunately for my social life, most crimes are committed in the middle of the night. But if I saw a hooker on the corner at that time, then chances are she or he was there on the night of the crime as well. Ditto for the drug dealers, pimps, and people coming home from their night job.

Another lesson I had learned was that sometimes the mountain just won't come to Muhammad. As a rookie, on my first serious drug case, I needed to interview several undercover police officers to present the case to the grand jury for indictment. The only problem was that every time I called the precinct to schedule the interviews in my office, they were out in the field on another undercover operation. They weren't blowing off the system—they were good, seasoned cops. But they sure as hell weren't going to take time off from active investigations and come all the way downtown to be interviewed by a rookie. It just wasn't done. So, after a week of failed attempts, I learned from a cop in their team, a former Marine, that the following morning at six A.M. they were all being briefed on a new operation in an old converted warehouse way uptown in the West 130s. So, I found an all-night bakery, got a dozen coffees and two dozen doughnuts, and had everything waiting for them when they arrived for their briefing. After a few tense moments ("How the hell did you get in here?"), they laughed, drank the coffee, ate the doughnuts, and gave me all the information I needed to prosecute the dealers.

Afghanistan was no different. In front of the guards, I would impatiently gesture to Nash as if to say, "Why are they keeping us waiting?" I'd also walk into the wrong offices on purpose. "Oh, I'm sorry, what is your name?" Meanwhile, Nash would burst out laughing. "Oh, that's a good one, boss. Let's see what you're going to say now!"

Eventually, I stumbled into an office to see someone who someone else had said might know someone who might be helpful about something. It was the best lead of the week. This supposedly helpful person was at lunch, or maybe he was just not in or maybe he didn't even exist. While I was talking to the underling who *was* there, another guy— let's call him Jamal—kept walking in and out of the room. Several people were trying to get the attention of the bureaucrats, so I let them all go ahead of me with their questions. Meanwhile, I waited, and Jamal kept coming in and out, looking nervous, and fumbling with some binders on a shelf. After a while I took the hint and followed him out into the hallway. Looking over his shoulder, he walked into a second room, a small, messy office with a desk and boxes on the floor and big ledgers everywhere. "Where are you from?" he asked me.

When I told him New York, he told me how sorry he was about what had happened on 9/11. He told me about seeing Mullah Omar in the building one day and described how that ministry had celebrated the hijackers' attacks on the World Trade Center and the Pentagon. So I decided to run with it. I started talking about friends lost, about my apartment being destroyed, what a horrible day it was, my children seeing the fire.

"Do you have any children?" I asked him.

He had two girls, one of whom was six months older than my Diana. So we talked about our kids. We talked about family and children and what it was like under the Taliban.

"Will you now be able to teach your daughters to read the Koran?" I asked him.

At that point he explained to me that I didn't have to convince him of how bad the Taliban were. In the 1980s he had worked for the Soviets, and so in the 1990s, the Taliban tortured him with electricity, jolting him again and again until he lost hearing in one ear. Then they decided they could trust him and hired him in the same job he had held under the Soviets.

So I began asking about records and whether there were any photographs from the years of the Taliban, from 1996 to 2001. It was a long shot—in Islam, realistic images, including photographs, are considered profane.

He looked at me and said, "Don't you want the book?"

"I'll be a son of a bitch," I thought. The Holy Grail exists.

So we went to get it.

I said, "I need to scan the photos. That means I need the book. I have to take it with me." At the same time I was thinking that I could be walking into a trap. If things went south, would they shoot an American? Unlikely. Certainly it would be a strategic mistake followed by the sincerest of apologies. But that isn't to say that they wouldn't make that mistake. After all, as they would surely point out, I was not in uniform and what was I doing in the building anyway?

I went to the bathroom to move my actual concealed weapon to a more comfortable and accessible location. I pulled out the magazine and replaced it to make sure it was properly seated with a round in the chamber and the hammer cocked. I wasn't sure what good it would do—maybe I could fire some shots out the window to bring in my security that was waiting out on the street. At the least, I was taking somebody with me. The latter, by the way, was not the comforting thought I had expected it to be. Another cinematic myth shattered.

Once I had the books in hand (there were two volumes), I still had to get them past the guards and out of the building. I put one under my body armor and gave the other one to Nash to tuck under his shirt. He was a gutsy kid and said, "Give me both," but I told him that didn't make any sense: It's harder to shoot two moving targets than one. I told him, "Walk right past the guards. Don't speak Dari, and don't stop."

When the first guard told us to stop, we pretended not to hear him. We smiled and greeted everyone and just kept going. When we got to the guy who had confiscated my rifle and decoy pistol earlier, I put on a big smile and said, "You should get a job in America, no one can get a weapon past you."

Out on the street I nodded to the guys to get in the car. Once the door had slammed shut, I said, "The embassy. Now."

We had all the necessary equipment in the car, but we needed a place with absolute privacy in order to assess the Book. The fewer people who saw what we had, the better. Not only to protect my source's life, but also for more practical reasons: If the bad guys knew the book had been compromised, they would make the necessary adjustments. Everything depended on exploiting the information before they knew we had it.

The guard shack at the embassy was perfect. I was counting on the fact that embassies are secured by Marines, and I knew I could enlist their help to get onto the compound and into the shack unannounced. We got to a secure room and opened the book and there they were—pages after pages of headshots. It was like the yearbook from an all-male school with bad grooming practices, and no glee club.

We spent hours scanning photographs and all of the accompanying data. The intelligence guys were ecstatic. "Omigod, this is so-and-so! This is it!" Vinnie's brother John, one of the best intelligence officers I have ever served with, was in the room with us, and I could tell he couldn't wait to call and tell his big brother, who had left Afghanistan a week or so earlier, that he had been right all along.

Around five in the afternoon Nash and I had to perform the second part of the trick—we had to bring the book back to the office where we'd found it. Returning to my guard at the door, I said, "Let's see what you can find this time." He found the gun he was supposed to find. I said Nash and I were coming back to see the guy who was gone when I'd come earlier in the day. I walked in, located the room where the books had been, and put them back in place. I never did learn why Jamal had trusted me so fast, and so far. I suspect it had a lot to do with the torture. Or maybe it was for his kids.

7

EXFILTRATION AND INFILTRATION

As each challenge arises, if you considered everything
that could go wrong, you would never act.—Herodotus

BY THE TIME we nailed the Taliban Book, most of the guys from Task Force Bowie had already left for home. The tenth Mountain Division had destroyed al-Qaeda's forces in the Shah-i-Kot Valley during Operation Anaconda, the terrorist leadership had fled, and we had established at least the semblance of an infrastructure for border security. Time to go.

But before General Harrell left a week earlier, he had warned me, "Don't go straight home. Take a few days." I knew I wasn't quite ready for the "world" just yet, so I stopped in Heidelberg. For two days and one night in that old university town, I spent my time eating leisurely meals (I had lost about fifteen pounds), reading *Beyond Good and Evil*, and running up and down hills and in and out of streets with no route planned. I hadn't run for five months, and for the first mile or so of that first run, I was stiff and sluggish. As I began to loosen up, it started to rain, mixing with the sweat that had by then soaked through my shirt. I couldn't help noticing that there were no land mines to watch out for, no ambushes to protect against, and not a single AK-47 anywhere in sight.

I did not speak to a soul the entire time except to check in and check out of my hotel, and to order food. I was an American, in Germany, with a military haircut, so it was not hard to remain isolated. I had time to consider Nietzsche's admonition, "Whoever fights monsters must ensure that in the process he does not become a monster himself. And when you look long into the abyss, the abyss also looks into you." Maybe Gary Harrell had read Nietzsche—or experienced it himself. Maybe that's why he said not to go straight home.

From Heidelberg, I arranged for travel through Kennedy Airport, with a couple of days in New York. I landed somewhere between one and two in the morning, and by the time I got to my apartment it was around three A.M.

Rule number one, as any parent knows, is that you never wake up the kids. So while my wife stayed in the other room, I crept in just to see their faces, smell their skin, and touch their hair. I felt like the kid in the middle of the night on Christmas Eve. I just wasn't strong enough to wait until the morning, but I had to figure out a way to wake Michael and Diana at the same instant so that neither felt slighted. Their beds made an L in the corner of the room, so I sat half on each and gently jostled them. I waited. They rubbed their eyes, slowly adjusting to the darkness. Then they started screaming, "Daddy's home! Daddy's home!" They must have screamed it ten times, jumping up and down and squealing and waking baby Jason. They wouldn't stop hugging and kissing me. It was exactly the homecoming I had dreamed about.

After about ten minutes, though, Michael said in a small voice, "Daddy, do you have to leave now?" I was devastated, but he knew the score. I had ninety-six hours. And during the time I was home, they followed me from room to room. Every time I opened the door to take the garbage down the hall, Diana came with me. Michael hid my uniform under the bed, assuming that if I couldn't find it, I couldn't leave.

Seeing their dread of my next departure was the worst, but the second-hardest thing about being back in the world was learning to talk about nonessentials again—to have a *conversation*. To discuss anything not involving immediate life and death seemed trivial, a waste of breath. The veterans I had met before Afghanistan had always been loath to talk about their service with anyone who hadn't been there. I suddenly understood why: No matter what I said or how long I spoke, there was no way I could ever convey one fraction of what it had been like. In *Twilight of the Idols*, Nietzsche said, "That for which we find words is already dead in our hearts." How could I explain the fear mixed with periods of the most serene calm, the elation and the total boredom, or the utter loneliness that underlay a complete sense of belonging? I couldn't. So I didn't bother.

There were other inhibiting factors as well. CENTCOM had received intelligence that individuals returning to Tampa from service in Afghanistan had been targeted by al-Qaeda. Nothing specific, but enough to get our attention. The Tenth Mountain Division was based in New York State. Army Special Forces had come out of Kentucky, Alabama, North Carolina and Colorado, so that narrowed the pool. Task Force Bowie was one of only two Tampa-based units that had been stationed in Afghanistan that first winter—Special Operations Command being the other. That narrowed the pool a lot. There were no names, and they would have to kill a whole lot more important people before I got to the top of the list, but standard risk analysis (probability of the harm times the magnitude of the harm) indicated prudence.

One of Task Force Bowie's intelligence officers forwarded an unclassified portion of the report to the head of the gun-licensing board at the New York City Police Department. Being a prosecutor, I had already covered any tracks that led back to my personal life. You won't find my home address listed anywhere, and I have always done a quick, almost involuntary scan of every room I enter, making sure I know where the windows and doors are. After all, whether it's from al-Qaeda or from a pissed-off gangbanger I had sent upstate, a bullet is bullet, and—as Woody Allen said—just because you're paranoid doesn't mean they're not out to get you. As a prosecutor, you have to believe that the old Mafia code of not killing cops and DAs is still honored. Whether it is or not, isn't the point. To do our job, we have to believe we are off-limits. Fear can freeze you in a courtroom every bit as much as it does on the battlefield. That kind of mental gymnastics was a luxury I could no longer afford. Not with kids. And not after Afghanistan. There is still no fear, but I'll be carrying a concealed weapon for the rest of my life. Now I look for the hands of every stranger. I used to carry my books or coffee in my left hand to leave my right free for greeting. Now it is my left (shooting) hand that is always free.

Back in Tampa, General Franks picked Gary Harrell to become the head of all of special operations for CENTCOM. Harrell wanted to take our whole unit with him, but by this time General Franks had seen the force-multiplying benefits of having an interagency unit assigned to CENTCOM, so we stayed put and Harrell moved up.

But before he left, we had our own version of *On the Town*. Like most of us, General Harrell was a big fan of Rudy Giuliani's, and when he found out that I had met the mayor several times as a DA and knew a senior member of the mayor's staff, a former DA himself, the general asked me to set something up. We had a conference scheduled in New York with the NYPD's Joint Terrorism Task Force. So I arranged a meeting with the mayor and had an al-Qaeda bayonet mounted on a plaque to bring to Mr. Giuliani as a gift. By this time, of course, Mr. Giuliani had returned to private life, and Michael Bloomberg was in the mayor's office. I had a second plaque made for him as well.

I flew up to New York a day in advance to work out the security and logistical details: a tour of Ground Zero by New York's Finest, complete with a flag-raising; a private ceremony at Mr. Giuliani's office, followed by another private ceremony at City Hall with Mayor Bloomberg; and capped off by an NYPD helicopter ride over the city to assess security readiness. I also stopped by Tavern on the Green, one of the swankiest places in the city, and asked if they could seat a party of twelve for lunch. That was asking a lot on such short notice, and while the maître d' checked his seating chart, I filled the silence with "You know, we just got back from Afghanistan . . ."

He said, "You coming in uniform?"

"Sure."

"You come in uniform and I'll guarantee you the best table in the room."

The rest of the team arrived that night, and we all went out to an Italian restaurant in the Bronx, an NYPD favorite. But meanwhile, all hell had broken loose in Mr. Giuliani's private life—his divorce case had started that morning and nobody in New York was talking about much else.

"Matthew, are you sure the mayor's going to have time to see us with all this going on?" the general asked me.

"Not to worry, boss," I replied. "He does what he says he's going to do." Later that night, at some point between the calamari and the cannoli, Mr. Giuliani's press secretary called me on my cell phone.

"Sunny, I hope you're not calling to cancel."

"Actually," she said, "Rudy would like to honor your team's service in a more public way. Would you mind if we had a press conference tomorrow?"

"All for it," I said. "But you're telling me you can set this up on less than twelve hours' notice?"

She called back half an hour later. "Ten o'clock sharp," she said. "On the *Intrepid*." The USS *Intrepid*, one of the most successful aircraft carriers in military history, was now a floating museum berthed on the Hudson River in midtown Manhattan.

So the mayor and the general were thrilled to meet each other. At one point after the ceremony, Mr. Giuliani leaned over to ask what we did to get the bayonet. I turned to the general, who leaned forward and, in hushed tones, told him.

The guys from Task Force Bowie got the royal treatment on a tour of the ship, raised a flag at Ground Zero, went to City Hall (setting off every metal detector in sight with our uniforms and concealed weapons), and then had our lunch at the best table at Tavern on the Green. I was proud of the way my city treated our team. As we walked from the Battery to Central Park in our uniforms, dozens of New Yorkers stopped to say, "Thank you."

But once we got back to Tampa and business as usual, the lovefest was over. The general had recruited virtually everyone in Task Force Bowie for the standard six-month deployment—mostly on nothing more than a handshake. Now that the six months were up, all of the agency representatives went back to their agencies, all of the special forces guys went back to their units, and all of the retirees went back to retirement. By the summer of 2002, we had fewer than twenty personnel left. Worse still, there were forces at work calling into question whether the unit should exist at all.

Big Army, as in "Big Army wouldn't like that," is an insult that can apply to any branch of the service. It refers to the brass-hat mentality that everything must go through proper channels, preferably in triplicate, and usually ending in "No." Yet the entire rationale for an interagency task force is to blow past those kinds of restrictions. From the get-go, Big Army had seen us as a bunch of cowboys out there snooping and pooping. Big Army in Washington and in Tampa said, "Where is the doctrine? There are no guidelines. So how do we know if you're doing it right?" They saw us as a threat to their worldview, a challenge to their entire way of life.

General Harrell's replacement was Brigadier General James Schwitters, a no-nonsense former Delta commander who was as sharp and savvy as they come. For reasons I never really understood, he appointed me the deputy director, the guy who actually runs things day to day. Eight months earlier, I had been the NFG; now I was the boss—even though several people in the unit were senior to me in rank. It wasn't until six months after I was put in charge that I was promoted to colonel, making it a little easier—but once again, I was the NFG, this time in the world of generals, where it was all politics, all the time.

My first task was to avoid annihilation, then build the team back up to functional size, ideally thirty military and seventy from other agencies. This meant pulling out our Rolodexes and calling up guys we had served with in the past. I was simply repeating the practice that had gotten me to CENTCOM in the first place. When Lieutenant Colonel Drew Schlaepfer—probably the finest Marine officer I have ever served with—called me back in 1998 to ask me to join him at CENTCOM, much of the reason I joined was because of who it was that had asked. I was hoping to get the same response to my calls. For conversations with a Marine, I usually started by quoting President Reagan: "Some people spend an entire lifetime wondering if they have made a difference in the world. Marines don't have that problem." It usually ended with the voice on the other end of the line saying, "Okay, but give me a week to figure out how I'm gonna tell my wife."

One of my first calls had been to New York state trooper—and Marine lieutenant colonel—James J. Maxwell. We'd been junior officers and sparring partners together. And there were more than a few fine establishments that had asked us never to return. He had New York street smarts, a wicked left hook, and a strong background in intelligence. I asked for a year; he gave me two.

At CENTCOM, the standard was, "But what have you done for me *lately*?" So while we were building the organization for future operations, we were also gathering intelligence for current operations, trying to come up with more success stories. In September 2002, General Franks formally approved our continued existence but, as a concession to Big Army, changed our name to the Joint Interagency Coordination Group. Task forces such as Bowie "execute," a difficult concept for some at headquarters to understand. Coordination groups, on the other hand, "coordinate and facilitate," a much more comforting concept for them. Of course, it changed nothing about how we operated.

As Iraq became the leading candidate for our next deployment, we saw ourselves needing fewer trigger-pullers and more investigators—more cops and customs officers. In Iraq, we would do counterterrorism the way Eliot Ness had fought Al Capone in the twenties—if you can't get them for murder, get them for tax evasion. We would be a full-service shop, searching for evidence of terrorist financing networks, weapons of mass destruction, weapons that could reach Tel Aviv (a violation of the UN Security Council resolutions), and any other prohibited materials, such as dual-use technologies—stuff that could be used for lawful purposes, but that could also be put to use developing weapons for terrorists.

We went back to recruiting volunteers, but we needed senior people with high-demand, low-density specialties, and we needed them from throughout the executive branch. After September 2002, I conducted months of briefings at a dozen agencies in Washington, D.C., to enlist support for what ultimately became Operation Iraqi Freedom. Using former Marines, personal contacts, and drinking buddies, I would scout out and brief those in that agency's hierarchy who might support the JIACG concept. Based on that briefing, I would tailor my request for the next person up the chain. I got to the point where I could do three briefs in a day and still get back to headquarters that night.

In December 2002, there was still no war in Iraq, but we were engaged in hot spots such as Yemen, Djibouti, and Afghanistan. No matter what happened with Iraq, I knew we were in it for the long haul and I wanted to get my people some R&R for Christmas. So I gave everyone a holiday and I took the duty. It was the second Christmas in a row that I had missed being home. Ironically, I missed Christmas of 2001 because I was the NFG; and I missed Christmas 2002 because I was the boss. I was just carrying on a family tradition: Dad had the family work every holiday in the restaurant so the staff could have time off.

One of our best pickups—later to become my mentor—was Jay Freres, a retired Foreign Service officer with more than thirty years in the State Department, including two tours in Afghanistan. In January 2003, however, we only had two dozen people, most of whom were military. To turn up the heat, I invited about sixty-five midlevel decision-makers from a dozen different agencies to a three-day brainstorming session in Tampa. I wanted press-the-flesh face time, because it is much harder to say no after you've been out drinking together the night before. I offered good weather, golf courses, and the officers' club. But I did my homework too, pulling up every single agency director's last budget testimony before Congress. That's when you get to see how agencies measure their success: by what they tell Congress they're doing in order to get more money. They needed to justify sending their agents into harm's way, I needed to show them how. When the group arrived, I had outlined each agency's director's testimony so that I could say to each one, "I can get you such and such."

The FBI said they wanted to have the ability to interview every Iraqi fighter found with an American phone number or a U.S.-postmarked envelope in his pocket. Done deal.

Immigration and Customs Enforcement (ICE) wanted a line into any shipping documents that indicated the movement of dual-use technologies. My comeback was "Absolutely, I couldn't agree more. Of course, I might not know a dual-use technology when I saw one. So it might be helpful to have a customs guy right there next to me."

Treasury wanted to record the serial numbers of any large cash seizures, the CIA wanted access to human intelligence sources. And on and on. Each time, my answer was the same: "Absolutely. But there's no substitute for physical presence and I might forget to call. It'd probably be better if you were there."

Then it was come-to-Jesus time, when they had to say what they would commit. Various agencies ponied up five, ten, even twenty guys. Then Kevin Power, the ICE agent who had been with me for the eight months since Afghanistan, got up and said, "Sorry, Colonel, one riot, one ranger. We're sending one person."

I knew Kevin. He loved the action. He needed the action. His father, an Air Force retiree, had just passed away. I knew Kevin would still be the one guy, and a good one. But this idea of a solo performance was devastating, to me and to another ICE agent named Bill Puff, a former Army captain who really believed in the mission and who wanted to be a part of it. Like me, he knew that if it was going to be just one person, it was going to be Kevin. So Bill went back up to Washington dejected, but not defeated, and in February he called and asked me if I could come up to D.C. I told him, "I'm flying to the Persian Gulf tomorrow. I've been in D.C. two days a week doing briefings since Thanksgiving."

He said, "If you come one more time, I can get you some agents."

"I'll reroute my flight."

I got on a plane and Bill picked me up at the airport in his "G-ride," the bland domestic sedan with black-wall tires and government license plates. He brought me to ICE headquarters at the Reagan Building on Fourteenth Street. He had assembled twelve people, some very senior—far more senior than I expected.

Because I was traveling commercial, I was not carrying classified information with me, which meant that I had to re-create a great deal of data for them. So we went to a classified room, and I gave them a classified briefing on a white eraser board, detailing as many contingencies and possibilities as I could remember from an operations order that ran to the hundreds of pages. It helped that I had been on the team that had actually drafted the first three phases of Operation Iraqi Freedom. I laid out what I could do for them, and what I needed them to do for me, carefully letting it slip that their archrival, the FBI, was providing fifteen agents.

At the end of an hour, the senior official in the room said, "How many people do you want?"

I said, "Give me seven guys."

He said, "I'll give you fifteen." I'm sure it was a coincidence that it was the same number as the FBI. And of course, Bill was one of the fifteen.

As it turned out, nine of those fifteen customs people wound up on the museum team, absolutely essential to the investigation in Baghdad.

On the ride out to Dulles, Bill was ecstatic. "I can't believe we're really doing this thing. Man, you really brought your A game today."

Maybe, but had it not been for Bill Puff's "irrational tenth," his true belief in this mission, it would never have happened.

Sand degrades everything you bring into the desert. This is true of tanks, trucks, computers, boots, rifles, and morale. Combat troops living in tents with nothing to do get stale; living in tents in the Persian Gulf subjects them to missile attacks as well.

I landed in the small Arab nation of Qatar, direct from Washington, and joined a small JIACG contingent for planning and rehearsals, about a dozen guys, getting ready for the final run-through. This crowd was heavy on the technical expertise, setting up computers and doing communications checks. All the functional reach-back to other agencies would now operate from Camp as-Sayliyah, CENTCOM's forward headquarters in Qatar. Built by the United States after Desert Storm, it had the advantages of being nearer the action, in the same time zone, and similar in climate.

In Qatar, we lived in modular units that looked like steel shipping containers, the kind that come right off freighters and onto railroad cars. We needed hundreds of separate meeting places, so for office space we set up tents inside a huge hangar. Each tent was filled with electronics, and so much electricity was buzzing that you constantly felt it in your hair. There were video feeds, satellite feeds, video teleconferences (once a day we were hooked up with Washington), and always the computers.

Aside from the fine sand that got into everything, the heat was tough on hardware, so the computers went down all the time. Whenever General Franks held a video-teleconference with Washington, it would steal all the bandwidth and everything else would crash. All the while, the temperature outside was 120 degrees and climbing. We did training with gas masks for NBC (nuclear, biological, and chemical) attacks. We needed to test all the gear, to hydrate, and to acclimatize the body to the heat and to getting no sleep.

I had left a small contingent behind in Tampa for further liaison and to respond to requests from the Office of the Secretary of Defense. Initially, I left Senior in the rear with the gear. I felt that he had done his share of "forward position" time in Afghanistan, but I soon realized that I needed him in Qatar with me. Qatar, of course, was the worst of everything— the hardships without the action. The staff was there primarily as a planning element, but also to manage up, by feeding the monster with endless status reports and operational briefings. If you don't feed the monster, you screw yourself, because the monster sets priorities and allocates resources. Of course, it was never enough. If I play Batman for one hour, Jason wants two. The Pentagon is a lot like that.

I also had to look after the rest of our area of responsibility. I had to send people to Pakistan, Afghanistan, and Yemen, as well as a small team to Djibouti covering the Horn of Africa.

Before we could enter Iraq, there were three other significant issues to be tacked. Legally, and for good historical reasons, military personnel could not tell representatives of civilian agencies what to do. However reasonable that is stateside or in peacetime, it is unacceptable in combat where the slightest hesitation kills. To overcome this, a half dozen of us got together and agreed—which is another way of saying "made up"—that each agency's headquarters would retain tasking authority (what we call operational control) of all of its deployed members, but that I would have control of all movements (what we call tactical control) of those members. Although unorthodox, it worked. Second, as a former military lawyer, I knew that the Geneva Convention and the

Hague Protocols only covered uniformed combatants. I was concerned that all of the nonmilitary members of my team not only comply with the Geneva Convention, but receive its protections as well. As another made-up fix, we agreed that all deploying civilians would wear desert camouflage uniforms (without rank insignia) and carry military-issued identification cards.

Finally, shortly before we crossed the border, someone in Big Army decreed that everyone in JIACG had to carry the same weapons. On the surface, it made perfect sense: every single law-enforcement agency has its own procurement and training program, resulting in weapons specifically suited to that agency's needs. The FBI uses .40-caliber pistols, ICE uses 9 mm. But the already overburdened military supply system is geared to provide one caliber of ammunition (9 mm) for pistols and one (5.56 mm) for rifles, and military armorers are trained to repair weapons in these same calibers. Moreover, in a combat situation, if your weapon breaks or jams, you want to be able to simply pick up the weapon of the man next to you and keep firing, or combine the parts of two broken weapons to make one functioning weapon. That is all well and good. But if I'm going to get in a firefight, I sure as hell want the men on my left and right to be firing weapons on which they have trained, and not ones they picked up a week ago for the first time. This issue generated more argument and discussion than any other. Ultimately, General Renuart agreed and decided that because those who operate in a combat zone should carry the firearms on which they have trained, each nonmilitary member could deploy with his standard-issue weapons, despite the logistical challenges created.

As the guys from the other agencies began to show up, we met them and learned what their capabilities were, as well as their personal take on their agency's priorities. These were all experienced agents who kicked down doors for a living. From the FBI, we got their hostage rescue team, as well as some of their best interrogators and document examiners. From ICE, we got computer experts, smuggling experts, and a few of their SWAT guys. On the military side, it was still predominantly Special Forces and Marines.

With the invasion becoming more certain, General Franks deployed Special Ops, ready to take out Saddam's SCUD missiles and to blow up border observation posts. He sent in reconnaissance units to secure bridges that we knew would be set for demolition, and we planned surgical bomb strikes. Once the oil fields had been secured, and because we had reps from the Department of Energy embedded with us, we would also play a part in helping contain any damage. Fifteen hundred wellheads were vulnerable to sabotage, but our concern was not just preserving the fuel. We wanted to avoid the kind of environmental disaster Hussein had caused in 1991 when he blew up the Kuwaiti oil fields. Moreover, an oil-field explosion produces enough smoke to create battlefield disasters, with zero visibility and soldiers choking on fumes.

In the second week of March, I moved a detachment of my JIACG team up from Qatar to Kuwait, the last-minute staging area for our launch. We needed to lease vehicles, as well as trailers for the extra gear. But the press had blown through first, and we didn't have CNN's equipment budget. The Office of Reconstruction and Humanitarian Assistance (ORHA) actually found that they couldn't buy anything in Kuwait or Qatar because it had all been snatched up by reporters and film crews. The Feds had to spend a fortune shipping stuff into the country.

But, fortunately, anywhere in the world, a cop is a cop is a cop. My NYPD cops made friends with Kuwaiti cops, and my U.S. customs guys made friends with Kuwaiti customs, showing exceptional resourcefulness in finding and funding vehicles and trailers for us. The vendors said, "You won't be bringing this equipment into Iraq, will you?" Playing along, we told them what they wanted to hear and signed where we needed to sign.

Camp Doha, in Kuwait, headquarters for the Third Army in the Gulf region, was where the communications capability was, along with all the bosses. So for about five weeks, I flew back and forth between Camp as-Sayliyah in Qatar and Camp Doha in Kuwait, coordinating with the multiple planning cells that were setting up multiple missions. Because Camp Doha was well over capacity, they set up an expeditionary camp called Camp Udari, a couple of hundred tents out in the middle of the desert for units trying to stay sharp. I had a liaison officer there, Lieutenant Colonel Brad McAllister—another of my recruitment phone calls. We had served together in the Second Battalion, Twenty-fifth Marine Regiment, when I was the commanding officer of Weapons Company in 1995, and I remembered him as a lanky captain with a lot of potential. When I called this time, he was a thirty-seven-year-old stock trader, making big money in Philadelphia. "Brad," I said, "I can offer you a substantial pay cut, lousy hours, miserable living conditions, and the chance to be shot at." Three years later, he is still in JIACG.

Brad said he wanted me to meet this guy named Dave who was

billeted in the same tent, a Navy commander detailed to the Defense Threat Reduction Agency (DTRA). Within the Department of Defense, DTRA focuses on weapons of mass destruction, biological warfare, nuclear weapons, and ultrahigh explosives—conventional fireworks that can do damage equivalent to that of nuclear weapons. When I dropped by to meet DTRA Dave (as we called him), he was in his running shorts, tanned, relaxed, unshaven, hair long. Essentially, he was a surfer dude with a tricked-up M4 and extreme operational capabilities.

We shook hands, but there was something simply too laid-back about this guy, too California, just like some people think I'm too New York. So, there we were like two male dogs circling each other and checking out the smells on the fire hydrant, at which point Brad tactfully disappeared. I was a CO and Dave was a CO, but I was in a T-shirt, with no indication of my rank. As a commander (the Navy equivalent of a lieutenant colonel), he was one grade below me, and somehow I got backed into slipping something into the conversation about my rank, which I instantly regretted. I got the eye roll I deserved, and we were off on the wrong foot. Nonetheless, I think we recognized that each of us could do something for the other. I was looking for a little extra beef and firepower; he was looking for the access that I had commanding a special unit of investigators. If DTRA worked with my guys, who represented all the agencies that would need to get the information he was trying to develop, they could get their findings into the system much more quickly, and without being held up by any one of a half-dozen managers who could find five different reasons for not sharing. So I made the proposition: "If you want to cross with us, I think we can make it work for both of us." His response was something to the effect of "Yeah, cool." It was not exactly the overwhelming gratitude or gung-ho cooperative spirit I had hoped for.

DTRA Dave didn't say "sir" and he didn't salute—that just wasn't his style. It rankled me, but I just bit my lip.

We met once more to firm up some of the details, and actually, I had second thoughts about bringing him in on such a delicate mission. The other guys in his team were cut from the same "action-figure" mold— hard-core trigger-pullers: buffed-up, bandanna headbands, mirrored sunglasses, maybe they'd shave once a month. But there was something about Commander David Beckett (who I later learned was a devoted father of three boys) and his team that told me they could be counted on at crunch time.

I decided to bring them, but I told Dave that he would have to trust me, because in a combat zone each unit can only have one boss. I would never take operational control and order him to participate in missions that were outside his lane, but I had to have tactical control over all movements. Actually, what I said was "Dave, if you're comfortable with TACON, I give you my word no OPCON."

"Cool."

On March 17, President Bush gave Saddam Hussein an ultimatum to leave, then summoned his commanders for a final gut check. Seconds after the forty-eight-hour grace period expired, B-2 stealth bombers hit Saddam's bunker in a decapitation strike intended to end the war before it began.

Marines immediately moved in from the south and captured the oil fields. Marines and British forces moved east to the port city of Umm Qasr and north to Basra, while protecting the right flank of the U.S. Third Army moving up the middle. Up north, we had to protect the Kurds from both the Turks and the Iraqis while keeping them from staging their own uprising. Special Forces, meanwhile, destroyed the SCUDS in the west. Coalition forces in the south covered half the distance to Baghdad in two days, using speed to keep the enemy, at least initially, from retreating into urban centers and regrouping. We were so successful that we feared that we had been pulled into a draw play. Intelligence had earlier warned that once we crossed a certain line, the Iraqis might unleash chemical agents. Now we learned that Republican Guard units had been found carrying self-injecting atropine tubes, along with new chemical suits. Atropine is an antidote for chemical weapons. We were not pleased with the implication.

Shortly after the nineteenth, I led a small recon team from Kuwait into Iraq in our SUVs, sliding quickly from the modern world into the third world. We were, at most, two hours' drive from the strip in Kuwait City, where you could get everything from the biggest gold bracelets to the flattest TV screens I'd ever seen. Yet here, a sign said PLEASE DO NOT FEED THE KIDS. The prospect of food brought starving Iraqi children out onto the roads where they might get killed by passing cars.

We passed a few straggly palm trees and miles and miles of desert punctuated by the litter of human poverty. Camels clopped along in front of us, bedouins herded goats from pickup trucks, and children in Dumpster clothing stood beside squalid shacks. You could see the layers of dust on everything, including the camels, which are always nasty, spitting, and biting. They are one of the few animals that will take a bite out of you for absolutely no reason. I wanted to shoot them.

As Journalist Matt Labash pointed out, "Before politics can become local, it is biological, about shelter and water, food and drink." But, especially in Iraq, the first biological imperative is safety, and for that I had to coordinate with the British Royal Marines, who owned the real estate in the south. I had a very "Victorian" tea with their sangfroid commanding officer, briefing each other on our respective missions, as nearby explosions rattled the cups. I half expected Sean Connery and Michael Caine to walk through the door bemoaning the Iraqis' failure to put up a jolly good fight. The Brits needed to know who we were and where we went in their sector, because having free agents on the battlefield is a recipe for disaster. Most U.S. units had a Blue Force tracking system with transponders feeding back their exact location to headquarters. We had never requested any. That way we couldn't get reprimanded when they accidentally stopped working. When your objective is a new way of doing things, sometimes it's better to beg forgiveness than to ask permission.

After the recon, I had to get back down to Qatar to brief General Renuart and get final clearance. Here are my objectives and resources, here are the units I have coordinated with, and here is my force protection plan, which now included DTRA Dave and—for all appearances—his well-armed biker gang. The team also included Army chief warrant officer Scott Patterson—as sharp as he was surly—and Senior. By this time, I realized I needed Senior's experience and judgment immediately at hand to keep me out of trouble. As later events will show, he had only limited success.

We got the green light, but as a new organization we had no supply tail, no account numbers, no charge cards, and no requisitioning authority. We had made a half-dozen nobody-is-looking trips to the Army's supply depot in Kuwait, but all we could get was enough food and water for about a week. The fuel and ammo were locked down tight. What any Marine will tell you, however, is that a dead end is just the beginning of another trail. Adapt, improvise, and overcome.

On our way up to the border we saw an MRE box staked up like a road sign with an arrow pointing thataway, and the words CAMP COMMANDO. Each vehicle had a walkie-talkie, and I said, "Gentlemen, right turn. We are going to Camp Commando."

Some of the team began to squawk. "What're we doing?"

I said, "We need supplies."

These guys knew governmental bureaucracy and many were former military—though only one had been in the Marines. They said, "But you didn't call ahead, you haven't filled out any forms. We'll be wasting our time."

I said, "Gentlemen, this is a Marine Corps unit."

Had this camp been run by one of the other services, there would have been fifteen people outranking me, which would have meant fifteen separate people needing to sign off, half of whom would have said no. Those who were agreeable would have allocated six rounds of ammo per person, then at the end of war they would have asked for those same six rounds back, or a report in triplicate explaining when and why the rounds were expended—bill to follow.

But the Marines keep it lean and mean. I dropped by one tent to find the deputy commander, Major General Keith J. Stalder, whom I had known when he was the Deputy Director of Plans at CENTCOM.

I said, "Sir. I just wanted to let you know that we were passing through." I gave him a quick brief on our mission, the agencies involved, and the coordination I had already done. He offered some good advice, and then I told him that I would check in with his "G-3" [operations officer] and maybe his "G-4" [logistics and supply officer]. The former was a matter of courtesy; the latter was more of a feeler with a big question mark at the end. He could have asked why I needed to see the G-4. After all, he needed his supplies for his own push north. But Keith Stalder was a Marine.

"No problem. Whatever you need, Matthew. Carry on."

So after briefing his operations officer, our next stop was the supply depot, where a Marine gunnery sergeant was in charge.

I said, "Gunny. I've got a civilian team here, a counterterrorism task force. DTRA, FBI, Customs. We're heading north. I can't use Big Army resupply channels, and I need whatever food, water, ammo, fuel, and other supplies you can spare. I've got no paperwork."

He thought for a moment, then looked at me and said, "You know what, sir? I'm about to go on my lunch break. I'll probably be gone for about an hour."

I had to laugh. Marines don't "do lunch" and we certainly don't go on "lunch breaks." How many times had he heard that line in some war movie, I wondered. He'd probably been waiting years to use it, just like all the drill instructors that had sharpened their routines watching Lee

Ermey, the drill instructor in *Full Metal Jacket*. But I needed to know he wasn't caving in because of my rank. I said, "You don't have to do this, Gunny."

"I don't know what you're talking about, sir, I'm going on my lunch break." Then he paused. "*Semper Fi*, sir." The Marine motto, short for *semper fidelis*, "always faithful."

"*Semper Fi*, Gunny."

As he walked away, I turned to the guys and said, "We've got an hour."

They couldn't believe it, but that didn't prevent them from taking everything that would fit inside the SUVs, in the trailers, or on top of the roofs. And in case anyone ever asks, maybe he wasn't a Gunny. Maybe he was a Corporal. Maybe it never even happened.

We headed north, and just short of the border, we had a prearranged rendezvous with some other stray cats eager to hitch a ride—seven guys from the 513th Military Intelligence Brigade, as well as some others from a certain unnamed agency. Altogether, we had twenty-seven people in twelve vehicles. We had big fuzzy dice—black, red, white, blue—hanging from the rearview mirrors as radio call signs among ourselves, plus, for the flyboys, "don't shoot us" panels on the hoods in colors that were supposed to change every day. We had enough food, water, fuel, and ammunition for at least two weeks. Therefore, the official duration for our mission was precisely two weeks. But we were still thin-skinned—no armor, no crew-served weapons—so trouble was something we would have to avoid or outrun.

Our first objective took us along the bay from Kuwait City to Umm Qasr, a port on the Persian Gulf needed for shipping in humanitarian supplies. During a debate in the House of Commons in March 2003, the British defense secretary unwisely compared Umm Qasr to the English city of Southampton. The analogy was met with skepticism among the British troops on the ground. The media picked up the response of one Royal Marine: "There's no beer, no prostitutes, and people are shooting at us. It's more like Portsmouth."

Traditionally, Basra had been the more significant port. But after the Gulf War, the citizens there had followed George H. W. Bush's urging to rise up against the Hussein regime. Instead of support from the West, their reward was mass executions and the transfer of shipping traffic to Umm Qasr.

JIACG was the first real forensic exploitation (i.e., examination) unit into these southern towns. So for the most part, we saw them just as the

Ba'athists had left them. Many of Hussein's loyalists were disguising themselves, often as women, and continuing the fight underground, retreating to hospitals, schools, and other protected buildings, as well as to mosques and museums.

Later, we would add to our mission set crime-scene examinations of any bombings with U.S. civilian casualties, but our first priority was to find out what Saddam Hussein had been shipping in and out. Our job was to investigate UN Security Council resolution violations and evidence of terrorist activity. Forensic examination for weapons and money—missiles in warehouses, money in vaults. Follow the money, follow the shipping label—track it back to wherever it came from and then shut down that operation.

DTRA was looking for fissile material, nuclear, biological, and chemical weapons, as well as megabombs. Their mission was to identify and eliminate; ours was to track down how the stuff got here: Who violated the laws? Who paid the freight? Where was it going? Looking for the same thing from different perspectives, we were a match made in tough-guy heaven.

Frequently, the Royal Marines' Forty-two Commando Battalion under Colonel Paul Howes provided us with guides. As a matter of courtesy, we would always go to the operations officer of that unit and say, "Here's the intelligence that we have, and here's where we are going. Can you provide us with security and give us the radio frequency for your quick reaction force. We'll share whatever we find."

The south, of course, was the land of the half million marsh Arabs that Hussein had uprooted and tried to wipe out, as well as home to the Shi'ites that Hussein had massacred. So we were getting incredible information, far more than we could process. We had a team doing physical inspections, a team conducting document and media (computer) exploitation, an interview team developing human intelligence, and a team responsible for WMD. The customs guys were vital to everything; so I spread them around.

Tracking weapons began with finding documents, then tracing all of the government employees whose names were on those documents. With funny money, you find ledgers, and then you trace it back to find out where the money came from. This meant day after day of looking through files—with an interpreter—a daily grind of very unsexy detective work.

We also interviewed thousands of men in a triage process. Who were the senior Ba'ath Party members? Who had been wearing a Republican Guard uniform yesterday and is now in a *dishdasha* (floor-length robe for men), or even an *abaya* (floor-length robe for women)? We were looking for the short haircut, the chafe marks from boots on the leg, a little more muscle perhaps. We would do the first five-minute interview, then pass them along.

For force protection, the team that had convoyed in together—nine from U.S. customs, seven from the 513th Military Intelligence Brigade, three from DTRA, three military members of JIACG, and five others—all bunked together in the same warehouse rooms, office buildings, wherever. We could then spin off on our various missions, with a little "you help me, I'll help you" along the way.

By the end of March, coalition forces in Iraq seemed poised to start shaping events, to bring the chaos under control. But this was also when Hussein chose to empty his jails. Then the police force quit, and some genius decided to disband the Iraqi army, leaving a power vacuum just as thirty years of rage at the regime was unleashed.

On April 1, the Army took Karbala, fifty miles south of the capital and home to two Republican Guard divisions. The next day, Marines crossed the Tigris, and on the day after that, the Army pushed through the Karbala Gap. Marines secured the airbase outside Kut, forty miles south of Baghdad, and the 101st Airborne took control of Najaf. The same day, we launched a ground assault on Baghdad International Airport southwest of the city. On April 4, we took the airport, and the Marines closed in from Kut. Forty-eight hours later, Baghdad was encircled, and the first C-130s began their hot-LZ landings at Baghdad International Airport. On April 7, tanks entered the city in the first of their "thunder runs," and two days later Iraqis were celebrating in the streets. The statue of Hussein was toppled on April 9, 2003.

Meanwhile, in the south, we were still digging through files in grimy warehouse offices, looking for evidence of weapons shipments. We were also reading through bank records, looking for terrorist-financing networks and terrorist activity linked to the United States. Dual-use technology was keeping us fully occupied, but the stuff we found did not appear to be black market. It was not smuggled in. Instead, it was government to government—truckloads of it. We read these shipping labels carefully. We also collected the business cards of the American,

German, French, Russian, Chinese, and Jordanian reps who had sold this equipment in clear violation of the UN sanctions.

People had told us about a lot of late-night shipments in a lot of trucks at the UN compound, along with unregistered ships and unregistered shipments. While we were looking for violations of sanctions, what two of our guys—ICE Special Agents Sean McElroy and Abdul-Rahman "Bud" Adada—found instead were two sets of books for the Oil-for-Food Program, meaning two sets of prices for what appeared to be the same shipment. China, Russia, and France (the most vocal critics of our effort to topple Saddam) seemed heavily invested in this creative bookkeeping. We had no forensic capability beyond rudimentary triage, so we passed it along to investigative teams further back in the pipeline. In the months that followed, this discovery emerged in the world press as what General Tommy Franks dubbed the "Oil for Palaces" scandal that some estimates put at $21 billion.

A company would agree to pay $2 billion for oil worth only $1 billion. Saddam skimmed half, the company skimmed half, and then it delivered the food. So after the graft and chicanery, $2 billion worth of oil might provide about $500,000 worth of food to the people. Bernard Guillet, diplomatic adviser to the French minister of the interior, was arrested at home in Paris in connection with the inquiry. Interior Minister Charles Pasqua resigned and was subsequently elected to the French Senate, where he enjoys immunity from criminal prosecution.

We kept searching in a widening circle along the coast, following the money and doing what detectives do everywhere—developing sources—and by April 12 we had shifted our investigative focus to Basra, which sits on the Shatt al-Arab, the "River of the Arabs," the confluence of the Tigris and the Euphrates, and the border with Iran.

Basra had fallen to the Brits on April 6, 2003. Heavily Shi'ite, this city was the first place I saw residents stoning returning police officers because of their past association with Saddam Hussein. I thought about explaining to the crowds that, logically, the police officers who were returning were probably not the bad ones. But I suspected logic was not at play. The Brits ushered the officers to safety and we continued on our mission. Shortly thereafter, the first of an endless string of car bombs would explode outside the police station, killing seventy-four people.

Basra has a long tradition of legal scholarship and Islamic heresies. Supposedly, it was also the port from which Sinbad the Sailor left on his adventures. Kuwaitis built summer homes here, and families once strolled along its corniche in the evening, buying grilled kebabs from street vendors. On September 22, 1980, Hussein used the question of which point in the river constituted the Iran-Iraq border as a flimsy pretext to attack Iran and begin an eight-year war in which he used chemical weapons on the Iranians and which resulted in the deaths of perhaps a million souls. Today, squatters live in the partially submerged freighters now lying derelict in the harbor.

While we were in Basra, the U.S. and British navies were running patrols in that harbor and also along the Shatt al-Arab, all the way up to al-Qurna, the putative site for the Garden of Eden, where the Tigris and Euphrates meet. The senior ICE agent, Steve Mocsary—his Navy SEAL past calling—and I would ride along to check out little alcoves amid the reeds and the tattered palm trees, finding weapons caches in odd little buildings seen best from the water.

But mostly we focused on the major shipping docks, teaming up with the Brits' Seventeen Port Maritime Brigade, the unit that was now running and maintaining the port and commanded by Lieutenant Colonel Paul Ash. In one warehouse alone, we discovered dozens of Chinese-made Seersucker antiship cruise missiles (a variant on the Silkworm missile), along with shipping documents indicating that a different, otherwise friendly, nation had been servicing those weapons up to just a month or so before the war. Ditto with the al-Fath missiles we found later.

We also hit the banks, blowing open safe after safe, and finding more of Hussein's stolen money than we knew what to do with. Usually, we had to drag the safes out into the desert because there is no way to tell whether there was something inside to set off a secondary explosion. Given their sheer size, we did have to blow one or two in place. In one instance, a company of Gurkhas were billeted nearby, and glass shards pelted several of them. These Nepalese troops were immortalized by Kipling for their ferocity and for their loyalty to the crown since the first Gurkha regiment was raised in 1815. The exceedingly "old school" Gurkha lieutenant, his mustache trimmed into a work of art, came over to voice their displeasure. "Sir, would you mind not blowing up the building on my men. It's making for a rather unpleasant afternoon."

We were recovering so much money, both Iraqi dinars and U.S. greenbacks, that we could not count it all and had to resort to the scale. (For the record, one million dollars in hundred-dollar bills weighs twenty-two pounds.) We processed the U.S. currency and found an

Army unit to take the money back to Camp Udari, still a staging area inside Kuwaiti. I tried to convince the Office of Reconstruction and Humanitarian Assistance (ORHA) to take the tens of millions of Ba'ath Party dinars we were recovering and reintroduce them back into the economy.

"Thanks for the advice, Colonel," I was told, with a decided emphasis on the word *advice*. As in "Don't bother us, Colonel, with your harebrained ideas." Months later, I read how ORHA was trying to reinvigorate the Iraqi economy by infusing it with seized Ba'ath Party dinars. Wish I'd thought of that.

These were days of sensory overload with no time for reflection. The Marines captured a terrorist camp run by al-Qaeda. The British found torture chambers and mass graves, as well as warehouses filled with bodies.

The people needed electricity, water, and food. Yet everywhere we went we were still being mobbed by grateful Iraqis, screaming *"Shukran, shukran"* (thank you) and "U.S. number one." Steve and I were still being dragged, literally, into house after house to drink tea and see pictures of loved ones who had simply vanished. Saddam Hussein, we learned, was nothing if not efficient in his ruthlessness. The Iraqis handed us their white and blue and yellow ration cards, asking what they should do with them now. I didn't have the answer then, I don't have the answer now.

There were other complications as well. When a foreign national comes up to you in a war zone and raises his arms, is he thanking you or about to kill you? You spend all your time trying to identify friend from foe, and the stress becomes debilitating.

One day, I had teamed up with a British Royal Marine "leftenant colonel" and a retired U.S. Army colonel who was working as a contractor. They were doing a recon in an area that I also needed to see, and they had one empty seat in their convoy. They were kind enough to offer it. I had watched them operate a couple of days earlier and seen that they were professionals, so I trusted them enough to take it. I left Steve in charge of JIACG in my absence.

We had reached a fairly dodgy area when two young men approached us. They looked healthy, a little more muscular than the average Iraqi, good haircuts—all the signs of former military. So each of us unobtrusively and silently put a hand on his weapon. The Royal Marine had his bull-pup-design SA80, a sweet assault rifle; we had M4s. But the young men, who spoke a little English, said, "Please, you have to help us, our sister is dying."

I remember thinking, "This is not my show. I don't get to call the shots." But the three of us looked at each other with that kind of "What the hell?" look.

We went back to our vehicle and talked about the likelihood of being ambushed. I remember laughing and saying, "I can see the sitrep [situation report] now—not just one colonel hoodwinked and killed, but three!" Each of us checked the chambers of our weapons. Then we got in our car and followed their car to the courtyard of a makeshift hospital a good fifteen to twenty minutes away. We just kept getting stupider and stupider.

The hospital was obviously without staff and without resources. Dozens of people were waiting in the heat of the courtyard, dead bodies mingled in with the living, and the smell of burnt flesh was appalling. The young men took us to their sister, a teenager, who had burns over her entire body. She had been trying to light an oil stove in the kitchen and it blew up. Even in a war zone, accidents still happen in kitchens. The brothers, who were in their twenties, started to cry, pleading with us. A man in the room volunteered his flatbed truck, and then each of us took a corner of the mattress she was lying on, and we carried her to the truck. There was no morphine, so every bump and jostle must have caused her excruciating pain. The British lieutenant colonel and retired U.S. colonel rode in the flatbed, I drove the car following. We convoyed to a British base nearby where the UK officer arranged for the girl to be flown to London that night. I never found out what happened to her. I really didn't want to know—because in my mind, she recovered perfectly without a scar.

In all the suffering, this was like a grain of sand, but what else are you going to do? They asked for our help, we did what we could. Was it fair to all the people who weren't going to be helped that day? I can't answer that. We tried to help this one girl because her brothers asked us to.

We could not solve all the human needs of the Iraqi people in twenty days, but a single mission, Operation Desert Scorpion, managed to detain a thousand Saddam loyalists and confiscate $9,463,000 in U.S. currency, as well as 1,557,000,000 Iraqi dinars, along with 1,071 gold bars and numerous unsanctioned weapons.

But still, not everyone was pleased with what we were doing.

On April 15, I was again in Basra when a British journalist approached me with rage in her eyes, screaming, "You macho assholes are down here looking for missiles and money, and the finest museum in the world in Baghdad has just been looted."

I called Senior back in Umm Qasr and said, "What the hell is she talking about?'

He said, "I'll find out, sir."

I said, "I want it now."

8

BABYLON

*This is the wall of Uruk, which no city
on earth can equal. See its ramparts gleam
like copper in the Sun.*—The Epic of Gilgamesh

B ACK IN U MM Qasr, Senior set up the satellite and went online.
When I got back the next day, he said, "Sir, you gotta see this. She's
not kidding."

Then he showed me the headlines:

MUSEUM TREASURES NOW WAR BOOTY. "Everything that could be
carried out has disappeared from the museum." Associated Press, April
12, 2003.

PILLAGERS STRIP IRAQ MUSEUM OF ITS TREASURE. "It took only 48 hours
for the museum to be destroyed, with at least 170,000 artifacts carried
away by looters." *New York Times*, April 13, 2003.

U.S. BLAMED FOR FAILURE TO STOP SACKING OF MUSEUM. "Not a single
pot or display case remained intact." *Independent*, April 14, 2003.

Senior went through a couple more, then said, "Sir, that's our mission."

I said, "Damn straight it's our mission. We've got the only law-
enforcement expertise in the country."

What we did not have was a full appreciation of the storm brewing.

UN Secretary-General Kofi Annan issued a statement "deploring the
catastrophic losses." The United Nations Educational, Scientific and
Cultural Organization (UNESCO) immediately convened an emergency meeting of thirty experts from fourteen countries, its director

general, Koichiro Matsuura, calling on American authorities "to take immediate measures of protection and surveillance of Iraqi archaeological sites and cultural institutions."

Meanwhile, a chorus worthy of Sophocles was taking the stage, outraged journalists and like-minded academics ready to chime in on the dithyramb. Johns Hopkins University Assyriologist Jerry Cooper was actually among the more restrained when he told the *Washington Post*, "It's as if the entire Mall—the National Archives and the Smithsonian—had been looted, along with the Library of Congress."

Then military tactics became the piñata at which every guest could take a swing. The *New York Times* wrote, "The American and British forces are clearly to blame for the destruction and displacement of [Iraq's] cultural treasures." Michael Petzel, the president of the International Council on Monuments and Sites, went so far as to claim that the United States was guilty of committing "a crime against humanity" for failing to protect the museum.

Counterpunch took an especially wild cut: "And like the Mongols, U.S. troops stood by while Iraqi mobs looted and destroyed artifacts . . . The looting and wanton destruction of the Baghdad museum . . . falls well within the jurisdiction of the International Criminal Court."

Dozens of other countries expressed their concern about the U.S. government's failure to prevent this catastrophe, and Mr. Rumsfeld's first response, while technically accurate, was not exactly a masterstroke of public relations. He reminded the world, "Bad things happen in life, and people do loot."

I called back to CENTCOM headquarters in Qatar and spoke to my second-in-command, Marine colonel Rich Jakucs—another one of my recruitment phone calls. We had served together in both Desert Storm and Lithuania—and I knew him to be a pro who put mission first.

I told Rich that I wanted to assemble a small team to get to Baghdad and secure the museum. Right away, he sounded the wrong note: "It doesn't sound like our mission. And it's definitely not the right time. It's still Indian country up there." His tone was a bit discouraging, especially since he was the guy rubbing elbows with all the executive officers of the organizations whose permissions we needed.

"If not us, then who?" I shot back. "If not now, then when?" These were not rhetorical questions.

I waited for a moment or two, then said, "You don't have an answer?" More silence.

"Then staff it. I'll send you the proposal in a few hours."

"You're the boss," Rich replied.

Staff it means to clear the plan through all the staff sections within the chain of command. Administration, intelligence, operations, logistics, planning, legal—J1, J2, J3, J4, J5, SJA. And then for us, of course, there were all the nonmilitary agencies affected as well—FBI, CIA, State, ICE, Energy. Basically, everyone in Qatar with a ballpoint had to sign off on the mission.

I put together a one-page information paper laying out what I wanted to do. All I proposed in the beginning was to go in and get ground truth, to stabilize the situation and stop the bleeding. I wasn't talking about a full-scale investigation, just a quick crime-scene analysis, get a sense of what was missing, then seal the area. I asked for three to five days. We could talk about what to do in the long term after that.

I e-mailed the one-pager to Rich. His job was to take it around and get consensus. That would be no small feat, but I believed he could do it. Then I grabbed some coffee in a canteen cup, walked off by myself, pulled my small commander's notebook out of the cargo pocket of my cammies, and started to work out the details. I did not yet have any specifics about what was missing, but I knew from grad school that if there had ever been a literal "cradle" where civilization was born, you could not get closer to it than the female face in limestone known as the Mask of Warka, and the Sacred Vase from the same ancient city. If someone had walked off with these things, we had to get them back.

By this time, I had more than fifty JIACG members in Iraq and another fifty in Kuwait and Qatar. We had half a dozen other missions going on at the same time, including interrogations. I decided that those who weren't going to Baghdad had to physically pull back to a more secure area. The military and the nonmilitary agencies had already gone out on a limb for the interagency concept, and in most cases based on nothing more than a handshake. Given that it was my hand they had shaken, I didn't feel right leaving their people digging around waterfront warehouses on their own. So, I decided to break up JIACG into smaller task-organized teams based on their skill sets and embed them into larger units throughout Iraq. This enabled my teams to accomplish our missions while being provided both force protection and life support (food, water, ammo, etc.). So far, so good.

With a map and a grease pencil, I began working out the specifics for the Baghdad team. I had to determine how we would travel, how many vehicles, who does security, how many weapons in each vehicle, and so on. I had Army captain Dave Wachsmuth put his analytical wizardry to use working out the fuel, water, food, and mileage issues. I then told Air Force major Rich Pearson, my determined and talented intelligence officer, to get me everything available on the routes between Umm Qasr and the capital. He briefed me a couple hours later. He said that it was basically a shooting gallery from Najaf to Baghdad.

I thought for a minute, then said, "We have tanks and Bradleys [armored personnel carriers] up in Baghdad, right?"

He nodded.

"They need fuel and parts, right?"

"Yes, sir." He paused. "I see where you're going."

"See if we can hitch a ride on the next resupply convoy."

"I'm all over it, sir."

But then the bad news. The next convoy for Baghdad wasn't leaving for at least three days. Even worse, permission to ride with it had to come not only from Qatar (CENTCOM headquarters), but also from Kuwait (Third Army headquarters) and Washington.

"Are you kidding me?"

"No, sir. There is actually a sergeant in the Pentagon who coordinates all vehicles traveling to Baghdad." Maybe I'd get all of the necessary permissions in time, I thought to myself. And maybe when I woke up tomorrow I'd be six feet tall and good-looking too. I was not all that excited about traveling with unknown logistics units whose size alone made them a prime target, but the alternative was a couple dozen of us in SUVs, tearing across the desert with the bad guys on the loose who knew where. Have a plan. Then have a backup plan, my old Gunny used to say, because the first one probably won't work.

Bending the rules was one thing. Getting people killed was another. Getting *my* people killed was quite another still. The choices were starting to suck. It was already past midnight, so I hit the rack to let all of this settle into the more optimistic and creative regions of my brain.

The next morning I called Rich Jakucs back in Qatar. He said, "I'm getting nothing but 'nonconcur.' Basically, staff sections are saying, 'Are you out of your mind? This is an active combat zone. You can't have nonmilitary investigators there.'"

He did have a point, up to a point. As he ran down the objections of each staff section, I knew these were legitimate arguments by reasonable people. It wasn't that they didn't want us to investigate what had happened. It was that they sincerely believed that the risks far outweighed any possible gains. One death, one casualty, or worse, one captured and tortured member of my unit on al-Jazeera and this multiple-agency experiment would have been over. The consensus was that I was being unreasonable. I thought about hitting them with Shaw—"All progress depends on the unreasonable man"—but I still wouldn't have gotten in the door. If I took it straight to General Franks, his assistant would have said, "You're bringing me something to which the general's lawyer and five other sections have already said no?"

I considered my options, but Rich already knew where I was going to come out. "Matthew, don't do it," he said. "This is stupid. You're risking your career. I know how pigheaded you are, but don't do it. It's a terrible idea."

"Got it, Rich, thanks." I hung up with him and started to imagine the first question at my court-martial. "Colonel, what exactly did you think you were doing with all of those civilians in a military war zone without approval and without adequate force protection?" I did not want to think about what the widows would say. At the time, I was reading *Defeat into Victory*, Field Marshal Viscount William Slim's classic account of guerrilla warfare in the jungles of Burma in World War II, and I remembered how he stressed that "acting without orders, in anticipation of orders, or without waiting for approval, yet always within the overall intention, must become second nature in any form of warfare."

I decided it was time to test that theory. I called back to Qatar one more time and asked to speak with General Renuart. When I got the general on my satellite phone, I said, "Sir, I've heard about this looting in Baghdad, and this could really hurt us. You know, sir, half my unit are cops and the other half are cops in uniform, but I'm having a lot of trouble selling the idea of an investigation."

He said, "Matthew, can you get there?"

"Yes, sir," I answered. There was silence on the line. Gene Renuart had taken over JIACG back in September 2002, and he was a good boss who often asked for my advice in a room full of officers more senior than I—not a tactic designed to win the popularity contests that neither of us cared much about anyway. But this was different.

"Matthew, don't give me your Marine 'I don't know how to fail' bullshit. Can you do this?" He had a good sense of humor, but this was not the time for a witty comeback.

"Yes, sir. I can."

"How fast can you get there?"

"Forty-eight hours, sir."

"Well, Matthew, you work for me. You don't need to go through anyone else. Do you understand? Get there and fix it. Just fix it. But goddamn it, Matthew, don't fail and don't get killed. That's an order."

Tommy Franks had always called General Renuart his "fifty-pound brain." He had fifty-pound balls as well.

"Sir, there's one more thing. Some German media are reporting that U.S. forces were involved in the looting. You know I'm going to do a thorough investigation. And God help any U.S. forces that were involved."

He said, "You know that 'Pit Bull' thing you do in New York?"

Pit Bull was the nickname I'd picked up back home, prosecuting tabloid cases like Puff Daddy and "the Baby-Faced Butcher."

I said, "Roger that, sir."

"Well, you do that Pit Bull thing in Baghdad."

That was all the guidance I received—or needed. The general had put his ass on the line because it was the right thing to do. I owed it to him to see to it that any fallout would stop with me. We would simply have to get to the museum before the naysayers knew what we were up to, then stay below the radar screen until we had some success.

I went to Supervisory Special Agent Steve Mocsary, the senior ICE official on the ground, to get his buy-in. He may have been a couple years away from retirement, and I had only known him for a month, but every day in Basra he had impressed the hell out of me. I knew about his background in underwater demolition, and I knew he liked storming around Florida on his motorcycle, so I figured he was a pretty easy sell. "Steve, this is your chance to get to Baghdad. Only catch is, we've got no top cover and no convoy security. It's you and me."

Then I added an old Special Forces phrase I knew would resonate: "Alone and unafraid."

He looked at me with a wry smile—a smirk really—and said, "What the hell."

There was no way I could justify DTRA Dave and his gang as part of the museum mission—they didn't have the requisite smuggling and detective skills and they still had their own work to do—but I wanted them along for the ride. Dave Beckett was unflappable and I had come to rely on his superior combat instincts.

That night in Umm Qasr I discussed all the angles with Steve and

Dave and with a select few of the others I knew I wanted on the team. "I don't know where you are on this, but I need you to be with me," I told each of them individually. But all they had to hear was *Baghdad* and every one of them was on board.

I assume that the DTRA (Defense Threat Reduction Agency) guys chose to go because it served their purposes. But I also think Dave liked the "what the hell" aspect of this convoy. He was beginning to see that just because we shave in combat, Marines aren't only about "doing it by the book." When necessary, we write the book as we go along.

I mentally divided everyone into one of three categories: those I wanted for the mission, those whose skills were needed for other ongoing missions somewhere else in Iraq, and those who had already begun to show the stress of operating in a combat zone. This last group was surprisingly large, and their exclusion from the Baghdad mission had to be handled with care, particularly since everyone with me had volunteered to be there in the first place.

At its most basic, preparation for combat consists of three things: superior physical fitness, extensive study of both history and TTPs (tactics, techniques, and procedures), and endless training to build muscle memory and confidence. But even those who do everything in their power to prepare aren't always able to cope with the demands placed on them. The lack of sleep, the stress of life-and-death decisions, injuries and infections, and the constant flow of adrenaline are all physiologically and psychologically corrosive. One of the keys to being a leader is to recognize the warning signs as quickly as possible. The movie version—the guy who cracks and starts screaming—is rare. But short tempers, loss of ability to concentrate, difficulty with repetitive tasks, slower decision-making cycles, and especially the desire to sleep—are all common under conditions of combat stress. In fact, those who are approaching total meltdown start to crave sleep more than anything else.

I needed trigger-pullers on the trip north, but once we got to Baghdad, I needed investigators. So the list I worked up totaled twenty-four people. Ten for force protection—with whom we would part ways once we got to a "secure" perimeter in Baghdad—and fourteen for the museum investigation itself. This latter group was top-heavy with ICE—nine agents—because they know investigations, and they know smuggling. They also had great interrogators and interpreters. The other five were military.

The next morning, I brought everyone together for the group hug, and I put it to the whole crew. I laid it out for them the same way I would lay it out for a jury. I never bullshit juries. When I don't have an eyewitness, the first thing I say is, "Ladies and gentlemen, I don't have a single eyewitness. I wish I did. But let me tell you what I do have."

I told the guys about the museum. I told them I needed volunteers to go to Baghdad to conduct an initial investigation. I pointed out that we had no formal written authorization, no top cover, no crew-served weapons, and that we would be traveling alone. If we got hit on the way, I added, we'd be on our own. No backup and no air support on call to pull us out of trouble.

"Colonel, stop trying to sugarcoat it," Bud Rogers chimed in.

I smiled and went on, "When we get to Baghdad, we won't have a place to stay or any formal way of getting resupplied. We will, however, be surrounded by a treasure trove of evidence and information."

I was giving them the truth, but it was a bit like Chesty Puller's truth. When a single Marine division was surrounded by eight Chinese divisions at the Chosin Reservoir in Korea, he brought his staff together and said, "Gentlemen, we have Chinese to the left and right, we have Chinese to the front and rear. They can't get away from us this time."

In the minds of many of these ICE agents, going to Baghdad to track down stolen antiquities had nothing to do with them. We had been turning up good stuff in Umm Qasr and Basra. We were getting great feedback from Washington, and we had even been the subject of a complimentary BBC documentary. To some, the museum investigation was not just a waste of time, it would take us away from our core mission—counterterrorism. One senior agent in particular was the most outspoken. He had been complaining nonstop about everything from the heat to the living conditions since he'd left the hotel in Kuwait. He made it clear to Steve that he was going to share his concerns with headquarters, specifically telling them that Steve was jeopardizing his entire team for a bunch of rocks. Steve offered to dial the phone for him. True to form, he declined. Later that day, we concocted a "mission" that required him to return to Kuwait and then the States. He did—to a hero's welcome, and I'm pretty sure, a promotion.

But for the others, getting to Baghdad sooner rather than later was the name of the game. They had already uncovered evidence that French, German, and some U.S. companies had been dealing with Hussein despite the UN embargo. There were more files in Baghdad. They wanted to see those files before they disappeared.

We were standing outside, behind a berm the British Royal Marines had thrown up along the Umm Qasr docks to prevent direct-fire and vehicular assaults. I knew that offering the rationale of the world's shared cultural heritage and the archaeological importance of the objects in question was not going to cut it. This was a "St. Crispin's Day" moment, and I was simply going to have to do my best Henry V.

What I came up with was something along the lines of "That way lies Kuwait City"—I pointed south with my left hand—"and a nice buffet with hot food and a nice clean bed in an air-conditioned room at the Radisson Hotel."

Then I held up my right hand, pointing north.

"This way lies Baghdad."

Most of these guys did not have their Shakespeare open for comparison, and at the very least I got their attention.

The left hand: "That way lies dolphins and a swim in the Persian Gulf."

Then the right hand: "This way lies Baghdad.

"That way lies safety and the C-130 that's going to take you back to your world, to your wife, to your kids.

"This way lies Baghdad.

"That way lies safety.

"This way lies the guns."

Then I stepped away and let them talk it over. I wanted to give them a little time, but not enough time to sleep on it. I got my answer that night: of the ones that I had already selected in my mind, we were twenty-four for twenty-four. If there's one thing I know, it's how to pick a jury.

We saddled up and left Umm Qasr just after first light the next morning, with one convoy following the Euphrates River north toward Nasiriyah and Diwaniyah, and the other south headed toward Kuwait and other missions. We did not want to go through the Karbala Gap at night, so we had to make time. I had coordinated with each of the units that "controlled" each sector we would be passing through, but those units were hundreds of miles apart. The only safe perimeter we could count on was at the end of the ride, at the Baghdad International Airport.

Places like Najaf, Nasiriyah, and Diwaniyah had been bypassed by the assault forces on the thrust to Baghdad, with the idea that pockets of resistance could be cleaned up later. *Pockets of resistance* sounds nice and contained, almost benign, until you realize it means people shooting at you. So it was for good reason that you were not (officially) allowed to travel without armor or at least crew-served, mounted machine guns.

For long stretches, Iraq's Route 8 is like a fairly decent state highway in some state like Nevada. We flew past the scrubby desert vegetation and in and out of a couple of sandstorms where we had to pull over for half an hour or so. It was a normal two-lane blacktop, only with burned-out tanks every hundred meters on the side of the road. We had rehearsed our counterambush drills and every man had his assigned visual quadrant to scan for threats.

I found the desolation outside the window both amazing and disturbing. This was the birthplace of agriculture, the birthplace of civilization. So where was the "Fertile Crescent"? Where were the "Hanging Gardens of Babylon"? I knew that thousands of years of irrigation were partly to blame. The increasingly brackish water evaporated, leaving behind the salt that seeped into the farmland and eventually destroyed it.

But thousands of years of bad ideas had also taken a toll. Geography plays a role in a nation's rise and fall, but so does what economists call social technology. The rule of law, solid property rights, a lack of corruption—these are even more important than natural resources. An open market for talent leads to prosperity; a "Big Man" keeping all the goodies for himself, or doling them out to family and friends, leads to stagnation and decline. Witness Saddam Hussein.

We had been on the road for many hours, and ruminating about these things, my mind kept drifting back to a speck on the map that had caught my attention earlier.

Without crew-served weapons we were already an "illegal" convoy, on a mission that had not officially been staffed. In for a penny, in for a pound. I proposed that we take advantage of this once-in-a-lifetime opportunity.

I said, "Gentlemen, we need to see Babylon." The site of those Hanging Gardens, and the ruins of that legendary city, was just about a half hour off the highway.

Reactions varied, but suffice it to say that not everyone was pleased. Admittedly, in terms of military tactics and force protection, one could question the decision. But one of the advantages of the "life is short, art is long" formulation is the recognition that an hour and a half was not going to be critical to the survival of the objects we had set out to rescue. And a little introduction to the spirit of ancient civilizations might even prove useful.

As it was, some of the ICE guys complained loud and clear, but I relied on Steve to win them over. "The Tower of Babel, Steve. The Hanging Gardens. Half the Old Testament is Babylon. You can tell your grandkids you saw *Babylon.*"

We took a vote, and everyone agreed that we would take a moment to see the site.

The river had changed its course and left this legendary city behind long ago. To reach the ruins, you have to drive in a winding, roundabout way through the scrub. The road was divided like a boulevard, with lanes in either direction, but instead of a grassy esplanade between them there was an irrigation canal. The heat was oppressive, the glare through the windshield blinding. Then up ahead, in the middle of nowhere, we saw a modern statue of Hammurabi. It was right there by the canal.

"Gentlemen, pit stop," I said over the radio.

The men got out to look, and I threw out a few facts about Hammurabi's code: " 'An eye for an eye'—this is that guy. He codified existing customs into a system of laws in 1792 B.C., the first Babylonian dynasty."

They had some questions, so I tried to give them a little more perspective on what we would be seeing once we got to the ruins, but the hardest thing to get across was just how old civilization was in the Middle East.

When Hammurabi tacked up his list of rules almost four thousand years ago, Babylon had already been a capital in continuous operation for at least six centuries. That's roughly equivalent to the time from Henry V to us. But then Hammurabi's empire fell to the Hittites. In 689 B.C., an Assyrian king opened the canals and flooded Babylon, destroying the walls of Gilgamesh. But sixty years later, the Babylonians extricated themselves from Assyrian rule, and the man who led the way had a grandson named Nebuchadnezzar. He rebuilt the walls and the temple and the famed Ishtar gate, and supposedly, he built miraculous gardens for his wife, who missed all the greenery of her home in the northern mountains. He also sacked Jerusalem.

Most of what Westerners know about this comes from the Bible. "By the rivers of Babylon," it says in the Psalms, "there we sat down, yea, we wept, when we remembered Zion." Much of the Old Testament is, in fact, the story of the Jews having it out with the peoples from this part of the world. Every time the Hebrew children fell short in their faith, Jehovah would arrange for someone to "smite" them, and the someone was usually a king from Mesopotamia. Assyrians conquered "the Ten Lost Tribes" of the Israelites in the eighth century B.C., and the Babylonians conquered Judah in 586 B.C.

Anticipating the day the Hebrews got their act together, Jeremiah prophesied, "The broad walls of Babylon shall be utterly overthrown, and her high gates shall be burned with fire." Isaiah said of Babylon that "wild beasts of the desert shall live there . . . wild goats shall dance there . . . wolves shall cry in their castles." They didn't have to wait long for the decline. Daniel tells of Nebuchadnezzar going mad and eating grass. In 539 B.C., the Persian king Cyrus captured Babylon and, according to Herodotus, diverted the river and drained the marsh—much as Hussein was to do twenty-five hundred years later.

Alexander the Great employed ten thousand men to clear the dirt and rubble and rebuild the temple, but then he died, at Babylon, in 323 B.C. In the fourth century A.D., in seeming confirmation of Isaiah, St. Jerome described Babylon as being used as a wild-game park for the amusement of Persian dignitaries.

When we got to the ruins some twenty-three hundred years after Alexander, the first thing that struck me, standing in what had once been the center of the universe—the New York or London of its day—was how incredibly quiet it was, and how long it had been "over" for these people. There was a village a few clicks (kilometers) away, but the ancient city stood in the dust by itself.

There was a small museum that had been looted and boarded up, along with its gift shop. We found a few kids wandering around, so we gave them some MREs. These kids tried to sell us what appeared to be pottery shards, three for five dollars. They also told us they knew where we could get better artifacts.

Babylon was one of the few "sights" in the world that thoroughly lived up to expectations, such as Pompeii, Knossos, and the Parthenon. But to have that spine-tingling experience you had to look beyond the desecration. In recent years, Saddam Hussein had tried to turn the site into a tourist attraction. He began "restoring" the ruins, which for him meant putting up fake walls that looked like cardboard cutouts or Disney on the cheap. On the edge of town he erected a billboard showing himself shoulder to shoulder with Nebuchadnezzar behind a couple of straining chariot horses. Many of the bricks he used in his "reconstruction" were inscribed with the phrase "This was built by Saddam Hussein, son of Nebuchadnezzar."

On the hill just behind the site, Hussein had built one of his seventy-nine palaces. He scattered these throughout the country, building sixty-seven of them after the sanctions of 1990 had supposedly cut off his money—Oil for Palaces. Cool breezes blew through the shaded terraces. Behind a columned, marble border we had a view that was perhaps 180 degrees. Eating our MREs on that terrace, we looked down into the ancient city as if it were a museum diorama. Although the palace was a cheesy reproduction of Nebuchadnezzar's, I still walked through every room. The marble floors and the high ceilings kept it cool, and looters had given it a new simplicity. Not a stick of furniture was left. The place had been absolutely stripped to the bones. Faucets, toilets, even exposed water pipes had been removed.

Kings had been building palaces in these parts for close to ten thousand years, outfitting them with whatever glories they could assemble. And for just as long, invaders have been ransacking those palaces, and carrying off the loot to embellish another palace down the road. "Loot" was a standard and expected form of compensation for armies throughout the ancient world. Assyrian friezes show parades of soldiers carrying off baskets of stuff; sometimes, images of loot hang above their heads like the radiant angels that also occupy that space. The Old Testament goes on at great length itemizing the hardware stolen from one king by another, back and forth. When Nebuchadnezzar sacked Jerusalem, destroying the temple, and bringing the Jews to the Euphrates for their "Babylonian captivity," Ezra tells of fifty-four hundred vessels of gold and silver he looted from the temple. Looking ahead, I had no idea what was in store for us at the museum in Baghdad. But one thing I knew for sure, looting was nothing new.

Once we were back on the road again, the sun was moving low in the sky and I realized that our detour meant that we would not make the airport before nightfall. Driving at night was out of the question—the area immediately south of the city was one of those "pockets of resistance" I had been briefed on earlier. But where to stay? Studying my map for a way out of this Hobson's choice, I was silently—but vigorously—reproaching myself for having jeopardized my team's safety with my grad-student indulgence.

But listening to the conversation in the car, I realized that the sweep of history that Babylon presented had gotten through to the guys. It impressed them, and that impressed me. Before Babylon, the overwhelming emotion was, okay, if the colonel is all worked up over a couple rocks, what the hell? If that's what it takes to get to Baghdad, so be it. After Babylon, they started to see what this mission was all about. The irrational tenth at play once again.

But that still didn't solve the problem of what we were going to do when the sun dropped below the horizon. Worse, two of the vehicles did not have enough gas to make it to Baghdad, regardless of when we arrived. Just as I was deciding where to call a stop and break the news to the team, we saw a couple Marines guarding the entrance to a large field. "Cheer up," I could hear Sophocles whispering in my ear. "Fortune is never on the side of the fainthearted."

We pulled over and learned that the Marines' Fifth Regimental Combat Team had just pulled into that site a few hours earlier. I walked over to the CO to ask for some fuel and a place to stay.

Colonel Joe Dunford, a real warrior who looked as if he hadn't slept for weeks, was sitting on an MRE box in the dust and drinking coffee from his canteen cup. *"Mi casa,"* he said as he waved his right arm toward the barren field in front of him, *"es su casa."*

I made a show of looking around. "I'd like to think about it and get back to you," I replied.

The next morning we hit the road early and covered the last leg of the journey.

We reached the Baghdad airport on Sunday the twentieth. We were eager to get on the case, but truth be told, I didn't even know where the Iraq Museum was located. Fortunately, I had radioed ahead for a security escort. So, after we arrived at the airport, Steve and I immediately headed off in two vehicles, with three men in each, to do a leader's reconnaissance. Steve always drove—after a month on patrol together we were like an old married couple that way. Cops are the same way. We had SUVs in the middle sandwiched in front and back by Humvees with heavy machine guns mounted on top—exactly the way we should have come from Umm Qasr in the first place.

At its best, Baghdad has the look of an East L.A. strip mall in the middle of summer. But in April of 2003, there was also Arabic graffiti on the walls, overpasses blown up, smoke rising in the distance, and the sound of automatic weapons all day and night. And this was when the resistance was at a lull. The supporters of l'ancien régime were keeping their heads down, licking their wounds, and trying to reorganize themselves. Like us, they were figuring out what to do next.

No electricity meant no traffic lights, but there were no traffic cops either, which led to chaos on the roads, with wrong-way traffic on the major thoroughfares. As in the south, and entirely consistent with the personality cult of a dictator, there were Hussein statues, murals, pictures, and busts everywhere. Every street corner, every office building, every few feet, no matter where you were, there was Saddam. And every Saddam was now defaced. In fact, there were so many of these that the troops began using them to give directions. "Take a right at the asshole with the bullet holes between the eyes. Then, when you get to the asshole with three red X's over his face, hook a left . . ."

After barreling through the city for about half an hour, we rounded a corner and I saw the sandstone walls, turrets, and palm trees of the museum compound. Just then, several explosions went off across the street from the entrance. Drawing closer, I saw the giant hole made by the tank round above the entrance to the Children's Museum. Over the main entrance to the offices was the handwritten warning DEATH TO ALL ZIONISTS AND AMERICAN PIGS. For anyone eager to be a part of the action, it seemed that Baghdad would not disappoint.

We pulled up to the main gate, guarded by a tank platoon that had been at the museum since securing the compound on the morning of the sixteenth. I introduced myself and told the platoon commander that we were there to do a quick crime-scene analysis. It sounded convincing as I said it, but the truth is, I had no idea how we were going to conduct a police investigation in all this "Mad Max" confusion. Obviously, we were going to have to do it the Marine way—adapt, improvise, and overcome.

"Whatever you need, sir," the lieutenant responded. Then he explained that the boss inside was named Dr. Jaber Khaleel Ibrahim al-Tikriti. I immediately noted the significance of the tribal name. Whoever this Dr. Jaber was, his name indicated that he was from Hussein's hometown of Tikrit, which we had to assume was not incidental to his advancement. The lieutenant then directed us to the administrative offices, where I introduced myself to the first Iraqi at the door as representative of the U.S. government here to conduct an investigation into the theft of antiquities.

The Iraqi motioned for us to follow. Just inside the door, he led us through a grand rotunda with pictures of Hussein, too high up to have been defaced. We followed a long hallway off to the right, which in the absence of electricity was lit only by the bit of daylight coming in through the small windows. I could see that in the offices to the right and left, books and museum records had been thrown everywhere. Safes had been broken into and ransacked. Anything worth the trouble had been destroyed or taken, right down to the telephones and the paper clips.

We came to an anteroom with a secretary's desk, very small, almost like the furniture in a child's room. This was the first step in a dance, not a show of force, so I asked Steve and Senior to wait outside (and observe by watching) as I stepped into Dr. Jaber's office.

Dr. Jaber was chairman of the State Board of Antiquities and Heritage, of which the Iraq Museum was one part. The administrators of the Iraq Museum in Baghdad reported to him, as did those of every other museum in the country, each of which was a satellite of the Iraq Museum. In his academic pursuits, he specialized in pre-Islamic periods, particularly Hatran, around the time of Christ, when this city southwest of modern-day Mosul was one of the great commercial crossroads of the world. No surprise, given his name and his appointed position, Dr. Jaber was a senior Ba'ath Party official.

His office was Spartan, with a desk that looked like surplus from the Korean War. Behind him was a door that led to the security office. In front of his desk were several seated men who were not introduced to me. They could have been friends, cousins, colleagues. They could have been Jaber's Ba'ath Party supervisors. I don't know, because I didn't get their names and I never saw them again.

After the obligatory greetings, I began slowly to explain our presence.

"I have heard that people have stolen antiquities from the museum," I said. Without my translator, this was going to be a stilted conversation, mostly in the present tense. "I am here to protect the museum, to find out what happened, and to get back whatever we can. I would like your permission to do this."

Hemingway described meeting a man who smelled of death. Dr. Jaber smelled of defeat. Even though his friends had come through the first Gulf War still in place, it was fairly obvious that for the Ba'ath Party this time, the party was over. He smiled in a benign, slightly distant way, then said, "You are the first to come to help us. We thought we would see the UN first, but they have not come. You are welcome." At that moment, a woman came in and began to serve tea. She was older. Of course, she wore the *khimar*, the Muslim head scarf.

"You wish to make an assessment?" Jaber asked me.

"I'll let the UN make the assessment," I replied. "I'm here to do, not to assess."

He smiled. Actually, he always smiled. "When would you like to start?"

I immediately thought back to my law-school mentor, the late Harold Rothwax. Whenever a lawyer asked this legendary New York judge when he wanted to start the trial, Rothwax, as brilliant as he was acerbic, always replied, "If it were done when 'tis done, then 'twere well it were done quickly." But I decided *Macbeth* might be a little over the top.

"Today is a good day," I said.

He cocked his head to the side, then blinked. Starting "today" is not a concept in Iraqi culture. Everything is *Insha'Allah*. God willing. "Tomorrow, *Insha'Allah*."

He was not offended, just taken aback.

The woman handed me a cup of tea, and Jaber once again tilted his head. "Oh, yes. This is Dr. Nawala. She is the director of the Iraq Museum."

I jumped to my feet, nearly spilling my tea. "I'm the hired help," I said. "I should be serving *you*."

She looked at me for a moment, and then I saw what might have been a faltering, precursory smile.

Dr. Nawala al-Mutwali was a world-renowned expert in cuneiform. She had been with the Iraq Museum since 1977, but had only recently been promoted to director from her position as head of the Department of Cuneiform Studies. Over time, I would hear her described by other archaeologists and museum staff as "Dr. No," but from the moment I said that bit about serving her tea, she and I hit it off.

I sat down, looked once again at Dr. Jaber, and said, "With your permission, I would like to stay here. Is there a place to live here? I have fourteen men including myself. We have four vehicles."

He thought for a moment, and then in his soft, lilting voice he said, "Oh, yes. The library is good."

As it turned out, the library was perfect. I needed a place that was secure—no windows—but also not in the fourth room in the back of the museum. I wanted to be able to move on a raid, and of course, I also wanted to be able to get out fast if bullets started flying. It had the additional advantage of being separated from the museum galleries and storage areas. Caesar's wife must be beyond reproach, and our being in the museum proper could enable someone in the future to accuse us of looting.

"We must do this together—my men and your staff," I said. "Together we can fix this. We can determine what happened and we can get back the property of the Iraqi people." For the next several months that would be my mantra: *the property of the Iraqi people.*

Over the next hour or so, we learned what we needed to know, then drove back to the airport, where DTRA and the men from the 513th military intelligence unit were preparing to return to their commands. They were going to work out of the airport or downtown or another country—I had no idea because, just like that, it was no longer any of my business.

Dave and I had managed to survive as partners for a whole month. He didn't know me from a hole in the wall and I didn't know him, and we had definitely not hit it off in the beginning. But I think he and his guys had come to see that there was a method to my madness, and, I do confess it, he and his men had grown on me as well.

I went over to say good-bye, and I wanted to pay them my highest compliment. "Gentlemen," I said, "I'd go through a door with you guys anytime." Then I paused.

"We'll do it again someday."

I turned to go, but then over my shoulder I heard, "Actually, sir, there is *one* more thing." I didn't know what he was talking about. But as I turned around, he called his team to attention and snapped a crisp, professional salute. It's one of the best damn salutes I've ever received.

9

LIFE AMONG THE RUINS

*If you could heal sorrow by weeping or
raise the dead with tears, grief would be more
prized than gold.*—Sophocles

GERTRUDE BELL, THE brilliant and headstrong daughter of a
wealthy English industrialist, first came to Mesopotamia in 1892.
She learned Arabic and archaeology, and by 1907, she was instructing
T. E. Lawrence on fieldwork at a dig in Carchemish on the west bank
of the Euphrates in modern-day Turkey. During World War I, in Basra,
she drew the map the British Army used to get to Baghdad. She turned
up next with British intelligence in Cairo, providing Lawrence (now
"of Arabia") with the tribal and topographical knowledge he needed to
lead the Arabs in revolt against the kaiser's ally, the Turks. In 1921, she
was the only woman summoned to the colonial secretary's conference
to decide the future of what the British troops called *Mespot*. There, she
drew another essential map, the one that created modern Iraq by splic-
ing together three provinces from the recently defeated Ottoman
Empire—not necessarily a good call. She also proposed the new nation's new ruler—Prince Faisal, the recently deposed king of Syria,
who was descended from the prophet Muhammad's great-grandfather.
She then became his most trusted adviser.

In 1923, on the east bank of the Tigris near Baghdad's old souq, or
marketplace, in al-Qushlah, the building housing the seat of government, Gertrude Bell set aside a single room for an Iraqi Museum of

Antiquities. The collection was soon moved to a separate building on Mamoun Street, at the foot of al-Shuhada Bridge, still on the east bank, and officially named the Iraq Museum, with Bell as its first director. It was a position she held until her death in 1926. Then in 1957, the government began construction of a two-story brick building arranged around a central fifty-meter-square courtyard in the Karkh district, across the river in the heart of central Baghdad. It was officially opened on November 9, 1966, and then a second identical square courtyard structure was added in 1986, creating a compound of forty-five thousand square meters, more than eleven acres.

Baghdad has always been a treasure house, as well as a center of scholarship. Without its libraries, and those of other great cities from Egypt to Persia, the works of Greek and Roman literature, science, and philosophy would never have been preserved to be rediscovered and retransmitted—in a sense, repatriated—when Europe emerged from its Dark Ages. The height of the city's splendor was Europe's nadir, the eighth century A.D., when Baghdad was ruled by the fifth Abbasid caliph, Harun al-Rashid, whose fabulous court served as the frame story for *A Thousand and One Nights*.

At night, Harun was known to skulk about his city in disguise, trying to take, as a modern press secretary might put it, "the pulse" of his people, much like Henry V more than five hundred years later, who walked from campfire to campfire in disguise before the battle of Agincourt to give his men "a touch of Harry in the night." Five hundred years after that, when Theodore Roosevelt was New York City police commissioner and rambling at night to catch cops sleeping on post, the tabloids of the day called him "Haroun-al-Roosevelt." Harun's diplomacy extended to China in the east and to the great Charlemagne in the west. The gifts he sent to the Frankish ruler—silks, ivory chessmen, an elephant, a mechanical water clock—are said to have strongly influenced Carolingian art. On the military front, his maneuvers westward—he camped on the heights overlooking Constantinople—led to years when the Byzantine emperors regularly paid him tribute. When Byzantine policy changed with a new administration and the tribute stopped, Harun came back with his armies and looted everything right up to the walls of Constantinople. Luckily for the Byzantines, he died before he could ransack the capital itself—enabling it to survive another 650 years.

The residents of Baghdad were not so fortunate when in A.D. 1258 the Mongols decided to steal everything that was not nailed down. The waters of the Tigris supposedly turned red with the blood of eight hundred thousand massacred souls, and black with the ink of a million manuscripts dumped in the river. But the way the Mongols looked at it, most of the treasure held in Baghdad had already been looted from somewhere else.

In the 1950s, Faisal II (the grandson of Gertrude Bell's political choice) was flush with oil money, and he decided to rebuild the city, commissioning Frank Lloyd Wright to do it. The great American architect sketched out a plan that replicated Baghdad's ancient, circular design, but which looked like something between a drip sand castle and "ziggurats from outer space." Even the Arabs laughed. Nobody wanted to recall the past. They wanted strip-mall modern.

When my team arrived in April 2003, Baghdad's glory days had been over for almost eight hundred years. The huge lead in philosophy, science, and medicine once maintained by the Arab world had been squandered by religious strictures and economic stagnation. But their decline was caused by outside forces as well.

The Ottoman Turks, the British colonialists, the three kings of the Hashemite family (Faisal I, Ghazi, Faisal II), and the fascist-leaning Ba'ath Party had all taken their toll, climaxed by a decade-long war with neighboring Iran, a humiliating defeat in the first Gulf War, and then another decade of UN sanctions and trade restrictions. By the time we showed up, cultural decline in Baghdad meant intermittent electricity, which often meant no running water. Garbage rotted as it piled up in the streets, and robed imams, men of god, passed by flanked by bodyguards carrying AK-47s. Looters, not restricted to antiquities, roamed far and wide, stealing anything they could. And each morning's call to prayer, after each night's interrupted sleep owing to sand fleas and the whirring of our electrical generator, was followed by the rumbling of American tanks.

On that first Monday, April 21, the entire team, having spent the night in one of the abandoned passenger terminals at the Baghdad airport, came to the museum early. We were met by sixteen young soldiers from C Company, Task Force 1-64, whose platoon of four tanks were stationed at the four corners of the museum compound. With the four-man tank crews rotating around the clock, they bunked when they could just inside the library's alcove. I told them that Dr. Jaber had offered us the library's anteroom, just inside the front door, and we began to make it our home. Hauling our stuff into the library, we cut the anteroom in half—it was about thirty feet by fifteen feet— by moving three seven-foot-high bookshelves. We created the partition partly to provide privacy for sleeping, but also because we were dealing with classified information. We took one side, the tankers took the other.

These were great kids, but they were kids, average age roughly nineteen. We let them use our satellite phones to call home—which made us popular. They had their own music and their own reading material, and to them we were a bunch of old men, only with very cool "toys:" weapons and electronics. Their "old man," the platoon commander, was a twenty-three-year-old West Pointer, Second Lieutenant Erik Balascik. His senior enlisted was battle-hardened Sergeant First Class David Richard, a former Marine who took more than his share of ribbing from me for having wound up God knows how in the U.S. Army.

Around nine o'clock, the museum staff began to arrive, with Dr. Donny George Youkhanna leading the way. He was Director of Research at the museum, and when not traveling to London, Amman, Lyons, Paris, or Istanbul to attend conferences on the plight of the museum, he was also the jocular and urbane museum spokesman. Because of his excellent English, worldwide reputation, and expansive personality, it was his face that the world came to associate with the museum. It was also his friendship I came to treasure most.

Before I could even begin to think about beginning an investigation, I had to do a reconnaissance, what we call an initial site survey. This was an eleven-acre walled compound with a dozen buildings, each one a maze of long corridors, dark rooms, and overlooking windows—all potential danger areas. With Donny showing the way, we conducted our first tour, starting with the exterior walls and working in decreasing concentric circles until we got to the many interior courtyards and the administrative offices.

Even before we began, I pointed out the handwritten sign over the main administrative entrance: DEATH TO ALL AMERICANS AND ZIONIST PIGS.

"I'll have it painted over," Donny said. "Don't let it upset you."

Turning to my left, I could not help but notice two well-placed and well-prepared firing positions dug into the ground in the front of the compound, surrounded by live hand grenades and spent cartridges. When we came upon the third firing position in the rear courtyard (there was also a fourth on the eastern side of the compound), I climbed inside and saw the dirt parapet, the aiming sticks (marking a shooter's assigned sector), and the clear field of fire. I said to Steve, "That's a damn fine firing position."

"Those are not firing positions," Donny assured me. "They are bomb shelters. We must protect the employees." Then, as if to explain: "We know you would not bomb the museum on purpose, of course, but maybe by accident."

Steve cracked up. "Sheets of tin with dirt on top aren't going to do much against a five-hundred-pound bomb," he said. "And what about the box of hand grenades next to one of those 'bomb shelters'?"

It was too soon for overt skepticism. So I gave him a look, and he put his game face back on.

When we came to the western side of the compound, we saw the ten-foot-high wall that ran along the edge of the buildings creating a completely concealed six-foot-wide passageway between the front and back of the compound. "I don't get it," Senior told me. "Why would they have built this wall when they already have a wall around the entire compound? And why did they build it along only one side—it's open at both ends. It doesn't seem to do anything."

"It connects the front and rear firing positions," I answered. "It's like an urban version of the old Vietnamese spider holes. Fighters can move between the positions without being seen, and without being shot at. Whoever did this knew what he was doing."

Donny overheard and he said, "Oh, no, this was just put up as protection from looters."

"But looters could just walk around the wall," Senior came back. "It's open at both ends."

I gave Senior the same look I'd given Steve a few moments earlier, and then we moved on.

There were expended rocket-propelled grenades scattered throughout the compound. Developed and supplied by the Russians, this shoulder-fired weapon uses an 85 mm, armor-piercing, shaped warhead capable of penetrating up to thirty-five centimeters of steel. It's very effective up to five hundred meters against a stationary target and three hundred meters against a moving target. It is known by its more common name: RPG-7.

Even more disturbing, we found a box of live (not yet fired) RPGs on the roof of the library and another on the roof of the Children's Museum. The grounds were littered with 7.62 mm shell casings, the bullets used by an AK-47—U.S. assault rifles use 5.56 mm. We also found more than a dozen Iraqi army uniforms, as well as human out-lines painted on a back wall for target practice and military maps in one of the buildings in the back of the compound.

But I had absolutely no intention of confronting Donny or anyone else about any of it. This was an investigation into the looting of the mu-seum, not into the former regime. No one is treated with suspicion, but everyone *is* a suspect until proven otherwise. And any individual's past is irrelevant, except to the extent it tells me something about where the missing antiquities are. No assumptions, no moral judgments. The only consideration is can they tell us anything of value. "Just the facts, ma'am."

Of course, the basic fact confronting us was that this place was a disaster. For all their sandbags and foam padding, and their "shelters" for the staff, they seemed to have prepared well for bombing, but not so well for pillage and plunder. And all three of the administrators I had met seemed to be living in an alternate universe. Dr. Jaber on Planet Despair, Nawala scowl-ing and serving tea, and Donny, the implacable charmer spinning stories that even he knew were implausible. But there was something in the way each of them accepted me—albeit tentatively at first—that made me want to help them even more than when I had first heard about the looting.

This first "walk-around" took all day, without ever entering the galleries or the storage areas. Later, when I mentioned to Donny that I needed to go into a certain room, he told me to ask Nawala. He wasn't being nasty or uncooperative. He simply didn't have the authority or the appropriate key. That's when I discovered the Byzantine complexity of separate do-mains, and separate rings of security, that existed throughout the museum.

After a long, hot day, a tasteless MRE back at the library, then a cou-ple of hours writing my daily reports, I thought, "My God, what have I gotten myself into?" We had security issues, cultural issues, political issues, logistical issues. And that's before we ever got around to sorting out a ransacked museum collection and an outraged press corps waiting at the gate. I'd done it this time. I had truly overreached. This was chaos, and I was in hell.

We had generators to power computers, but lights at night attracted snipers. So after the other guys sacked out, Senior, Bud, Steve, and I gathered in the cheery glow of a flashlight. "Okay, guys," I said. "Among us we've got a hundred years of experience in law enforce-ment. What the hell are we going to do?"

There was no judicial apparatus whatsoever: no court system, no judges, no cops, no prosecutors, and no defense attorneys. We were the whole ball game. So the first big decision was that this would be a re-covery operation, not a prosecution. We wouldn't worry about com-piling evidence; we would focus on getting the stuff back as fast as possible before it went underground. To do this, however, we would have to develop a new methodology, from scratch. And that is exactly what we did. We made it up.

We already knew that the first order of business was to identify what was missing and get photographs of the missing items to the interna-tional law-enforcement and art communities to help prevent the smug-gling of the stolen treasures. But then what?

Marines never come out of the field without an amnesty box, a place for kids to drop off any "trophies" they may "accidentally" have picked up on the rifle range or the battlefield. So my Marine Corps mentality led me to say let's institute an amnesty. Only instead of just having one small amnesty box, let's make the entire country an amnesty box. Let's declare amnesty for anyone returning artifacts belonging to the museum or an archaeological site. We kicked around the idea of saying you are in the amnesty program until it is proven that you are some kind of ring-leader or major offender, but finally I vetoed it. It was all or nothing. Our decision to grant amnesty, of course, was based on no authority whatsoever. Except the best authority of all: It seemed like a good idea.

Working against us, however, was the Iraqi fear that history would re-peat itself: that the United States would leave and the former regime would come back with a vengeance, massacring just as before anyone who had given offense to Saddam. We were constantly told that Ba'ath Party spies were everywhere, and that they were taking notes. In this re-spect, the situation was like the year before in Afghanistan, when the fears of a resurgent Taliban kept parents from sending their kids to school.

So we decided to make the amnesty program a part of a larger com-munity outreach. We would meet with local imams and other leaders who could communicate our policy to the public. We would advertise the program in local newspapers and radio stations. We would make it clear that the only question we would ask anyone returning an artifact was, "Would you like some tea?"

After the other senior guys had gone to bed, I strapped the flashlight to my forehead and went into the library stacks. Luckily we had plenty of batteries—another one of the items we had liberated in quantity from Camp Commando. The shelves were packed in so tight that I could barely pass through. On many nights to come, you would find

Plate 1. The Children's Museum, upon our arrival in Baghdad in April 2003. Countless Web sites and articles feature a similar picture showing the front of the Children's Museum with the hole created by the tank round. What they usually fail to mention is that the tank had fired in response to RPG shooters who had fired on the tank from that building.

Plate 2. Front of the museum compound taken from the roof of the library, showing the galleries (straight ahead), two of the firing positions (in the middle), and the team's white SUVs with supplies. The administrative offices are to the right.

Plate 3. Our "home" for months in the museum's library. Notice how squared away my bedroom is.

Plate 4. Our "shower" facilities in the courtyard behind the library. Because it abutted an apartment building, we hung a poncho for privacy. Some of the guys later set up water bladders for limited, sun-heated water.

Plate 5. The administrative offices of the museum, as we found them in April 2003.

Plate 6. A eureka moment in April 2003 coming across the first artifact that I had actually studied in school, a black basalt stela from Uruk depicting the king as lion hunter. The oldest stone carving of its size ever recovered in Iraq and the first known attempt at indicating perspective in bas-relief, this was, miraculously, untouched.

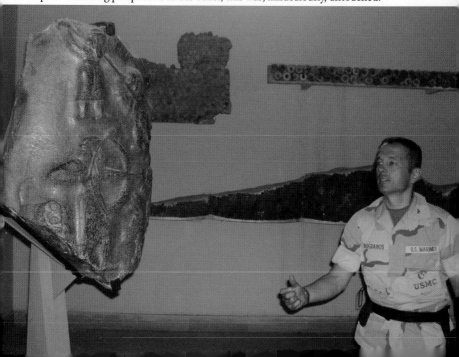

Plate 7. The Sacred Vase of Warka, the world's oldest known carved stone ritual vessel, ca. 3200 B.C. The 1.06-meter alabaster vase was discovered by a German archaeological team in 1940 at Warka, near al-Samawa, in southern Iraq.

Plate 8. The pedestal that once held the Sacred Vase of Warka, in the Sumerian room on the second floor of the Iraq Museum, as found in April 2003.

Plate 9. U.S. Army (and NYPD) Captain John Durkin armed and ready on a raid in Baghdad in June 2003.

Plate 10. Immigration and Customs Enforcement Supervisory Special Agents Steve Mocsary and Bud Rogers looking for weapons and antiquities on an afternoon stroll through the streets of Baghdad in May 2003.

Plate 11. After an item was recovered via amnesty or raid, it was placed on this table and photographed. In this shot, from May 2003, are everything from extraordinary fourth millennium B.C. pieces to fakes (made in Damascus) to an item stolen from the gift shop (the black head of Hammurabi).

Plate 12. The remote corner of the basement as we found it on May 2, 2003. The brown cabinets with the coins and cylinder seals are untouched and the 103 plastic boxes are strewn everywhere.

Plate 13. The keys to the storage cabinets that the thieves dropped in the dark and fumes, as we found them in one of the boxes on May 12, 2003.

Plate 14. On May 12, 2003, Steve Mocsary examines some of the gold coins that the thieves failed to get from the collection in the basement.

Plate 15. Stopping at Babylon in April 2003. With Steve Mocsary, Defense Threat Reduction Agency Commander Dave Beckett, and Bud Rogers.

Plate 16. Dr. Jaber's office in May 2003. With Dr. Donny George and Dr. Jaber Ibrahim.

Plate 17. The British Museum in July 2003. With Senior Master Sergeant Roberto Piñeiro and Dr. Nawala al-Mutwali.

Plate 18. The lobby of the Central Bank of Iraq as it appeared in April 2003 when we began our search for the treasures of the royal tombs of Ur and Nimrud.

Plate 19. One of the underground vaults of the Central Bank in May 2003, partially demolished after an unknown thief fired an RPG point-blank at its door. Another failed entry was discovered in the bank's old building, where two bodies were found, presumably would-be robbers who happened on the same vault. Rather than join forces, they appear to have shot and killed each other. Neither vault contained the treasures of Ur or Nimrud.

Plate 20. The helmet of King Meskalamdug, ca. 2500 B.C. Weighing more than one kilogram, it was constructed of a single sheet of gold, masterfully hammered to reproduce the hairstyle of the period.

Plate 21. The opening of the first box containing the treasure from the royal tombs of Ur in an underground vault of the Central Bank of Iraq in June 2003.

Plate 22. The treasure of Nimrud. The box was opened in an underground vault of the Central Bank of Iraq at 1:43 P.M. local time, June 5, 2003.

Plate 23. One minute after opening the box containing the treasure of Nimrud. These gold anklets, ca. 900–800 B.C., weigh over a kilogram.

Plate 24. One of the finest examples of gold jewelry ever found in the Near East. This crown, ca. 900–800 B.C., was first discovered in one of the royal tombs in Nimrud, the ancient Assyrian capital.

Plate 25. *The Lioness Attacking a Nubian*, ca. 8th century B.C., a chryselephantine ivory plaque inlaid with lapis and carnelian and overlaid with gold.

Plate 26. The solid gold bull's head that adorned Queen Puabi's (Shub-Ad) Golden Harp of Ur, from the Early Dynastic III Period, ca. 2600–2500 B.C.

Plate 27. Cylinder seals, the earliest of which date from the Uruk period, ca. 3500 B.C., were worn on a string and then rolled with pressure on clay to leave a design or "signature" in relief. Varying in size, but usually smaller than a human thumb, single cylinder seals have sold for more than $250,000. This Akkadian cylinder seal, ca. 2334–2154 B.C., photographed beside its modern impression, depicts a water god in his enclosure, approached by gods with flames and a gatepost keeper.

Plate 28. The Mask of Warka. An exquisite life-size limestone head, ca. 3100 B.C., generally believed to be the world's oldest known naturalistic depiction of a human face, possibly representing the goddess Inanna.

Plate 29. The Akkadian Bassetki Statue. Cast in pure copper and weighing about 150 kilograms, this is one of the earliest known examples of the lost-wax technique of casting. Dating to the Akkadian period, ca. 2250 B.C., it is pictured here after it was recovered in November 2003.

Plate 30. With some of the team in front of one of Saddam Hussein's palaces in Basra in April 2003. From left to right: Steve Mocsary, Immigration and Customs Enforcement (ICE) Special Agent (and interpreter) Dave Denton, Dave Beckett, ICE Supervisory Special Agent Mark Garrand, a British lieutenant colonel, ICE Special Agent Kevin Power, and Roberto Piñeiro.

Plate 31. Conducting a press conference at the Pentagon on September 10, 2003.

Plate 32. With Afghan children in Kabul in March 2002, on the first day of school since the Taliban took power in 1996.

Plate 33. Presenting an al-Qaeda bayonet to Rudy Giuliani aboard the USS *Intrepid* in August 2002, with then–Brigadier General Gary Harrell. Lieutenant Colonel Terry Sopher (left) and Major Ashton Naylor (right) are visible in the back.

Plate 34. Wearing an NYPD shirt, with Afghan fighters on the Shomali Plains in Afghanistan in February 2002. Nasrullah, the interpreter, is wearing a hood.

Plate 35 (above). On a helicopter in June 2004.

Plate 36 (above right). With District Attorney Robert M. Morgenthau at the Museum of Jewish Heritage in downtown Manhattan in May 2005.

Plate 37 (right). Still boxing, here with my trainer Darryl Pierre during a bout at Church Street Boxing Gym in New York in January 2004.

Plate 38. Claudia and family the day Nicole was born in 2005. Michael (6) is in blue, Jason (3) is in white, and Diana (5) is seated.

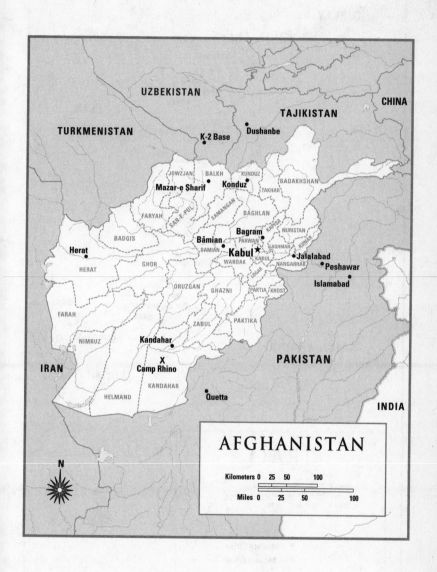

TURKMENISTAN

UZBEKISTAN

TAJIKISTAN

CHINA

K-2 Base • Dushanbe

JOWZJAN
BALKH
KUNDUZ
BADAKHSHAN
Mazar-e Sharif • Konduz
TAKHAR
FARYAB
SAR-E-PUL
SAMANGAN
BAGHLAN
BADGIS
Herat
GHOR
BAMIAN
Bâmian •
PARWAN
Bagram •
Kabul ★
WARDAK
KABUL
LOGAR
NURISTAN
KUNAR
KAPISA
LAGHMAN
Jalalabad
NANGARHAR
Peshawar
Islamabad
HERAT
ORUZGAN
GHAZNI
PAKTIA
KHOST
FARAH
ZABUL
PAKTIKA
NIMRUZ
Kandahar •
X
Camp Rhino
KANDAHAR
HELMAND
IRAN
Quetta •
PAKISTAN
INDIA

N

AFGHANISTAN

Kilometers 0   25   50   100

Miles 0   25   50   100

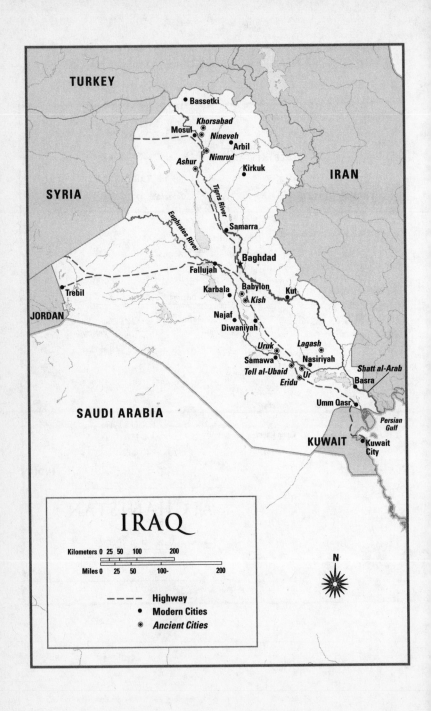

TURKEY

• Bassetki

Khorsabad
◉

Mosul • *Nineveh*
        ◉
        • Arbil
Ashur *Nimrud*
◉   ◉
              • Kirkuk

SYRIA

IRAN

Tigris River

Euphrates River

• Samarra

Baghdad

• Fallujah

• Karbala   **Babylon**
                ◉   • Kut
                Kish
                ◉

• Trebil

JORDAN

• Najaf
• Diwaniyah

                    Lagash
                    ◉
        Uruk
        ◉
• Samawa   • Nasiriyah
Tell al-Ubaid   ◉ Ur
◉   *Eridu*   *Shatt al-Arab*
                          • Basra

SAUDI ARABIA

• Umm Qasr

Persian Gulf

KUWAIT
        • Kuwait
          City

IRAQ

Kilometers 0 25 50 100   200

Miles 0   25   50   100-   200

N

– – – Highway
• Modern Cities
◉ *Ancient Cities*

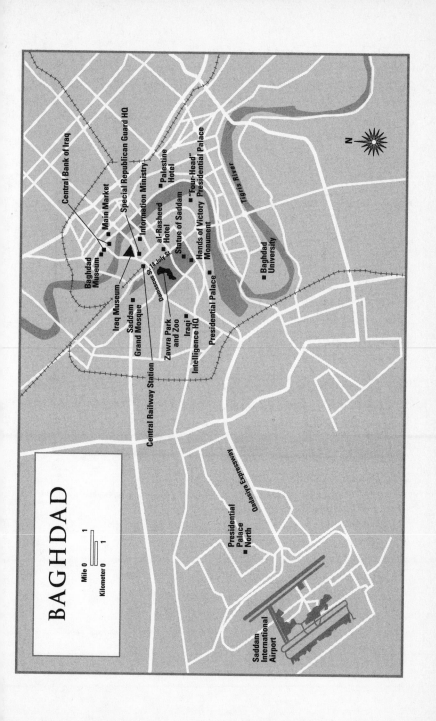

BAGHDAD

Mile 0 ⊢——⊣ 1
Kilometer 0 ⊢——⊣ 1

N

Central Bank of Iraq

Special Republican Guard HQ

Main Market

Information Ministry

Palestine Hotel

"Four-Head"
Presidential Palace

al-Rasheed
Hotel

Statue of Saddam

Hands of Victory
Monument

Baghdad
Museum

Iraq Museum

Saddam
Grand Mosque

Damascus St.

14 July St.

Zawra Park
and Zoo

Iraqi
Intelligence HQ

Presidential Palace

Central Railway Station

Baghdad
University

Tigris River

Qdaasiya Expressway

Presidential
Palace
North

Saddam
International
Airport

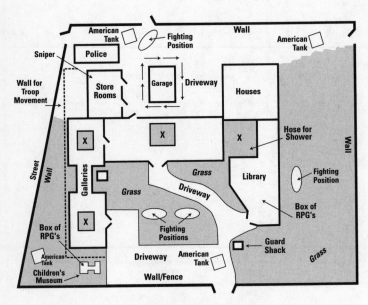

Iraq Museum Compound

Sketch prepared by Colonel Bogdanos and Senior Master Sergeant Piñeiro

X = Courtyard

(NOT TO SCALE)

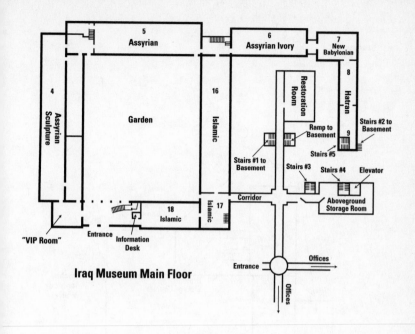

Iraq Museum Main Floor

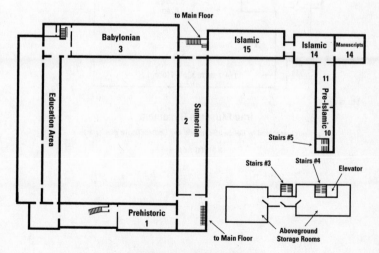

Iraq Museum Second Floor

Sketches prepared by Colonel Bogdanos and Captain David Wachsmuth

(NOT TO SCALE)

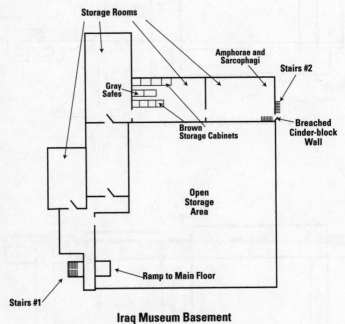

Iraq Museum Basement

Sketch prepared by Colonel Bogdanos and Captain David Wachsmuth

(NOT TO SCALE)

me seated on the floor in one of those dusty, dank aisles, reading for hours about the museum, about the country, about the people. I also pored through the English-language art history and Iraq Museum books that Donny would bring me, and the ten to twenty articles on recent antiquities-related events that Senior would print every day. This was going to be like grad school, only with live ammunition. I did not have time to educate and inform myself and then act. Everything would be happening at the same time, with me improvising to try to keep up with the evolving situation.

The next morning, after little sleep, Steve and I briefed the rest of the team. Like the P.M. executive sessions with Steve, Bud, and Senior, the A.M. briefing would become part of an unvarying routine. On that Tuesday, I laid out the plan for the day, then checked with Steve to determine which of his men would come with us on the day's inspection.

Our objective this second day was the galleries and the aboveground storage areas. But this would still be a quick walk-through, with no forensic assessment or measurements. Before we could do a forensic search, and certainly before we could put the staff back to work cleaning out or reorganizing things, we first had to "clear" the rooms, which meant a military survey to make sure that there were no weapons, mines, or booby traps.

Inspections from nine in the morning and continuing until two or three in the afternoon—this too would become a pattern. But having quickly realized the limits of Donny's authority, I came to rely on Nawala as my guide. She was director of the museum proper, and thus keeper of the keys for the twenty-eight rooms, landings, and alcoves that constituted the public galleries, as well as for the storage areas. Weeks later, when we got to room twenty-eight, we started all over again with room one, looking at each aspect with greater understanding and new eyes. And then we did it again, peeling off one more layer of the onion with each pass.

On first entering the public display area, my initial reaction was surprise at the relative lack of damage, especially having seen what the administrative offices looked like. There, the crowd had given full expression to their anger against Saddam, stealing typewriters and office furniture and throwing books and papers into bonfires on the floor. And the much-photographed long corridor leading from the offices to the galleries had half a dozen smashed amphorae (storage jars) and one cracked sarcophagus. But once in the galleries themselves, they showed, if not restraint from greed, then at least astonishing restraint from vandalism. Some statues did have scars where looters had tried to chip away at them, and one of the larger pieces had been toppled over onto its protective foam, as if the looters were hoping to use the padding to drag it away. But altogether, fewer than a dozen pieces in the galleries showed any sign of damage, and of the 451 display cases, only 28 had their glass broken. Maybe the crowd had spent its anger in the offices, hallways, and restoration rooms. Maybe that destruction had proved cathartic. But just maybe the silent majesty of these fragments of antiquity, cast in natural light from the high windows, had somehow worked its magic and dampened the enthusiasm for violence.

Seeing all those empty display cases, my second thought was that the "170,000 artifacts carried away by looters" as reported in the *New York Times* could not possibly be accurate. I had always doubted that "looters" could steal 170,000 items in forty-eight hours—if those numbers and timing were accurate, those were highly organized thieves. But now I saw there was simply not enough *emptiness*—empty cases, shelves, or pedestals—in the entire museum to support anything resembling that claim.

My next thought was, "Okay, get me on your computer. Show me your inventory system."

I wanted a simple checklist of the museum's holdings so that we could do an inventory to see what was missing. The Iraqi approach was to wait and see what came back, or turned up on the black market, then confirm whether or not it had been stolen. As Dr. Nawala was so fond of saying, "Insha'Allah." God willing.

I soon discovered the reason why: their record keeping was about on a par with the system the Sumerians used five thousand years ago. The museum divided all arriving artifacts into one of five different categories and then manually entered all of their holdings on index cards. This hopelessly confusing and incomplete handwritten "system" might have worked back in 1923, when they could fit everything in one room, but the Iraq Museum now held over five hundred thousand separate items, with tens of thousands more arriving every year from active sites. The undersourced and undertrained staffers were so far behind on their inventories that thousands of artifacts from recent digs had not yet been logged in from the excavation catalogues for each site.

On top of that, many of the index cards had been destroyed in the many fires set in the museum, forcing us, ultimately, to review all of the excavation catalogues that were stored throughout the museum.

The storage area was where this trust in Allah over Pentium processors really took its toll. After the BBC arrived, they captured a typical exchange between Nawala and me, standing by the kind of metal shelving you see in suburban two-car garages. I always had my black commander's notebook stuck into the back of my pants, and on the film you can see me pulling it out to take notes. In a matter-of-fact voice, I asked her, "So, when can I have an inventory of what's on the shelf?"

She said, "Oh, it's very difficult."

"But tomorrow, perhaps . . ."

"Oh, no, no, not tomorrow."

"Okay, next week . . ."

She laughed nervously, as if she hoped I was kidding, but she couldn't be sure. I smiled, waited a beat, then asked her, "So, can anybody give me the number of boxes that were here on April sixth?" There was no response.

I said, "How will we be able to tell if any boxes are missing? If someone took this box, would you know? I don't see a number on it."

Nawala seemed confused.

"Okay. If I take this, how do you know? How do you know it's gone?"

She looked down and shrugged.

"Is there a list?"

"No, there is no list for the boxes."

"Can anyone tell me if there's seventy-five in here—"

"Seventy-five?"

"Or one hundred—"

"A hundred?"

"Can anyone give me . . . ?" I was getting a little worked up, so I had to calm down. This was a major encounter of social delicacy, where she needed to save face.

"Can somebody give me a number of the boxes that were here on April sixth?"

"It's difficult."

I gave her my best smile. "Difficult . . . or impossible?"

"It's not impossible, but it's difficult, it's very difficult. If any boxes come back, we will know if they are our boxes."

I laughed. "I know you can tell me if the box is back, but I want to know if you can tell me if the box is missing."

"Yes. From downstairs."

"From up here. Can you tell if a box is missing?"

"At least the ladies, when they prepare the lists. Maybe they can have an idea. Approximately."

"Approximately is okay. Maybe we can have that list tomorrow?"

"Wow!" she replied, by this time knowing me well enough to know I was not joking.

"*Insha'Allah*," I said.

We had this kind of interchange every day. It was always challenging, it was always frustrating, but it was also always laced with humor and affection—hence the constant teasing about our "affair." Somehow, in the cultural no-man's-land between us, we arrived at our best approximation of the truth.

Given the recent damage, the incomplete cataloguing, and the general state of disarray, Nawala and also I agreed to a not-so-secret code. Time and again, I would look at a room or shelf that was in complete disarray and ask whether this or that was "as it is." *As it is* meant that, yes, this was the way a particular piece, shelf, or room looked before the war. Nawala often blushed, stammered, and hesitated, then embarrassedly admitted that whatever mess I saw was indeed "as it is."

It is in the nature of ancient artifacts to have fractures and missing pieces. It was also true that the museum had been understaffed and underfinanced for years. And in a country hemmed in by sanctions and with a regime that chose to spend what money it did have on presidential palaces and statues of Saddam, straightening up was not a matter of hiring temps or running over to Staples for plastic organizer trays. Despite their best efforts, the place was in a hell of a state, further adding to the confusion.

In time, Nawala also revealed to me that entire shelves in the storage rooms contained fakes that had been confiscated over the years from counterfeiters. Many of the items stolen from the aboveground storage rooms were, in fact, fakes from this collection. Some of these copies were truly exceptional. Sometimes it took the staff weeks to determine that something was not authentic. But at times, Donny George would look at one of these and say, "Oh, yeah, Damascus. You go down fifty meters, and it's the vendor on the right." Or, "Amman. Yes, he keeps getting better and better."

There was a special marking system—the inscribed letters *MZ* (for *muzawer*, Arabic for "fake")—to indicate that something was a copy. The museum staff did not want to have to spend time re-authenticating artifacts that they had confiscated or allow those copies to be reintroduced into the marketplace. So they kept these copies separate and used them for training and educational purposes.

The Iraq Museum, colocated with the State Board of Antiquities and Heritage, the umbrella organization headed by Dr. Jaber, was also the central repository for all artifacts excavated in Iraq. The museum's storage rooms contained hundreds of thousands of catalogued items and not-yet-catalogued pieces from more than thirty sites of extensive excavation throughout the country. In addition, as the invasion loomed more and more certain, various items from outlying museums in Mosul and elsewhere had been transported to the central museum for safekeeping.

Working from the other direction, our equally vexing problem was that, during almost thirty years under a dictator who considered the museum, like the country, his personal amusement park, many Iraqis told us that Saddam had raided the holdings over and over, taking priceless artifacts and hiding them throughout Iraq.

And in all things, Iraq moves to the ticking of a very different clock. There are two kinds of businesses in Iraq—those that come back after the midday break to escape the enervating heat, and those that do not. A nonprofit museum almost never open to the public fell decidedly into the latter category. Museum workers started their day at nine thirty or ten, and the women (excepting Nawala, who would stay later as a personal favor to me) never worked past one or two in the afternoon because the fathers or brothers would say it was not safe and they would come to pick them up to get them home before nightfall. Thus, although we walked through the museum together from the time Nawala arrived in the morning until she left, we were never able to thoroughly inspect more than one room a day.

For an institution responsible for more than five hundred thousand objects, these administrative and procedural anomalies presented problems enough, but then there was the human dimension. The entire museum did not possess a single conference table, because no one ever talked to anyone else in any structured way. The first time I said that I would like to sit in on their regular staff meetings, everyone looked at me slightly perplexed. What are you talking about? Whoever heard of a staff meeting?

And certainly not all was sweetness and light among the staff. Donny and Nawala—though both were cooperative—were rarely at the same spot at the same time, and when they were, they were usually contradicting each other. Nawala was understandably bitter for having been treated like dog meat during twenty-six years of service at the museum. But as a Christian in an Islamic country, Donny George often seemed an outsider as well.

Others on the staff were decidedly uncooperative, and their statements were frequently proven false. The museum compound was a free-fire zone for accusations—some accurate, some bogus. Some were sincerely believed and sincerely motivated; some were a function of past grievances, political differences, or simply the desire for another person's job.

The Office of Reconstruction and Humanitarian Assistance (ORHA) had warned me off dealing with any Ba'ath Party members. But I did not have that luxury. Some proponents of de-Ba'athification wanted us to clean house. In a museum run by Ba'ath Party operatives, however, you can't fire everybody. And there is a difference between Ba'ath Party members who truly believed and Ba'ath Party members who simply needed a job and therefore had to check the appropriate box on the application.

Even among staffers who tried to be helpful, there were often inconsistencies as to when an item had last been seen. Sometimes a "witness" was clearly relying on hearsay; sometimes the witness was just as clearly lying. But it was the prior regime's systematic "removal" of items over the last several decades and the multiple locations used throughout Iraq to house those treasures that made an otherwise difficult task truly Herculean. Often, two witnesses swore to have been present when an item or group of items were removed, but told a completely different story about where it had been moved and why. Without access to more credible witnesses, more museum documentation, and the government officials whose names appeared on various orders to move certain objects to different locations, we were like the blind men groping the elephant. There were more problems to come.

During our initial inspection of the administrative offices, we observed that an unknown number of the registration cards appeared to have been destroyed in the many fires lit throughout those offices. Because many of the oldest archaeological sites in Iraq were originally excavated by foreign expeditions, we began developing a plan to assemble inventories from those countries to re-create the cards. Fortunately, that proved to be unnecessary: although many cards were destroyed, the excavation catalogues were intact. We nonetheless realized that we needed to back up this flimsy system and create a single database of the museum's holdings. Later, when specially trained units from the carabinieri, Italy's paramilitary national police force, arrived, they worked on this as well.

They also began safeguarding some of the archaeological sites, highlighting another problem—just as grave—over which we had no control whatsoever: the nonstop looting of the sites throughout Iraq. All the great cities of the ancient past were made of mud and mud bricks, and when they were abandoned or destroyed, new inhabitants built from the rubble of older buildings on the same spot. In time, the level rose, and when these villages were abandoned, centuries of wind and rain and sandstorms weathered them, leaving behind great mounds of dirt called tells. It is these tells that archaeologists explore, and that looters exploit. There are six hundred tells in Iraq, over thirty of which have been sounded. But in another respect, with ten thousand years of continuous habitation, the entire country of Iraq is an archaeological site.

Like investigators at a crime scene, archaeologists are meticulous about looking at objects in context. When they approach a tell, they go to great pains testing strata and exposing cross sections. Much of the information they extract from any one clay pot, for instance, depends on the depth and level at which it was found, and what was found near it at the same depth and level. This is called a cultural stratum. The tragedy of the recent lootings is that looters intent on finding artifacts for sale dig into the tells randomly, often with bulldozers. We simply did not have the manpower to both recover the museum's stolen holdings and protect the sites. We didn't even have enough people for the investigation.

In addition to the physical obstacles facing us, there were more personal ones as well. My prosecutorial mind-set had limited my initial view of the Iraqis. Except for the persecuted Kurds in the north or the terrified Shi'ites in the south, I saw them as the enemy. Many had been part of a brutal regime. They had invaded two other Arab countries, murdered over one million of their fellow Muslims, and—according to Amnesty International and Human Rights Watch—buried over 290,000 of these people in mass graves. I didn't understand these people and their issues and I didn't want to understand them. But that was exactly what I had to do—understand them—to help sort out this mess.

This was never truer than when I started hearing about "the secret place."

Nawala was the first to allude to it. As the weeks progressed and my relationship with both Donny and Nawala deepened, I started to learn more and more about the extent and limits of their authority and knowledge about the museum, its practices, and its holdings. Two weeks into the investigation, I showed Nawala a list of items Donny had told me were missing. She went down the list, crossing off every item, telling me they had not been stolen. When this scene repeated itself more than once, I mentioned it to Donny, who admitted that Nawala would have a better handle on what was and was not missing.

During every inspection thereafter, whenever Donny would point to an empty display case or pedestal, indicating its contents had been stolen, I would go to Nawala for confirmation. One morning, all three of us were walking in one of the galleries—Nawala and I a step or two behind—and Donny pointed to an empty pedestal and said, "Alas, it is gone," mourning the loss of another piece. I leaned back and glanced at Nawala, and she winked at me and said, "It's safe."

I didn't know what was more surprising, that they still couldn't get their story straight or that she had winked.

Members of the staff would be talking, and one would say, "It's here," and then another would say, "No, it's there," and then they would mutter in Arabic among themselves. Clearly, we were not in on the joke. Several of the ICE agents spoke Arabic, and what they kept hearing was the Arabic phrase for "the secret place."

After a while, I began to make allusions to "the place" or "the safe place," and they would say, "Oh, sure, yeah, you mean the secret place." And I would say, "Oh, yeah, that place, the secret place." There was no sense of shame, no sense that they were being devious in hiding information from me. But no one volunteered more information. Clearly this was a matter of some delicacy. Not even Donny George had been entrusted with this information.

More disturbing to me, the project of moving items to the secret place resulted in at least one bald-faced lie. When I first toured the galleries, a member of the museum staff named Moshan Hassan—who spoke very little English—called my attention to the Neanderthal display, pointing out the indentations where the dozen or so grave goods had rested. He told me that they had all been stolen. It was not until a few more gallery inspections, when I thought about the display case—the heavy lid that had to be slid off and then back on, the absence of *any* fingerprints anywhere on the glass—that I realized that his story didn't make any sense. Weeks later, when I confronted him, Mohsan suddenly "remembered" that it was staffers who had slid back the lid and then replaced it. Most importantly, they had taken the grave goods to the secret place. When I asked whether there were any other "stolen" items that had been moved to the secret place, he complained of chest pains and went home.

As I discovered over time, the location of the secret place was known only to five museum officials, each of whom had sworn on the Koran not to divulge its location until a new government in Iraq was established and U.S. forces had left the country. Donny George had been at the museum for twenty-seven years. He had served as director of documentation on the State Board of Antiquities and Heritage and assistant director general of antiquities before becoming director of research. But because he was a Christian, he could not swear on the Koran and was not one of the five.

To understand why this distinction kept him out of the inner circle, you have to understand the place that the Koran holds in Islam. It is not just revered the way the Bible is by Christians. In Christianity, Christ is the incarnation of the Word, the ultimate mystery. In Islam, not even Muhammad holds that exalted position. Instead of an incarnation of the Word in any human form, Islam maintains belief in an inlibration of the Word, i.e., the Koran. So in Islam, the rough equivalent to Jesus Christ is not the Prophet Muhammad, but the Koran.

To understand why I didn't just come out and say, "Nawala, how about it? What's with the secret place?" you have to understand a thing or two about the dance that goes on between prosecutors and the people they question. Cutting to the chase—the vast majority of interviews between prosecutors and suspects end in some sort of confession. I'm not talking about a full "here is what I did and here is how I did it" confession. Those happen, but they are rare. I'm talking about the fact that the suspect usually admits to being involved in the act—but puts it in the best possible light as he sees it. He was "dissed." He had no choice. He was only the driver, and on and on. I'm not saying that perpetrators tell the truth—they almost never do. In a four-defendant robbery-murder, for example, every one of them will tell you he was the lookout or the driver of the getaway car. But a portion of the truth always leaks out.

Second, and despite what defense attorneys would like juries to believe, the reason perpetrators admit their involvement is not physical coercion or even the threat of physical coercion. Professionals don't use physical abuse for a host of ethical and legal reasons. But there are also practical ones, not the least of which is that when what is "spilled" has been co-erced, it is usually a lie. No, with any suspect, my greatest leverage as a prosecutor is that when I walk in the room, he doesn't know what I know (from witnesses or physical evidence). This is why suspects rarely ask for an attorney: they want to learn what I know. But my greatest psychological asset is that we both know he did it. Once you see the investigator-suspect dynamic in this light, some kind of confession be-comes inevitable. There are, of course, exceptions to the rule. The patho-logical liar who has convinced himself of his innocence, or the suspect who has been well-rehearsed by his lawyer—think Puff Daddy—are unlikely to admit anything. For everyone else, it's usually not a question of *if* he'll tell you, but *when*. Your job is to convince him through body language and other indirect indicators that you *know* he did it, occasion-ally leaking out how you know. But you never tell him everything you know and you never—ever—ask the defendant, "Did you do it?"

It works the same way with witnesses. The tough questions wait for last. You certainly never ask those questions before you have earned their trust, before you have earned the right to have your questions an-swered. That would be like going to those lockers in the basement storage room right away. Rookie mistakes all. You never want to put your witnesses—and *your* witnesses is how you must think—in a posi-tion where they are forced to lie. If you let them appear to get away with the lie, then you have lost credibility. If you call them on it, you hurt their pride and you lose the bond.

With Nawala, when I began to home in on the secret place, my ques-tion took the form of "Is it safe?" She told me that it was, then sighed with evident relief when there were no follow-up questions. It was not an easy thing to ask Nawala to break her vow, but true to my instincts as a DA, I put a tail on her. One day, I pressed her for specific informa-tion. "How can you be sure it's safe? Have you seen it recently? Could you give me an exact count?" She then went about her business and re-turned in a few hours with the information, having never left the com-pound. I know because I had told the soldier guarding the gate to watch her movements all day. In this way I ascertained that "the secret place" was within the museum compound.

It would take another five weeks of drinking tea and building trust before we talked about it more directly.

"Perhaps you would like to tell me about the secret place?"

"Of course."

"But until now you have not told me about this place."

"You never asked!" I had to laugh. This was so much like my drug informants back in New York whenever I would ask why they hadn't told me about one secret or another. "You never asked!" We both knew, of course, that if I had asked earlier, she would not have told me.

The compounding irony of their employing a religious test for being trusted with the knowledge was that Donny George—the museum spokesman—was always out of the loop. Whereas Jaber's English was marginal and Nawala's conversant, Donny's was perfectly fluent. He had become skilled at dealing with the press during the first Gulf War, and reporters invariably went to him for quotes this time around as well. But given the combination of his limited access and authority, his information was often wrong.

"We cannot tell the precise moment when friendship is formed," James Boswell wrote in his *Life of Samuel Johnson*. "As in filling a vessel drop by drop, there is at last a drop which makes it run over; so in a series of kindnesses there is at last one which makes the heart run over." That was—is—Donny and I.

My initial perception of Donny was that he was, above all else, a survivor. I knew him to be a dedicated professional who cared deeply about preserving Iraq's past. I also knew Donny had overseen Saddam's god-awful "reconstruction" of Babylon, had supervised the digging of the firing positions he insisted were bomb shelters, and was known to have prided himself on the fact that Saddam made marginal notes in his reports.

Donny reminded me of Claude Rains's Louie, the French police chief who became pals with Bogart's Rick in *Casablanca*. Detractors—most of whom have never had to live under a brutal dictatorship—have questioned his shifting loyalties. Others have said that he was merely a realist whose heart (though not necessarily each of his actions) occupied the right place.

Even though his instant affection for me might be viewed as a manifestation of his realism, I believe it was genuine. And because I became so fond of him, it was important that I make the boundaries of our relationship clear. With a nod to his girth, I joked that even if I came across a size 42 Republican Guard uniform in a staff locker someplace, it made no difference to me whatsoever. But turning serious, I also said that if I ever discovered he was guilty of a war crime or a crime against humanity, he needed to know this: I would never allow him to be taken in by a stranger. It would break my heart, but I would do it myself.

With Nawala, on the other hand, the friendship came from a completely different place. Although it was primed from our first meeting, that did not keep her from being defensive about the museum's prelooting disarray, as well as the military buildup inside the compound walls. But I never projected suspicion and she never projected hostility. From the get-go, I treated her like my witness. From the get-go, she repaid my efforts. And I was always honest.

Several years before, when I'd questioned Jennifer Lopez for the Puff Daddy trial, "my" witness had come to the DA's Office with an entourage numbering in the double digits. One of them, best I could tell, served no purpose other than to ensure that she had a never-ending supply of orange juice. During hours and hours of interviews and debriefings over several weeks, Ms. Lopez would alternate between tearful pleas and equally melodramatic outbursts of anger, all the while evading every question of substance. Rather than call her on it, I intentionally but mistakenly opted for a mode I thought she would be more comfortable with—I patronized her. As a result, I never got to the point where I could trust her enough to call her as a witness. But, then, neither could the defense. A valuable lesson. Faced with evasiveness from Nawala, I was empathetic, but I didn't overdo it. I was always honest.

In many ways, Nawala was also a victim, and people who have been traumatized by crime often make a kind of transference onto the prosecutor. This was as true of Nawala as it had been years earlier with Natania Reuben, the remarkable mother of two who was an innocent bystander shot in the face by Jamal "Shyne" Barrow during the shootout that led to Puff Daddy's prosecution. When asked to make a statement to the court at Barrow's sentencing, Ms. Reuben spoke about how much she had lost as a result of the shooting. But then she spoke about how much she had gained, and at the top of her list was her friendship with the prosecutor. That affection runs in both directions. Whenever I am asked a question about the "Puff Daddy" case, I have to do a quick translation in my head before answering, because in my mind it will always be the "Natania Reuben" case. And whenever I meet a new victim, I wonder if he or she will prove to be as courageous as Ms. Reuben.

For a witness or a victim, the prosecutor is also the person who can provide physical safety. For a witness who might be considered an accomplice, he or she can provide safety from criminal prosecution as well—at least to the extent that the witness cooperates and brings value. Sometimes the prosecutor is the father figure, sometimes the protective big brother, sometimes father confessor, sometimes the tell-it-like-it-is friend. All of these aspects were present in my relationship with Nawala, and they were all, I think, genuine. Witnesses, however, always need to put their traumatic events and the people associated with those events in the past. So the closeness—however genuine—is usually short-lived.

With Dr. Jaber, the relationship was more formal, a matter of deference. I would end every day at the museum by having a last cup of tea with him. As a further gesture of respect, I always gave him the chance to answer any question I might have before I asked other staff members. His responses, however, were usually noncommittal, if not evasive. During the entire time I was with him, and during dozens and dozens of meetings, he never once told me a single fact that I had not already known. Not once. But he was always good to me, and visually expressive—you could always tell what he was thinking. "Oh, yes," he would say in his sweet, sighing voice, "of course we can do this for you."

Like Jaber, Nawala was always friendly to me and always open—even when she too was being evasive. She even wanted pictures taken of us together and was particularly annoyed during the week National Geographic's Lisa Ling showed up, asking me "Why does she have to be here?"

Our daily exchanges about "today" versus *Insha'Allah* always had the same level of good humor, but hidden under my good humor was a sense of forcefulness that seemed to leave the Iraqis a little taken aback. Nawala seemed to think it was cute: "The American is doing it again." It was as if they looked on me as a child, as if thinking, "Doesn't he understand this is the Middle East, and he's not going to get it today or tomorrow or even next week?" These good people have had ten thousand years doing things in their own good time. Even if I started the clock at the heyday of the Greek tradition I value so much, they still had a seven-thousand-year head start on me.

But there was a problematic aspect of the goodwill between Nawala and me as well. Time and again, as the investigation proceeded, she would inform members of the team as well as members of the international community that she would communicate only in the presence of Colonel Bogdanos. After she refused to speak with a member of the British Museum and another from UNESCO without my being present, I began to worry about the appearance that I was controlling her in some way. Even the BBC joined in, noting that "this stubborn, taciturn woman . . . was much taken with Bogdanos." When I asked her directly why she would only speak about the looting if I was present, she looked down. "Because you don't make me serve tea," she replied.

10

KEEPING HEADS

Nothing is stable in human affairs. So avoid
excess joy in prosperity or excess despair
in adversity.—Socrates

MEMBERS OF THE museum staff were fond of showing visitors the head of a human-headed bull from the palace of Sargon II in Khorsabad that lay on the floor of the Assyrian gallery. Some Mosul businessmen had stolen the statue after the first Gulf War and cut off the head to transport it out of the country. They were caught at the Jordanian border, brought back to Baghdad, and in 1999, all ten were executed on state-run television. The manner of execution, the staff pointed out—with a sense of irony, if not poetic justice—was beheading.

Because of the close association between authority and brutality in Iraq—three decades of Ba'athist death squads, gang rapes, and mass graves—the job of recovery was complicated by the need to convince potential allies among the people that everyone would be keeping his head.

On Wednesday, April 23, 2003, immediately after completing our initial inspection of the public galleries, we began our "IO," information operations, campaign with our first foray into the community. We went to the nearby mosque and spoke to one of the imams. Later that afternoon, he had a chest full of stolen manuscripts delivered to the museum. On our behalf, he also issued a fatwa. I was pleased with his level of cooperation, but his edict against looting or possessing stolen goods was a tad more than I had asked for. I grew concerned that we were now one step away from an intifada.

While we spent each day until about two o'clock or so inspecting the museum, we spent the rest of the daylight hours trying to build relationships with the community. Not just to promote the amnesty program, but also to start developing potential informants that might bear fruit—so long as they didn't get us killed first. Being out and about required careful attention to social cues that were alien to us. This was a guest culture that had changed little since Hammurabi was making lists of rules.

Starting at the local mosques, we then branched out to playing backgammon in the neighborhood cafés. We strolled from marketplace to marketplace, drinking more tea than I thought humanly possible. We also got sick repeatedly from unwashed glasses and unclean water that never quite reached the boiling point. Graciousness was, however, one of the few orders on which I brooked no discussion: "You will drink any cup of tea offered to you. I don't care if you saw the guy scoop the water out of the Tigris then spit in it, you will say *shukran*, and you will drink it with a smile. That's why they invented Imodium."

In my view, there are only two kinds of people in an investigation: potential informants and the people I haven't met yet. Rule number three in any investigation (number one is that everybody is a suspect until proven otherwise, and number two is that moral judgments have no place in an investigation) is that to build trust, you have to show trust. My show of trust, force-protection concerns notwithstanding, was that I never wore a helmet. Helmets look menacing. Like mirrored sunglasses on state troopers, they create a barrier to more than shrapnel. I left the choice up to the guys—this was by no means an order—but two thirds of them chose to follow suit.

We had not just fallen off the pumpkin truck, however, and like Cervantes, we decided to "trust in God, but keep our powder dry." Each of us, therefore, carried a side arm and an M4 on a sling. We wore body armor (I wore the lighter version under my uniform, others wore the heavier, more protective version outside their uniforms), we rarely moved with fewer than four team members, and we were (almost) never out of sight of our assigned partner.

On Thursday, our fourth full day at the museum, our site assessment moved on to the aboveground storage rooms. Here, as Nawala led the way, I began to see a pattern. Passing by row upon row of shelves, we came upon traces in the dust that looked as if someone had scooped into a sack whatever had been sitting there. Three or four rows over, we would find another arm sweep, and artifacts unceremoniously piled on the floor. Numbers stick in my head—I paid for college and law school by counting cards, after all—so I recognized that the items piled below the second arm sweep belonged on the shelf back where we had seen the first arm sweep. The artifacts had been left behind, but first they had been moved. My hasty conclusion was that this was definitely the work of an impulse shopper. He found something he liked better. So he dumped out what was in his sack and took the second batch.

It was becoming obvious that, in my initial statement of objectives, I had anticipated the way events would play out exactly wrong. I had said that we were going to do a quick survey and inventory of the missing items, but that the recovery of the loot would take years. As it turned out, it was going to take years to complete the survey and cataloguing, but the recovery began immediately.

Our first walk-in visitor showed up on April 24, 2003. A neighborhood resident, a young pianist, pulled up in his van with one of the twin copper bulls from Ninhursag (about 2500 B.C.), as well as a roughly four-foot-high statue of the Assyrian king Shalmaneser III (about 850 B.C.). He said he had taken them for safekeeping. He seemed like a nice kid, but just about everyone we met had taken it for "safekeeping," just as every defendant is "innocent," and every inmate was "framed." There was no reason to spend time wondering why he—or anyone—had really taken the item. On the human level, we invited him to the reopening of the museum, and the New York Times wrote a nice piece about him. But for investigative purposes, "nothing but the facts, ma'am."

This was also the day Senior found the fire with fragments of Ba'ath Party identification cards smoldering in the ashes. I chose to ignore this, just as we had ignored the DEATH TO THE AMERICANS sign, the weapons and firing positions, and the contradictory accounts about how the positions had come to be there.

Late that night, architectural historian and art commentator Dan Cruickshank showed up with a film crew from the BBC, looking for a place to stay. It wasn't so long ago that we had similarly been homeless and Marine colonel Joe Dunford had taken us in. We let Cruickshank and company camp with us in the compound and offered what we had: MREs and lukewarm water. Next day, as a bellwether for the recovery effort, the BBC team sent out their driver with two hundred dollars to see what he could pick up. At the thieves' market in Baghdad, you can find old computers, telephones, used dentures, artificial legs—just about everything, no problem. The driver came back with a wide selection of artifacts—pale red and green beads, an amber ring, shards of pottery—many with markings from the Iraq Museum.

Back at the compound, another guy came in off the street—this time with forty-six antiquities, mostly small stuff, but we kept our word and treated him well. "Would you like some tea?" we said. Later in the day he came back with eight more artifacts. "Another cup of tea, perhaps?" Then he came back for a third time, bringing with him a plastic garbage bag containing a seven-thousand-year-old clay pot—predating the wheel by about two thousand years—that Donny told me came from Tell Hassuna. Gazing at the characteristic reddish, linear design, my tough-guy investigators were visibly moved by the sight of something so beautiful and so old. Every one of them pulled out his camera, and we spent the next thirty minutes photographing the vase in each team member's hands—including mine. This was another "eureka" moment for the guys, and one of several turning points that occurred in rapid succession.

From that time forward, we always had one of our Arabic-speaking ICE agents, Ramsey Korban, Bud Adada, or David Denton, "working the gate," that is, standing on the sidewalk in front of the compound soliciting walk-in business. From then on, a day didn't go by that one of them didn't come back into the library with a bag or a box of something. In fact, they kicked up a friendly rivalry among themselves over who could recover more items during gate patrol. They were all good, but Ramsey had a streetwise rap that never failed to produce.

Another big breakthrough came that first Friday when Jonathan Hunt from Fox News came by to interview me. Although I would agree with Thomas Jefferson that it is better to have newspapers without government than government without newspapers, I had been putting off the media, my head still reeling as we tried to sort out even the basics of what had happened since April 8. But I relented when I realized that his absence of agenda was exceeded only by his persistence. A day later, on Saturday, it was Bill Glauber of the *Chicago Tribune*, quickly followed by Alexandra Zavis of the Associated Press. After these interviews appeared, the press became genuine allies. After all the hype and hostility of the initial reports, I thought the fourth estate owed me one.

And they delivered. Reporters started coming through for us with information, informants, and other shared resources. Everything involved the same war-zone horse-trading that we had been doing since Basra. You give me the informant and I'll give you the exclusive on whatever follows from it. Sometimes, when the correspondents wanted to go out with us on a raid, they would have to hang around six or eight hours waiting, and they were damn good company. Among the most gracious was Jane Arraf of CNN, who even came by with Starbucks, sometimes the ground coffee, sometimes the hot stuff in a thermos. Reporters know how to pack.

I had long ago learned that in a world of finite resources, the more publicity an investigation receives, the more resources it is likely to receive. Moreover, publicity would help alert border officials. When border guards are on alert, smugglers don't move the goods. If the smugglers don't move the goods, you can work your informants in the local area to get your stuff back. The better you work your informants in the local area, the more likely the bad guys are to risk moving it, and therefore the more likely you are to recover it in transit. Putting the bad guys in that kind of squeeze is an investigator's dream.

So from this point on, I spent one to two hours every afternoon speaking with the press, detailing each day's discoveries. I also put Senior to work searching the Web and printing out each day's press reports. I needed to see what the world was saying about the investigation. Mostly I wanted to benefit from all the digging being done by all these high-priced but fearless reporters running around Baghdad. The news stories from Tuesday would help me develop my to-do list for Wednesday. Sometimes I would say, "Go grab the NBC guy." When he showed up, I'd say, "You want a tour of the museum? Then give me the whole interview of that clip from yesterday. I want to go over what that guy was saying." Then I would watch the video with an Arabic speaker in the reporter's makeshift studio or on a little handheld viewer I would have borrowed from another journalist. Sometimes when I recognized someone we had interviewed earlier, I wound up shouting at the screen, "You lying son of a gun! You tell them that? You didn't tell me that." So we would go back and see that museum employee or archaeologist and interview him or her again. But there were also plenty of "oops" moments where I realized that we had missed something that a sharp journalist had nailed, or where I realized we needed to reinterview a witness in light of subsequent developments.

We began disseminating photographs of the missing items, not only to customs and border officials from the neighboring countries, but

also to the International Criminal Police Organization (Interpol)—
and through them to their 184 member countries—as well as to prosecutors and police departments in the major destination cities of
London and New York. When we did not have access to a decent photograph of the artifact itself (sometimes they were of poor quality;
sometimes they had been destroyed during the looting of the administrative offices; sometimes they had never existed in the first place), we
used the photograph of a similar item. On occasion, I found a similar
photograph in an art book on one of my solitary midnight forays into
the library stacks.

Lieutenant Giuseppe Marseglia of the Italian carabinieri, an archaeologist with their special art-crimes unit that arrived in June, took over
the role of scanning and logging the missing cylinder seals into the international databases used by museums, dealers, and law enforcement
agencies. Together, he and Claude Davenport ensured that law enforcement around the globe had the most accurate and up-to-date information upon which to act. The images also told art dealers and collectors
(assuming they played by the rules) what not to buy. The distribution
process along with the publicity blitz also told the world what was being done to recover the stolen treasures.

The American media eats up the idea of "the Marines have landed,
the situation is well in hand," but in these first few days, reporters—
maybe desperate for something light—picked up on the supposed
"man bites dog" novelty of a slightly "egghead" Marine running
around Baghdad quoting Cicero. I explained that I was nothing special,
a grunt, an 03 (Marine-speak for an infantry officer), and I suggested
that inquiring minds check out the backgrounds of many of my fellow
officers. And while it was nice that they gave me credit for being reasonably articulate, their "surprise" reminded me of my classmates at
Columbia Law School. On the first day of civil procedure, the legendary professor Hans Smit—the prototype for *One L* and all the other
terrifying law-school professors on television—walked to the black-
board and wrote out a phrase in classical Greek. Bemoaning the defi-
ciencies in modern undergraduate education, he asked if anyone could
tell him what it said. "Of the anger of Achilles, sing heavenly muse," I
told him. Then I politely pointed out that he had one of the diacritical
(breathing) markings wrong. My classmates were already cutting the
guy with the white-sidewalls haircut and Marine uniform a wide
berth. But after that, some of them told me they thought I was "inter-

esting," even "amusing." Professor Smit, on the other hand, asked me to come to his office—and then arranged for me to get a joint degree in law and classics.

Twenty years later, there were still those who seemed to think that anyone in the military is a Neanderthal. Sarah Collins, a British Museum curator, came to Baghdad to do her duty—I will give her credit for that. But I could be speaking with someone and she would come up and without so much as a "How d'you do" interrupt and start talking to that person. Haughty arrogance would have been an improvement. In fact, she treated me as if I didn't exist. She could never accept that we (the military) had done anything positive. But it was her treatment of Nawala that really bothered me. On one occasion she asked why I didn't just get rid of her. "She's not mine to get rid of," I replied.

So I was still trying to bridge that cultural gap, and still a bit gun-shy with reporters. What really revved up the confusion, however, were those initial accounts carrying the mystical number 170,000—as in, 170,000 items stolen. And once that number entered the public consciousness, it was adopted as a rallying cry of outrage by archaeologists, journalists, and government officials around the world. Subsequently, this huge error, and the need to correct it, led to a media obsession with box scores. The museum looting could be turned into a sports story too. One that was all about batting averages. Forget the complex issues. How many chunks of rock are missing? Don't bore me with process and nuance. How many doodads have been returned? Gimme the stats.

The number 170,000 first appeared in Reuters. They quoted Nabhal Amin, identified as the museum's deputy director, as saying, "They have looted or destroyed 170,000 items of antiquity" from the museum. That number was picked up by the BBC News online and Voice of America News, and then it appeared in the *New York Times*, *USA Today*—just about everywhere. As we would soon discover, Nabhal Amin (true name "Nedhal") was not even a current museum employee, let alone the deputy director. She had, however, been an employee years before.

From the limited emptiness, I had known the first time I stepped into the galleries that this number had to be wrong. Within seventy-two hours, I knew the number was intentionally false, a fiction perpetrated first by some museum staff, and then (in most cases, innocently) repeated by the press.

As it turns out, there *are* approximately 170,000 IM (for Iraq Museum) numbers that have been given out since 1923, with such numbers representing anywhere from one object to a dozen (when they are of the same type and found together). This, of course, is the likely source for the number Amin reported. But it does not explain why her actual statement did not refer to IM numbers, but to 170,000 "looted or destroyed . . . items of antiquity."

There are not 170,000 "items of antiquity" in the museum, but well over 500,000. As I learned from Dr. Lamia al-Gailani—another in a long line of remarkable, accomplished, and strong-opinioned women produced by the land between the two rivers—the museum had a clearly defined method of screening. According to Lamia, an acknowledged expert in cylinder seals who joined the museum staff in 1961, whenever an antiquity arrived at the museum from an archaeological site prior to 1988, it was compared against the accompanying excavation catalogue(s) and then examined for one of four possible designations. *A* (for "Arabic") was inscribed on all Islamic pieces dated after the fall of Iraq to Arab forces in A.D. 637 (consisting of antique Islamic sculptures, ornaments, furniture, and porcelain), and *MS* was used for all coins (totaling more than 100,000). All other antiquities were then screened to determine whether they would receive an *IM* (for "Iraq Museum") number or simply maintain their original excavation numbers received at the archaeological site. Tens of thousands of pieces in the museum, never intended to receive IM numbers, carried only excavation numbers (by site) as their permanent designation. The museum staff no longer used the A designation after 1988; but the other three designations remained in effect. The fifth possible designation was the *MZ,* (for "muzawer") for all fakes. Once this screening process was completed, the staff then catalogued the object, i.e., prepared an index card for each item with its description, designation, and—sometimes—its photograph.

After we exposed the number 170,000 as bogus, commentators began engaging in all sorts of rhetorical gymnastics to account for why the press got it wrong. "Perhaps the first reporters on the scene, confronted with an empty museum, inquired about the total number of registered objects and reported that figure as a loss." But that does not account for the fact that Amin made her statement on April 12, 2003, while "she led a small group of journalists through the museum," each of whom quoted her exactly the same. It is unlikely in the extreme that they all "misunderstood" her with such precise uniformity. The media certainly uncritically accepted and dramatically repeated the number. But they did not make it up.

More to the point, for the number 170,000 to have been a truthful answer, the question would have had to have been "How many non-coin, nonfake, non-Islamic (unless received after 1988), pre-A.D. 637 objects that had already been screened and given IM numbers to replace excavation-site numbers were in the museum at the time of the looting?" I strongly suspect that in the heat of the moment, with bullets flying, no reporter asked her that question. In other words, the press was duped.

From a Machiavellian perspective, you could argue that there were advantages to all the exaggerations. The dramatic numbers mobilized world opinion to look into the problem, and, in that heightened atmosphere, I was able to bring in the most talented people in the war zone to help work on the case. Indeed, but for the reporting of such grossly inflated numbers, it is unlikely my team would have been dispatched at all. The flip side, of course, was that, once it became clear that initial reports overshot the truth by at least a factor of ten, many public voices gave a sigh of relief that "only" fourteen thousand objects had been stolen—completely losing sight of the fact that one missing antiquity is too many. This *only* allowed many governmental agencies, private organizations, and media outlets to dismiss the entire tragedy as overblown and move on to the "next" crisis and the next news cycle.

Mark Twain once noted that the only difference between a cat and a lie is that a cat has only nine lives. Well, that's how we felt about the numbers. Even after we had dug down to the truth, the inflated numbers lived on. And it was largely to counter these wildly fluctuating accounts that we started conducting daily press briefings. Of course, the use of such raw numbers missed the point. It made it sound as if we were counting ears of corn. In this game, each bead, pin, pottery shard, piece of shell, and the Sacred Vase of Warka count as one item. But surely the loss of certain legendary artifacts is an order of magnitude greater than the loss of a pottery shard.

Some media began reporting as early as April 16, 2003, that "in fact, in the main collection, it now appears that few items are missing, and very little seems to have been the victim of mob violence." But then four days later, the London-based *Guardian*, without citing a single source, cranked the number of missing items back up to 270,000. Fortunately, this number was just too absurd to gain traction and it dropped from sight.

Others insisted that the misleading numbers were a smoke screen because the staff was in on the thefts. At the same time, I was told by visiting archaeologists that I was "wasting my time" investigating the staff, that I should be looking at art collectors and dealers. And then, of course, there were still others who told me never to trust visiting archaeologists, who had their own axes to grind. Under the circumstances, we chose to reject preconceived biases, relying instead on anyone and everyone who could possibly provide information.

And it worked. Within the first three days after our arrival, we had recovered well over one hundred pieces. With each piece we would check for museum identification numbers, photograph the piece, scan the picture into our computer, and enter the photo and number into our own inventory system. Nawala had given us a list of pieces stolen from the museum, so I told computer whiz Claude Davenport to subtract these hundred from the list of the missing items. He came back and said no can do. Nothing that had been returned was on that list. Not even the pianist's copper bull from Ninhursag or the statue of Shalmaneser.

Before I could even process this incongruity, we received word from Dr. Ahmed Chalabi, now a deputy prime minister, but then leader of the Iraqi National Congress (INC), that he had pulled off one of the largest single seizures. At a checkpoint near Kut in southern Iraq, his INC forces stopped a truck supposedly bound for Iran. The smugglers escaped, but the security forces were able to confiscate a metal footlocker containing 465 artifacts, mostly cuneiform tablets, amulets, pendants, and some cylinder seals, all stolen from the Iraq Museum. The footlocker itself had Iraq Museum markings all over it.

When Chalabi sent word of the recovery, I rounded up some of the team and we went to his compound to see what he had. Dr. Chalabi would become a controversial figure to say the least, but throughout our investigation he was one of our biggest assets. Other officials provided ongoing criticism and impressive lamentation—reminding me of what Cicero had said about the foolishness of tearing one's hair in grief, as though sorrow would be made less by baldness—but Ahmed Chalabi provided access to witnesses, security when we needed to travel outside Baghdad, and sound advice on possible leads.

He and his men operated out of an old hunting lodge in Baghdad, luxurious in a nineteenth-century, "Great Game of Empire" kind of way. When we pulled up in our convoy in our first week in Baghdad, we were stopped in front of a roll of concertina wire by Iraqi fighters wielding AK-47s, warlord style. We told them we were there to inspect the antiquities. They said impossible. After a little further discussion, they said we would have to leave our weapons outside. We said no. And after a little more discussion, they dragged the concertina wire aside and let us into the compound. Of course, I was thinking back to all of my foolishness in Afghanistan and wondering if I was being given a second chance to play it safe. Instead, I fell prey once again to that irrational tenth.

The compound had concentric circles of security, and I knew I was going to have to talk to six crew bosses to get to Chalabi. You go past an outer perimeter, then beyond some buildings, and finally into a courtyard. Each circle has its own level of security, and each time you pass through one barrier, you have to explain yourself all over again. And each time I began to explain myself, the response was the same—impossible. It can't be done. But then it would go from it can't be done to it can't be done with those weapons. As we made our way through the gauntlet, even I was a little surprised at the level of armament.

On the other hand, there were people in the armed crowd that I recognized. I could not share this with anyone else in our group, but I had come across these men before in a different setting, maybe even a different country. They were men who I knew were not going to be a problem, men who may, in fact, have worked for the very same government that I worked for, or who were at least allies. Still, it was limited comfort, considering that the Iraqis had what appeared to be an unlimited amount of heavy weapons, and I wasn't sure the "friendlies" would blow their cover for us.

Eventually, we made it to the inner circle, and Steve and I met Dr. Chalabi. When he saw my name stitched over my front pocket, he immediately asked if I was of Greek ancestry. When I told him I was, he ran down a list of Iraqi innovations for which the Greeks had always received credit (the Pythagorean theorem, tapered columns in architecture), and I immediately shot back with a few that were indisputably Greek (tragedy, democracy). When we started comparing the relative merits of *Gilgamesh* and the *Iliad*, he insisted we stay for lunch.

Afterwards, he showed us the seized antiquities. Then he allowed us to pack up the cache and take it back to the museum—on one condition: that he and I continue our discussion on another day. Lunch with Dr. Chalabi and his equally brilliant daughter Tamara became for me a thoroughly enjoyable weekly event. Half the time was spent discussing joint strategies in stopping the trade in illicit antiquities, but the other half was a good-humored, hotly contested debate about our respective heritages. He often won those debates. Not because I gave in—he would have been furious—but because the evidence was on his side. After all, they *did* invent the Pythagorean theorem (or a version of it) well before Pythagoras.

Dr. Chalabi had been a pleasant surprise. The unpleasant surprise was when we got back to the compound. Some of the ICE agents spoke privately to Steve. "We ain't doing that again," some of them said. All those AK-47s and all those hard stares from dark, bearded faces had spooked them. It's a hard lesson that just because an armed force shares your hatred of a particular tyrant, it does not follow that they necessarily welcome your presence in their country. "The enemy of my enemy is my friend" is often true only to the moment of regime change. Pro that he was, Steve didn't tell me about those conversations until years later over a beer. To allow his guys to save face, he simply started finding other missions that did not require leaving the museum compound for many of his team. Not every investigator is necessarily a door-kicker. We were still able to round up enough guys for full-blown raids, but we never again went out with the entire team. And whenever we went out on one of our "let's go have a cup of tea" trips, it was often just me, Steve, Bud Rogers, and Ramsey.

Shortly after we returned from Dr. Chalabi's, Jonathan Hunt from Fox News brought us an informant who had told him about a bomb shelter in western Baghdad filled with manuscripts. Months before the war, someone had removed 337 boxes containing approximately 39,500 ancient books, Islamic manuscripts, and scrolls from the nearby Saddam House of Manuscripts, subsequently renamed the Iraqi House of Manuscripts. The informant had come forward, he explained, because the neighborhood residents who had been standing guard no longer believed they could protect the contents from thieves.

The larger question, of course, was who had removed these items in the first place, and why? Were the manuscripts relocated for safekeeping, or for easier loading onto some kind of transport out of the country?

In exchange for the information, I promised Hunt he could ride along and film our actions. But first I wanted to do a quick recon. "Steve, you know how the world was created, right?" He rolled his eyes, expecting another lesson in Mesopotamian cosmology. "On the seventh day God may have rested, but Marines filled sandbags. We're going out again." We put our sweaty vests back on, checked our weapons, grabbed a few other team members, and took off in a small convoy of SUVs, our fuzzy dice hanging from the rearview mirrors. We were armed and dangerous, alert for trouble, pumped up for the chase. We barreled into al-Mansur, a wealthy neighborhood, all stucco and bright bougainvillea, about twenty minutes to the southwest. It looked like Santa Monica without the beach. We located the bomb shelter, and the neighborhood residents who showed us the bullet holes in the walls described with obvious pride all they had done to drive the would-be-thieves away. Then we inspected some of the boxes. They did, in fact, contain manuscripts, many over a thousand years old, and beyond valuation.

We walked around the neighborhood and had tea in three different houses. I explained to my hosts that I wanted to bring a television news crew to capture their story. I told them that I wanted the world to know of their bravery and dedication in protecting these cultural treasures from at least one armed attempt to steal them and asked for their permission to do so. It was also part of my IO, information ops, campaign: I hoped other Iraqis would see this coverage and want to help us.

In one of the houses, a little girl came out. She had long hair, and she was wearing a white dress just like one my daughter Diana has. Of course I fell in love with her immediately and began playing with her in a peekaboo sort of way. She would run off, and then she would shyly come back. I reminded myself that I had to carry more candy, because I was running out. Then Senior, ever the voice of reason, told me, "Sir, we have to go. It's getting dark."

Since we needed trucks to move this stuff to safety, I told the residents we would return in the morning with the trucks and a television film crew. As we left, the neighborhood residents spoke brightly about what a wonderful day tomorrow would be when the cameras rolled and we ceremoniously returned the boxes to the museum. But I was disappointed because the little girl was nowhere to be seen and I wasn't going to be able to say good-bye to her. At just the last moment, she came running up to me with a tiny flower. She had picked it along the side of the road. She gave it to me and I stuck it in the lapel of my uniform, no doubt violating three governmental regulations.

The next morning, I located the head of the manuscript museum and told him the good news. Actually, I had spoken to him earlier, when I'd first heard about the missing manuscripts, but he'd never mentioned that they had been removed for safekeeping or that he knew where they were. Perhaps he didn't trust me enough yet to tell me. Perhaps he had other reasons for not telling me. Once again, there was no investigative purpose to be served by asking. So I never asked. But when I suggested that he come with us to reclaim this prize and to confirm that the manuscripts were from his museum, he was hesitant. I was a little surprised by his reluctance, but I persisted, and eventually he agreed to come with us. This was a case when the alarm system in the gut that should have gone off did not. As an investigator, it was careless. As a Marine, it was dangerous. As a boss, it was inexcusable.

When we arrived at the bomb shelter with the team from Fox News and trucks borrowed from Third Infantry, I introduced the head of the museum to the neighborhood residents and suggested that he thank these ordinary citizens who had protected this cultural treasure. No sooner had he climbed up on one of the trucks than all hell broke loose. He had yet to utter his first sentence, and the same, joyful people we had met the previous day kicked up a full-scale riot, screaming and threatening bloody murder.

I turned to my interpreter. "What the hell's going on?"

"They're shouting that you have betrayed them," he said.

I threw myself into the crowd, bobbing and weaving the way I do in the ring. I had to find the leaders I had sipped tea with just the day before. When I reached them, I asked what had happened. What had I done?

They jabbed their fingers at the museum director on the back of the truck. "Why are you giving the boxes back to the Ba'athists!" they yelled.

I had completely missed the fact that this museum director would be viewed by the entire community first and foremost as a senior Ba'ath Party official. Whether he was actually a good guy or a bad guy was irrelevant—seeing him, they thought that the fix was in and that they were being double-crossed.

Given the number of trucks and the size of the bomb shelter, I had requested and received additional army troops for drivers and security. My biggest problem at that point was that I didn't know these kids— and kids they were—and I didn't know how they would react if an Iraqi pushed them, punched them, or worse, grabbed their weapon. On our arrival, I had posted two-man security teams at the four corners of the block—standard procedure—and now I sprinted to each of those sets of nineteen-year-olds to make sure they understood that these were "friendlies," despite appearances to the contrary.

"What's your first name?"

"John, sir."

"John, look at me. Take a deep breath and look at me."

"Yes, sir."

"Keep your rifle pointed at the ground and smile at the civilians, but don't let them get too close to you and don't let them touch your weapon. Don't let them force you into a shoot/no-shoot decision. You are allowed to fire if you believe someone is about to shoot you or one of us, but for God sakes be sure. You're a good man and you can do this."

"Roger that, sir."

Then I did it three more times. The eye contact was as much for me as for each of those kids. It took a minute or two, but it was all I needed to be sure. These were good, cool, well-disciplined kids. A credit to their unit and to the high school sweethearts they had at home. Then I ran to find those who appeared to be in charge. It was difficult to hear with all of the screaming and difficult to move in a crowd that was growing angrier by the minute. But we began negotiating, and after a tense hour or so we reached an agreement. We agreed to leave the boxes in the bomb shelter—returning those dozen we had already started loading onto the trucks—and they agreed to permit us to enter the shelter to count the boxes and check their locks. They also agreed to establish a twenty-four-hour neighborhood watch over the boxes until a new Iraqi government was instituted.

Back at the compound, Jonathan Hunt, who has spent more time in Gaza, Iraq, and other war-torn areas than in his native England, said, "I don't think I make enough money for this. I *know* you don't." But Hunt continued to bring us informants and accompany us on other raids. I never saw the museum director again—although I had seen him often at the museum in the days preceding—but a television crew from Australian *Dateline* managed to find the director, and about six months later I watched the program. They had interviewed that same museum director, referring to him as the "hero" who had saved the manuscripts. They completely missed the point that it was the presence of this Ba'athist apparatchik that had caused the riot in the first place.

It was the end of the month, we had been there ten days, and we had seven hundred pieces in the "recovered" column. And still, not one of these items appeared on Nawala's list of missing objects. This prompted me to have a long talk with our dour museum director, though to what effect I do not know. The facts were that she had given me a list, and they had squat for an inventory system. Anything beyond that would have been an assumption.

Lousy bookkeeping can work both ways, of course. About this time, artifacts that had not been in the restoration room on Monday would appear there on Tuesday. Reacting to this mystery in view of all available staff members required the full measure of our thespian talents: "Senior, we have got to clean up our act! How can we be so sloppy? How could we have missed this? We can't come back here every day to recount. It's going to be at least three days—maybe until around one in the afternoon, maybe one thirty on Thursday—before we're going to be able to visit this room again, you know." Sure enough, three days later we would find more objects and replay the scene all over again. After the third or fourth time, Senior asked if I wouldn't mind "yelling" at someone else for the failure to properly "clear" the restoration room.

On May 1, with the BBC film crew in tow, we made our first methodical inspection of the aboveground storage area. It became the second major turning point in the investigation. This was an area filled with Torah scrolls, one of which had what looked like a feeler sticking out the top. No sooner had we discovered this potential trip wire than one of the guys tripped over it. On the BBC tape, you can hear me shouting, "Do you have a death wish!"

It turned out to be nothing, but then Senior called me over to a far corner. A window slit had been broken open from the inside and boxes moved against the wall. The height was just about right for a man's eye to line up with the slit—a classic sniper position.

Near the sniper's window, one of only two that offered a clear field of fire onto the street running along the western side of the museum, we found AK-47 parts and a box. Steve used bottled water to wash dust off the case so we could read it. The alphabet was Cyrillic, but I knew from experience what it said: RAKETNIY PROTIVOTANKOVIY GRANATOMET: rocket-propelled grenades (RPGs). We were able to track the bullet hole we found nearby, determining that one burst from a Bradley Fighting Vehicle's 25 mm chain gun penetrated the wall and barely missed the shooter about midthigh height. Tracing the shot across the room, Bud Rogers found the spot where the shell had disintegrated into the back wall.

We also found an old, Soviet-style hand grenade, its pin lying a few feet away. We had everyone stand clear except for Steve, Senior, and me. This was, of course, completely wrong. The kill range of a grenade is five meters, so you don't want three senior people standing over the same grenade. Luckily, it had no firing mechanism.

Nawala was upset when we came upon all this hardware and I pointed out that they were Soviet-made, which meant Iraqi army.

"Iraqi army? There was no Iraqi army in here."

I reassured her that we assigned no blame. I also assured her that I was certain that they had come in after the staff had left. I wasn't certain, of course, but it made no sense to share any concerns I did have.

Then we found a part of an Iraqi uniform lying on the floor, and then, about every hundred feet, more pieces of more uniforms. The way these remnants of military service were scattered about they seemed to make a trail—for the exits. And then it hit me. Snipers usually work as a team—the spotter and the triggerman. For these two, it appears, the burst from the chain gun tipped the balance toward career change, and a return to civilian life. These guys were in such a hurry to get back to mama that they started stripping off their clothes and, like six-year-olds heading to the bathroom, left the door open—the door to the aboveground storage area.

"Well, I'll be a son of a . . . ," I said to myself. "Crime number two."

It was like what had happened to that burned girl back in Basra, the one whose oil stove had exploded—accidents continue to happen even in wartime, and accidents continue to happen during civil unrest. Looters got into this area because fleeing Iraqi soldiers had left the door open. That accident makes the aboveground storage rooms an entirely different incident from crime number one, the looting of the galleries and the restoration room. When you find blond hair at a crime scene and then you find black hair, you don't conflate them. You've got two different patterns. So you put the strands of hair in two different evidence bags, and you put the bags in two different cardboard boxes. And you tease out each pattern separately.

But if the looters got into the aboveground storage area through a door left unlocked by retreating military, how did the military get in? In the fourteenth century, William of Occam recommended the principle of parsimony, which he expressed as Occam's Razor: Never increase beyond what is necessary the number of entities required to explain anything. In the case of the aboveground storage rooms, only one entity is necessary: the museum staff—either voluntarily or at gunpoint—had provided keys.

It was the very next day, May 2, that we came upon the breaching of the walled-up entrance to the underground storage area and discovered crime number three. Nawala told me about the value of the coins in the lockers only after we'd found the chipped-out cinder blocks at the bottom of that narrow stairway. When she passed out, ending that day's examination, I thought it was because of the apparent loss of the coins, along with her sudden awareness—the one empty locker standing open—that it was an inside job. A day later, she told me that her concern was not just for the world's greatest collection of coins from antiquity, but—oh, by the way—the world's indisputably greatest collection of five-thousand-year-old cylinder seals.

With this awareness of three distinct patterns—the theft in the galleries, the looting of the aboveground storage area, and the inside job in the basement—I was like a writer ready to start on the second draft. So from May 2 to May 12, while we waited for the forensic team to arrive and examine the basement crime scene, we went back outside and did it all again, only with new eyes. It's not until you reach the end of your first draft that you can begin to see how the pieces of your story really fit—or don't fit. That's why they say writing is actually rewriting. God is in the details.

On our "second draft" tour I was no longer the guest, so I could pick my guide for each survey of the grounds, and vary my company depending on what I wanted to learn. We went to the Children's Museum to measure the point of entry and the trajectory of the tank round. We went back to every site on the eleven-acre compound and compulsively examined it again and again. Yet another reason detective work is usually more exciting to read about than to conduct. Meanwhile, the afternoons and early evenings were still spent out in the streets, developing information and acting on that information. My nights were still spent discussing strategy, writing reports, and reading on the floor in the library stacks.

On May 9, around three P.M., after another long day spent with a fine-tooth comb and a magnifying glass, I was having my usual cup of tea with Jaber. One of the Army kids from the tank platoon burst into the room and said, "Sir, there's trouble outside. You need to be there."

The "trouble" was in the main courtyard—more than a hundred sign-carrying people jumping up and down and screaming. I had another riot on my hands.

Even a happy, peaceful crowd in the Middle East can be pretty noisy. These people were thrusting their fists into the air and doing the high-pitched ululations that Lawrence found so bone-chilling during his adventures in Arabia. The signs they held up in Arabic and English said, JABER IS A DICTATOR! and REMOVE ALL BA'ATH PARTY MEMBERS! These were past or present museum employees. One guy brandished a leather strap he said had been used to beat the workers. I declined to ask how it came into his possession.

Two men in particular looked to be the cheerleaders. They were shouting at the crowd, waving their arms "Up! Up!" and whipping everyone into a frenzy. Then I saw them bend down and pick up their camera and sound equipment. They were a film crew from al-Jazeera, trying to turn this demonstration into a riot, and a better photo op. I no longer felt like a guest or an outsider at the museum. I had started to feel at home. So instantly I saw red. You do this in *my* house?

It was déjà vu all over again as, without a word, I dived into the angry crowd. I knew Steve, Bud, and Senior—wherever they were—would cover my back. Once again, I needed to find the man in charge and get control of the situation. The crowd at the bomb shelter had been scattered pockets, but here it was a solid mass of people. After just a few seconds, I must have disappeared from sight, because Steve and Senior later told me how they had panicked for my safety. In India, twenty-three hundred years ago, Alexander had jumped into a crowd of the enemy and disappeared. When his men saw him again a minute later, a dozen Malli lay dead at his feet, but he had an arrow sticking out of his chest and had passed out with his sword still in his hand. Word spread that their beloved Alexander was dead. His Macedonians went berserk in the literal sense of the word. By nightfall, there was not a single living inhabitant of that city. All seventy thousand had been killed. Later, Alexander recovered.

The question for us on that day was whether any of the rioters had weapons hidden under their clothing. The compound was guarded by U.S. soldiers, and everyone who entered had to show ID. But as a gesture of goodwill, we had declined to search individuals who the staff said worked in the museum. After the riot, of course, we searched everyone, even the press. But on this day I used a variant of an approach I'd learned a decade earlier. I'd been meeting a less-than-savory witness with NYPD detective Rob Mooney, and Rob playfully put an arm around the guy, commenting how he appeared to have been working out. Just when I was wondering about Rob's new gentle side, he whispered to me, "The guy's clean." He had just done a patdown for weapons.

Once I found the ringleader and "accidentally" stumbled into him—he was "clean"—I convinced him to go into the museum library with me so we could discuss his grievances "like civilized men." We spoke for about an hour, with Donny joining us at the end. Ultimately, the protest leader agreed to leave the compound without any further demonstrations, but only after I agreed to forward his petition, signed by more than 130 of the 185 returning staff members of the museum or State Board of Antiquities and Heritage, to the Coalition Provisional Authority. I also promised to read his poetry. He kept his word and so did I. He returned the next day with his poems, and I read them. Another Rumi he was not.

After things had settled down, and I came up to Steve and Senior, they were genuinely upset at my recklessness in entering the crowd alone. Each of them asked to speak to me privately in the back. It was the first time either of them had ever gotten so emotional in my presence. Senior especially, as an enlisted man, was struggling to keep his temper and not rip this hotheaded colonel up one side and down the other. Steve was not nearly as restrained. I knew they were right and I apologized.

As for the petition, it turned out that, while some of the rioters who signed it sincerely believed that the museum's leaders were all Ba'ath Party loyalists, a large number thought that they were signing a petition to resume getting paid.

The very next day, an elderly couple came to us breathless and distraught. They identified themselves as the caretakers of the Saddam House of Manuscripts, the museum whose manuscripts had been moved to the bomb shelter. They told us armed looters had just entered their museum. If we wanted to save whatever sticks of furniture still remained and catch the thieves, there was no time to waste.

Within five minutes, and despite the 115-degree heat, twelve team members in twenty pounds of body armor flew out of the compound in four vehicles. We had no time for reconnaissance, so we did it the Marine way—improvising on the fly and developing the tactical plan as we hauled ass down the street.

As we pulled up, we saw that the museum was a three-story building—once inside, we also learned that it had a square central atrium surrounded by an interior stairway. Bad guys expect you to work from the ground up, which is why it's better to hit the roof and work your way down. You move faster running downstairs, and it's easier to shoot down. So while we would have preferred to reach the roof from an adjoining building and then clear each floor working from top to bottom, nothing was close enough. Buildings were sufficiently close, however, to offer clear fields of fire on us as we came and went.

We had no choice but to go in the front. We left one three-man team to cover the front. Then the other three teams entered and began methodically clearing all three floors.

When you raid a building, you do each floor, one by one. You go up the stairs in pairs, with the second man's hand on the shoulder of the man in front. He has left and you go right. You go room to room and slam open each door, yelling "Clear" when you are sure. Even if you have reason to believe nobody's home, you always plan for the worst, because for all you know the bad guy and his cousin just came in the window and are sitting there with two sawed-off shotguns. That's why you slam open the door, hoping for shock value. The same with stun grenades or flash bangs. (You don't use fragmentation grenades unless the tactical situation demands it because it could be the bad guy's grandmother and his three-month-old baby sitting there.) What you want is that "deer in the headlights" half-second that lets you get the drop on them, sort it out, and, if need be, take them out.

The trouble is, once you clear a room, it's only clear for that brief moment, it's not clear five minutes later, or even fifteen seconds later. You have to leave security, which means weapons and eyes on each location. So as you're going up the stairs, you're necessarily losing people, leaving them behind to maintain a secure rear.

On this particular raid, not until we got to the roof did we realize that we had been had: There were no looters and there had not been any that day.

Back at the compound, the elderly couple told us the truth. It had been a test and we had "passed." Looters had been there the day before and were coming back in a day or two to steal what little remained. The caretakers had come to us to learn whether we would respond and, if so, to prove to potential thieves how fast the Americans could and would react. We felt used and told them so, but I also stressed that if they had told the truth initially, we would have conducted the raid anyway, but more safely as a rehearsal. Interestingly, from that day on, not only did the amount of information we receive increase, but we also started receiving almost daily trays of Iraqi food.

While our temporary home within the museum compound was beginning to feel more secure, it had become clear that Nawala's two gun-toting henchmen were not the only dubious characters on the premises. Mohsan Hassan was another staff member who kept following us around, always pretending to be doing something else. I was always trying to steer Nawala away from him. He seemed to have no official duty, yet he also seemed to have power. In the old Soviet Union you had the commissar watching the colonel, and I hoped that kind of arrangement wasn't in play here. Time and time again, Mohsan was the one who would appear with the keys to open doors for us. But just as often, he would be the one saying that we can't go in because we don't have the keys. It was also Mohsan who would later take us on a wild-goose chase when we were searching for the treasures from the royal tombs of Ur and Nimrud.

Another ray of darkness was Dr. Hana Abdul Khaliq. A senior member of the museum, she was a mean, nasty woman who was all the more terrifying to the young women on the staff because her brother was a big shot in the Ba'ath Party, in fact #41 on the U.S. government's Top 55 most wanted list. Only one of the women told me directly how much they were afraid of her, but not one would ever talk to me when she was present, and no staff member ever smiled when she was around. She could make the temperature in a room drop just by showing up. And when she did show up, everyone would scatter. She would never go on the tours with Nawala or Donny. She was never in the office when I would have my tea with Jaber. But she was always there in spirit, like a shark lurking just a few feet away where the bottom drops off and the water turns dark.

My interview of her about the museum looting was brief: she "saw, heard, and knew nothing."

Meanwhile, questions began to arise back at headquarters. Rich, my number two back in Qatar, had remained negative about this mission. After a few days, I called to check in with him and he said, "I don't think you understand the controversy back here. Have you forgotten that everybody except General Renuart nonconcurred on this mission? And he only gave you three to five days. You're getting a lot of good press, but a lot of generals are starting to ask what the hell it is you're doing up there. I think you need to get back to Qatar before they pull you out. You've got to think about your career."

"Thanks, Rich," I said. "But I'm not done. Buy me some more time and cover my back as long as you can." He was right. I'd been given three to five days to assess the situation and stop the bleeding. I had exceeded those orders. Only one career would be affected if things went south.

Time to pick up the pace, but for that I needed reinforcements. So I went back up on the roof of the museum to call New York City police captain John Durkin back in Manhattan, duty captain of ESU, the Emergency Services Unit, and Jerome's former boss. I needed more men, preferably cops. But John had another qualification: He had been a Marine rifleman twenty years earlier—complete with the "Devil Dog" tattoo. When he tried to get back into the reserves, the Army offered him an officer's commission and John took it. His favorite phrase was, "I'm a Marine Corps rifleman in an Army captain's uniform."

I said, "John, can you give me six months? I really need you out here." I knew his twins were ten years old, I knew his wife wouldn't be happy, and I knew I was asking a lot. Without a moment's hesitation, he replied, "You got it, bro . . . sir." Recalled to active duty, he was in Baghdad a couple weeks later. On his belt were Jerome's handcuffs—later put to good use.

Other things were looking up as well. Iraqis were dropping off artifacts with GIs directing traffic or manning checkpoints. Local people approached us to ask what would happen to their "friend" if he returned an antiquity. Some said they knew someone who might know someone who might know something about an artifact. Others wanted to know about rewards. No matter the question, our answer was always the same: "Why don't we talk about it over a cup of tea."

Like our young pianist who brought back the bull's head and the statue, many of these people assured us that they had taken the items merely for safekeeping, intending to return them as soon as it was safe to do so. I think we can reasonably say that a certain number of these stole the stuff and then experienced a change of heart on realizing that they were not stealing from Saddam—the biggest crook of all—but from their own heritage. The vast majority simply lost their nerve. Mothers turned in items stolen by sons; sons turned in items stolen by friends; employees turned in items stolen by their bosses.

Sometimes they came to the museum; sometimes we met up at some remote street corner. Sometimes they approached empty-handed, needing a little extra persuasion at the last moment. Sometimes they dropped a bag at the gate and ran away. Sometimes they approached with the artifacts in hand. But always, it took guts for them to come forward and deal with us.

Steve had gotten ICE headquarters to allocate about two thousand dollars total for buybacks, but we barely used half. The trouble with buying back antiquities is that you're providing an incentive for people to go out and steal something. On one occasion, we had a guy come in with a tablet that had been stolen from Babylon a couple of days earlier, and he said, "I want to turn this in for the reward." We said, "You just stole it. Here's what you're going to get. Let's go have a cup of tea. Then you can leave and not get arrested. How's that for a reward?"

Our need for informants was no different from that of any other investigation. And just as in a murder case in New York or a robbery in Istanbul, each informant had his own reason for coming forward. Some wanted to help us catch the bad guys. Some were after a reward, plain and simple. Some were rival dealers in antiquities—this works the same way with drug dealers—hoping to put their competition out of business.

In New York, we have to worry about the informant's motivation only insofar as it reflects on the reliability of the information. In Baghdad, the question of motivation led to an additional question: Are we being led into an ambush? You have to take certain risks to get the job done. You also have to listen when your gut says: "This doesn't feel right." For our reality checks, we usually relied on the four senior people. "Okay, guys, what's the gut?"

One café in particular was known as a hangout for smugglers. It was also the hangout for a former pro boxer. He was a big, good-humored, guy probably in his forties, but slightly punch-drunk. He swept up at the café and appeared to have been adopted as a sort of mascot. I came in one day and he and I talked about the sweet science. He told me about his brush with the big time when he had lived in L.A., and I told him how I still boxed for the Widows and Orphans Fund for the New York City Police Department.

After we left, an informant told us that we could meet a certain weapons and antiquities dealer at this place—he would be wearing such and such. We showed up at the cáfe again the next day. The informant did not want to be seen connecting the American with the arms dealer, but we were never sure we were going to be able to find the guy again. So Steve suggested I create a little diversion while he and the informant snuggled up to the dealer.

I went up to the big guy from the day before and said, "Hey, come on. Yesterday, you said you were a boxer. So let's box." He was very much a heavyweight and I weigh 160—okay, so maybe I'm up to 164. I worked with Ramsey, our ICE interpreter, to make sure that the concept of "Nice and easy, you're a big guy" was getting across. We were in the front of the café, and I began sparring a bit in a friendly sort of way, and this heavyweight was as smooth as he was big. The Iraqis left their hookahs and their backgammon games to gather around and they cheered us on. But one serious punch from this guy and I would have been going head over heels the way they do in cartoons.

When you box, you mentally sit down in order to lower your center of gravity, so it all comes from the abdominal core. It's all about angles. My best shot in any fight is usually to slip the right hand, step in, pivot, and go for the kidney with a left hook or for the ribs with an uppercut, because that's what takes the wind out. A few times, I've done it just right and the guy does spiral toward the ground, falling to one knee with the color drained from his face. A good fighter named Rich Plansky once told me that after I hit him, he could feel himself crumpling to the mat but couldn't do anything to stop it.

But before you can move inside, you've got to test the waters. Most people have never had the wind knocked out of them by someone who is trying to hurt them. So the first thing you do in a fight—in the ring or in the street—is to hit them in the solar plexus, right over the heart, hard enough to make them take a little air. It also makes his heart skip a beat. But you have to be looking in the guy's face to see how he reacts or there's no point. If nothing happens, then you're screwed. It means he's not afraid. But usually, it's shocking to their confidence, as well as to their cardiovascular system. He gets an immediate sense that he could lose this thing, that he might just shuffle off this mortal coil.

That's when you move in for the kidneys. You also want to hit him on the button—the nose—because it makes the eyes tear. Lots of things hurt, but tearing eyes also cuts down vision, and he loses sight of your hands. It's another way of seeing what he's about.

At the café, however, we were just playing, and the entire place cheered as he put up his hands and I punched at them, and then I put my hands up and he punched—until one jab really connected and my whole arm went numb.

I looked over at Steve, who was in the back playing cards, as if to say, "Okay? We're done, right?" And he gave me the sign that said, "Two more minutes." I shook my head as if to say, "I don't have two more minutes!" But luckily this guy was being a real gentleman, and eventually I grabbed him in a big bear hug and wrestled him around, laughing. By this time, Steve had made his connection without burning the informant and we got what we needed. Me? I had sore hands for a week.

The rest of our effort was classic law-enforcement: random car-stops at checkpoints throughout the country, and increased vigilance at international borders. Altogether, I went on well over thirty raids, but not all "raids" are what you think. Some are the full-blown "kick the door in" type, but far more common are the "walk in gun at the ready" and the "Would you mind if we looked around while the water for tea is boiling?" types. Of course, you are never sure which one it will be before you get there—so you are always mentally prepared for the worst. Sometimes the "raid" (in whatever form) was for people, sometimes it was for boxes, and sometimes it was for information. Often, the place was empty, sometimes it wasn't. Often, the press came along, sometimes they didn't. Regardless of the type of "raid," there comes a time when you realize you're just way, way too old to be doing that sort of thing.

Months later, I was having a drink with a good friend of mine, New York City detective Joe Sweeney—one of the guys who had been on baby patrol a couple years earlier. I knew Joe had kicked in his share of doors in his life, and after telling him how I'd hurt my shoulder hitting one door, I asked for his advice on how to do it better the next time when I returned to Iraq.

"That's easy," he said, speaking softly. "All you have to do is three things. First, be ten years younger. Second, gain twenty pounds. And third, get someone else to do it." Then, raising his voice considerably, he added, "What the hell are you thinking? You're the boss!" He knew

I did it *because* I was the boss, of course, but his point was well taken. There were plenty of guys on the team who took down doors for a living, and while there is something to be said for never asking your team to do something you are not prepared to do yourself, there is a fine line between earning respect and feeding your ego. I wanted to believe that it was all about leadership, but truth be told, there was more than a little ego at play as well.

My interaction with Bud Rogers, the guy who crawled over the wall into the basement storage area with me, on the other hand, was 100 percent good-natured, fun-filled, laugh-out-loud ego. We were always competing for the lead position for anything that involved action, competition, or risk. It was always Bud and me—usually in that order. All I had to do back at the library after a raid was to quote Cicero's "A man who has no time to care for his body is like a carpenter who has no time to care for his tools" and the shirts would be off and we'd be one-upping each other in some form of exercise—pull-ups hanging from the doorjamb, push-ups on MRE boxes, dips between display cases. If I did fifteen, he would do sixteen. Senior even joined in on occasion, but Steve would look at us with the amused smile of an indulgent parent. Our favorite competition, however, was trading quotes. I was notorious for running around "quoting dead guys," as my men so elegantly put it. So we played something like "Six Degrees of Kevin Bacon" only with Shakespeare or Kipling or Thucydides. We would do it by topic or theme, and Bud was good.

Our competition took other forms as well. On one occasion, Bud and I were running to get to the same door on a rooftop. You can't use your rifle stock for busting down doors in real life because they're plastic, so you have to use your shoulder. To get there first, I literally flung myself off the ground and launched into it. But what we didn't know was that it was locked solid and bolted from the inside. I think it was the only steel door outside the museum that we ever came across in Baghdad, and all I remember is going numb, but then the adrenaline kicked in, and I was fine. Of course, Bud proceeded to throw his body into it as well—fortunately for my ego, he couldn't budge it either.

Once, Kevin Power and I had just pulled up to a building. He's a big, burly guy, a SWAT team leader with ICE, and we were going to hit the door together, Kevin on the left and I on the right. I'm a lefty, and when you're going to hit a door, you always try to use your nonshooting shoulder, so as not to numb your shooting hand. So in my case I would start with my right shoulder pressed into the doorframe on the right side of the door. Kevin and I had our weapons at the ready, and I nodded to him and said, "Ready to roll?"

He said, "No." It had been kind of a rhetorical question. I mean, I didn't expect an answer. So I screwed up my face and said, "What?"

He said, "You haven't quoted a dead guy." It took a beat, but I realized that this man, who usually countered my quotes with his from Rodney Dangerfield and Bart Simpson, was serious. So I gave him Yeats: "Think where man's glory most begins and ends, and say mine was I had such friends."

He nodded, furrowed his brow, and then said, "Okay, now I'm ready."

Not long after this little episode, one of my teams was rotating home and another was rotating in. So I flew back to Qatar to say good-bye to some and welcome others, the time-honored "hail and farewell." That's what you do when you lead people. The most important times you spend with those in your charge are the first ten minutes they're in your organization and the last ten minutes. And I'll be damned if I was going to let a war prevent me from discharging my duties.

This trip was the first time I ever had my own jet, a four-seater. I was a little embarrassed, because it was just me, but the crew said they had not been up in a few days and needed the flying time.

Down in Qatar I also met the new, incoming team, and to them I said, "You gentlemen I've just met. You don't know this about your outgoing colleagues here, but I am about to pay them the greatest compliment I can pay, which is to say, 'I would go through a door with you anytime.'" It was true, but it is equally true that not everyone was eager to go through that door.

When you take a door, you're not doing some kind of careful analysis, thinking there's someone back there, look to the left, look to the right. That's all muscle memory from the training. What you're really *thinking* while your body is on autopilot is "Please don't let me screw up. Don't let me be the guy who gets somebody killed. Let me acquit myself well in the eyes of those whose opinions, within the entire universe, at this moment in time, are the only ones that count." And you don't play it safe. Like an injured athlete, when you play it safe, you're not on top of your game. When you play it safe, you hold back, so you're slow, your instincts aren't fully engaged. Playing it safe can get you—and others—killed.

It made me all the more grateful for men who, when it's time to take a door, will fight over who gets to go first. It reminded me of guys fighting for the check at my father's restaurant. "My turn!" Of course in this case, they're fighting over the opportunity to take the greatest risk of getting killed.

Some guys are "heroes" to the point of being reckless and flamboyant, and they usually wind up dead, and sometimes they get other people killed as well. When you assume a risk, it has to be for a good reason, and there has to be an upside. I have no use for people who act heroically more out of self-interest than out of a desire to save others. On the other hand, I have seen many legitimate heroes who have done things that have astounded me. "A hero is no braver than an ordinary man," Emerson tells us, "but he is brave five minutes longer." Those people, those ordinary men and women in extraordinary circumstances, are the stuff of legend. I am not one of them. I am not even in their league. And because I'm not, I appreciate them all the more. I'm just the guy trying to get the job done and get everybody home for Christmas.

On the other hand, even within the select community of law enforcement and career military, there are guys who, the moment risk enters into the discussion, say, "Discussion over." In Iraq, especially after the visit to the Chalabi compound, I discovered that a surprising number of men who carry guns for a living are not necessarily gung-ho risk-takers. Some agencies, for instance, often attract people who are simply looking for a steady government job with a strong sense of moral purpose. Even some guys in SWAT or ESU are risk-averse. But for others, the risk of death is just another factor to consider—it does not end the discussion. Then again, some guys I've met in the Marines and in Special Forces need the risk of death just to keep it interesting.

But our work in Baghdad was not all guns 'n' ammo, nor all recovery of antiquities. The JIACG team had become like a Marine expeditionary unit in miniature, self-contained, and capable of dealing with whatever came up. Our freedom of movement allowed us to be princes of the city. Steve was the best at stopping at every checkpoint to say, "What's up, guys? Find any antiquities today? Find any weapons?" Steve could—and did—chat up everyone and anyone who would listen.

All the while, I lived in fear of General Renuart being forced to step in to say it's over. I may occasionally not ask for permission, but I never disobey a direct order. And you do not argue after the ship has sailed. So I was keenly aware of the need to keep producing results in terms of the primary mission. So while probably two thirds of our time was taken up with the museum, various team members would routinely spin off to track down documents, weapons, money, and bad actors.

As in Basra, we went through plenty of warehouses, but here in Baghdad, we could also hit the headquarters of Iraqi customs, as well as the headquarters of the IIS, the Iraqi Intelligence Service. And while the museum was our primary base of operations, we also worked out of the airport. The museum, however, was always my baby, and I would draw on the crew as needed. "Okay, today I need both computer guys, I need the fingerprint guy, and all three interpreters."

All the work involved consensual leadership, a team concept. We would put together teams specific to whatever mission was at hand, figuring out how many FBI interrogators or how many computer specialists we needed. Sometimes this required a bit of inducement to bring them on board. When something big would come up, I would tell them, "Hey, guys, I've got the lead story for your sitrep [situation report] for today. I got your next press release." And they would respond, "Okay, I can give you six guys."

The FBI might develop the information, and it might speak to the FBI mission statement, but it wasn't ever as if it were an FBI mission in isolation. We would all lend a hand, especially in terms of force protection. We came in together, and we would all leave together.

I remember one time we were on our way to a raid, and we had already set up our tactical plan and were totally focused. Steve was driving and I was in the front seat—the old married couple once again—and two guys were in the back. Urban combat is three-dimensional, meaning that you can become a target from street-level, above, or below. So you need many sets of eyes looking out for threats.

We were scanning the streets, looking at the rooftops, rehearsing all the what-ifs in our minds. And then suddenly what should pop into my head but a Stephen Sondheim song, "Sorry-Grateful."

Now, first, you may ask, "What is a heterosexual man doing replaying lyrics from a Broadway show tune as he goes into an armed confrontation?" It was a song from *Company*. One of the guys in the musical is single, in his thirties, and on the outside looking in, observing the ups and downs in the relationships of four couples and asking what it's like to be married. Another character responds with a great song that begins, "You're always sorry, you're always grateful. . . . Everything's different, nothing's changed." And then the clincher: "Good things get better, bad get worse. Wait, I think I meant that in reverse."

That's life in a combat zone. Your eyesight is better. Your hearing is better. Things taste better. The water quenches your thirst better. The sky is the brightest blue you've ever seen. You never get tired. And you're with the best friends you'll ever have. The good things get better, but the bad things get worse. You are more afraid. You are more anxious. Your stomach hurts all the time. Your feet hurt. It's always way too hot or way too cold. Everything is more. It's not for everyone, but not every trial lawyer tries cases. Not every door-kicker kicks down doors. Not every tool needs to be a hammer.

11

BEWARE THE RABBIT IN A RAGE

He makes no friend who never made a foe.—Alfred, Lord Tennyson

O N MUHAMMAD'S BIRTHDAY, a holiday, the driver of a big SUV stopped at the museum gate, had a brief exchange with the guard, and then pulled into the courtyard. From where I was standing in the alcove in front of the administrative offices, I could see this was a UN vehicle. The cavalry had arrived, I thought.

The car stopped in front of the entrance to the administrative offices, and a man leapt out. He wore well-cut slacks and an open-collar blue shirt like a man out for a stroll, but he was closing the distance between us way too fast. You only do that if you're overcompensating, or if you want to intimidate. I had my right hand out, arm extended, planning on giving him the warmest welcome he'd had all day. He too had his hand out, but in it was his card. Without saying a word, this representative of the UN thrust the card at me like a weapon. All I could figure was that the guards had given him a hard time. That's the only way I could account for his being so "pre-enraged."

"I'm grateful you're here, sir," I said. "We've been waiting for you. How can I help you?"

I don't need your help, he replied. I'm going in.

"I'm sorry, sir, but no one is here today, the doors are locked, and I don't have the keys." This seemed to upset him even more, so I added,

"It's a holiday, sir." And then I smiled. "Caesar's wife must be beyond re-proach." That was my standard reply to the question of why I didn't have my own set of keys. From our billet in the library, we had no immediate access to the galleries or the storage rooms without a staff member pres-ent to unlock the doors. Exactly the way I wanted it. It usually got a chuckle. Not this time. He simply raised his voice. He had the president of UNESCO coming in two days, he yelled—or maybe it was the vice president. It was hard to understand him in all his apoplectic fury. The staff must be alerted and everything must be properly prepared. In other words, he was the advance man.

But his manner—haughty, officious, loud—was the real story. It was as if my being an American was enough to push him over the edge. And being an American in uniform dropped me back about sixty thou-sand years on the evolutionary scale.

"Since you're here, can I show you around the grounds? Perhaps I can fill you in on the situation, and our work." But he said he didn't need a tour. In fact, he told me, he kept an office there. He *did* strut as if he owned the place. Yet, for an "owner" of such a troubled property, he looked surprisingly rested. To avoid reacting, I amused myself by imag-ining he was a prewar guy who had decamped before the war and was coming back after a few weeks on Corfu.

"Fantastic," I said. "There's a million ways the UN could help. We need forensic examiners, interpreters, translators. We need office equip-ment, especially computers and scanners. We need to get these people back on their feet. I don't want to do the investigation and then recon-struct the museum—I'd like to do them simultaneously, but to do that I have to have staff."

"This is your mess!" he spit out. I stepped back, flabbergasted.

Then he went off on the standard diatribe I had heard countless times before about the U.S. having "protected" the oil ministry, speaking in the tone he might use with a maid who had just scorched his favorite shirt.

And then he reached his punch line:

"I am not here to help you. I am here to watch you fail."

I was a forty-five-year-old homicide prosecutor from New York City, but I had never dealt in diplomatic circles before, or in the inter-national circles of nongovernmental organizations. For the first time, I was face-to-face with the kind of man who could agree to sacrifice ten thousand lives to make a point, and then order dessert.

No matter how much this man might hate George W. Bush or object to the U.S. invasion, how could he wish us to fail when failure meant chaos and civil war? More to the point, why would he want my team to fail on a mission to preserve cultural treasures? In my perhaps naïve optimism, these ancient objects rose above the level of politics or nationality or religion. The Mask of Warka is not Christian, Islamic, or Judaic. It is older than all that. It's primal. Universal. Transcendent.

But hearing this vehemence from a public official was as if someone had opened a door and let in a cold draft. I knew I was just the convenient punching bag, but it was still shocking.

Then this ice-cold diplomat blew out just as quickly as he had blown in.

Shortly after noon, a few of the staff began to show because we had other visitors coming. A U.S. ambassador would arrive at three, along with a minister from the Japanese government and his entourage, along with all the journalists covering the fact-finding mission. This meant about thirty guests at the museum, but only three staffers had arrived to oversee their tour. This was still a crime scene, and I couldn't vouch for its integrity with anything more than a two-to-one guest-to-staff ratio. Anyone beyond that number couldn't properly be supervised inside the museum, and I would have to search them when they came out. I was not about to search a high official of the Japanese government in front of a dozen guys with Nikons around their necks.

The museum staff suggested the only reasonable solution: to break the party into three smaller groups and take turns going through the museum. I informed the ambassador and the Japanese minister, both of whom smiled and passed by. Then I stood at the door counting heads to make up the first group of ten. Unfortunately, the eleventh guy in line was somebody who, at least in his own eyes, was very important. He was startled when I stepped in front of him. "Do you have any idea who I am?" he said. I smiled and told him I was sorry but that I would get him in the museum in just a few moments. I didn't know who he was—it turned out he was something like a chief of staff—but of course I said, "Oh, yes, sir, I appreciate your position, which is why I will take you through myself in just a few moments." At which point he literally started jumping up and down. He could not believe that he did not make the first cut.

This was the second time in the same day that my attempt at charm and diplomacy had proved a miserable failure. I tried to calm him down, but meanwhile the tour was starting without me, and ten was the right number of visitors only if I was in there too. Looking over my shoulder, trying to move on, I said, "Sir, I'm so sorry, but as I told the minister, you just can't go in now. I'll do this as many times as necessary and everyone will get a tour."

My attempt to be reasonable made him go even more ballistic.

"I have your name!" he screamed. His face was bright red, and the cords in his neck were like ropes. "I'll have you thrown out of the country!"

At which point John Durkin, the recently arrived NYPD captain, came over and more than proved his value (as if it had ever been in doubt). John moves as only an Irish cop can move. He's not a particularly imposing guy, but he smells of cop. You see him in the park with his kids or on the beach in a swimsuit and you say, "Excuse me, Officer . . ."

He looked at me and said, "Sir, I got it."

And now the Japanese guy was screaming even louder because we were talking about him. I said, "John, are you sure, because this guy, I mean, this guy is nuts!"

In my head I was already reading the diplomatic protest this incident was sure to generate.

John smiled at me and said, "Sir, I've been doing UN details for seventeen years—this is nothing."

He put his hands behind his back, cop-style. The Japanese guy had no issue with John, but he wanted to tear my head off, and he was trying to crawl over John to get to me. All John did was give his body a sudden flex, and the Japanese guy bounced back a couple feet. The whole thing was imperceptible. John's hands never moved, his face never changed expression, so it never happened. At least, no one could ever say it happened, but he had just given the guy a message about the limits of diplomatic immunity. I remember thinking, "Damn, he's good."

When the diplomatic note—which is nothing more than a formal complaint with a lot of words like *whereas* and *hereby* and *wherefore*—did come, General Renuart seemed more amused than angry. He said, "Matthew, you know—when I said that thing about being a 'pit bull,' I didn't necessarily mean with foreign delegations." I later learned from John that the tone of the note had been softened by a well-received bottle of Scotch courtesy of CNN.

But it wasn't just the international community. Even within the American command structure, there were plenty of people we rubbed the wrong way. Usually, people have to meet me before they develop a strong dislike. Not in Baghdad. Administrators and officers often showed up hating my guts on spec. Most of the senior officers I ran into on the streets of Baghdad were at my level or below—except for "hands-on" officers like General Harrell, colonel is the last rank where you really are still a doer out in the field—and it was only by virtue of my rank that I was not constantly hearing, "Step back, Jack."

One of the perception problems was that our team lay outside normal reporting channels. We did not answer to Ambassador Paul Bremer at the Coalition Provisional Authority. We did not report to the U.S. Army's Task Force 1-64, who owned the real estate, or to CFLCC (the coalition forces land component commander, the commander of all ground forces in Iraq). We were sort of a throwback to the Napoleonic era, when the emperor had inspectors general reporting back directly to him, an arrangement that, of course, pissed off his marshals to no end. The same kind of resentment brewed up against us. Most everyone saw us as free agents on the battlefield, rogue cops, cowboys.

"Who do you report to?" they'd ask me.

"General Franks," I'd answer, resisting the temptation to tell them it was *whom*.

"Yeah, yeah. But who do you really report to?"

Sometimes this same sentiment was more elegantly phrased as, "Who the hell are you guys? How come you assholes get to go wherever you want?" Special Forces has that degree of freedom, but they operate outside U.S.-controlled areas and apart from conventional forces. So out of sight, out of mind. We occupied the same time-space continuum as the conventional forces, however, so our mere presence was enough to piss some people off. To make themselves feel better, many units just fit us into the Special Forces context: "Okay, special mission. Snoop and poop. Spooks."

Even our mission confused matters. Museums are usually the bailiwick of Civil Affairs—that's why they have curators and historians in their unit. "So why the hell weren't *they* given this mission?" I was asked pretty much every day. "Well," I would think to myself, "no one was 'given' this mission. Someone saw it as needing to be done and did it." What I said, however, still working on my diplomatic skills, was that this was an investigation, not a conservation. It was us or nobody.

My rank and our early successes enabled us to navigate most of these rocky waters, but once we started looking for the treasures of Ur and Nimrud, it was this same kind of friction that almost got me kicked out of the country.

Our hunt began with a letter we found, dated August 12, 1990, acknowledging receipt by a bank official of sealed crates containing gold from the museum. This was ten days after Saddam Hussein invaded Kuwait and started the first Gulf War. As fate would have it, the week we found the letter, I was approached by Jason Williams, a British anthropologist and filmmaker working on a documentary for National Geographic. However inclined I was to keep him at arm's length, he was impressively persistent, the embodiment of Shakespeare's "fellows of infinite tongue that can rhyme themselves" into your favor. But it was the story he brought, more than his charm, that really captured my interest.

He had found a tipster, a former bank employee who claimed to have been present when Saddam's son Qusay removed $1 billion worth of U.S. currency from a vault in the Central Bank. Interesting enough, but then the informant claimed that he had also seen Qusay move a spectacular collection of gold. Hearing the mention of gold, Jason and I looked at each other, and he mouthed a single word: "Nimrud."

In the annals of great archaeological discoveries of the last hundred years, the treasure of Nimrud is second only to King Tutankhamen's tomb. A spectacular collection of more than a thousand pieces of gold jewelry and precious stones from the eighth and ninth centuries B.C., it had been displayed in public only once, very briefly in 1989. Then, shortly before the first Gulf War, it was moved, supposedly for "safe-keeping," to the Central Bank of Iraq. Whether it was still in the bank vaults in April 2003 was anybody's guess. It could have been melted down. It could have been given to one of Saddam's mistresses and hocked in a pawnshop in Biarritz.

We asked the source whether the gold Qusay had moved was in the form of bars or jewelry. He said he did not know, but he had the impression that the boxes were not heavy enough to have contained gold bars. This was not a good sign. But while Qusay put the money in a truck and drove away, the informant said the gold was simply relocated from one vault to another. Of course, Qusay planned to take everything he could get his hands on before fleeing. Most likely, he was moving the treasure to make it more accessible when he had the chance to come back for it. My hope was that he needed one more day to complete the heist, and that it was a day he never got.

The treasure of Nimrud represents Assyrian civilization at its zenith. The Assyrians, like the Jews, are an ancient people who have survived into modern times despite conquests by the Medes, Parthians, Romans, Sassanid Persians, Arab caliphates, Mongols, and Ottoman Turks. Along with the Armenians, they were one of the earliest peoples to convert to Christianity, after which they became known by their ecclesiastical designations: Nestorians, Chaldeans, Jacobites, and Melchites. In the twentieth century, again like the Armenians, they were subject to systematic extermination attempts. They had a highly advanced civilization when Europeans prided themselves on flint tools. The treasure of Nimrud is their heritage.

Referred to in the Bible as Calah (Assyrian name Kahlu), Nimrud is in northern Iraq, on the Tigris, a little southeast of modern-day Mosul. Scholars say that it was inhabited in the early third millennium, but it appears to have been in ruins by the thirteenth century B.C. Then, in the ninth century B.C., the Assyrian king Ashurnasirpal II, relocated his capital there from Assur (the basis for the name Assyrian), rebuilt the city, and erected a magnificent palace. The city then flourished as the capital from the ninth century B.C. until it was destroyed in 612 B.C. by a combined force of Medes and Babylonians.

Sir Henry Layard rediscovered the site in 1845, and in 1950, British archaeologist Max Mallowan (also known as Agatha Christie's second husband) excavated the northwest palace. He cleared a room in the harem, but failed to notice that the pattern of the floor tiles had at some point been slightly altered.

Not until 1988 did anyone notice the uneven floor. The prize for this observation goes to Iraqi archaeologist Dr. Muzahim Hussein Mahmud, who spotted the irregular pattern in the tiles and started digging. The tomb held a sealed sarcophagus containing the body of a queen. Buried with this well-tended lady was an array of grave goods that included at least thirty-one exquisitely crafted gold and silver necklaces, bowls, fibulae, rings, and other jewelry.

Motivated by the first find, Dr. Muzahim reexamined every square inch of that area and the next year discovered another burial chamber, marked by a stone tablet with a cuneiform inscription. Just like in the movies, the inscription was a curse: "Whoever lays hands on my jewelry with evil intent or breaks open the seal of this tomb, may his spirit wander for all eternity." For Dr. Muzahim, a little restlessness in the afterlife was probably worth it and he opened the sarcophagus. Inside were two female bodies later identified as Queen Yaba and Queen Atalia, from the eighth century B.C. Beside them were some of the finest examples of gold jewelry ever found in the Near East, including more than 700 tiny gold rosettes, more than 90 necklaces, an uncounted number of gold and carnelian beads, and 157 gold objects (a crown, a diadem, 79 earrings, 6 necklaces, 4 chains, 14 bracelets, 30 rings, 15 vessels, 3 bowls, and 4 anklets—one of which weighed almost three pounds). Additional gold objects were on the floor of the tomb as well.

Four months later, Dr. Muzahim found a third vaulted crypt belonging to the ninth-century B.C. queen Mullissu, the wife of Ashurnasirpal II, the king who had built the northwest palace in the first place. In this tomb were fifty pounds of gold and silver jewelry, 449 separate pieces that make Harry Winston look like K-Mart.

In 1990, Dr. Muzahim uncovered a fourth vault, but, unfortunately, grave robbers had found it first.

Many precious items are described as "priceless," but few truly are. A few years after it was discovered, an exhibit of the Nimrud gold was planned for the Romische-Germanisches Museum. But it was canceled because no underwriter was willing to insure the treasure. That's what we mean by priceless.

Our first step was to find and interview the individuals who had moved the crates from the museum to the bank in the first place, primary among them being Mohsan, the always present and usually underemployed museum staffer. Unless he had some special Ba'ath Party juice, you would have to wonder why a midlevel, deputy director would have been chosen for such a task.

The Central Bank consists of two buildings on Rashid Street on the east side of the Tigris, just over al-Ahrar bridge. Facing the bank from the street, the new wing is on the left, closer to the bridge, and the old wing is on the right. Mohsan told us that he had transferred twenty-one boxes from the museum to the Central Bank's old building. Only one box contained the treasure of Nimrud. Sixteen boxes contained the Iraq's Royal Family collection. The other four contained the contents of a different set of tombs that were almost two thousand years older than those of Nimrud. They were from the ancient Sumerian city of Ur.

The treasures from Ur came to light between 1922 and 1934, when Sir Leonard Woolley and his British-American archaeological team excavated approximately eighteen hundred graves of "common folk," as well as sixteen tombs he described as "royal." These dated from the Early Dynastic III period of the Sumerian era, approximately 2600–2500 B.C. This was about five hundred years before the biblical Abraham was said to have lived in "Ur of the Chaldees."

In the grave marked PG-1273, but referred to by Woolley as the "great death pit," he found seventy-four skeletons laid side by side in rows surrounding the central, and presumably royal, deceased. Based on the remnants of their dress, he determined that these were fully armed soldiers, ladies-in-waiting in silk with gold embroidery, and servants and musicians, all following their king to his grave. Woolley also found sledges and chariots, including the requisite horses and oxen, helmets and copper spears, ritual gold daggers, gold and silver cups, and thousands of small beads of lapis lazuli.

In the separate grave of Queen Shub-Ad, he found the remains of more than a dozen ladies-in-waiting in equally splendid regalia. The approach to the queen's burial chamber had been "guarded" by five men with copper daggers, and in the corner sat a harpist to provide accompaniment for the queen in the next life. The instrument had a mother-of-pearl inlay and was adorned with a bull's head of gold.

Selma al-Radi, an Iraqi-born archaeologist and tour de force of brilliance, energy, and spunk, was visiting the museum just about the time Jason Williams and I began our search. Like her equally dynamic cousin, Lamia al-Gailani, Selma had a four-decade-long association with the museum, but had been forced to leave under Hussein. Lamia went to London and Selma split her time between Yemen and Manhattan. In May 2003, her first day back at the museum as part of an assessment team, Selma looked around, shed a few tears, then rolled up her sleeves and said, "Okay, Colonel, let's get to work." Nothing fazed that woman: not the heat, not the damage, and not the dangers. So when I saw her grief upon learning that the treasures of Ur and Nimrud might have been stolen, I began to understand that these were no ordinary boxes of jewelry.

Yet another problem was that an exact count of the treasure of Nimrud has never been published—the collection had been taken from the museum too quickly after its discovery. Even the seminal book purported to contain a complete inventory of the treasure has many entries that read "beads," "ornaments," "earrings," and the like, without providing exact numbers. According to Selma, though, the two treasures of Ur and Nimrud combined contained approximately 7,360 objects.

Although Mohsan had told us that the boxes had been moved to the Central Bank's old building, we later found a seemingly reliable informant who claimed to have seen the treasure in the new building. Only one of these accounts could be accurate, but which one? And knowing which building to search was not enough. We also needed to find a bank employee who could tell us in which of the dozens of vaults in the bank the treasure had most recently been seen. So we took out ads on local radio and in newspapers asking anyone with information to contact us. While it was certainly an unorthodox approach to finding potential informants, it was no crazier than declaring amnesty for the whole country or, for that matter, diverting a significant potion of a counterterrorist team to tracking down a bunch of rocks in a war zone.

Rashid Street is Iraq's financial center, an evolutionary outgrowth of an ancient marketplace that still exists there. During the invasion, the area had been heavily bombed. By the time we got there in April, the bank buildings were surrounded by enough tanks and barbed wire to look like Berlin, 1945.

The two bank buildings themselves, secured by an Army scout platoon, had been reduced to a mass of twisted steel and dangling cables by a single precision-guided bomb. But the big surprise was underground. The basement that housed the vaults in the new building was under about twenty feet of water. The old building was also wet, but only about ankle deep. On our first trip to Rashid Street, it was Steve and I as always just walking around and observing a lot by watching. The basement of the old building was an endless maze on several levels of dark, winding hallways. Violating pretty much every rule of patrolling ever devised, Steve and I split up to cover more ground. Down one of the hallways, I found two bodies in front of a vault. Violating the rule of no assumptions, I can only suppose that they were both would-be robbers who happened on the same vault at the same time. Rather than join forces, it appears they opened fire and shot each other dead.

When I got back to ground level, I walked up to one of the grinning soldiers who asked if I had found "the surprise." I told him I had, thank you very much. Then I reminded him that they were a health hazard.

He assured me he had found the bodies only a few hours ago and had already made the appropriate notifications for disposal.

In the next week, we took Mohsan to the bank several times and had him re-create the scene of moving the boxes. Every time he told the story, he "remembered" putting the boxes in a vault on a different level in the basement, or down a different hallway, or with a different front door. At one point, even the ever-patient Ramsey snapped at him, "You don't want us to find the treasure, do you?" Once, after our third day in a row down another long, dark hallway that turned out to be wrong, I told him we were going to do this every day until we got it right. As when I had confronted him about the "missing" grave goods from the Neanderthal display, Mohsan complained of chest pain and told me he did not think he could come to the bank anymore.

So it was up to us to search for other witnesses, finally identifying the right vault a month later. On May 26, we opened it and found the sixteen boxes containing approximately 6,744 pieces of jewelry, pottery, and gold from the collection of the Royal Family. Beautiful and valuable, but not what we had been hoping to find. The five boxes containing the burial goods from Ur and Nimrud were gone.

During the month we spent going through the motions with Mohsan, we were also bringing other witnesses to the bank. That's what you do with witnesses to test their credibility. You bring them to the scene and say, "Show me." Time and again, we heard the same thing: the new building, not—as Mohsan had told us—the old one. The only problem was that the basement of the new building was completely submerged in water.

From the beginning, there was nobody to turn to for assistance, either in investigating the whereabouts of the missing treasures, or in draining the new building so that we could take a look. The governing body, the Coalition Provisional Authority (CPA), had no law-enforcement agents, and they were still moving into Four-Head Palace, at the same time struggling with the more pressing issues of restoring water, food, electricity, and some semblance of law and order to Baghdad. Steve knew underwater demolition, but scuba equipment was hard to come by in Baghdad, all the more so during a land war.

Sensing an opportunity, Jason Williams, the filmmaker for National Geographic, said, "I'll pump it, but I need an exclusive."

This was May 9. "You've got yourself a deal," I said, without really thinking it through. After all, the "permission" was not exactly mine to give. Jason knew that I didn't have the authority to approve the pumping. And I knew he knew. But we also knew that it was the right thing to do and that time was of the essence. So, we shook hands as, perhaps, our very different forebears had done countless times before in different eras, in different regions of the world. Only this time we weren't dividing up the land of some conquered people, we were trying to get newly freed people back their treasure. Immediately, Jason hired some local labor and started pumping out the water, diesel fuel, and debris from the wreckage above.

By May 14, we had located yet another informant, and we went back to the new building to do what we had done countless times before. Several members of the team were with me, and another group was already there. Right away we were set upon by a man who, even before he told me his name, informed me that he was "the senior Treasury agent in Iraq." It's always a dangerous sign when someone tells you *what* they are before they tell you *who* they are. Of course, the use of the definite article *the* in any introduction is also usually an indication of bad things to come.

He walked up wearing one of those "shoot me first" khaki vests popular with visiting politicians and the Coalition Provisional Authority, an accessory meant to add a little panache, I suppose, to those eight-by-ten glossies destined for the wall back in the office.

"What do you think you're doing?" he asked us.

I said, "Sir, I am conducting an investigation."

He immediately ripped back into me, asking who authorized me to conduct an investigation.

My first thought was "Whoa there, big fella." The third rule of confrontation is to take your time. You never want to go too far too fast—unless you have no choice—because once you're there, you can't back up without backing down. In a confrontation, the key is about finding common ground, a stance you can both live with. Backing down never gets you there because you feel "had," and it makes the other guy think that he can get more.

But here for the third time in two days—the French and Japanese incidents had been the previous day—somebody in a position of importance was going from zero to sixty in about two seconds, and directing all that energy at me. If you asked yourself, "What's the common denominator here?" you might come up with Colonel Matthew Bogdanos. And I will admit that I tend to bring out that kind of aggression in some people. But it's usually part of an overall plan, and I certainly don't try to bring out that reaction in my "superiors." As a military officer, I am not in the habit of dissing authority, and I thought this Treasury guy outranked me. Of course, like the French diplomat, he wasn't really seeing *me*. He was seeing Donald Rumsfeld. He was seeing the Pentagon and the entire military command structure trying to bully him out of doing his job. Back home, he was an accountant, but here he was "the senior Treasury agent in Iraq," and maybe for the first time in his life it was as if he had a set of balls and was feeling the funk. But it may also have been because I was so deferential that this little weenie thought he could take the first alpha-male moment of his life and run with it. And run he did. I asked him if he wouldn't mind walking away from the crowd (and I had slowly been inching away, hoping he'd follow). But it was as if these were his fifteen minutes of fame and he wasn't going to be deprived of them.

His assistant was an Army captain. He and I made eye contact, and then out of respect for me, he turned around and stepped out of earshot. He couldn't bear what he was hearing. "Sir, I have a witness and I want him to corroborate his story."

He screamed back at me that we weren't going anywhere near the vault because he had heard that we blew up bank vaults all the time.

I was going to tell him that we hadn't blown a bank vault since Basra, but I decided that this wasn't the time. Instead, I said, "Sir, I have no intention of blowing up a bank vault here. I'm trying to track down antiquities removed from the museum."

He puffed up like a frog, then croaked out that there was no way he would allow it, sending forth a mouthful of spittle.

I said, "Sir, I have to conduct my investigation," still treating him as I would a superior officer.

He gave me his best, most intense stare, then said that if I set one foot inside that bank I will be out of the country by the end of the day.

I thought, well, that's a distinct possibility, but what am I going to do? Superior or not, "the senior Treasury official" was not in my chain of command. So strictly speaking, he could not order me to do or not do anything. He could, however, get me in a lot of trouble. So I nodded respectfully, then escorted my witness on past him into the bank.

At that point, there was little reason to stop. If he had any juice with Bremer, I was already screwed. Neither Major General Renuart nor

General Franks was going to test the lines of authority to go to bat for me. So I figured I had at most twenty-four hours. And even if this weenie didn't somehow pressure the military into pulling me out, it was going to mean the end of my freedom of action. With General Renuart, like General Harrell before him, the procedure had always been, "Matthew, you don't need to ask permission to do something. Do what you think is right. Just let me know what you did." The unwritten premise is that you never want to force your boss to screw himself by saying yes or to screw you by saying no. So you don't ask.

But here this guy was ripping me a new asshole, and I took it because I thought he held rank. A day or two later, when I found out he was only a GS-15, meaning we were basically equivalent—one military, one civilian—I was incensed. For about a nanosecond, I considered "talking" to him in private, but it wouldn't have served any purpose.

This two-day period, with the Japanese diplomatic note and the dressing-downs from the UN guy and the Treasury weenie, truly was the low point of my time in Iraq. And it was about to get worse.

Rich Jakucs, my number two back in Qatar, was becoming more insistent that we stop the museum mission and turn our attention full-time to counterterrorist operations. I knew that the museum investigation was going to take more, not less, of my time, and that the day would come when the other missions would suffer.

To stop this from happening, I realized that, at least in the short term, we needed two deputies, me and someone else. Rich had been with me the longest, and we'd been friends for fifteen years. But I had another colonel in Tampa, and my gut told me he'd be the perfect fit. U.S. Army colonel Mike Dietz had been a Fort Lauderdale cop for twenty-three years before he was recalled to active duty and assigned to me at the end of 2002. He'd commanded troops in Bosnia, and he had a fundamental decency and core of common sense that had always impressed me. He'd even gone through Marine Officer Candidate School in 1973, but like John Durkin, he was offered a better deal by the Army. So he took it.

Whichever of the two wasn't appointed deputy would probably spend the rest of his tour in Qatar or Tampa, but not in Iraq, where the action was. To a military officer, not to be able to march to the sound of the guns is devastating. Whatever decision I made, I owed it to both of them to do it in person. I needed another half a dozen vehicles and about twenty or thirty more people anyway, so I asked both of them to bring a convoy up to Baghdad.

Before Oliver Wendell Holmes was a Supreme Court justice, he was a damn good Army officer in the American Civil War. He observed that the "prize of the general is not a bigger tent, but command." I was already pretty sure that Mike would be my choice, so I put Rich at the head of the convoy to give him his moment of command. They made it without incident, but when they arrived, I could see that Rich was spent. Six months of insane hours in Qatar had taken their toll. I told each of them privately that Mike would be the acting deputy in my absence, and that he would be my choice as permanent deputy when I left.

It didn't make it any easier to break the news, but it was the right decision and we all knew it. Over two years later, Mike Dietz is still the deputy.

I also decided that it was time to move up two press conferences that were already in the works. With the threat of expulsion looming, I wanted these events as closure. On the other hand, I thought just maybe, if the press conferences were on the docket, I might not get kicked out because it would look bad.

The first of these was a live broadcast on May 16 for the Pentagon's daily briefing from the video-conferencing facility in Saddam's palace. And the second was a press conference in the museum courtyard later the same night. Victoria Clarke, assistant secretary of defense for public affairs, had set these in motion after an e-mail exchange with General Renuart. One of them had said, oh, by the way, this guy can talk and we need a good news story. For the video feed to Washington I needed to use the Coalition Provisional Authority's equipment, but when I walked into Four-Head Palace to set it up, an Army colonel I had never met before said, "What the hell do you want?"

I said, "Excuse me?"

He said, "We all know who you are. What do you want here?"

I said, "This is the approach you take with people when you first meet them?"

Obviously, he had heard about the exchange with the Treasury guy—no doubt over a few frosty ones at the palace cantina—because he repeated many of the same phrases almost word for word. But there also seemed to be an underlying resentment primed, I think, because the people here couldn't so much as leave the palace grounds without permission. Every trip across town was three phone calls and two reports in triplicate. Not only did I have a freedom on the field of battle unknown to them, but my men and I were about to get some public recognition. Usually the only time a bureaucrat gets to see himself on TV is if he's been indicted.

The irony is that these kinds of rivalries and resentments had led to our initial impulse to stay under the radar. But by now publicity had become an essential tool for carrying out the mission. We had started out with a deep "credibility deficit" created by the widely inaccurate initial reporting—and it wasn't just the 170,000 number. The *Daily Telegraph* reported, "Twenty-six statues of Assyrian kings, all 2,000 years old, had been decapitated." Every one of the heads depicted in the accompanying photograph and all of the ones in the vaults were "as it is" *before* the war and none of them had been stolen. There were exactly five heads stolen from the museum, and all five were from Greek and Roman pieces from the Hatran galleries. But only one of them had been decapitated by the looters. The other four heads had been severed long before. Later, the director-general of UNESCO held a press conference in which he claimed that the Iraq Museum's entire collection of eighty thousand cuneiform tablets had been stolen. It would have been devasting . . . if true. In fact, that entire collection was secure and undamaged.

In truth, everything about the war had become politicized and "spun" long before we ever got to Baghdad. Everyone had his or her own agenda, which he or she then tried to piggyback onto whatever was happening. Even the excellent new translation of *The Epic of Gilgamesh* couldn't resist a footnote describing how the ancient king had preemptively attacked a monster, and how we might learn a lesson from that.

On the museum front, we had been trying to overcome all the initial confusion, and find the middle course, working for almost a month to convince both the "everything was taken" critics and the "nothing was taken" skeptics that both were wrong and that neither was serving any constructive purpose. We learned that the intensity with which people held on to the inflated numbers and certain other misperceptions was usually in direct proportion to the intensity of that person's opposition to the war. Similarly, the belief that nothing was stolen tended to rise in direct proportion to the intensity of that person's support for the war. As usual, the truth was somewhere in the middle.

With so many critics on both sides of the aisle, I decided that my press briefings should simply lay it all out there. Opinions are good, opinions are welcomed. But they should at least be based on facts. My goal with these two events, then, was nothing more than setting the record straight, getting the facts out to as many people as possible so that they could have an informed opinion. We did the big Pentagon briefing via video-teleconference, then we drove like hell across town to stand in front of the microphones at the museum and answer questions from the Baghdad press contingent. This time Donny George answered questions alongside me, exactly the way it should be.

I don't know if I can credit my scheduling strategy exactly, but I did make it through the next few days without expulsion, and then after all that airtime, the various raging rabbits quieted down. At least for a while, almost everyone seemed genuinely pleased. Once, I was doing a live feed with CNN that had originally been scheduled for two minutes when one of the studio anchors said, "Keep it running." On another occasion, I got word that a CNN executive had remarked, "The colonel turned a public relations disaster of global proportions into the only success story of the war."

Afterward, the Pentagon public affairs office starting forwarding me e-mails of requests for further interviews. "A positive spin like I've never seen in all the time I've been here," one of them said. "A great bounce," they explained, in PR lingo. Once again, my expectations were backward. One of the reasons I had done the press conferences was to be able to stay in Baghdad. My reward for progress and the good PR? To be pulled away on a press junket just as things were looking up.

It is in the nature of the profession of arms that "good-byes" are frequent and often final. There is, of course, the ever-present possibility of getting killed. Live every day as if it were going to be your last, Byron once noted. For one day you are sure to be right.

But there is also the understanding that you each have your own life and family to go back to in the "world." And even if you do "keep in touch," it'll never be with the same intensity, and it'll never again be as pure as it was when I had your "six," your six o'clock, your back, and you had mine.

So we never take our good-byes for granted. We're not morbid or melodramatic about them; just serious.

Thus, although I knew that I would be back in a few days, I rounded up Senior, Steve, Bud, John, and a couple others to say good-bye. "That a man might know the end of this day's business before it comes," I began, walking up to each man and shaking his hand as I was speaking. "But it suffices that the day will end and then the end is known." Bud recognized the lines from *Julius Caesar* and smiled at me as if to say, "Good choice."

"And whether we shall meet again, I know not. Therefore our everlasting farewell take. . . . If we do meet again, why, we shall smile. If not, why then, this parting was well made."

12

OF HAMMERED GOLD

What is now proved was once only imagin'd.—William Blake

EVERYONE WHO TRAVELS military class has a favorite seat on a C-130. We tell ourselves that no shoulder-fired antiaircraft missile—a Stinger, for instance—has ever taken down one of these lumbering giants. But choosing a seat, like so much else you do in a combat zone, is all about the role probability plays in your particular belief system. I think that sitting closest to the cockpit is probably the safest because a ground-based shooter is not going to lead enough to hit anything but the tail. But that is not why I prefer to sit up front. I choose the front, specifically the second seat—not the very first—because there's a window, and during the day, it gives great light for reading.

As it turned out, the C-130 for my flight out of Baghdad had recently taken a hit from a 12.7 mm anti-aircraft gun—probably a Soviet-made DShKM-38/46. The hole was still visible. More to the point, it had struck and killed the guy who had been sitting in my favorite seat. The crew maintained a kind of gallows humor about it. They weren't taking the man's death lightly, but what are you going to do? Everyone thought Zorba was nuts when his son died and he danced on the grave, but he would have gone crazy if he had not danced.

This was an Australian plane. In a hot LZ, Aussie pilots follow the op-

posite strategy from the Americans. They go for miles along the con-
tours of the earth, staying under the radar of surface-to-air missiles,
called SAMs. "I don't worry about small arms," the pilot told me, "I
just don't want to be hit with a SAM." However reasonable this
approach, it had not worked out so well for the guy who had been sitting in my seat. Testing the laws of probability even further, this flight
would be making two stops in northern Iraq to pick up Special Forces
guys before heading south toward Kuwait. This was, however, the only
C-130 scheduled to leave Baghdad that day.

My psychological options were "bad juju" versus "lightning never
strikes twice." I was already moving for my usual seat before they told
me about the bullet hole, and damned if I was going to change course
and admit that I was spooked. I pulled out my book and sat where I always sit.

I didn't start reading right away, however. Looking out the window
and across the runway, thinking about this insanely ancient and exotic
town, I actually felt a little nostalgic. An hour or so before, as I had been
leaving the museum, Donny had come around to say good-bye, and we
had given each other a hug. I looked at him and could see he was upset. "Hey, what's the matter, brother? I'm only going for a few days. I'll
be back."

He nodded, and that was it. A reporter who had been nearby came
over after Donny left and said, "Donny was upset."

I shrugged. Then she said, "So, is he upset because he's afraid of losing
a friend, or is he worked up because he's afraid of losing a protector?"

"When did they stop being the same thing?" I asked.

We taxied down the runway and took off low, Australian style, and I
leaned back and opened my book, but then I realized that this was the
first time since we'd crossed the border into Iraq that I didn't have to be
ready to act at any given moment. You don't have to be Wordsworth to
realize that a little tranquillity can improve your ability to think straight.
There was a lot to think about. We banked left and I looked down over
the Tigris. Then I pulled out my Day-Timer, a pen, and my commander's notebook.

With the threat of court-martial and expulsion off my back, it was
time for me to start figuring out what I had, and what I knew—the
pattern in the pattern recognition. Back in the States, the questions
from the press were not going to get any easier than they had been in
Baghdad, and if not for the reporters, then just for myself, I wanted to

use the flying time—six hours on the first leg alone—to sum up the state of play so far.

But beyond any analysis of the looting and our ongoing plans for recovery, there were other, larger questions that needed to be sorted out once and for all. U.S. forces had taken a lot of heat in the beginning. The "Why didn't you prevent the looting?" question had emerged right from the start, during the period that British columnist David Aaronovitch had summed up with "You cannot say anything too bad about the Yanks and not be believed."

I thought about the Swedish paper that had quoted a man they said "happened to be there just as U.S. forces told people to commence looting." The story was translated into English and posted around the world. This sole source, however, had gone to Baghdad to act as a human shield in opposition to the invasion—the kind of blatant bias, motive to misrepresent, and conflict of interest that generally discredits a witness in the legal system. Reputable journalism usually takes that kind of bias into account and moves on as well, but the very next day, CNN's Jim Clancy reported, "There have been rumors that U.S. Marines were involved in this [the looting] opening the doors to the museum." What CNN neglected to mention was that no U.S. Marines were stationed anywhere near the museum. The most outrageous account, however, had come from a German publication that quoted an alleged witness who said he had seen American troops—and Kuwaitis, for some reason—loading artifacts onto military trucks and driving away, surrounded by "armored cars." "They broke open the side door and stayed inside for a while. Then they shouted to the people gathering outside, 'Come in!' That's how the looting began."

The academics had weighed in too. I particularly liked one of Professor Eleanor Robson's comments because they were wrong in every respect. In an article ironically entitled "Iraq's Museums: What Really Happened," she reported, "Fedayeen broke into a storage room and set up a machine gun nest at a window." In fact, no one broke in. As we determined, the doors were opened with keys. And the men in there were not fedayeen; they were Iraqi Army, probably Special Republican Guard. And, while I'm sure it's six of one, half a dozen of another to most Oxford dons, it was not a machine gun nest, but a sniper position.

Almost immediately, these journalists and scholars with no experience in, and a healthy contempt for, the military, also started offering opinions on the tactics U.S. forces should have employed. When asked

about the looting, Elizabeth Stone, a specialist in Iraqi archaeology at
the State University of New York, told the *Guardian*, "You have got to
kill some people to stop this." So who exactly was supposed to shoot
these unarmed civilians—me and my men?

The galvanizing symbol of our perception problem, however, had to
be the giant hole above the entrance to the Children's Museum. That
hole made a great photograph, and it was almost invariably offered as a
sign of American callousness. Hardly anyone reported why that hole
had come to be there—which was Iraqis firing rocket-propelled
grenades at our tanks from that building's rooftop.

But mostly, journalists and archaeologists who had never before
heard a shot fired in anger still fixated on the question of why U.S.
forces, in particular, Task Force 1-64, could not have moved just one
of its tanks just five hundred yards closer to protect the museum.
"All it would have taken was a tank parked at the gate," said Jane
Waldbaum, president of the American Institute of Archaeology.

So why had the United States not "done more" to protect the museum? Between Senior's Googling, our team's hundreds of interviews,
and my countless hours of forensic examinations of the entire museum
compound—inside and out—here's what I knew.

Two months before the war began, in January 2003, the Archaeological Institute of America had called on "all governments" to protect
cultural sites in the event of an invasion. A group of scholars, museum
directors, and antiquities dealers also met with Pentagon officials to discuss their fears about the threat to the museum's collection. McGuire
Gibson of the University of Chicago's Oriental Institute went back
twice more, and he and his colleagues continued to barrage DOD officials with e-mail reminders. They could not have done more.

As a cautionary tale, Gibson cited what had happened during and immediately after the first Gulf War. In 1991, during the bombing of
Baghdad, allied forces had been scrupulously precise in avoiding Iraqi
cultural sites. One attack completely leveled the telecommunications
facility across the street, but put only a shrapnel dent in the Iraq Museum's front door, while also dislodging a ceiling tile. But the end of
the first war against Saddam unleashed a wave of looting at archaeological sites across Iraq, which fed an already sophisticated network for
smuggling, which in turn thrived on artifacts from poorly guarded sites
being dug up and hauled away. "We wanted to make sure this didn't
happen again," Gibson told the *Washington Post*.

Gibson and his colleagues were heard. But only partly. The Pentagon ordered the Iraq Museum placed on the coalition's no-strike list, and CENTCOM obliged, listing it as #3. But the planners had no idea of the extent to which the average Iraqi viewed the museum as Saddam's gift shop. Accordingly, they did not anticipate that the museum—unlike the poorly guarded archaeological sites—would be ransacked or, for that matter, looted. Even museum officials, who brought in sand-bags and foam-rubber padding against possible bomb damage, were caught by surprise. Donny George told the *Wall Street Journal*, "We thought there would be some sort of bombing at the museum. We never thought it could be looted."

Some critics made a big deal about how we protected the oil min-istry, but not the museum. What they failed to take into account is that to "secure" a building in combat, you usually have to physically occupy it, at least temporarily. If the building is fortified, that means a battle. In this comparison, there are three facts that such critics blithely ignored. First, the "securing" of the oil ministry began with U.S. air strikes on April 9. It was a lawful target, and we dropped a bomb on it. We were not going to bomb the museum. Second, the oil ministry did not con-tain soldiers—it had not been turned into a fortress that housed people who were trying to kill us. The museum was filled with Republican Guards shooting at Americans with automatic weapons and tank-killer rocket-propelled grenades. Finally, the oil ministry is just one building—the coalition "secured" it in less than an hour. The museum was an eleven-acre complex of interconnecting and overlapping buildings and courtyards. Securing it would have required a serious firefight that would likely have reduced the place to expensive rubble. Comparing the museum with the oil ministry, then, is comparing apples and elephants.

The law of armed conflict holds that cultural property should be protected against any act of hostility. But the same international agree-ments that protect cultural property—the Geneva Convention of 1949 and its two protocols of 1977, and the Hague Convention of 1954 and its two protocols of 1954 and 1999—*absolutely prohibit* the military use of otherwise protected cultural sites, specifying that such sites lose their protections when so used.

In clear violation of those provisions, the Iraqi Army had turned the museum into a fortress. Hussein's elite Special Republican Guard was stationed across the street. The RPG position at the Children's Museum was aimed toward a traffic circle, offering an unobstructed field of fire on the high-speed avenue of approach that ran in front of the compound. That street, running between the museum and the Special Republican Guard facility, led to the strategically important al-Ahrar Bridge across the Tigris, nine hundred meters away. The sniper's position in the aboveground storage room provided a perfect flanking shot on any U.S. forces moving through the marketplace to reinforce any battle in front of the museum. The sniper's window also overlooked the ten-foot wall that protected soldiers running from the battle position in the back to the battle positions in the front courtyard. Each of those fighting holes, equipped with dirt ramparts and aiming sticks, provided interlocking fire.

All of this was run from the makeshift command post that had been set up in the back of the museum compound. And all of it took months to prepare. The museum staff, of course, had to have participated. But was their participation willing or unwilling? Did they fill sandbags right alongside the soldiers? Did they object to the fortifications, fearing that such preparations would lead to a destructive battle? Or did they merely acquiesce, knowing the penalty for defying the regime?

Nawala denied knowing anything at all about military preparations—and it made no sense to press her on that issue. But Donny admitted that during the invasion he handed out guns to the staff. Individual staff members say that he told them to use the weapons to shoot Americans; he says he handed out the guns to protect against looters—the same looters he told the *Wall Street Journal* he thought weren't coming. The fact is, Donny had done nothing illegal: he was entirely within his rights to hand out guns to shoot either invaders or armed looters.

I came back to Sherlock Holmes's "eliminate the impossible and whatever remains, however improbable, must be the truth." So what did remain? Writing in my notebook, I worked out a timeline for what the evidence told me happened before, during, and after the fighting near the museum.

On the morning of April 8, armed Iraqi soldiers took up their previously prepared firing positions in the museum compound. The museum staff, including all museum guards, had already left, decamping when U.S. forces hit the outskirts of the city on April 5. The only exceptions were Dr. Jaber and Donny, along with a driver and an elderly archaeologist who lived in the rear of the museum compound. They had planned to stay throughout the invasion, but decided to leave when they realized the level of violence that was imminent.

The violence in question was, in fact, part of a brilliant campaign to attack Baghdad from the inside out. With all the Iraqi defenses facing the perimeter, General Tommy Franks had opted for "thunder runs" into the center of the city with tanks and mechanized infantry. Desperately hoping to avoid a Stalingrad situation of siege warfare or guerrilla resistance, with potential casualties in the tens of thousands, coalition forces would race through the center of town with an armored force, overwhelming the enemy with speed and power and probing for weak spots. They would then work back out toward the edge of town, repeating the tactic as often as necessary. In the event, only two thunder runs were required. By outstripping the ability of the Iraqi forces to react, this emphasis on speed—although it bypassed large pockets of resistance and left large areas unprotected—saved lives. Crumbling from the inside out, Baghdad fell in days instead of months. One of these "thunder runs" ran directly in front of the museum. And the intensity of the fighting in the vicinity of the museum and the Special Republican Guard compound opposite it was directly proportional to this area's strategic importance.

At approximately eleven A.M. on April 8, after ensuring that all of the doors to the museum and the storage rooms were locked, the four museum staffers left through the rear exit, locking it behind them. They then crossed the Tigris into eastern Baghdad, hoping to return later the same day. As they left, the nearest U.S. forces were about fifteen hundred meters west of the museum, receiving heavy mortar fire as they proceeded in the direction of the museum. When Donny and his colleagues from the museum tried to come back several hours later, heavy fighting pinned them down on the other side of the river.

On April 9, a tank company from Task Force 1-64, the only U.S. unit in that part of Baghdad, moved to an intersection about five hundred meters west and slightly south of the museum. Their orders were to keep that crossroads open as a lifeline to support U.S. forces engaged in combat in the northern part of the city. Throughout that day, they took fire from the Children's Museum, the main building, the library, and the building to the rear of the museum that had previously been used as a police station. The tank company commander on the scene, U.S. Army captain Jason Conroy, estimated that approximately 100 to 150 enemy fighters were within the museum compound firing on U.S. forces. Some of these fighters were dressed in Special Republican Guard uniforms and some in civilian clothes. They were carrying RPGs or AK-47s.

Later, many neighborhood residents told Roger Atwood, who was writing for the *Wall Street Journal*, that "the Americans had come under attack from inside the museum grounds and that fighting in the area was heavy." They told me the same story, but they were merely confirming what the museum grounds and its spent shell casings and RPGs had already told me: This was a fiercely contested battleground. Indeed, the fighting was so heavy that for forty-eight hours, between April 8 and 10, some U.S. soldiers in Task Force 1-64's C Company never left the inside of their tanks.

According to several accounts from nearby residents, it was during this time—on the ninth—that two Iraqi Army vehicles drove up to the back of the museum (near where the impromptu command post had been) and spent several hours loading boxes from the museum onto the vehicles before they left. On the following day, April 10, Second Lieutenant Erik Balascik's platoon received word of looting "in the area of the museum and the hospital." They passed this information up to the Task Force 1-64 commander, Lieutenant Colonel Eric Schwartz, who ordered them to move closer to investigate. As soon as they did so, they began receiving intense fire from the compound. Because of that fire, and because, from their position to the west, the Children's Museum blocked their view into the main compound, they never advanced close enough to determine what was actually going on within the compound, let alone within the galleries and the storage areas of the museum itself.

By going to investigate, the platoon had created what American law calls an "attractive nuisance." The Americans' mere presence was drawing direct fire from the Children's Museum. This forced one of the tanks to fire a single round in return from its 120 mm main gun, which took out the RPG position, put the hole in the Children's Museum, captured the world's attention, and inflamed the critics.

What critics fail to consider is that when you take direct fire, under anyone's rules of engagement you fire back—no further discussion. No need to check with the boss. And because the Iraqis had fortified this cultural site and were firing at him from it, Second Lieutenant Balascik and his company commander, Captain Conroy, would have been entirely justified in taking any steps necessary to eliminate the threat. With the approval of the task force commander, they could have called in air support, dropped a two-thousand-pound bomb, and turned the entire compound and its contents to rubble. But even if they had simply stood their ground and fought back with ground-based supporting fire, there would have been nothing left of the museum either to save or to loot.

Instead of conducting such an assault to "save" the museum, the moment that Schwartz—a former high school teacher—was informed of the situation, he made the tactically wrong but culturally brilliant decision to pull back those tanks from the museum. This was the only way to avoid the Hobson's choice between endangering his men and destroying the institution. It took real courage to pull back. It took real courage in the face of a hundred Special Republican Guard soldiers to hold fire. Because few journalists, not to mention archaeologists, understand military tactics, Lieutenant Colonel Schwartz, Captain Conroy, and Second Lieutenant Balascik generally get no credit for this. As I planned my comments for upcoming interviews, I wanted to give them that credit.

One of the residents we interviewed said that the looters—estimated by some witnesses to number between three or four hundred at their height—first appeared at the museum on the evening of April 10, entering through the back of the compound. If this single source was accurate, his account strongly suggests that the original fighters had left the museum by that date—April 10. There was, however, still intense fighting around the museum on the morning of the eleventh. It was on that day, at the intersection directly in front of the museum compound, that Captain Conroy's tank company destroyed an Iraqi Army truck and a Bronevaya Maschina Piekhota (BMP), a Soviet-built armored fighting vehicle. This fighting in the front of the compound on the eleventh prevented U.S. forces from either approaching the museum or determining that enemy forces no longer occupied the museum itself. The eleventh was, however, the last day that fighting was reported near the museum.

On the afternoon of the twelfth, the museum staff came back, courageously chasing looters from the museum, a moment famously captured by a German film crew. The soldiers had already left, but had they retreated an hour before, or the day before? It is entirely possible, especially considering all the uniforms lying around, that some of the looters carrying out antiquities had been in uniform and carrying AK-47s only hours—or even minutes—earlier. We simply don't know. Regardless of

when this retreat took place, however, it cannot be overstated how difficult it was for U.S. forces on the ground to have known when the last
fighter left, and whether it was safe to enter without a battle that would
destroy the museum. I rarely knew what was happening one hundred
meters away—let alone on the other side of an eleven-acre compound.

Some critics have contended that if journalists were able to get into
the museum on the twelfth, military forces should have been able to do
the same on that day or even on the eleventh. With rare exceptions,
however, journalists are not shot at simply because of who they are.
Putting on a military uniform makes anyone a lawful target. Journalists, protected—officially at least—by their "noncombatant" status, are
generally able to move more freely on the battlefield in order to report
on the conflict. This is not to suggest that journalists aren't vulnerable
to random fire, or that being a combat journalist doesn't take guts, or
that journalists are never targeted illegally. Rather, it is to point out that
neither journalists nor combatants should be judged by the distinct restrictions placed on, or the distinct freedoms enjoyed by, the other.

The only way uniformed military could have entered a compound
the size of the museum's is with guns blazing or by a "reconnaissance
in force." This means having troops advance in the hope that they don't
get shot. If no one shoots at them, it suggests that the building is clear.
Either that or it's an ambush. But if they *had* been fired on from the
museum, they would have been forced to call in supporting arms—
tanks, mortars, and crew-served weapons. In fact, even to prepare the
reconnaissance, the commander would have been obligated to request
preplanned targets (which means approved in advance by headquarters)
inside the museum compound. Because the museum was on the no-
strike list, any request for preplanned targets would have been denied,
and any soldiers would have had to enter unsupported—with the risk
that the football-field-sized open area between the compound wall and
the buildings would become a killing ground.

By April 12, the fighting in Baghdad had subsided, and the damage to
the museum and its holdings was done. Once the staff was back on-site
to guard the museum, there was no more looting.

On the afternoon of the twelfth and then again on the thirteenth,
with the compound no longer a battlefield, Donny George and others
approached Task Force 1-64, the Army tank unit, and asked for help.
That much is fact. But surrounding those simple requests for assistance,
an urban legend grew up, the Legend of the Heartless Tank Crew.

The legend began in the *New York Times* with the account of an archaeologist named Raid Abdul Ridhar Muhammad, who supposedly "went into the street in the Karkh district, a short distance from the eastern bank of the Tigris, about 1 p.m. on Thursday [April 10] to find American troops to quell the looting . . . Mr. Muhammad said that he had found an American Abrams tank in Museum Square, about 300 yards away, and that five Marines had followed him back into the museum and opened fire above the looters' heads. That drove several thousand of the marauders out of the museum complex in minutes, he said, but when the tank crewmen left about 30 minutes later, the looters returned."

It made for a sensational story that justified its front-page placement, but the account is geographically impossible and internally inconsistent. To put it more bluntly, the evidence strongly suggests that it never happened. The *Times* report had Muhammad going "a short distance from the eastern bank of the Tigris . . . to find American troops." However, the Iraq Museum is not on the eastern bank of the Tigris, but nine hundred meters *west* of the river. Assuming that "Muhammad" existed at all and did what he said he did, he had to have been talking about some other museum. The only one possible is the Baghdad Museum (containing twentieth-century artifacts), on Mamoun Street, which is, in fact, "a short distance from the eastern bank of the Tigris." Any reporter working in Baghdad in April 2003 knew, or at least should have known, the difference between the Iraq Museum in Baghdad's al-Karkh district, on the western side of the Tigris, and the Baghdad Museum in Baghdad's al-Rusafa district, on the eastern side of the Tigris.

This obvious error in geography helps to explain many other problems with the story. Despite Muhammad's claim to having found five Marines "300 yards away," there were no Marines near the Iraq Museum on April 10—it was not their sector. There were, however, Marines assigned to the *eastern* side of the Tigris, where the Baghdad Museum is located.

The sector in which the Iraq Museum is located was assigned to Captain Conroy's tank company. They were the only unit in the vicinity of the museum on April 10 and were still engaged in combat on that day. They did report that an unknown Iraqi approached them—on April 10—and told them of looting "in the vicinity of the hospital and the museum." Immediately thereafter, a second Iraqi approached the same tank crew and told them to shoot the first Iraqi because he was fedayeen. Then both men ran away. When the crew reported this slightly surreal encounter—the fog of war in all its glory—they were ordered to advance toward the museum to investigate. That is when they drew fire from the Children's Museum, fired the single round in response, and then pulled back.

But there are other flaws in the Muhammad story that appear obvious to anyone who knows the first thing about the military. Military personnel follow orders. They don't wander off on their own just to see what's going on down the block. No soldier or Marine would ever—as the article claims—have left his battle position, during combat, to follow an unknown informant into a potential ambush. Even the number of "Marines" alleged to have followed him (five) rings false: a fire team (the smallest tactical unit), like a tank crew, has four men.

Finally, the *Times* description of "thousands of men, women, and children" in the crowd contradicts every other witness we ever interviewed about the looting, every one of whom numbered the crowd at fewer than four hundred. There have never been any reports of children, and although some of the looters appear to have had rifles (former fighters?), not a single other witness ever reported seeing the colorful "rifles, pistols, axes, knives and clubs."

But the legend was already born, and legends spawn sequels, and the details change with each telling. In the *New York Times*, the request for assistance came on April 10, but the *Guardian* soon shifted it to April 11: "The Americans returned with tanks at one point on Friday [April 11] and sent the looters fleeing, but as soon as the tanks rumbled away, the gangs came back to finish the job." Then it became April 12: "[A] single tank crew responded . . . for about 30 minutes on April 12." Then, as in a kids' "choose your own adventure" game, the assistance seeker became a "shape-shifter." In the *New York Times*, he was Muhammad. Then he became "Muhsin, the guard [who] tried to convince the American tank crew positioned nearby to come and protect the museum—they came once and drove off the looters but refused to remain." Eventually, he became "museum staff and journalists in Baghdad [who] repeatedly urged American tank crews to go and protect the museum until they finally went for half an hour to chase away looters." In other accounts, the tank crew never even moved at all: "One tank crew was within 50 yards of the building . . . but its commanders refused emotional pleas from museum staff to move any closer."

Like the earlier controversy over the number of looted items, the Legend of the Heartless Tank Crew says far more about the quality of some of the early reporting than it does about what really happened at the museum.

Among the few solid facts to emerge from all this urban folklore, however, is that on the twelfth and thirteenth, Donny and others *did* seek help from an army tank unit on the street, as well as from a lieutenant colonel at the Palestine Hotel.

So why didn't U.S. forces just do what Donny and others asked and move a tank closer to the museum?

First of all, you can't just go hail a tank the way you hail a taxi. Unless you're requesting a suicide mission, you need a tank platoon. What Monday morning field marshals like Jane Waldbaum—an excellent archaeologist but a lousy tactician—do not understand is that a single, stationary tank is a death trap. While intimidating to look at, tanks are far from invulnerable—one well-placed round from an antitank weapon and you would need to use dog tags to identify the charred remains of the four men inside. The only way a tank can survive in combat, especially urban combat, is by virtue of speed and maneuverability, and by the firepower provided by other tanks. You have to have, at the least, tanks in pairs. You also need a squad of infantry alongside them, because tanks have blind spots. But mostly, once you draw fire, you have to return fire until you have eliminated the threat—right down to the plumbing in the basement—if that's what it takes to protect your men.

Okay, so it's not as simple as sending in a tank. Then why not send in some ground troops instead? Committing "just" ground troops would have been criminally irresponsible on the part of the commander, whose obligation is to protect the lives of the men under his command. A proper military assault would have required supporting arms. And this once again brings us back to the specter of the museum reduced to rubble.

Moreover, if their mere presence had not dispersed the crowd what would these ground troops have done, anyway—shoot the looters? Perhaps the critics would like to have been there with an M16, mowing down the local residents swarming through the museum. But people who know the law of war know that deadly force can only be used in response to a hostile act or a demonstration of hostile intent. Shooting unarmed looters in civilian clothes who were not presenting a risk to human life would have been a violation of the law of armed conflict and prosecutable for murder under Article 118 of the Uniform Code of Military Justice.

Well, couldn't they have just fired some itsy-bitsy warning shots?

Here we see the influence of movies on assumptions about what is possible in a law enforcement or military engagement. A warning shot only works if you are a member of the Screen Actors Guild. In real life, firing a weapon merely escalates the situation, usually causing unarmed participants to arm themselves, which once again means drawing return fire. Moreover, the bullets fired from the muzzle of a weapon—be they "warning shots" or shots aimed at center mass—do not just disappear into the ether. Eventually, they come back to earth and hit something—often with fatal effect—which happens all the time when revelers fire celebratory shots into the air during holidays and weddings.

The bottom line here is that any suggestion that U.S. forces could have done more than they did to secure the museum before the twelfth is based on wishful thinking rather than on any rational appreciation of military tactics, the reality of the conflict on the ground, the law of war, or the laws of physics. "If I'd raced up from south Baghdad to the museum, I'd have had a lot of dead soldiers outside the museum," the tank commander for this sector, Lieutenant Colonel Eric Schwartz, told the BBC. "It wasn't the museum anymore—it was a fighting position."

The blame for the looting must lie squarely on the looters. But the blame for creating chaos at the museum from the eighth through the evening of the eleventh, that allowed the looting to occur must lie with the Iraqi Army. It was they who chose to take up fighting positions within the museum, they who chose to fire on the American tanks, and they who kept American forces from investigating the reports they had received of looting "in the area of the museum." But after the eleventh, the blame does shift to the U.S.

The U.S. Army showed up to secure the compound at ten A.M. on the morning of the sixteenth. This force consisted of our future roommates from C Company. If critics want to question U.S. reaction, the delay between the twelfth to the sixteenth is fair game. I will go one step further: this delay was inexcusable. Although nothing was taken during this period, that does not make the indictment any less valid—because our forces had no way of knowing that looters wouldn't come back. You can thank the museum staff for guarding the compound for those four days and not the U.S. military.

This leaves us with the more pointed question—the one that is never asked: Before the battle, why was no unit assigned the specific mission of moving in to protect the museum the moment Baghdad was secure?

There are two basic kinds of orders in the military. The first is the standard type that directs a unit to achieve a specific objective at a specific time. "At 0800 tomorrow, you will seize the beachhead and advance to the cliff wall." Then there are the kinds of orders that warn a unit that they will be expected to achieve a specific objective at a time yet to be determined. This is a get-ready order, telling that unit to be prepared to execute that mission. Such be-prepared-to orders enable the commander on the ground to conduct proper reconnaissance, develop a tactical plan, and identify personnel and resources needed for the mission when it *is* ordered.

No such be-prepared-to-execute order was issued for the museum, and therefore no unit was either assigned or prepared to be assigned to secure it until the tank platoon showed up on the morning of the sixteenth. Why wasn't such an order issued? Why was there such a delay in responding to repeated requests for assistance on April 12 and 13? The answer is the same for both questions—and it is neither complicated nor entirely satisfactory.

Ultimately, the same "catastrophic success" on the battlefield that outstripped the ability of the Iraqi forces to react also outstripped the ability of coalition planners to anticipate security needs once Baghdad fell. In the case of the museum, this was exacerbated by a lack of a sense of urgency on the part of military planners, grounded in a failure to recognize the extent to which Iraqis identified the museum with the former regime. Thus, despite the prior warnings, planners simply did not believe that the museum—unlike the presidential palaces and governmental buildings that were more overt manifestations of the regime—would be looted. Even if they had properly planned for the museum, however, given the lack of sufficient forces in country, there would have been no spare units to assign anyway. As I said, not entirely satisfactory. But not sinister or callous either—just human error.

Along with pattern recognition, any forensic or criminal investigation requires an appreciation of the unity of time and place. Once I had the timeline for the fighting worked out, I began to use it as a template to sort through the rest of what had happened. I needed this structure to help explain the unfolding of the three distinctly different crimes: the thefts in the public galleries and restoration area, in the aboveground storage area, and in the basement storage area.

In Baghdad, we did not have access to the kind of judicial and governmental apparatus that would have allowed us to determine precisely how many missing antiquities had been stolen in the years or even decades before the war—though sources told us the number was high. Because the museum had been open to the public only once since 1991—on April 28, 2000, Saddam's birthday—and closed again shortly thereafter, we could not even turn to museum visitors for independent verification as to what was in the museum just prior to the arrival of coalition forces. So even when we were able to determine what was missing, we were not always able to determine—independent of what the staff told us—when it was *first* missing. This didn't affect our day-to-day operations, however, because our primary job was simply to get the stuff back.

In order to do *that*, though, we had to come up with three different investigative approaches to begin tracking down three different types of thieves—professionals, people off the street, and insiders. These three different categories of crooks had taken three different kinds of loot—marquee items from the galleries, random artifacts from the storage area, and high-value smaller pieces from the basement.

From the twenty-eight galleries and landings on two floors, and from the nearby restoration room, thieves stole forty of the museum's most treasured pieces. All evidence suggests that these marquee items were carefully chosen, implying that the thefts were professional. Whether or not these thieves were assisted by museum staff, the selection and removal of these items showed the mark of a professional. Likewise, the underworld connections necessary to move and sell these items required a level of professionalism beyond that of a low-level staff member or neighborhood looter. Indeed, we had been told that professionals had come in just before the war—possibly through Jordan—waiting for the fog of war and the opportunity of a lifetime.

One of the most telling clues to the professional eye of these thieves was that they passed right by the unmarked copies and lesser pieces and went straight for the highest-ticket items. There was one exhibit in particular that had twenty-seven cuneiform bricks running from Sumerian through Akkadian and Old Babylonian to New Babylonian. The nine most exquisite bricks were taken—selected from each time period—and all the others were left behind. That kind of selectivity happened repeatedly, also implying some measure of organization. Of course, some observers have given credit where it wasn't due, citing, for instance, the fact that the stela containing Hammurabi's code was untouched. But it would not have required a master thief to read the large sign next to the display telling anyone in Arabic and English that this is a copy, and that the original is in the Louvre.

Others used the discovery of a pair of glass cutters as further evidence of professionalism and the advance planning that goes with it. But this tool was a rusty relic that should have been junked long ago, and it was never used on any of the glass inside the museum. Moreover, why would a pro bother bringing along such a tool to a museum with neither a security system nor guards on the scene?

To me, the rusty glass cutters argued just the opposite—that while the professionals went about their business, they no doubt had to put up with any number of bumbling amateurs getting in their way. Would-be looters in off the street knocked over statues and, unsuccessfully, tried to drag them away on their foam-rubber padding. We could trace every single heavy piece that did leave the museum by following the trail of skid marks left in the floor. It's safe to say that these guys had never done this sort of thing before and had no idea what they were getting into. This is not to say that some random bumblers in the gallery area didn't get lucky. The guys who walked off with the Sacred Vase, after all, were average joes, not an experienced gang of thieves imported for the occasion.

Altogether, in the galleries, corridors, and nearby restoration room, twenty-five pieces or exhibits were damaged by this sort of activity, including eight clay pots, four statues, three sarcophagi, three ivory reliefs, two rosettes, and what remained of the Golden Harp of Ur. (Fortunately, the golden bull's head that was stolen from the harp while it lay in the restoration room was a modern replica. Unbeknownst to most of the staff, the original had been removed to the Central Bank of Iraq before the first Gulf War.) Sadly, one of the damaged statues was a two-foot-high terra-cotta lion from Tell Harmal dating from the Old Babylonian period of approximately 1800 B.C.

It is also safe to say that some of the thievery in the galleries had been carried out by a third category of persons. That so many pieces originally missing from the galleries "miraculously" showed up on the restoration-room floor strongly suggests that they had been lifted by sticky-fingered staff who later chose to take advantage of our amnesty program. Moreover, seven of the most precious items from the museum had been collected and left in the restoration room: the Golden Harp of Ur, the Mask of Warka, the Lioness Attacking a Nubian, two plates inlaid with shell depicting ritual scenes from the royal tombs of Ur (2600–2500 B.C.), a large ninth-century B.C. Assyrian ivory-relief headboard, and a ninth-century B.C. wheeled wooden firebox from

Nimrud. Although the room itself had two small safes that could have housed the Mask, the Lioness, and the plates, none of the objects were secured. Instead, everything was left on a table and stolen, except for the wooden body of the harp, a reproduction that was severely damaged, the fragments of its intricate ivory inlay left scattered across the room.

Dr. Chalabi offered the opinion that the forty big-ticket items that had been stolen from the galleries might have been bought and sold as part of a long-standing arrangement. He was probably right. They could have been ordered on the heels of the first Gulf War, with patient thieves waiting for the right moment. Of course, not many people in the world have the wealth, along with the perverse willingness, to spend $50 million on an object so conspicuously "hot" that they'd have to hide it in a secret vault in some secluded location. Accordingly, the trail to those big-ticket items would depend on monitoring a rarefied group of known buyers and on developing confidential sources within the art community, most of whom would be museum employees and university professors. But because potential whistle-blowers risked losing their jobs, the challenge was, first, to find them, and, second, to protect their identities. I knew we would also have to tighten borders in the hopes of interdicting the loot before it got to the collector.

From the two aboveground storage rooms, 3,138 excavation-site pieces (jars, vessels, pottery shards, etc.) were stolen—though I knew that number would surely grow by another one to two thousand when inventories were finally completed. Valuable in their own right, they were of significantly less value than the signature pieces that had been in the public galleries. This was largely the work of random looters— indiscriminate, or at least undiscerning. This is where we saw the traces in the dust where an arm had swept across an entire shelf, dragging anything and everything into a sack—and then dumping out the contents of the sack a few aisles away. Somebody took an entire shelf of fakes, leaving untouched an adjacent shelf containing pieces of infinitely greater value.

But these rookie mistakes do not rule out the possibility that our other bad actors made the amateur heist a lot easier. Neither of the two storage rooms that were looted showed any signs of forced entry on their exterior steel doors. One of the looted rooms was on the first floor, and the other was on the second, and both were connected by an interior stairwell so that entry to one automatically enabled entry to the other. The second-floor room was where the sniper team was located. So our best judgment was that the looters gained access—even to the first-floor storage room—when the sniper team decamped, leaving the door open behind them. But it was also possible that either the professionals who stole the high-end artifacts or the insider(s) with the keys to the basement may have left the doors open—intentionally. Crowds destroy evidence and help cover tracks.

While our amnesty program and our raids over the past month had recovered many of these items, there was still plenty more work to be done.

As for the underground storage area, while the "insiders" who had breached the wall had never managed to open the lockers to get the big prize, they did steal from the plastic tackle boxes scattered across the floor—our best count to date—5,144 cylinder seals, as well as 5,542 pins, glass bottles, beads, amulets, and other small items of jewelry.

They may have screwed the pooch, but they knew how to get in, they knew where to find the keys, and they knew what they were looking for. Given this level of preparation, it follows that the loot they took was more likely to have a middleman buyer and make its way into the hands of organized smugglers able to move it out of Iraq and into the international market. Like Louie in *Casablanca*, many officials of bordering countries would be "shocked" to discover that their borders were well-worn thoroughfares for stolen goods. It remained to be seen if such newfound awareness would actually cause them to do anything about it.

Nonetheless, I realized that the most likely way of recovering loot from more sophisticated thieves, especially when the items in question were small and easily hidden, was still at border crossings, where law and custom allow inspection of baggage on less than probable cause. I knew that, as a result of Iraq's neighbors increasing the effectiveness of their border-security and inspection programs to thwart terrorists, they were also intercepting many antiquities that would otherwise have slipped through. While relevant borders were far from airtight, and antiquities smuggling had become a quasi–cottage industry in many regions, the increased effectiveness of border inspections had probably discouraged many less experienced smugglers from even making the attempt. But I also knew that the old hands would simply increase their patience and resourcefulness.

Increasing inspection rates, alone, then, would never be enough to stop the traffic. A law enforcement official must be able to articulate a rationale in order to seize an item in transit, and at a glance these smaller artifacts were not necessarily recognizable as contraband. The key strategy, going forward, would be to educate law enforcement authorities so that they could immediately recognize illicit antiquities and therefore be justified in seizing what they found.

We needed to treat recoveries inside Iraq and interdiction at the borders not as separate approaches, but as two prongs of the same pincer designed to work together to put the squeeze on the bad guys. Increased border inspections increase the risk of trying to move stolen goods out of the country, which keeps them in Iraq, which makes them more likely to be seized through raids based on good intelligence inside the country. But the pressure of seizures inside Iraq pushes smugglers to risk export, which makes them more susceptible to interdiction at a border with improved inspection programs and better-educated guards. These actions would be further enhanced by the increased scrutiny and investigative resources that would result from heightened public interest and improved public awareness that would result from a well-received press junket. So maybe it was a good thing that I was going to New York to try to get the story out as widely as I could.

With recent events and future strategies straight in my head, I turned off my reading light, closed my eyes, and fell asleep.

I arrived at Newark Airport late Monday night, May 19. My wife had assembled a group of about fifty—including every Bogdanos she could find—with a giant WELCOME HOME banner. This was the first time since 9/11 that she had allowed herself to cry—and it was about two years' worth of tears. She had pulled off quite a feat of logistics. Everyone was wearing a T-shirt indicating their relationship with me. MY DAD IS A HERO, MY SON IS A HERO, MY HUSBAND IS A HERO, MY BUDDY IS A HERO. The best part was that the kids had tipped me off over the phone. "Remember, Daddy, it's a secret. You can't tell anybody," Michael had said, never quite factoring in from which person this secret was to be kept.

The kids also told me about their new game. If they ate a good dinner, Claudia would turn on the TV after dessert and let them watch CNN or Fox News. If a story about the Iraq Museum came on, they would race to see who could be first to kiss my mug on the screen. Always prepared, she had taped some earlier news shows as a backup. If I didn't come on in the first fifteen minutes, she would secretly hit PLAY.

Once we got home, I maintained a low profile. I wanted to spend time just with my family, but I also wanted to avoid unnecessary conversations. I felt as if I were from another planet, and there was no point trying to bridge the distance. How do I respond to "So, Matthew, how was Iraq?" Do I say, "Great, Evan, it was great. How are things with you?" Or do I describe to Melissa the smell of burnt flesh in that makeshift hospital where the two young men took us to their sister?

On Wednesday, I did a radio talk show hosted by attorney Ed Hayes, a former Bronx DA and the real-life model for the scrappy lawyer in *The Bonfire of the Vanities*. Now a high-priced defense attorney, he got more than his share of acquittals, but never at the expense of his honor or his respect for the law. He invited me to attend a formal dinner before the program at the Museum of Television Arts, organized to discuss the role of TV in promoting justice and the impact of publicity on the fairness of a trial. I told him I would be there, but that I would be late. I wasn't going anywhere until I had put my kids to bed at eight.

When I arrived, I was thrilled to see New York Supreme Court judges Edwin Torres and Leslie Crocker Snyder—two of my role models. Respected by defense attorneys and prosecutors alike, they had lost count of how many defendants had put out contracts on their lives. Some people are as tough as nails; these two made nails look soft. As enjoyable as the evening was, however, it didn't feel right sitting in an air-conditioned room eating hot food and drinking chilled white wine while my team was still in Baghdad eating MREs in the dark to foil snipers. Forty-eight hours earlier, I had been sharing their dangers; now I was sipping an espresso.

I had to remind myself that, for these few days, it was my duty in support of our mission to be back in New York talking to the world. I still felt guilty, but it couldn't dampen the pleasure of being back with Claudia and the kids. "When the voices of children are heard on the green and laughing is heard on the hill," William Blake wrote, "my heart is at rest within my breast and everything else is still." When I was with them, it wasn't so much that the world made more sense. It was more that the rest of the world just ceased to exist.

Once, when Michael was about six months old, my only witness in a murder trial had been threatened by the defendant's drug gang and refused to testify. The judge gave me forty-eight hours to change her mind or dismiss the case. I put her in a hotel with police officers at the door, walked to my apartment, and sat by Michael's crib. He didn't do anything cute. He just lay there sleeping and I watched him breathe. That's all. Just breathe. At about midnight, I realized that I had forgotten all about the trial.

In New York, on Thursday, I was interviewed for a story to appear in the *Times* Sunday magazine. I think I gave the reporter some good stuff—the reporter certainly thought so—but the piece never ran. I later got word through a friend on the staff that it was "not a good time" at the great gray *Times* for a positive piece about Iraq. It seems that they and the *Washington Post* were going through a period of self-examination for not having been more vocal in opposing the war early on. After the *New York Times*, I did an interview with the *Hellenic Times*, because that's a paper dear to my father's heart, and then with the *Wall Street Journal*. I also did some TV interviews, ranging from the *News-Hour* to *Fox & Friends*.

I don't think anyone at the Pentagon or elsewhere anticipated the staying power of this story. They thought the looting in Baghdad might be worth one or two news cycles. But during that spring and summer, if you had Googled my name, you would have come up with several thousand hits. There was something about trying to safeguard things of lasting beauty in the middle of a war that struck a nerve, worldwide.

While some interviewers came from the "Don't confuse me with the facts" school, others were not only well prepared but admirably open-minded. Jeff Brown of the *NewsHour* knew as much about the investigation as I did. Alan Riding of the *New York Times* and Eric Gibson of the *Wall Street Journal* posed tough questions that actually caused me to refine our recovery strategies. Bill Glauber of the *Chicago Tribune* and Alexandra Zavis of the Associated Press consistently impressed me with their keen insights.

And while I realized that there was a serious purpose to my role as a talking head, the whole time I was doing media I was never quite "there." The job I really cared about was investigator, not show pony. That's why I invested what spare time I had visiting the Metropolitan Museum, looking for, and often not finding, the statement of origin called the "provenance" down at the bottom of the descriptive plaques. I also made the rounds at the archaeology departments of the major universities in the metro area, searching for people who could help me break down the wall between law enforcement and the art world.

While I was gone, John Durkin was in charge back in Baghdad. We spoke on the phone every day, and whenever we needed a secure connection to discuss classified information, I walked over to the FBI's Joint Terrorism Task Force office a few blocks from my apartment.

They had lousy coffee, but good communications capabilities. I also reviewed all of his daily situation reports to make sure they were written in the passive voice, to give John plausible deniability should anything go wrong in my absence. Fortunately, thanks to John, things went right. On May 22, a walk-in tipster directed him to a vehicle driven by two Iraqis. When the team stopped the car at a predetermined military checkpoint, they discovered two boxes containing 425 pieces of loot.

But much of their effort went to more mundane matters. One of these included just getting workers to show up. Despite one members' personal desire to watch us fail, UNESCO had agreed to provide two vans and a sedan to help transport staff, including twenty-one workers who were trying to do an inventory of the collection. But no one paid the drivers, a matter we had to rectify posthaste. No sooner had we solved that problem, however, and managed to get a full staff at work, than the museum generator crapped out and everyone had to go home again.

A frequent visitor during this period was Ambassador Pietro Cordone, an Italian diplomat who, based on a long career spent largely in the Middle East, was appointed the Coalition Provisional Authority's senior adviser for culture in May 2003.

His first order of business was to deal with Dr. Hana Abdul Khaliq. Because of her high-level Ba'ath Party membership and all-round nastiness, he removed her from her position and banned her from the museum grounds. While most of the staff celebrated, they also wanted him to go further. Ten former employees appeared at the library entrance trying to make an appointment with Ambassador Cordone, still agitating for Dr. Jaber's removal and replacement by an "elected" museum director.

When the ambassador expressed displeasure with Nawala about the slow and highly uneven pace of inventorying the collection and what was missing, as well as the lack of progress in cleaning up the museum, Nawala said, "It's not my job." The ambassador told her that it was indeed her job and that she had better start doing it.

Back in Baghdad before the end of the month, I benefited from the ambassador's interventions, but I think it was a good thing that I was on hand to soften his somewhat austere approach, such as frequently extending his deadlines to the staff after he left the compound. Nonetheless, the ambassador's daily inquiries, along with all the press attention, were useful in increasing the pressure on everyone, which, in turn, was leverage I could use in finally convincing Nawala and others to supply us with a complete inventory of the secret place. Given the religious connotations of the oath she and four others had taken, the discussion was a lot more complex than that. It took weeks, and it was an effort in which I reverted to unalloyed lawyer.

No matter to whom I spoke, I always started by stressing how much I respected the oath, but asked in turn that my need to know also be respected. I next pointed out that the oath was predicated on preserving the artifacts against U.S. forces as pillagers, and then asked if I was a pillager. Once each of them saw that the basis for the oath was no longer valid, then I hoped to convince them that the oath was no longer binding.

No one caved in on my first pass. It required three or four more conversations. And the frustration—in particular with Nawala—was that I could not build on what we had discussed and agreed the last time, but had to go back to the beginning each time.

"Nawala, do you trust me?"

"Of course."

"Nawala, do you think I'm going to give the stuff to the Israelis?"

"Well, no, of course not."

"Am I going to give it to the Kuwaitis?"

"No."

"Do you think I'm taking it home? You know, my apartment is so small. I really don't have room for much in the way of Iraqi antiquities. I can't even fit one of your boxes in my apartment!" I must have said that line to her five times, and each time it made her smile. Each conversation was a repetition of the last, but each iteration dug a little deeper. Finally, on June 2, Ambassador Cordone was there to lend his gravitas and told them that enough was enough. "We will do it this afternoon," he said.

"We will do it tomorrow," they responded. *"Insha'Allah"*

But the next day, the day appointed for the big unveiling, Dr. Jaber did not show up. He had suffered what he said was a heart attack. I visited him at the hospital two days later and he was in good spirits—for all appearances having made a rapid and complete recovery.

On June 4, several team members at long last opened up the bricked-over space that had been the museum's top-secret vault for more than a decade. It contained 179 locked trunks packed in tight because of a low ceiling. They had to use bolt cutters to get the locks open, because, once again, no one could lay his hands on the keys. Within each box, immediately on top, were loose pages listing what was in each box. Our guys were able to confirm that all the jewelry and ivories from the public galleries were safe. To be more precise, we were able to confirm that the 8,366 artifacts listed on the inventory sheets were in those 179 boxes. A cynic might ask how hard would it have been to replace a loose, nonserialized inventory sheet with one doctored to delete certain items. Not hard, I suppose, but there is no evidence that any of the sheets were doctored, and there will always be limits to our knowledge in this sublunar world. With the inventory complete, our team left, and the staff bricked up the wall again.

Meanwhile, the hunt for the treasures of Ur and Nimrud continued.

Unfortunately, my involvement in other parts of our mission kept me from being there at the finish line. Colonel Bogdanos, deputy director of JIACG, was engaged in counterterrorism activities elsewhere in Baghdad and Iraq, when Matthew, amateur classicist, would much rather have been leading the chase for the Nimrud gold.

By the end of May, the crew hired by Jason Williams succeeded at last in pumping out nearly five million gallons of water from the basement of the Central Bank. The scene revealed was gruesome: A heavy steel door at the end of a long tunnel was seriously scarred and dented. In front of the door lay an expended rocket-propelled grenade. Also on the floor was what remained of the not very bright shooter. Evidently, he had fired the RPG at point-blank range in that narrow chamber. Considering the dead men I had found in the other bank building, I made a note to read up on these four queens of Nimrud, whose treasure we were trying to find, and more specifically, on the curse inscribed on their tombs almost three thousand years earlier.

On June 1, 2003, with water still dripping from the girders, several of the team crept down the spiral staircase to the bank's basement. They shined portable fluorescent lights into another long, narrow hallway leading to the vault purported to hold the treasure. As everyone watched, Muhammad, the former bank manager, turned three keys in the three locks, spun three combination cylinders, and extracted three vault bolts. Then he pulled back the door.

The vault floor was still covered in about an inch of water. They shone their lights on several canvas sacks, later found to contain more than eight hundred million Iraqi dinars. Then they illuminated two large wooden boxes on casters, two smaller wooden boxes, and one metal footlocker. The wooden crates were waterlogged and spongy.

Their paint was flaking. Two of the wooden boxes lay on their sides, and a third lay on one end—the result of rising and falling water. Wrapped around them were thin wires holding small lead seals—unbroken. But it was the metal footlocker on which our hopes were riding.

Two of the guys lifted one of the smaller wooden boxes and water streamed out. At that point, Nawala expressed concern that opening the crates in these soggy conditions would cause damage to the artifacts. She insisted that the boxes be lifted out of the water and allowed to dry before they were opened. More frustration, more delay. The team re-sealed the vault and left.

On June 5, the team returned. At 9:48 in the morning, they opened the first four boxes, containing hundreds of superb pieces of gold and jewelry from the royal tombs of Ur. The first of those four boxes also contained the original golden bull's head from the Golden Harp of Ur (a replica sat atop the wooden harp in the restoration room), as well as the golden helmet of King Meskalamdug. Weighing more than one kilogram, this piece was made of a single sheet of gold, hammered to reproduce the hairstyle of the time. After two hours of slow and careful inspection of the boxes containing the treasure of Ur, Nawala wanted to move the last box to a dry vault in the old bank building before opening it.

Once the last box was moved, they broke the seal. At precisely 1:43 in the afternoon, they slowly opened the lid and exposed the gleaming gold within: exquisitely wrought crowns and bracelets, necklaces and armbands, rings and anklets. We could finally say that after nearly three thousand years, the treasure of Nimrud was safe.

In an interview later with the *Hartford Courant*, Jason Williams said, "The value of what's in that vault is the same as the value of the objects that sit in the Tower of London. You could not put a dollar figure to these items. They go to the very core and the heart and center of the people." Exactly.

Sharing pride in and mutual respect for each of the cultures that has flowed into the bloodstream of modern Iraq—Assyrian and Babylonian, Kurd and Shi'ite and Sunni—is the only hope of weaving these people, brought together by the British in a shotgun marriage eighty years ago, into a viable nation-state.

It was a moment to soften the hardest cynics.

13

WHAT DOES MILITARY DUTY LOOK LIKE?

Everyone lets the present moment slip by, and then looks for it as though it were somewhere else.—Hagakure

ON JUNE 7, I was sipping tea in Dr. Jaber's office with Donny and Nawala when Ambassador Pietro Cordone arrived. In good spirits, he suggested that we celebrate the recent discoveries by exhibiting the treasures of Ur and Nimrud in a one-day gala museum opening in July. My first thought was about security. It was not just the treasure that was at risk. By drawing so many dignitaries to the museum, the opening would turn the museum into a high-value target for terrorists. I also knew who would be tapped for the job of ensuring that nothing bad happened: Colonel Bogdanos, USMC.

Before I said anything, however, I wanted to allow the museum staff to weigh in on this idea, and each was characteristic in his or her response. Dr. Jaber tilted his head, but remained silent. Nawala said, "It is impossible in July. Maybe in September." Donny paused, then said, "We can do this."

Almost immediately, Donny began describing the room we should use and how it should be displayed, becoming more animated as he addressed each detail. In time, when the ambassador asked if I could develop a security plan sufficient to the occasion, I turned to Nawala and said, "As you wish." She looked down, smiled, then added a whispered "Yes."

When the ambassador asked the staff to pick a date, it was my turn to smile and avert my eyes. They told the ambassador that they wanted to be sure it was a date on which I could attend. We agreed on July 3. The next day, the museum staff surprised me and the ambassador with an unscheduled press conference to announce the opening. Their excitement was palpable.

On June 11, I had to leave for the States yet again, this time for an on-site module at the Army War College in Carlisle, Pennsylvania. Immediately after my promotion to colonel the year before, I had been accepted into their master's program in strategic studies. The two-year course consisted of two brief periods in residence, a thesis, and thirty papers written throughout ten modules of online learning. I wrote many of those papers by flashlight.

Thanks to Senior's good eye and to John Durkin's shrewd negotiating skills, the day after I left produced another big score. About ten days earlier, a guy had come in claiming to have some artifacts, saying that he wanted five hundred dollars as a reward for returning them. John said, "Show me what you got. Then we'll talk." A couple of days later, the guy came in again, this time carrying a badly lit Polaroid of ninety-six artifacts. Looking at all the stuff spread out in the photograph, Senior whispered, "Isn't that the Sacred Vase of Warka?" A rookie would have nailed the guy right then, with the likely result of coming up empty. A slick operator might have said, "Okay, but you get half now and half when you deliver it." And then he would have been out half the money with nothing to show.

John handed the picture back and said, "This is all crap." This was our only lead to the museum's single most precious missing item, but John let him walk out the door.

"Good call, John," I said, when we spoke about it later that day. "For the record and in case this goes south, I would have done the same thing. Just keep him on the hook."

This kind of thing is like landing a fish with a light tackle. You have to keep the connection, but you also have to give him running room or he could break the line. Mostly, though, the guy who comes to make the offer is usually just a middleman. If you try to hold him, you can blow your credibility. And a middleman never knows where the goods are anyway. The middleman is the mule, and they never tell the mule where the stuff is, because that's the only way they can be sure he won't be threatened or coerced or enticed into revealing the location.

The guy came back two more times trying to make his sale, and John finally said, "Okay, I can get you your five hundred dollars, but you have to show me some good faith. Bring the stuff in tomorrow." The next day, four different guys showed up with all ninety-six items, including the museum's pride and joy—the Sacred Vase of Warka—in the trunk of a car. Apparently, the five hundred dollars was the middleman's entrepreneurial improvisation, because the men never asked for money. Instead, they were rewarded with an invitation to the recently scheduled, one-day gala opening of the museum.

Thrilled with their recovery, John and Senior became despondent when they saw that it was in fourteen pieces. But then Dr. Ahmed Kamel, the museum's deputy director, examined the vase on the spot and told them it was in exactly the same condition as it had been when German archaeologists first discovered it at al-Samawa in 1940. As Dr. Kamel later told me during one of our long walks together, "It was in fourteen pieces then, it is in fourteen pieces now. We will restore it again."

Hearing that news, John and Senior were like two kids celebrating the winning touchdown. Then, about an hour later, the ambassador showed up with an Army colonel. They viewed the new recoveries displayed for them on our recovery table in the library. In Baghdad, the likelihood of any appearance by the Coalition Provisional Authority was always directly proportional to the likelihood of favorable press. Sure enough, the next day, Reuters described how the vase had been recovered by "CPA security staff." "He is here for the feasting, but was not there to help catch the game," observed Euripides. I had a good laugh at John's expense, but when serious people got important parts of the story wrong, we were not amused.

On its Web site, the University of Chicago's Oriental Institute published a photograph showing the vase as it had been before the invasion, side by side with how it looked when it was recovered—broken into fourteen pieces. Omitted from the site was any mention that the vase in the "before" photo was already heavily restored. Also omitted was that there was no new damage—despite the fact that both USA Today and the Associated Press reported this fact. A team from the British Museum passing through Baghdad just after the recovery stopped to inspect the vase and found no new breaks. Their report concluded, "The lower portions of the vase below the register of naked 'priests' are intact apart from some damage to the restored plaster of Paris foot and bowl. The upper portion of the vase has broken along old break lines into c. ten pieces."

Although most of the major press got it right, some still managed to get it wrong—none worse than the *Boston Globe*: "Looters discovered the delicately engraved 4-foot-tall vase and tipped over its support stand, shattering into 14 pieces a priceless treasure that had survived intact for five millennia." Not only had the vase been found in fourteen pieces in 1940, but it was also famous for being one of the first pieces known to have been restored in antiquity—the copper wire used to mend it thousands of years ago still visible to anyone who bothered to look.

Time to reflect and check the facts did not make the characterizations any more accurate. In the April 2004 issue of the Oriental Institute's journal, the "before" and "after" photos were again placed side by side, with the "after" caption reading, "The vessel was recovered, in pieces, in June." Again, no mention that there were no new breaks, despite the fact that the British Museum and I had already issued reports stating all the breaks were along the old fracture lines. As recently as May 2005, reports were still showing up that the vase was returned "in damaged condition," without mentioning that only the results of prior restorations had been damaged and not the vase itself.

By the time I got back to Iraq near the end of June, the JIACG team was recovering antiquities, carrying on a criminal investigation, dealing with more "family feud" staff issues, and making preparations for a formal reception at the one-day opening that would draw hundreds of press and international dignitaries. If people hadn't been getting killed throughout Iraq, it might have been comical, with my professional "tough guys" pinballing among detective work, landscape supervision, and party planning worthy of a June bride. But they had also been stonewalled and hamstrung by some military officers and other officials who took advantage of my absence. John and Senior gave me a "wouldn't mind if you chewed some ass" list, and though it was long, I think I managed to get to every name on it.

For the big one-day opening, Donny said that he wanted to use the main entrance to the public galleries, at that time still bricked up. Nawala insisted that the museum use the administration hallway, the entry then in daily use, and threatened to resign if her demand was not met. Donny refused to back down, and the main entrance was being readied. One of the first things I did when I got back was to ask Nawala not to resign. She stayed on.

On July 2, 2003, amid much fanfare and security, the treasure of Nimrud was moved to the museum to be displayed for the day in a room just off of the Assyrian Gallery. For the last twenty-five years, the Iraq Museum had been, in effect, Saddam's private treasure house, but on July 3, it was to be open to the public. The night before, it was my privilege to rest beside the treasure with a loaded M4.

The museum opening marked a high point. The media coverage was huge, the goodwill enormous, the staff in heaven. Even so, we had our detractors. The *Independent* quoted Elizabeth Stone, the archaeologist who had earlier called for the shooting of looters, as dismissing the opening as nothing more than "an act of propaganda." I can only pity anyone whose cynicism does not permit them to appreciate the dignity and empowerment that even such a small step as this one-day opening engendered. I saw the joy in the faces of the museum staff as they prepared *their* museum and the pride they showed on the day *their* treasure was displayed. I know that the opening proclaimed, if only for a few hours, the possibilities the future might hold for a museum, for a city, for a country.

Unfortunately, the museum opening was also a turning point.

Just a few hours after our celebration, at approximately eight thirty P.M. on July 3, 2003, one of the young soldiers who earlier in the day had served on our security detail was killed. Private First Class Edward J. Herrgott, aged twenty, from Shakopee, Minnesota, was shot to death by a sniper while manning the gunner's hatch of his Bradley armored vehicle. Two days later, an aspiring young reporter named Richard Wild was killed while standing on the street corner in front of Baghdad University in the Bab al-Muzzam district. An unidentified assailant simply walked up to him and shot him in the back of the head.

The "honeymoon" period was over.

It was also about this time when I realized we needed to expand our investigation to include transit and destination countries as well as the origin country of Iraq.

This next phase began with an e-mail I received from Manhattan assistant district attorney John Irwin. Apparently, an Immigration and Customs Enforcement (ICE) agent back in New York had been trying to get in touch with me concerning a seizure he thought might be related to my investigation. Although I had worked with ICE for years and had ICE agents in my team in Baghdad, ICE headquarters had not been able to "locate Colonel Bogdanos" and had asked the DA's Office for assistance. Because John was my best friend in the Office, he was given the task of contacting me.

Once I got John's e-mail, I called him on my satellite phone, and he gave me the name and number of an ICE agent in New York. John had just had triplets (two boys and a girl) and was telling me that if I thought Afghanistan or Iraq were tough, I should try changing three diapers at the same time. I thoroughly enjoyed the image of this longtime bachelor rubbing A & D ointment into every crevice, until a sudden burst of automatic weapons fire cut our call short.

When I phoned the ICE agent later that night, I had difficulty believing that what he was telling me wasn't just a bad joke. A week after our investigation had begun, on April 30, 2003, customs inspectors in Newark had seized four FedEx boxes containing 669 artifacts stolen from the museum, including 87 cylinder seals. The proper way to deal with such a cache is to use it as bait to catch a thief. Once you discover the loot, you keep your cool, wait until somebody shows up to claim it, then slap on the cuffs. If you're real good and you've got the resources, you let the middleman who picked up the goods actually complete the sale to the collector. Then you grab them all. While that kind of patient approach is extremely labor-intensive—you need to conduct surveillance on the players and on the stuff—and it requires real courage to allow an intercepted shipment to go back into transit, the rewards are enormous. You get everybody. We do it with drug shipments all the time. It's called a controlled delivery, and it usually ends with a jury saying "guilty."

That's not what happened in Newark. The frontline inspectors from Customs and Border Protection (CBP) had done a good job in identifying and impounding the goods. But they are not investigators and are not authorized to investigate any seizures. That's what ICE does. But CBP, the inspection section of what used to be the U.S. Customs Service, let thirty days go by before getting the message to ICE, the investigative section of what used to be the U.S. Customs Service. Another thirty days went by before the ICE investigative unit notified us. As a result, it was midsummer and those stolen goods were still waiting in a Newark warehouse.

By then it was too late. The intended recipient, a Madison Avenue art dealer, when notified of the seizure could say, "I don't know what you're talking about. I wasn't expecting that shipment. I would never do that. It must be some kind of mistake at the other end." The opportunity to prove that it wasn't a mistake—letting him sign for the shipment and bring it home—had been squandered. The thieves were probably out bulldozing archaeological sites, the European middleman shipper was licking more mailing labels, and the scheduled recipients, who should have been working on their "prison pallor," were soaking up the sun in the Hamptons or Vail.

I did not want this kind of missed opportunity to happen again, so, with our amnesty program firmly in place and a network of informants throughout Iraq, I decided that it was time for me to become a traveling emissary, soliciting assistance from, and providing detailed briefings on the investigation's findings to, anyone who would listen. Ultimately, that included eight law enforcement agencies in six countries. There was Interpol in Washington, D.C., and Lyon, France; U.S. customs in London, New York, and Washington, D.C.; Scotland Yard and Her Majesty's customs and excise in London; Jordanian customs in Amman; Kuwaiti customs in Kuwait City; Italian carabinieri in Iraq; and U.S. attorney's offices in New Jersey and New York.

Despite the media barrage and our earlier efforts to send photographs of the missing items to law enforcement authorities all over the globe, I was still concerned that customs and border officials throughout the world would not easily recognize certain types of antiquities as contraband. Therefore, they might not make a seizure even if they found the goods. Moreover, international law enforcement were so heavily occupied in addressing the full-scale war on terrorism that they had little time, energy, or resources left for antiquities. I had to show them how important this was, not only because of the antiquities themselves, but because of a simple fact about smugglers: the same people who were trafficking antiquities were also trafficking weapons as well.

UNESCO shared my concern and were so vehemently outraged by the looting that they actually had five meetings in the first three months alone. Meeting on April 17 in Paris, April 29 in London, May 6 in Lyon, June 23 in Vienna, and July 7 in London, these guys were obviously fired up, motivated, angry. But their preference for hitting the conference center rather than the streets reminded me of Cicero's friend Atticus, as described by French historian Gaston Boissier: "He always belonged to the best party, but he made it a rule not to serve his party. He was contented with giving it his good wishes, but these good wishes were the warmest imaginable. His reserve only began when it was necessary to act."

My first stop on a six-country tour that would take the better part of the next several months was London, to brief Scotland Yard. While there, I learned that the British Museum was hosting the 49th Rencontre Assyriologique Internationale, an annual gathering of some of the world's foremost authorities on Mesopotamian archaeology. I knew that the investigation would succeed only if the law enforcement and art and archaeological communities worked together. So, I decided to take the first step. Not afflicted by shyness, I invited myself to the last day of that conference.

Neil McGregor, the director of the British Museum, was kind enough to shuffle the schedule and permit me to brief the three hundred attendees on July 11. I wanted to provide accurate information on what had happened at the museum to the world's art and archaeological communities. But mostly, I wanted to enlist their support for the investigation. I learned much about art smuggling and walked away with a list of experts who volunteered to be "on call" whenever law enforcement authorities needed to verify the origin of a seizure or recovery.

In fact, one gutsy archaeologist was willing to do more than that. Buying into the idea that archaeology and law enforcement should be hand in glove, this individual agreed to go undercover to nail some dealers that had been suspected of illegal trafficking. We prepared this archaeologist thoroughly on what to say and do, to avoid anything constituting entrapment and to stay visible from the observation car across the street: Just go in and listen. Excited and nervous, this Arabic-speaking scholar walked into the shop and heard the unsuspecting dealers speak about specific Iraqi antiquities and the best way to avoid law enforcement. Our newest recruit came out minutes later completely revved up: "Arrest them right now! Right now!" But of course you have to wait to avoid making it obvious who the "undercover" informant was. The dealer was in custody before the end of the week.

There were some other pleasant surprises that summer.

Even when I was home on leave, the amnesty program and the media barrage continued to deliver. An individual who had learned about our investigation from watching CNN called up and said he had a "package" for me. We arranged to meet in a coffee shop in the middle of the day in midtown Manhattan. He handed me a brown-paper envelope, and as a result, a four-thousand-year-old Akkadian piece is now back in Baghdad, where it belongs.

Meanwhile, the recoveries in Iraq continued, the most notable being those made by the U.S. Army's 812th Military Police Company. Not part of my original team, they were led by U.S. Army captain Vance Kuhner (a recalled reservist from the Queens DA's Office) and U.S. Army sergeant Emmanuel Gonzalez (a recalled New York City police officer) and achieved remarkable successes.

Acting on a tip from an informant, on September 23, 2003, Kuhner's 812th Military Police Company dug up the Mask of Warka, the first naturalistic depiction of a human face, from about 3100 B.C., buried in back of a farmhouse in al-Rabbia, north of Baghdad. Inspired by success, Captain Kuhner and his men got into the spirit of the enterprise, using their own money to grease the wheels with informants. It paid off.

On November 3, 2003, they conducted another predawn raid, this time based on a tip about a smuggling ring operating in southeast Baghdad. They recovered a cache of small arms, along with the Nimrud brazier. This is the small wooden firebox, clad in bronze with bronze turrets and resting on a set of wheels, that was part of the loot taken from the restoration room. Early excavations at Nimrud had found small "tramlines" in grooves in the floor of Assyrian throne rooms. Archaeologists anticipated the function, but not until they reached the throne room of King Shalmaneser III (858–824 B.C.) did they find an actual brazier—the only one known to exist. With an image on its side of an enemy city in flames, the box was wheeled from place to place, wherever the king happened to be, to warm the royal feet.

Later that same day, using information acquired during the first seizure, Kuhner and his men raided a warehouse in Baghdad and recovered seventy-six pieces that had been stolen from the museum basement, including thirty-two cylinder seals. Then they looked in the cesspool behind the warehouse. Submerged in the muck, covered in grease, was the Bassetki Statue. This beautiful Akkadian piece, weighing 150 kilograms, and not quite a meter in diameter, shows the lower portion of a seated male figure, its legs curled around the base of a standard or doorpost. The youth depicted was no doubt the mythological figure with six large rings of hair that customarily guarded Akkadian doorways. It is a spectacularly naturalistic rendering, cast in pure copper almost two thousand years before the Golden Age of Athens. According to its inscription, it stood in the palace of King Naram-Sim in southern Iraq, yet it was found by a road crew at Bassetki, near the Turkish border in Kurdish northern Iraq. How did it get from southern Iraq to the north? Once again: there is nothing new about looting.

But there were losses as well.

On November 12, 2003, a truck broke through the gate in Nasiriyah and exploded in front of the Italian military headquarters. It killed twelve of the carabinieri who had been working the archaeological sites as well as five Italian army soldiers and sixteen Iraqi and Italian civilians. The day it happened, I was with Lieutenant Marseglia of the carabinieri at Interpol headquarters in Lyon. He was devastated, but despite the losses, the Italians continued their efforts.

James Sullivan, the director of Interpol's U.S. National Central Bureau, is a former Marine and an expert at harnessing the power and resources of the international law enforcement community. He invited me to attend the first meeting of the newly formed Interpol Tracking Task Force to Fight Illicit Trafficking in Cultural Property Stolen in Iraq (ITTF). When I arrived, I met the leaders of the task force, Germany's Karl-Heinz Kind and France's Jean-Pierre Jouanny, and I was impressed with both their enthusiasm and their experience. I offered to provide a formal briefing on the investigation to all of the member nations that had sent representatives (Iraq, Jordan, the United Kingdom, the United States, Italy, and France). They graciously fit me into the schedule for the international conference—no small feat—and my presentation coupled with their insightful questions and recommendations lasted the better part of the first day.

Before my arrival, I had drafted a detailed concept paper for the way ahead in the international investigation, laying out the importance of multiple investigations being conducted simultaneously in different countries in order to catch everyone involved. Having met Karl-Heinz and Jean-Pierre, I believed they could pull it off. Moreover, given that Interpol's exceptional databases linked 184 member nations, I realized that they were ideally set up to formally take over the role I had informally taken on during the last six months. When I presented my suggestion, I even offered to hold a press conference announcing that they were taking over, all the while willing to continue my efforts in the shadows. They thanked me kindly, were very respectful, then educated me on the realities of budgets and staffing. They had neither the resources nor the legal authorities to do what I so desperately—and foolishly—hoped they could.

I had taken my shot with Interpol, hoping through them that I could link the individual countries. Marines always adapt and improvise. So it was time to go to plan B: the individual countries. Things were about to get a whole lot worse. I met with one official from a country in continental Europe that shall remain nameless. When I proposed increased attention at the borders on Iraqi antiquities (and offered to develop a training program for his border officials), he told me that his country did not have a problem with Iraqi antiquities. When I said that I had interviewed witnesses who had told me that he did, he assured me that he could prove they had no problem. His proof? They had never made a seizure of Iraqi antiquities in his entire country! I respectfully declined pointing out that it *might* have been because they weren't looking hard enough.

I asked an official from another country to increase by a percentage point or two their random inspection rates. "Colonel," he replied, "do you have any idea what that would do?"

"Yes, sir. I think you would recover some antiquities and probably some weapons and other prohibited materials as well."

"No, I mean do you have any idea what that would do to our customs and excise revenues?"

By then, however, my involvement in the investigation was officially over—ignoring, of course, that it had never "officially" begun. I had been called to the Pentagon on September 10, 2003, to give the Department of Defense's final briefing on the investigation. When I pointed out that the investigation would require several more years, noting that I wasn't done yet, they said, "Yes, you are. Congratulations." In point of fact, I was hard-pressed to complain. At that point, CENTCOM had given me five months. They had allowed me to divert significant assets from our assigned counterterrorism mission to hunt down some pieces of rock with funny writing on them. But just because I understood their rationale didn't mean that I had to like it.

I was able to squeeze in another two months, but by the end of November 2003, any official role I had once held as the "head" of the investigation was over. And as I flew home for my first Thanksgiving in three years, it was clear that no one else was willing or able to follow in my footsteps.

When I was mobilized pursuant to presidential recall in October 2001, it was for a period of two years—the maximum authorized under the law. To complete some aspects of the museum investigation, as well as to ensure a smooth transition of my counterterrorist duties to Colonel Mike Dietz, I had already agreed to extend that two-year period by a few months. During this entire span, I had been home for a total of thirty days. Total. Two years, when it measures the difference between ages forty-four and forty-six, is not particularly crucial, because you remain basically the same person. But when that person is under the age of six? It is an order of magnitude difference, and I missed a great many of those changes as they took place in my children.

I had missed Jason's birth and I had missed Christmas twice. I missed Diana's second birthday while I was in Afghanistan; I missed her third birthday while I was in Iraq. I was resolved to do everything in my power not to miss any more meaningful days in their lives.

By the time I got back in November 2003, I had accrued more than sixty days of vacation time, and I took every single minute of it. The next two months were heaven—and also instructive. On one of my first nights back, Michael, Diana, and Jason were making a racket long past their bedtime. I rattled the doorknob to their room before I went in and could hear all three jumping back into their beds. But when I slowly poked my head in, Michael said, "It's okay guys, it's only Daddy." And then the three of them went back to jumping on their beds. Maybe Baghdad wasn't as hard as I thought. I did manage to teach Diana some Greek and Michael how to throw a baseball. And I tried to make up for having missed the first two years of Jason's life. I learned his favorite pajamas (elephants), his favorite stuffed animal (Simba), and his favorite song ("Bare Necessities" from *The Jungle Book*).

I also went back into the ring. Even at my age, as long as I have boxing, there will always be a part of me that is unspoiled. Fast jabs, short right hands, hard hooks, crisp uppercuts. Moving, bobbing, weaving. Slip the punch. Move inside. Deliver the combination and get back outside. Mists of sweat raining as each punch lands. Pushing. Wanting to stop. But not stopping. Not until the bell. Never stop until the bell. Sixty seconds to breathe. Then do it again.

I'd been with my new trainer, Darryl Pierre, for about five years, and he was every bit as good and as tough as Sammy. Our first fight as a team was one of my charity bouts for the New York City Police Department, and after I had stepped in the ring, I was nodding to a row of friends from the DA's Office.

"You fightin' anyone out there?" Darryl asked.

"No, I was just saying hello," I answered sheepishly.

"Let me introduce you to the man who you *are* fighting, because he wants to put you down."

"Yes, sir." He'd gotten my attention. "Keep your mind on your job and your job on your mind" was his mantra. Sammy believed in the simplicity of fundamentals; Darryl believes in the power of focus. Advice I have since put to good use in and out of the ring. The first time I walked back in the gym after two years, we hugged and then he said, "Yeah, I saw on TV that you'd gotten a little soft. Don't worry. We'll get it back. I'll get you a fight in six weeks." Then he jabbed me in the stomach. "I'd better make it seven." And he did.

We got a video camera for Christmas and went crazy taping everything the kids did for the next few weeks. Each night after they went to bed, I'd put that day's tape in the VCR and watch it. But then I'd put in one of the dozens of tapes I had from the museum, and I'd watch that as well. I'd also started watching the news again—but only after the kids went to bed—becoming addicted to accounts from Iraq and Afghanistan. Of course, I was watching these stories with different eyes. There might be a report of military action in Fallujah or Kandahar with x number of dead and wounded. But I would have known the neighborhood they were talking about, the reason for the action, and some of the participants.

Toward the end of my military leave, just when I was picking a date to go back to the DA's Office and start my life again, I got a phone call from Mike Dietz. "Can I speak to the founder of CENTCOM's Joint Interagency Coordination Group, please?" This didn't bode well.

"What's up, Mike?"

"Uh, Matthew . . . I know you've done your time and I've got no right to ask, but we need you. All the original guys are getting out at the end of their two years, and I've got a whole new group of guys that can't even spell *interagency*. Iraq, Afghanistan, and the Horn of Africa are all ramping up at the same time. The long and the short of it is, I need another colonel so we can split the region in half. Hell, you might even be recalled in ten months anyway. This way, you can call your shots. You know how well we work together." And then to lighten it up a little, he added, "Consider this payback for picking me to be the deputy."

Mike was a good friend and every word he said was true. The limit for presidential recall was twenty-four consecutive months, but the key word there is *consecutive*. I could have said no, gone back to my life, and been recalled again a year later. Emotionally, that would have been crushing to all of us: me, Claudia, and especially the kids.

We had always told the kids that my military duty was for two years. Of course, they don't understand two years any more than adults understand two thousand, but the point is that they understood that when a certain time is up, it's supposed to be up.

Trying to figure out where I was going to find the courage to tell the kids, I thought about a mountain pass called Thermopylae, where in 480 B.C., three hundred Spartans were hopelessly outnumbered by a reputed two million Persians. To stall the invaders, buying time for their fellow Greeks to mount a defense, the Spartans chose to stand their ground. When the Persian king, Xerxes, sent a messenger to the Spartan king, Leonidas, saying, "We do not want your lives, only your arms," Leonidas could have stepped aside, let the Persians advance, and lived to tell the tale. Instead he replied, "Molon labe"—come and get them. (Harrell adopted *Molon labe* as Task Force Bowie's official motto in Afghanistan.)

"But our archers are so numerous," continued the envoy, "that the flight of their arrows darkens the sun."

"So much the better," replied Dienekes, the second in command, "then we'll fight in the shade." The Spartans held out for seven days. Herodotus tells us they fought until their weapons broke, and then "with bare hands and teeth." A simple stone marks where they stood and died:

Go tell the Spartans, stranger passing by,
That here obedient to their laws we lie.

I didn't have that kind of courage. Nor did I have three hundred Spartans to mount a stalling maneuver. Fortunately, what I do have is a resourceful wife who came up with the perfect idea. "Daddy used to be on military duty and just visiting home," she told the kids. "From now on, he's going to be home, but just visiting military duty."

It simply had to be put into terms that had meaning for them. My six-year-old was elated. "Daddy, Daddy, it's so great. Now you're going to be home and just *visiting* military duty."

Telling my boss, Robert M. Morgenthau, New York's legendary district attorney since 1974 and the model for the DA on *Law & Order*, was much easier. A true leader, he'd served on destroyers in the U.S. Navy in World War II and seen action in both the Mediterranean and Pacific. We had already discussed ways I could increase the Office's role in counterterrorism investigations and—dear to my heart—setting up an antiquities task force. Now those would have to wait. "Take as much time as you need," he said. "You will always have a job here. Just get home safe."

"Roger that, sir."

And just like that, I was on the hook for another two years. Mike was right. There was plenty of work to be done, even for two of us. We ran counternarcotics operations in Afghanistan, trying to give those people a shot at a future without warlords living off the opium trade. We developed border-security initiatives in the Horn of Africa (Djibouti, Ethiopia, Somalia, and Sudan), trying to eliminate potential sanctuaries for terrorists fleeing their former refuges. And we worked out significant security issues in advance of the June 2004 transition to Iraqi rule. While crisscrossing the globe for these various missions, however, I always found time to work on the museum investigation.

I expanded my audience for talks about the investigation to include interested institutions and organizations such as the Archaeological Institute of America, Massachusetts Institute of Technology, State University of New York at Stony Brook, and the University of Cambridge and its famed McDonald Institute for Archaeological Research. Because I was no longer officially involved in the museum investigation, I used vacation time for these briefings, sometimes traveling at my own expense. Through such briefings, travels, and lectures, I began to build up a cadre of confidential informants (smugglers, curators, archaeologists, and dealers) for the future.

Following my lecture at the Archaeological Institute of America, I met New York University professor Joan Connelly, whose brilliant work interpreting the Parthenon frieze—also known as the Elgin Marbles—I'd read years earlier. I was even more thrilled when she invited me to visit the tiny island of Yeronisos off the coast of Cyprus where she and her team were excavating in the summer of 2004. Since I was scheduled to deploy to Iraq yet again in June 2004 to participate in the transition to Iraqi rule, I was able to work in the intermediate stop and spend a few days digging into the past.

Surrounded by the blue Mediterranean, this chalk-white island was slowly being worn away by the waves. Otherwise it was an unspoiled paradise. Dr. Connelly had a theory that Cleopatra had built a temple here for the birth of Caesarion, her son by Julius Caesar. Amazingly, the site had remained undisturbed for two thousand years. Everyone on the team was assigned his or her small part of the grid, a square meter or so that they would burrow into with the utmost care. I went to work like everybody else, digging and sifting, scraping away with a trowel and a brush. A couple of hours later, when Joan dropped by to see how I was doing, she broke out laughing. "You know you've just blown through about four centuries there, pal," she said.

I looked up, then glanced around, noticing for the first time that my hole was significantly deeper than anyone else's.

"You dig like a cop," she said.

She was right, but the fact is that I had waited all my life for this, and I was pretty revved up. Fortunately, my overweening enthusiasm did not lead to disaster. In fact, I actually found a small dish for votive offerings of grain or incense, a dish now in the good hands of conservators in Cyprus.

The members of our expedition were ferried over each day in small boats from the harbor at Paphos, where we all stayed. At the end of our visit, Dr. Connelly organized a party for the entire village, including, of course, the bearded and black-robed priest.

Even though I had to catch a plane early the next morning, it was the perfect night. We sang and danced and ate grilled fish and drank wine under the stars on a cliffside patio overlooking the sea, with white-washed cottages trailing off into the distance. It was Joan's birthday, and I had taught all the excavation volunteers to dance a Hassapiko and sing a Cypriot song. The celebration went on until "rosy-fingered dawn" appeared over "the wine-dark sea," and then I went straight to the airport and my flight back to the war zone.

The challenges of providing security for the transition meant that I was never able to get to the Museum during this second stint in Baghdad. Each day I would arrange for the necessary transportation and trigger-pullers, and then each day another mission would arise that would force me to cancel my trip and go elsewhere. Then I returned to the Army War College for graduation in July and learned that my master's thesis on conducting multiple-agency counterterrorist operations was forwarded to the 9/11 Commission, which favorably cited JIACG's efforts. One of several recommendations I had made in that paper was the creation of a single training program open to every U.S. governmental agency involved in national security. The goal was to develop a shared vision and a unified approach to the global war on terrorism. The thesis also made its way to the Pentagon.

The lesson here is to be careful what you ask for, because I was immediately assigned to the National Defense University in Washington, D.C., to assist renowned interagency savant Erik Kjonnerod in developing such a program. To backfill me overseas, I pulled out the Rolodex again. I hadn't seen former RF-4 Phantom jet pilot Joe Catan since we went through Officer Basic School together twenty five years earlier and I had to drive up to Vermont to meet his wife and three kids. "Prosperity is full of friends, but real friendship shows in times of trouble," Euripides observed. This copilot with American Airlines is now Lieutenant Colonel Catan in Iraq.

Once I got to D.C., one of my first stops was to see Paul McHale, Assistant Secretary of Defense for Homeland Defense, for his advice and guidance. Most knew him as the architect of a new way of thinking about national security. But I knew him as the commander who had mentored me when I was a still-wet-behind-the-ears captain thirteen years earlier. I also solicited and received help from every agent, cop, and former Marine inside the Beltway who I had ever served, drank, or had a case with. It took six months, but in February 2005, we conducted the first executive-branch-wide, operational-level, interagency course ever offered by the U.S. government, with 136 participants from eighteen agencies and all nine military combatant commands.

I received letters of commendation from a dozen different agencies and we trained a lot of people in a better way to conduct counterterrorist operations. I like to think that we also saved lives with the knowledge that was gained and shared. But if I couldn't be home in New York, I'd rather have been in Baghdad. On one occasion while I was there, however, Baghdad came to me. Donny had just been named director general of the Iraq Museum—with Nawala returning to her previous position as head of the Department of Cuneiform Studies. Dr. Jaber had returned to the University of Baghdad—with Dr. Abdul Aziz Hameed being named chair of the State Board of Antiquities and Heritage. In January 2005, Donny and Dr. Hameed visited the U.S. State Department to discuss funding for museum renovations.

Whenever Donny came to the United States, which was fairly often, we made it a point to get together if at all possible. For his visit to D.C., I picked a nice restaurant, and when we sat down, I said to my two guests from the Muslim world, "Gentlemen, I'm going to have a glass of wine, but if you don't want me to, I totally understand."

Dr. Hameed said, "Well, that's okay for you, but I'm going to have a Scotch."

"I guess a glass of wine's okay, then," I replied.

Donny trumped that with, "How about a bottle?" It was a very long night.

While I was still in Washington, Diana called me on the phone to ask, "Daddy, can you come to my birthday party this year?" No child should ever have to ask that. She should be able to assume. But her daddy was always on "military duty." I'd missed the last two, which was bad enough. But given that I'd been home for Michael's third, just before September 11, and for his fourth, between Afghanistan and Iraq, it was even harder. The contrast was difficult for a four-year-old girl to understand.

What really broke my heart was when she said, "Daddy, I wish you never joined the Marines."

"Why, sweetheart?"

"Because the Marines always take you away from your children."

"But you know why I leave, right?'

"To fight the bad men so they don't start another fire?"

"That's right."

She thought a moment, her four-year-old mind surveying the human condition.

"Daddy, did you join the Marines before I was in Mommy's tummy?"

"Yes, sweetheart. I joined before I even met Mommy."

And it was precisely the order in which I took on my major roles in life—Marine, DA, husband, father—that, I think, has enabled me to be the father I hope I am.

A few weeks later, when I was home on leave, Diana turned to me again and asked, "Daddy, what does military duty look like?" It had never occurred to me that the kids really had no way of understanding where I went when I wasn't with them. All they knew was that I was gone, and whatever I was doing, I was doing it with someone else. So I came up with a plan to have Michael and Diana spend a few days with me in D.C. I would have loved to bring Jason as well, but he was only three and I was also thinking in practical terms: two hands, two kids.

I picked a week when I could clear my calendar of briefings at the Pentagon and the other eighteen agencies I was working with. Inauguration week was ideal because no one in Washington did anything that week anyway, and most of my briefings had already been canceled. Searching for the perfect place for them, I moved hotels three times—the military uses residence hotels for such temporary assignments—

ultimately finding a place near Dupont Circle that was child-friendly. I sent photographs of the lobby atrium, complete with babbling fountain and ersatz jungle, where the kids could play.

We were all pretty excited. But if I was going to show them "what military duty looks like," I had to take them to my office at the National Defense University. Unfortunately, Diana develops car sickness on trips of more than twenty-five minutes. So every day I tried a different route between work and the hotel, trying to find the way with the fewest stoplights and the least traffic. I tried E Street, Potomac, Pennsylvania Avenue, Rock Creek, and on and on until I finally stumbled onto the perfect route.

They came and we had a glorious week in the capital visiting military duty, even if I did have to do most of my work after the kids had gone to sleep, usually finishing at about three or four in the morning. When it was time to turn out the light, I would walk into the bedroom and hover for a minute, watching them breathe, just as when they were babies. And not just because it's "comforting." When my kids are nearby, I sleep better. When I'm home with them, I get mad when the phone rings just because someone is calling and interrupting us. It could be my mother or my best friend, but my initial reaction is always anger. Being a father is like that red thread braided into all the lines on all the king's sailing ships in the Royal Navy—it's woven into everything I do.

People often ask me what my plans are for the future. What I am going to do when I finally get off active duty and come home. My answer is always the same: whatever it takes to make sure that none of my children ever has to ask me again, "Daddy, can you come to my birthday party this year?"

14

It's All About the Price

Every man is guilty of the good he didn't do.—Voltaire

In August 2004, a young man named Joseph Braude was brought to trial in Brooklyn Federal Court. I was not the prosecutor in that case but a witness. Still on active duty and therefore wearing my uniform, I was, according to the defense attorney, nothing more than "window dressing" for the prosecution.

The summer before, on June 11, 2003, Braude had been caught coming back through New York's JFK airport with three cylinder seals from the Iraq Museum in his shaving kit. His arrest was the first for attempting to smuggle Iraqi antiquities into the United States.

Braude existed in the murky world of nontenured academic achievement. The author of *The New Iraq*, he had studied Hebrew, Persian, and Arabic at Yale, then Islamic history at Princeton. In Iraq, he was a "consultant" to businesses, a bit of a journalist, and according to former CIA director James Woolsey, he had previously been "helpful to the U.S. government."

When caught, he claimed that he had been bringing the seals into the United States for safekeeping, guarding them until they could be handed over to the proper authorities. He seems to have been one of the few individuals who had missed the nonstop media barrage about the amnesty program and the procedure for returning artifacts in Iraq.

The larger irony was that Braude's defense attorney was Benjamin Brafman, the same high-profile lawyer who had defended Puff Daddy when I'd prosecuted the rapper in connection with a Manhattan shoot-out. Brafman was also for the defense in the case of the "Baby-Face Butchers," when I'd prosecuted Christopher Vasquez for his and Daphne Abdela's thrill killing in Central Park. According to Vasquez, he and Brafman's client, Ms. Abdela, who was reared in a posh Central Park West brownstone, stabbed and gutted the forty-two-year-old victim and then threw him into the lake to see if he would float. Abdela pled guilty to manslaughter and Vasquez was convicted at trial.

So how did a relatively obscure quasi-academic like Braude, a small fish with no money, charged with smuggling goods he says he purchased for two hundred dollars, get one of the highest-paid and best defense attorneys in the country, a lawyer whose clients usually leave the courthouse each day in a limo? This is not to suggest Ben Brafman did anything inappropriate in taking the case. But the first dot you have to connect is the number of well-placed individuals and the amount of "genteel" money involved in the antiquities trade. These people live on the Upper East Side and in Georgetown and in Pacific Heights, not in some Mafia enclave in Bensonhurst. But even more important, you have to understand that a trial like Braude's was all about the price. They have chairs and institutes at universities named after them. And they have good lawyers.

In real estate you need "comps," sales of similar houses in your area that establish market value. To establish market value in smuggling, you need a judgment from a court of law. The calculus the bad guys use is actually quite sophisticated. In addition to the actual value of the item itself (be it drugs, weapons, or antiquities), there is the risk associated with the smuggling operation from start to finish. The issues here are the risks of getting caught, and if caught, of getting charged; if charged, of getting convicted; and if convicted, of going to jail. Each factor represents an independent analysis. The bottom line with regard to Iraqi antiquities was that if the first guy who gets caught coming through customs gets a slap on the wrist, the price of smuggled antiquities goes down. If he does prison time, the price goes up.

Not surprisingly, then, I noticed some familiar faces—art collectors and dealers—in the courtroom the day I testified. When the well-prepared prosecutor, Assistant U.S. Attorney Deborah Mayer, put me on the stand, her purpose was to fill in all the details that would undermine the defense attorney's argument. I identified the cylinder seals in question, pointing out their IM numbers, indicating that they were from the museum—in fact, they had been stolen from the basement. She asked me about our outreach effort in Baghdad at the time, the twice-daily press conferences at the museum, all the TV news reports. And then she asked me to provide some additional information about Baghdad geography—where the military, Presidential Palace, and Four-Head Palace, the headquarters of the Coalition Provisional Authority (CPA), were.

The reason all this mattered was that Ben Brafman's main line of defense was that the well-intentioned Mr. Braude did not feel sufficiently safe in Baghdad in June 2003 to turn over his cylinder seals to either the museum or the CPA.

Deborah Mayer—a former Navy JAG who couldn't break the habit of calling me sir—knew what Brafman was going to argue, of course, because one of the foundations of the judicial process is "discovery," the period before the actual trial during which both sides lay their cards on the table. The prosecution lets the defense know all the evidence it has amassed in order to try to convict, the defense provides some of its counterevidence (they are under far fewer requirements), and each side provides a list of all witnesses to be called. There are also pretrial conferences in which the parties—the prosecution, the judge, and the defense—get together and talk turkey. Here deals are struck about what can be presented before that panel of twelve impartial citizens and thus entered into the record (and, more important, into the jurors' consciousness).

There is also a lesser-known process called Queen for a Day (named for the fifties TV show) before you even get to court. It doesn't happen for every case, but when it does, it involves the prosecutor, detective, defense attorney, and defendant. It is a chance for the defendant to tell his story with the understanding that, so long as he does not take the stand and contradict his Queen for a Day statement, nothing he says during this session can be entered into evidence. Even the prosecutor and the judge, then, are privy to this supposedly more candid account. But the simple reality is that trials do not operate on the basis of some Platonic ideal of "Truth"; they operate on the basis of admissible evidence. The real brilliance of the jury system is that, although juries almost never see all of the evidence, in the vast majority of the cases the "truth" wins anyway. But not always.

Under sharp questioning by ICE special agent Bryant Wong, Braude had spoken freely, if not necessarily honestly. Being a part of the investigation, I too knew all that he had said to Wong and to the others. In fact, we had originally hoped to use him as an informant. That he was guilty actually made him more useful, but ultimately I decided that he was just too unreliable.

When it came time for Ben Brafman to cross-examine me, I have to say it felt good to be sparring once again with my old adversary. Ben's goal was to convince the jury that Braude did not feel safe enough to hand over his cylinder seals to me in Baghdad—hoping the jury would forget that Braude had felt safe enough to go to the marketplace to buy the seals in the first place. Ben made much of the two killings that had taken place just after our museum opening, even though they occurred almost a month *after* Braude's arrest. He kept confusing Baghdad geography, even Iraq geography, trying to make it sound as if every act of violence anywhere in Iraq at the time was happening right on top of poor Braude. Ben mentioned that violence had broken out in Kirkuk; I pointed out that Braude was in Baghdad, hundreds of miles away.

Ben said to me, with some frustration, "Right now, with the exception of you, do you honestly believe that anybody in this room understands where Kirkuk is in Iraq."

I shot back, "Your client does," prompting an objection from the prosecutor because things had already gotten a little heated.

Then the judge, Allyne R. Ross, intervened, like a teacher breaking up one of my scuffles back in grade school. "Mr. Brafman, stop. Just move on."

Ben was well-known for his asides, usually delivered as much for the press as for the jury. Despite the judge's warning, he couldn't resist giving me one more shot—and it was a good one. "You're a witness, not a prosecutor."

"I know the truth," I replied.

The rest of the afternoon went on in a similar vein, and then on the second day of the trial, Ben kept handing me press clippings, trying to convince the jury that "everyone knew" that all hell was breaking loose in Baghdad in June 2003, that it was terribly unsafe, and that it is perfectly plausible that Braude would have been too afraid to come forward. But it wasn't holding water. We sparred over my answers again and again, with Brafman asking me about countless press reports—even if they were inaccurate and even if I had never seen them before. It's an old defense-counsel trick, trying to get the jury to hear the contents of those reports even though they were hearsay and therefore inadmissible.

In the skilled hands of Ben Brafman, that old trick usually works. The problem for Ben was that I knew what he was doing and was determined to make him play by the rules. I was displaying a certain frustration at the repetition, and Ben was showing similar signs of frustration because clearly I was not saying what he wanted me to say.

"I don't think you understand . . . ," I told him, trying to explain why I hadn't read another batch of press clippings that had nothing to do with the museum. "I wasn't sitting home in my apartment sipping coffee reading the newspaper."

When I made a similar comment a few moments later, he cut me off, but then the judge cut him off. "Please don't interrupt!" she swatted.

The courtroom is theater, and Ben and I were center stage. I was just home from the war, and Ben was in an exquisitely tailored suit. I could see several of the jurors making faces at Ben, while one even threw up her hands and another started shaking her head at him. Ben could see it too, but as a seasoned pro, he still had a job to do.

After another long round of press clippings, and some fairly taciturn responses from me, he said in exasperation, "You tell me you couldn't have read something if it came across your desk?"

"My desk!" I howled. "My desk?" I had already told the court how we had been camped out in the library and taking showers with a garden hose. Now Ben knew he had blown it. At which point the judge intervened again, pleading for mercy.

The next witness was an instantly likable and very sharp customs inspector, Marguerite Caropolo, also in uniform, and with a Brooklyn accent right out of central casting. She had met Braude at the door to his plane and escorted him to a private room at the airport terminal for further questioning. Obviously, someone had raised suspicions about Braude and told customs that he was on this particular flight, and had been to Iraq. But because Inspector Caropolo had intercepted Braude at the door to the aircraft, rather than in the normal customs control area, Ben proceeded to argue that Mr. Braude had been denied his rights.

In effect, Ben was saying, "Okay, my client lied. He lied on the written customs declaration about where he had been, and he had lied about the value of what he was carrying—both federal crimes. But, because he was nabbed at the door of the plane, he was denied the right to change his mind and correct the false statements. Because of this denial of a second chance to be honest, he deserves a pass." The jurors just weren't buying it. Neither was Ben—who had been urging Braude for months to plead guilty.

We broke for lunch, and when the judge reconvened, the defense folded. Braude changed his plea to guilty of all three charges in the indictment. However satisfying the conviction, the sentence of six months' house arrest and two years' probation was not what I had hoped for.

I could never be a defense attorney. I jokingly say it's because I don't want to have to sit at the same table with all those criminals, but really it's because I need to believe deeply not only in what I do but—most important for me—in the people I do it with. The Constitution says that everyone deserves a vigorous defense—and I firmly believe it. But others can take care of the defendant. I want to defend the victim. After the looting in Baghdad, I felt that the "victim" was not only each person deprived of seeing this part of the world's cultural heritage, but also each of these precious artifacts themselves.

Five thousand years ago, even mundane, commercial objects such as cylinder seals could be exquisitely handcrafted works of art. Other antiquities, such as votive statues, fertility goddesses, and small figurines meant to aid in childbirth, were, in fact, prayers in clay. As you look at these artifacts, you can see these ancient craftsmen trying to probe great mysteries. Today, when free markets are revered above all else, these sacred objects are bought and sold—and too often stolen—like stripped-out auto parts. In 1997, McGuire Gibson noted, "In one Bond Street shop, I was shown a bag of more than a hundred cylinder seals and received an apology because these were the poorer quality ones; I was told that the best items had been sold to Japanese and Taiwanese collectors a day or two before."

There are many players in the stolen-antiquities trade. And like the infamous "molasses to rum to slaves" trade of the eighteenth century, it could not exist without the active complicity of otherwise respectable society. While the first two components—the thieves and smugglers—make no bones about what they do, the last two in this chain—the dealer and the collector—often engage in self-deception of the highest order. But it is the even more covert and painstakingly rationalized participation of academics in the middle that makes this all possible.

Before anyone, collector or museum, pays for a stolen antiquity, it must first be authenticated as genuine, for a price, by an expert curator, dealer, or professor. The price, surprisingly, is not always money. Sometimes it is access to an item that no one else has ever seen or critically examined before. In some cases, it is the ability to publish a new finding that attracts the scholar, and for some, the allure appears to be overwhelming. The more valuable the item, the more visible the "name" necessary to assure the buyer that he's getting his money's worth. If you are going to spend a million dollars on a small statue, you are not going to be satisfied with the guarantees of a graduate student. You want the full professor or the head of an institute.

Dealers are just as necessary. In many cases, socially connected Madison Avenue and Bond Street dealers—the vital link between the smuggler and the collector—have made the sale before the theft. There are many more who would never sponsor a heist, but, like Pontius Pilate, know how to "wash their hands" of unpleasant realities. These facilitators who believe they are engaged in benign criminal activity (an oxymoron of the highest order) might be "shocked" to discover that they are helping finance the drug trade, as well as international terrorism. Smugglers don't care whether the cargo is drugs, weapons, or antiquities— they get paid for their ability to evade the law. And at least during the first leg of the journey out of Iraq, antiquities and weapons often travel together. We almost never recovered an antiquity without recovering weapons as well.

Antiquities smuggling is also helping to fund the insurgency in Iraq. In a series of simultaneous raids on a terrorist hideaway in the first three days of June 2005, north of Karmah in al-Anbar province in northwest Iraq, Marines operating alongside Iraqi security forces arrested five terrorists in their underground bunkers. The bunkers were filled with automatic weapons, ammunition stockpiles, black uniforms, ski masks, compasses, night-vision goggles, and a chest of more than thirty artifacts that had been stolen from the Iraq Museum. You connect the dots.

We need to get the community of scholars, museum directors, dealers, and collectors to stop kidding themselves and, like our undercover archaeologist in London, to lend a hand.

Archaeologists like John Russell, professor of art history at the Massachusetts College of Art, offer an example of what can be done and what more could be done if archaeologists worked more closely with law enforcement. Wanting to do more than just complain about the devastation of Iraq's archaeological sites, John raised his hand and said, "Not on my watch." Then he took a leave of absence and fearlessly served as the senior advisor to Iraq's Ministry of Culture from September 2003 until June 2004. Fifteen years earlier, he had gone to Nineveh and Nimrud to study the reliefs that had been left in situ. After the first Gulf War, he reported seeing these same pieces turning up for sale in the West. From Nineveh alone, he saw photographs of three relief fragments for sale in 1995, ten in 1996, and two more in 1997. Of the reliefs he saw in Nimrud, one later turned up for sale in London in 1996 and another in 1997. He also noted that when he last saw these pieces, they were in the hands of the Iraqi government in the Antiquities Department house on the site of Nimrud—adding, almost as an afterthought, "There is no evidence that Iraqi officials are involved in these thefts." Then how did they reach the market?

Maybe I do dig like a cop. But, as with the earlier claims about glass cutters and 170,000 stolen objects, even brave archaeologists sometimes investigate like college professors.

In 1995, London businessman and collector Shlomo Moussaieff offered the Bible Lands Museum in Israel a piece of an Assyrian relief for temporary display. To ensure the relief was genuine, the museum contacted John Russell. John immediately recognized it as one of the reliefs he had seen years earlier at Nineveh. Moussaieff told *New York Times* reporters Martin Gottlieb and Barry Meier that he had purchased the piece for fifteen thousand dollars in a warehouse at the Geneva airport. He later returned it to the Iraqi government—and they reimbursed him the purchase price.

That is what can be done when law enforcement and academics work together. To see what more could be done, consider the time John Russell was approached by a lawyer in November 1996 asking if he would authenticate ten Assyrian reliefs. When Russell told the lawyer that the pieces were authentic, but stolen, he never heard from the guy again, and, of course, those pieces have never been seen again. I know John is too decent a man to do business with these people, and he did the honorable thing by refusing. But my response as a prosecutor is, "Do business!" Or at least pretend to. "You bet," you tell them. "Bring 'em in tomorrow and let's have a look," and then you call the cops. Wear a wire. Record the conversation. Tell the collectors and dealers you'll do business anytime. You have to get your hands dirty, because tracking down criminals, even well-heeled, well-connected criminals, is dirty work—and we need to find the courage to do it.

There are indeed many different kinds of courage—the courage of Thermopylae, the courage to tell it straight to your kids, and the courage to tell the colleagues in your department that you are going to start co-operating with the police. Intellectual, moral, and artistic courage, as well as the courage valued in the three areas in which I spend most of my time—the courtroom, the boxing ring, and the battlefield—I see as all coming from the same place.

In my view, being efficient and ruthless on the battlefield is entirely consistent with being a loving, fully sensate human being. It is not so much a question of bouncing back and forth but of integrating. At times, being a good military officer means having compassion and sensi-tivity: witness Siegfried Sassoon, winner of the military cross for his bravery during the Battle of the Somme, who wrote poems from the trenches in World War I, expressing the same tender "watch while they sleep" concern for his men on the battlefield that I have experienced with my children. At times, being a good parent means being tough and demanding. Witness those parents sturdy enough to be the solid brick wall a teenager can rail against, even beat his fist against, without the in-hibiting fear of doing damage.

JIACG brought down the Chinese Wall between law enforcement and counterterrorism. Perhaps we should begin taking down the equally counterproductive wall we've set up between being fiercely loving and being occasionally fierce.

I used to quote a line from George Orwell because I liked the way it sounded. He said, "We sleep safe in our beds because rough men stand ready in the night to do violence to those who would harm us." I never intended to be one of those standing ready to do violence so that my kids could sleep safe.

But that is what we in the military do when we do it right. The military—like cops and boxers—has clearly defined codes of conduct, the very strength of which leads to outrage when they are violated, whether by a Mike Tyson biting off an ear in the ring, a cop physically abusing a suspect, or a Lieutenant Calley killing unarmed civilians at My Lai. The outrage is particularly acute among others who share the code. No one hates a bad cop more than a good cop.

In the world of illicit antiquities, people who would bulldoze an archaeological site—or indirectly pay for it by buying illicit antiquities—clearly have no honor, no code, no rules. One of the defining characteristics of terrorism is also the absence of honor, of codes, of rules. Not only children, but the children of the terrorists' own people are fair game. The cult of death among radical jihadists is so strong that they prep their younger cousins and little brothers and sisters to go on suicide missions. People who will sell out their own cultural heritage are bad enough, but when we stare into the abyss of terrorism, it stares back that much more deeply.

John Stuart Mill, one of the founders of modern liberalism, wrote, "War is an ugly thing, but not the ugliest of things, the degraded state of moral and patriotic feeling which thinks that nothing is worth war is much worse. The person who has nothing for which he is willing to fight . . . is a miserable creature." Yet far too many remain passive in the face of terrorism on the one hand and widespread looting and trafficking on the other. They stand across a wide cultural chasm that separates them from the warrior ethos of Leonidas or even the "get into the fight" ethos of law enforcement.

Confronted with serious threats to civilization—whether cultural theft or terrorism—how do we respond? Do we come back at it with the reasoned and compassionate consensus of the whole-foods collective or with the mindless savagery of a lynch mob? Ideally, neither. Instead, we must come at the homicidal rage of the one and the senseless disregard of history of the other with hard steel, informed strategies, and a rock-solid code of acceptable behavior for ourselves. Yet today's cultural bifurcation tries to force us to chose only one or the other—the inert idealist or the mindless brute.

Historically, the life of action and the life of the mind (or artistic sensibility) have always been two halves of a single whole. Today, when we conjure up the classical Greek ideals, we think of philosophy and art, but even in their greatest contribution to aesthetics, Greek society was all about *agon*—competition. Each year in Athens, the presentation of new plays was such a competition, with Aeschylus, Sophocles, and others vying for the prize in playwriting. But *agon* does not mean hostility. In most every boxing match since the ancient Olympics, you'll see the guys hug each other after the last round.

Consider Aeschylus—the first and in many respects greatest of Greek tragedians—famous today for his masterpiece, the *Oresteia* trilogy. That is not, however, how he saw himself. The inscription he wrote for his own gravestone mentioned not his theatrical renown, but what mattered most to him: "This gravestone covers Aeschylus... The field of Marathon will speak of his bravery, and so will the long-haired Mede [Persian] who learned it well." In his eyes, he was a warrior first. Sophocles was elected one of Athens's ten generals. Xenophon led ten thousand Greeks on an epic march out of Persia and then wrote an equally epic masterpiece describing their *Anabasis*. Socrates, the father of modern thought, fought with conspicuous bravery at Delium, Amphipolis, and at Potidaea. He also worked from time to time as a stonecutter, reminding us that a little blue-collar experience can be an instructive counterweight in a life spent with books.

As recently as the nineteenth century, General Sir William Butler, knighted for bravery, published author, and accomplished painter, said a "nation that will insist on drawing a broad line of demarcation between the fighting man and the thinking man is liable to find its fighting done by fools and its thinking done by cowards." Lord Byron, "rock star" Romantic poet, died while fighting for Greek liberty against the Turks. Winston Churchill, a product of the Royal Military Academy, fought hand to hand against the dervishes on the Nile, was a hero of the Boer War, served as first lord of the admiralty, won the Nobel Prize in literature, was not a bad painter, and will be remembered as perhaps the greatest statesman of the modern era.

Nor is this a feature of Western civilization only. Under Bushido, the code of the warrior, a samurai was expected to excel as much in poetry and calligraphy as in his swordsmanship. A revered seventeenth-century samurai text held that to focus only on the martial arts is to be a "samurai of little worth." Indeed, the most treasured mode of artistic expression for the samurai—valued for its serenity and simplicity—was the *Cha-no-yu*, the tea ceremony.

But the mechanization in World War I turned the warrior into a lamb for the slaughter, and it turned officers into bureaucrats. The draft and consequent democratization meant dilution, and the profession of arms ceased to be a profession. After Vietnam, recruiters were kicked off campuses, and except in the American South, the military, and alongside it the military code of honor, dropped in social cachet to about the level of chewing tobacco. And the idea of a promising person going off for a stint in the service became only slightly more common than going West to become a cattle drover. All of this contributed to the "culture war" that has left us with red staters and blue staters, yelling at each other on TV, unable to find common ground or arrive at sensible policies.

The fact that *honor* is a word now rarely used without irony costs us in other ways as well. To be an "idealist" is to be considered something of a flake. So what we're left with is the idealization of wealth and comfort, justified by Calvinist piety. It is worth remembering that when Socrates was condemned to death, it was for the crime of impiety or, as Voltaire put it, of being "the atheist who says there is only one God." A couple of thousand years later, another Greek, Nikos Kazantzakis, said, "In religions that have lost their creative spark, the gods eventually become nothing more than poetic motifs or ornaments for decorating human solitude and walls."

And the warrior's code has decayed along with those gods. There are things worth defending other than self, but the idea of the warrior as that defender has become another antiquated concept. And so the warrior must exist in parallel with the everyday world, John Keegan tells us. But is not of this world, and always follows at a distance. The warrior's ideals, like the warriors themselves, are forced ever farther to the margins of society.

I have to admit that riding a patrol boat on the Tigris or going through doors in Baghdad clears the head in a way that I enjoy. But for me the physical excitement or the ego stroke of having men trust me enough to move when I say so isn't the attraction. It's the ability to make a difference. And while it may sound a bit like a certain knight-errant from La Mancha, I like the idea of seeing something that is wrong and being able to fix it. That is why I'm a prosecutor rather than a considerably better paid defense attorney, and that's a large part of the reason why I stayed on active duty for four years after my recall, and why I transferred back into the reserves at the end of that hitch—knowing full well I could be called again—rather than retire.

Arête is the Greek concept of honor for the sake of honor, excellence for its own sake. But we don't have to say it in Greek for the concept to sound out of place. Even in English it's something of an anachronism. But honor is not some antique refinement, like knowing classical languages. Honor is a force multiplier. If you decide in advance to act honorably, then, when the moment arises, you know exactly what to do. It doesn't mean you do it—I'm living proof of the adage that we do what we can, not what we ought—but at least it points you in the right direction straight as the needle to the pole. The concept of honor, like the concept of bravery, is a form of mental conditioning. *Semper Fidelis*, "always faithful," is the Marine Corps motto. It is not just a phrase but—like Bushido—a way of life.

In the Marine Corps, everything we do, we rehearse until the correct response becomes reflexive. If you're going to do a raid, you practice that raid a hundred times. It's all about conditioning and each individual's muscle memory. Culture and custom, codes and systems of honor, are society's version of the same kind of conditioning—only in this case, it's a form of *societal* muscle memory. Cultural artifacts—especially those from the distant past that resonate in an almost subconscious way—help guide us in this collective training. In a very real sense, then, they offer a possible answer to Juvenal's question of the first century, "Who will guard the guardians?" We all will as a society based on the code we have established. "What is honored in a country," Plato observed, "will be cultivated there."

It seems a great loss that the code of honor and physical courage that comes out of the warrior ideal is sometimes limited—without pressing the issue too far—to certain segments of society: military, police and firefighters. But these actors and doers are often less than tolerant of different ways of thinking or different lifestyles. On the other hand, there is a culture of highly developed aesthetic appreciation that is sometimes limited—again without painting with too broad a brush—to certain academics and a thin slice of the economic elite. These readers and thinkers are great on nuance and sensitivity, but even when they are "right" on the issues, they are often subject to paralysis by analysis.

Some people will always be the first to run out of a burning building, and then there are others like NYPD officer Jerome Dominguez and Court Officer Tommy Jurgens who always will be first to run in. There were financial types in the World Trade Center on 9/11 that relocated their offices to the suburbs, and there were some who reenlisted in the military.

Hemingway, who integrated both the aesthetic and the active side of life, put it this way: "If people bring so much courage to this world, the world has to kill them to break them, so of course it kills them . . . It kills the very good and the very gentle and the very brave impartially. If you are none of these, you can be sure it will kill you too. But there will no special hurry."

My idea of hell is being one of those for whom life is in no special hurry.

★ ★ ★

Hell on earth can take other forms as well. Late during my tenure at
the Iraq Museum—after all the original members of my team had deployed home—Dr. Chalabi told me about a mass grave that had been
uncovered about an hour south of Baghdad. I wanted to go without
anyone I knew, take as long as I needed, and not have to make conversation. So Dr. Chalabi offered to provide an escort to the site along
with appropriate protection.

After we left the city and got out into the desert, we came to an especially desolate stretch in an already desolate landscape. The sun was
blinding. A few of Chalabi's men milled about. I also noticed some international aid workers. I got out of the vehicle and walked toward the
trench. It was about six feet wide with vertical walls about three feet
deep. But the skeletons inside were not a tangle of arms and legs, as if
they had been dumped in. They were in good order, lying close together,
like soldiers in a row. Some were still wearing their blindfolds. But what
nearly brought me to my knees were the skeletons of children. As I
looked along the line of decayed bodies, I began to see family units—two
large skeletons, then maybe two smaller ones. At times it looked to me as
if I could detect a larger arm lying across a smaller form. I imagined a father comforting his child just before the gunshots.

After a moment I had to look away, which was when I saw a crying
woman dressed in black. She was wandering around the site, and when
she saw me, she reached out her arms and came forward. I was in uniform, and to her I guess I represented authority. Seeing her tears, I put my
hand over my heart—the Iraqi gesture of condolence. A kid of about
twelve came over and he translated. He said that the woman was trying
to locate the bones of her family. As we talked, I tried to move her away
from the gravesite through my gestures. I remember telling her that there
was no way I could know which were the bones of her family.

It was clear this site had already been disturbed and some of the
skeletal remains already removed—doubtless by other similarly grieved
family members. I told her that the only way she could know for sure
was to wait for international aid workers to check what remained of
the clothing on the bodies to see if there were any identifying cards or
papers. Perhaps she could find her family that way or even by a process
of elimination. Even as I said that, I knew I was lying to her; many of
the skeletons had no clothing remaining and it would be impossible to
know who they were.

She again pleaded, saying she didn't care. Only bones from the site would allow her to bury her grief. "Weep and be not consoled, but weep," Dostoyevsky wrote, "a long while yet will you keep that great mother's grief." I looked at her and I said, "What do you want?"

"This one," she said, "was his size. I am sure it is my son." So I knelt down with one foot in the trench and one knee on the edge and—may God forgive me—did what she asked. "*Shukran,*" she said. "Thank you."

It was time to get back in the car.

More than 270 mass graves have been reported in Iraq. By January 2004, 53 had been confirmed and the remainder were still awaiting an inspection team. According to Human Rights Watch, Saddam Hussein systematically "disappeared" as many as 290,000 Iraqis, mostly Kurds in the north and Shi'ites in the south, during his reign of terror. His 1989 plan for filling in the wetlands of southern Iraq was, essentially, geno-cide directed at the roughly half a million Iraqi marsh Arabs. In 2004, the *Journal of the American Medical Association* concluded a ten-year study and determined that "nearly one out of every two families in southern Iraq . . . directly experienced violent human rights abuses, such as beat-ings, kidnappings, amputations and killings."

But sad to say, while Saddam was gassing, executing, and torturing his own people, it was business as usual for some archaeologists. Between 1987 and 1989, Western archaeologists were digging at Nineveh and Nimrud, just a few miles away from the Anfal campaign that resulted in the "wholesale destruction of some 2,000 villages" and the "mass sum-mary executions and mass disappearance of tens of thousands of non-combatants, including many women and children and sometimes the entire population of villages."

Given the magnitude of the atrocities in proximity to major archaeo-logical sites, and given that excavation requires contact with local labor, as well as local transportation and local housing, it is astounding that, at least to the best of my knowledge, not one of the archaeologists who excavated in Iraq ever publicly protested any of Saddam's atrocities. To say that they did not know is to deny too much. It is to deny what was common knowledge. Even after the atrocities were well documented and publicized throughout the world years later, there was still silence. "Access meant success," and no one was willing to speak up.

Having for years "enjoyed the warm hospitality, great food, and excellent library of [the British School of Archaeology's expedition house in Baghdad]," some Western researchers even continued to visit

after the United Nations imposed sanctions. In March 2001, several
U.S. and British archaeologists went to Baghdad and were greeted by
Saddam's deputy prime minister, Tariq Aziz. They were then thanked
personally by Saddam's culture minister, Hamed Youssef Hamadi, re-
splendent in his military uniform, "for breaking the cultural embargo
on Iraq," an embargo that was, of course, instigated to help bring Saddam into compliance with the arms control and human rights standards
of the civilized world.

Then, in January 2003, seventy-five "archaeologists and other
scholars . . . [went] on record as opposing the current threat by the
Bush administration to wage war against Iraq." They howled in protest
about the U.S. intervention and the lives it would cost and later rose up
in indignation that the museum was ransacked, but they never said a
word about Saddam. Even their logic was faulty, proclaiming that "the
likelihood that [Iraq] would attack its neighbors is far greater in the
event of a U.S. attack," curiously having forgotten Hussein's unpro-
voked attacks on Iran in 1980 and Kuwait in 1990.

Some journalists live in similar glass houses. Many had lived and
worked in Iraq for years and had never reported a single atrocity. When
confronted about such silence, their answer is that they would have
been kicked out. My response to that is "And?" Maybe that's what
you're supposed to do—speak the truth and get kicked out if need be.

The British Museum was founded in 1753. Within a hundred years, excavating for private collections had become a passion among Europe's
genteel and well-heeled, which is why the Parthenon Marbles (commonly known as the Elgin Marbles, in honor of the man who took
them) are in London. It is also why the Pergamum altar is in Berlin, the
Law Code of Hammurabi and the Venus de Milo are in the Louvre, the
pediments from the Aphaia on Aegina are in the Munich Glyptothek,
and "Priam's Treasure" from Troy is in St. Petersburg and Moscow. By
modern standards, each of these acquisitions was an instance of looting.
And the debate over which culture, by rights, should have the privilege
of possessing and displaying such treasures has intensified. The countries of origin insist on the return of what they consider to be pillaged
artifacts, while those in possession argue that time is on their side.

Colin Renfrew, Lord Renfrew of Kaimsthorn, the founder of the
Illicit Antiquities Research Center at Cambridge University's McDonald Institute, dismisses these claims of continued ownership as disingen-

uous. He correctly points out that those making claims of ownership are often descendants not of the culture they wish to appropriate, but of subsequent conquerors who represent one more link in an endless line of looters and plunderers. It's a bit like the Seventh Calvary laying claim to grave goods from the Lakota Sioux.

But the much more serious problem is the ongoing, accelerating plunder of archaeological sites in the twenty-first century. This is not just a question of cultural pride or property rights—it is a question of losing irreplaceable historical data.

Archaeological discoveries require context in order to be fully meaningful. An object from the distant past for sale in a Baghdad marketplace or even properly preserved in a well-lit, climate-controlled museum accessible to grandmothers and schoolchildren tells us little. Objects become instructive and meaningful only when we know at what level they were found, and what else was found with them. The constellation and exact placement of objects illuminate how life was lived, and how social structures, art forms, and technologies progressed. That is why modern archaeology goes to great lengths, with dental picks and tiny brushes, to approach fieldwork in a carefully documented, stratigraphic fashion. It's a lot like detective work at a crime scene, moving inch by inch across a grid. And that is why having gun-toting looters bulldozing tells throughout Iraq is such a tragedy. These marauders are destroying opportunities to learn about the past that will never come again.

Some archaeological purists seem to insist that objects, once studied, should be returned to the ground. The majority of archaeologists, however, argue merely that any market for antiquities, however aboveboard, encourages the black market, which in turn encourages looting. Dealers counter—not unreasonably—that without a commercial trade to maintain market value, antiquities would be treated like so many cow pies on so many third-world construction sites. At the other extreme, some collectors argue for the complete legalization of the trade in antiquities, not coincidentally using the same morally bankrupt and legally false arguments some people make for the legalization of drugs.

Museums have also entered the fray. The laws of patrimony—where they exist—hold that everything that comes out of the ground belongs to the country in which the artifact is found. And many emerging nations now insist that antiquities should stay home. But if you carried patrimony to its logical conclusion, every single piece of Mesopotamian art would be in Baghdad and Egyptian art in Cairo. When you ask

Donny George about the treasure from Nineveh in the British Museum, he says with brilliant Donny flair, "It certainly belongs to Iraq. Let's consider it a long-term loan."

Museum directors insist that restricting antiquities to their country of origin would mean that most of the interested public would never see them. True enough, the only place most New Yorkers or Bostonians will ever see Mesopotamian objects is at New York's Metropolitan Museum of Art or Boston's Museum of Fine Arts. But then the Solomonic Lord Renfrew counters that this problem could be dealt with on the basis of museum loans—though less permanent than the kind the British Museum and Louvre seem to have in mind.

But it isn't just museums and collectors. Some countries have less interest in stopping the illegal trade than might be indicated by their public protestations, particularly because "open" borders are profitable borders. Moreover, the sheer volume of tonnage that passes through certain international ports and free-trade zones makes anything approaching a complete inspection impossible. Even the improved technology placed at such ports and borders as a result of September 11 does not solve the problem: Devices that detect weapons and explosives do not detect alabaster, lapis lazuli, and carnelian, which is as it should be. In the battle against terrorists, we don't need teacups or gift-shop statuettes setting off false alarms.

Perhaps in response to such lax enforcement, there is a movement not to allow any antiquities into the United States unless the source country verifies its origins. That's not fair either. Many objects that came out of the ground in the nineteenth and early twentieth centuries were lawfully excavated and owned (under the laws of that time), yet have no documented proof of that fact. What if the source country cannot or will not verify the origins of an arguably legal piece? More than likely, it would simply go underground. And if the piece was not lawfully excavated in the first place, all that the additional requirement would mean is one more official who has to be bribed.

For their part, the Collectors Association argues that all that should be required for the purchase and sale of antiquities is a "birth certificate" of sorts, a statement that is called "provenance" or "provenience." In the United States, *provenance* is the documentation; *provenience* is the exact location where the piece was found (latitude, longitude, height). In the UK, *provenance* means both. Trouble is, give me an hour and a decent counterfeiter and I can get you good paper.

All it takes to give something false provenance (paper) is to send it to an expert who can check to see if the piece has ever been seen, documented, or photographed. The same expert usually begins by making sure the piece is real and then determines if it has ever seen the light of day. But you have to pick the right expert. That's where the Nineveh thieves went wrong. They picked John Russell and he ratted them out. You can be sure that John is off the list, but you can be just as sure that the list has many more names. If the item has been seen or photographed before in situ or in a government-owned collection (take the Sacred Vase of Warka as an extreme example), then it can never surface and must stay underground forever. For those pieces, the seller must still authenticate, but need not produce provenance.

On the other hand, if the expert determines that the item has never been seen before, then after it is authenticated, you need to send it to a dealer to provide a fake history. McGuire Gibson has described visiting shops in which he often finds illicit "items . . . accompanied by written authentications, including dating and translation or at least indications of content, signed by well-known British colleagues."

Laws requiring that the archaeological find spot be indicated would add more of a challenge. Even this requirement can be gotten around. A crooked archaeologist could falsify his excavation catalogue. More commonly, though, a dealer claims that the item had been in his grandfather's collection. He then produces the paperwork indicating that, for an Iraqi artifact, it was received before 1923, and that, for an Egyptian artifact, it was received before 1983 (the years patrimony laws went into effect in those countries). Usually, the grandfather is conveniently dead when these dealers make such "discoveries."

Antiquities dealer Frederick Schultz is a classic example. In February 2002, he was found guilty of violating U.S. law by conspiring to receive stolen Egyptian antiquities. Using the standard cover, Schultz told potential buyers that the antiquities came from the Thomas Alcock Collection, which he said belonged to an English family since the 1920s—long before the Egyptian patrimony laws. Of course, the Thomas Alcock Collection was a complete fiction, created by Schultz and coconspirator-turned-prosecution-witness Jonathan Tokeley-Parry to hide the stolen nature of the antiquities.

The resourcefulness of the dealers engaged in the black market highlight the challenges facing law enforcement. But it gets worse. According to Lord Renfrew, although "unprovenanced" art is all but synonymous with "looted" art, some of the world's greatest museums fuel the illicit trade through their "no questions asked" acquisitions policies.

In the 1960s, the Metropolitan Museum of Art in New York acquired the "Lydian Hoard," a treasure from the time of King Croesus. When they put the objects on display in the 1980s, the showing aroused the suspicions of the Turkish government—Lydian sites had been notoriously subject to looting by local villagers. The Turks filed a complaint against the Met, and the museum was forced to produce such woefully inadequate documentation that, ultimately, they were obliged to return the objects to Turkey. Insufficient documentation creates other risks as well. Several years ago, the Getty Museum acquired a kouros, a statue of a Greek youth standing in a stylized position, for many millions of dollars. They appear not to have asked many questions—perhaps for fear of getting the wrong answers. The irony is that the statue was a fake, and the Getty people were taken for a serious ride. In 1995, the Getty claimed to adopt a more circumspect policy.

Over many years, museums and private collectors have developed other ways of establishing false provenance that don't require anything so crass—and transparently illegal—as forgery. All that's required for "antiquity laundering" is an exhibition in a respectable museum, however minor, and a catalogue that is purposefully vague about where, exactly, an object came from and who, exactly, might have held possession of it from the time of excavation to the time that it first appeared in public. English country estates and French châteaus have notoriously large attics, and previous ownership is easily attributable to any number of Victorian eccentrics or dotty grandmothers. It is also true that many a deceased expert has been shown to have authored a slightly dodgy provenance.

Auction houses also figure in the mix. At one time or another, Sotheby's, Christie's, and most of their ilk have been called to account for their practices. Sotheby's in London gave up dealing in antiquities altogether in 1997—though they continued to refer interested buyers to their New York office. Sotheby's stressed that the change was in response to "their concerns on issues of patrimony and heritage," and not as a result of the enormous smuggling scandal exposed by Peter Watson of Britain's Channel 4 television station just a few months earlier.

Despite claims that they have cleaned up their act, many otherwise reputable dealers, museums, and galleries continue their practices in the finest traditions of last century's robber barons—mixing the sleaziest underworld characters with the world's most "respectable" elites. Helping to drive the matchmaking, the U.S. tax code still allows dealers and benefactors to take huge tax breaks even from unprovenanced and almost assuredly "hot" antiquities that are donated to museums. And it is hard to assume "good faith" in the notorious "no questions asked" acquisitions policies of many of those museums.

The Illicit Antiquities Research Center makes two recommendations: stop clandestine excavations and establish standards for the licensing of dealers. Both ideas have merit, but do not go far enough. The standards should apply to all parties. Although many argue that the interests of dealers, collectors, museums, and archaeologists differ so dramatically that establishing a single code of conduct acceptable to all is impossible, such differences are no greater than those existing between prosecutors and criminal defense attorneys. Yet, the American Bar Association has adopted and actively enforces a single code of ethics applicable to every attorney admitted to the bar.

We need to do far more, however, to add teeth to these ideas. And it is not enough to suppress the market. "Suppressing" the market—without taking additional measures—actually creates supply-and-demand forces that drive up the price. Unfortunately, the history of legislation in this area shows far more gum than incisor.

The first international attempt to prevent the importation of cultural property stolen or illegally exported from source nations was UNESCO's 1970 Convention on the Means of Prohibiting and Preventing the Illicit Import, Export and Transfer of Ownership of Cultural Property. The crux of the agreement was to establish the assumption that anything unprovenanced after 1970 was looted unless proven otherwise. While a step in the right direction, this convention has proven largely ineffective. The enforcing mechanism for its protections in the United States is the 1983 Convention on Cultural Property Implementation Act (CPIA), which places the initial burden of proving the lawful possession of the artifacts on the possessor. It also provides for the implementation of import restrictions, either through bilateral agreements with the aggrieved country or through emergency actions in crisis situations.

Under this crisis provision, the U.S. Congress passed the Emergency Protection for Iraqi Cultural Antiquities Act of 2004 in November 2004, and President George W. Bush signed it into law three weeks later. We can see the power of dealers, collectors, and museums in that it took Congress nineteen months to pass a bill establishing more effective mechanisms to stop the illegal importation of stolen Iraqi antiquities into the country. The act permits the seizure of all undocumented cultural material being imported into the United States.

But there are still other legal hurdles to overcome. Under U.S. law, no one can acquire good title to stolen property. Someone who buys an object in good faith has to return it if it has been shown to have been stolen. In civil-code countries, however, particularly in Europe, a good-faith purchaser is favored over true owners. Thus, even when an item has been shown to have been stolen, if the current owner can show that he didn't know it was stolen at the time of purchase, he usually gets to keep it. Moreover, international legal restrictions are effective only after the date on which they are signed into law. That is why there are so many antiquities on the market with provenance indicating ownership before 1970—the year of the UNESCO convention.

Even after 1970, it is still possible for illegal antiquities to be "laundered." As long as the antiquities pass through, say, the Geneva Freeport (without being inspected, of course) and receive valid export stamps from the Swiss (whose policy is to allow the free movement of commerce in and out of its freeports), dealers and museums in New York and London can legally import those newly cleaned objects. Given the loose weave in this fabric of laws and regulations, we can see why so many embarrassing questions sit like an eight-hundred-pound floral centerpiece at a museum fund-raiser. The Rockefeller Wing of the Met contains a treasure trove of antiquities from Peru. But how did they get there? It is well-known that looting has ravaged Peru for decades. In other regions, looting is destroying sites as soon as they are discovered, crushing any hope of learning about previously unknown cultures.

And it cannot help when antiquities draw record prices at auction. When the throne room of Sennacherib was excavated by Henry Layard in 1849, some of the reliefs were taken to the British Museum, some to the University of Pennsylvania Museum, and another to the country estate of one of Layard's patrons, Lady Charlotte Guest. She constructed a display area for her treasures, a new wing called the Nineveh Porch. Over time, the country house was sold and became the site for the Canford School. Lady Charlotte's Nineveh Porch became the tuck-shop or snack bar. The relief was painted over and, when it was remembered at all, was thought to be a plaster cast. In 1992, John Russell determined that it was authentic. Shortly thereafter, the piece was cleaned up and sold at auction for 7.7 million pounds.

15

WHATEVER REMAINS

I know now that there is no one thing that is true—it is all true.
—Ernest Hemingway

IN THE YEARS after 9/11, there was a massive burnout within a New York City Police Department that had been worked to death. Because retirement pay is based on earnings during the last years on the job—and these cops knew they would never make so much overtime money again—it was time for many to hang it up. Retiring during that period worked out for their pensions and for their kids' college funds, but for me, it meant I was never able to have my "last case" with many of them, or even to say good-bye in person.

Once, while I was home on leave, I called up the Manhattan Robbery Squad to speak to the lieutenant, an old friend about to take the gold watch. He had sent out e-mails to all the people on his list, and I was calling him up to say congratulations, best of luck, and all that.

Some guy answered the phone, a voice I didn't recognize, and I said, "Hey, it's Matthew Bogdanos. Is the lieu around?"

"Who's this again?" asked the guy.

"Matthew Bogdanos. B-O-G-D-A-N-O-S. Colonel, USMC. Also an assistant district attorney."

He said, "Can I tell the lieu what this is in regards to?"

"Here's what you can do. You can tell him that Matthew Bogdanos wants to talk to him."

"And who are you again?"

"Where are you sitting?" I said.

"What're you talking about? I'm in the squad room."

"Where is your desk?"

He described it.

I said, "Okay, so you're sitting in Kevin Flanagan's old desk. Look over your right shoulder. You see a desk in the far corner near the lieutenant's door? There's a computer on it, and a lot of papers . . . that's my desk. It's been my desk for more than ten years and it will always be my desk."

"Yo, pal . . . meaning no disrespect, but I don't know you, you don't know me."

I said, "I know. Sorry. Just let me talk to Lieutenant O'Connor."

As soon as the lieutenant got on the line, I went off on a tear. "Paul, you're killing me. How could you do this to me?"

He said, "Yeah, yeah, I know. I've got five new guys. You gonna come back and help me train them?"

"Paul, do me a solid. Put up my picture or something, will ya?"

When Chesty Puller reached retirement and was asked about his thirty-seven-year career in the Marines, he said, "Well, I'd like to do it all over again. The whole thing. And more than that—more than anything—I'd like to see once again the face of every Marine I've ever served with."

I'll drink a glass of retsina to that. And not just to the Marines, but to the exceptional men and women from a variety of services and agencies with whom I served in JIACG. I'll also extend the sentiment well beyond the military, because there are other bonds I hold just as dear.

Before 2001, in almost seventeen years as a prosecutor in the federal, state, and military justice systems, I handled well over a thousand different cases, resulting in about six hundred felony indictments and almost two hundred felony trials. Over the years, I found my way onto many a victim's Christmas card mailing list. Some would even send pictures of their family—for a while at least. I saved all those cards, and just before I left for Afghanistan I spent hours reading every one of them. I read their thanks for convicting the man who had killed their son or father, brutally attacked their daughter, or changed their lives forever by putting a gun to their heads to rob them. But I wondered if *they* knew that for a few weeks or months—depending on the complexity of the case—each of them had been with me every waking moment. While I was shaving in the morning previewing that day's events in court. While I was sitting in my office long after the lights were out in the hall wondering if I had missed something that would mean the difference between conviction and acquittal—deciding I should go over the evidence just one more time to be sure. And while I was hitting the heavy bag with a steady stream of combinations, listening for the sweet sound the bag makes when you hit it just right, all the while reviewing the witnesses I would be calling to testify at the trial, wondering who would need extra attention the night before they took the stand.

As I read their letters, for just a moment I could see their faces. Not when they were at the morgue identifying the body. Not when they were still in the hospital describing their attacker. No, I saw them later, after the defendant had been convicted and they could allow themselves the luxury of starting to feel safe again. Even if I had the time, there was no way to contact the smallest fraction of these people. Many had died. Many had themselves later been incarcerated for their own crimes. Many had just vanished. Most, I suspected, would not have wanted to hear from me anyway, being forever attached as I was to a dark—usually the darkest—moment in their lives.

Another relationship I cherish is with my juries. Years after a trial, I'll be running along the river or through a park, and I'll hear someone yell, "Hey, DA!" and it's one of my jurors. These start out as twelve complete strangers who walk into a courtroom, and you ask them to trust you just because you are the prosecutor. Cicero once said that every time he made a speech, he felt as if he were submitting to judgment, "not only about my ability, but my character and honor." That is how I feel each time I enter the courtroom. The best way to describe this relationship is a courtship. There's the wooing phase, which is jury selection. You get to know me; I get to know you. I glimpse a little of you; I reveal a little of me. Jurors are expected to bare their souls and describe what they believe and if they hate police or if they are racists. The reason good prosecutors bare a little bit of their souls as well is so the jury knows that we are in it together. In other words, I show them that I'm prepared to do what I'm asking them to do.

Then there's the journey phase, where together the jury and I uncover the defendant's guilt, all the while building on—and never violating—the bond of trust between us. On this journey, I vow never to hide anything from them—even if it hurts "the case"—and never to present evidence I believe might be false. The jury vows never to allow bias or prejudice to enter their deliberations. Finally, there is the catharsis that comes with the verdict. If each of us has done his or her job, then whatever the verdict, we feel proud, and we are forever linked by the memory of what we have done together.

But right up there with "the face of every Marine I've ever served with," and the faces of so many jurors and victims' family members, I cherish the sorry mugs of a lot of smart, tough detectives. Mike Kennedy retired and started a second career as a Florida cop. Kevin Flanagan retired and makes good money as a security consultant. Some, like Jerome, are no longer with us. If I had the chance to see Jerome's face again, I wouldn't talk about how I've missed him or how he's still on my speed dial. No, I'd tell him what he'd really want to hear. I'd finally admit what I should have told him when I had the chance, that he was the better shot. The trust and camaraderie I've had with the men of the NYPD, the esprit de corps, is the same that I experienced in Afghanistan and Iraq. There's still plenty of door-kickers left—so *Insha'Allah*, my service with such remarkable people isn't over yet.

And then there are the judges. Of those I "grew up" with, who patiently and bravely suffered through my prosecutorial adolescence, few are left now. Soon there will be none. Harold Rothwax and Shirley Levitan have passed away. Herb Adlerberg and Alvin Schlesinger have retired. Eddie Torres is about to follow. Patricia Williams transferred to the Bronx, Dick Lowe is on the federal bench, and Leslie Crocker Snyder left the bench to seek public office. Micki Scherer was promoted to Administrative Judge for Manhattan and Juanita Bing Newton to Chief Administrative Judge of the Criminal Court—neither trying cases anymore. We did battle together; we did justice together. Sometimes I got mad at them, but I always respected them and I'll never stop missing them.

Can I ever have my old life again? After four years, will these relationships ever be the same? I don't know, but I am going to try. These are some of the reasons I returned to my old job at the District Attorney's Office after my release from active duty in October 2005. But the biggest reason, perhaps, is that it is in my blood, a part of who I am.

And then of course, there's my family. They'll always be there. But still, things change. My father's restaurants no longer exist, though the place across the street where I drunkenly got the idea of enlisting in the Marine Corps still does. Dad had been counting on his sons to run them, but we moved on to other things. (Mark, Deno, and David all opened their own restaurants, periodically going into real estate just to make enough money to start another.) So my father went from three restaurants to two to one. On the last one, the landlord raised the rent and my dad fell behind, until in 1993 the marshals had to padlock the front door. Most of them had been customers over the years, so they came in the day before to let us know when they were going to execute the warrant. We got a couple trucks, called every friend we knew—mostly cops—and hauled out everything we could: refrigerators, chairs, tables, glasses, silverware. We brought the deep freezer to my dad's apartment and he ate shrimp, octopus, and calamari for months. We even took the horses—my mother had bought wooden carousel horses from Palisades Park at auction years earlier—that had been ringing the restaurant's outer walls.

One of Dad's restaurants is now a massage parlor. Another is a limousine service. The third serves Afghan cuisine. I've never stepped inside any of them, but I could show you the alley at Twenty-sixth and Third where we used to play our own version of stickball. And I still have the front door—beautifully carved, with a porthole—as the door to my office at our place in the country.

As much as I want my old life back, and my old job back, I don't want to stop the hunt for Iraq's stolen heritage. So I received permission from Robert Morgenthau, the District Attorney of New York, to head New York's first investigative task force dedicated to the recovery of stolen artifacts. It won't be easy. I have learned that when it comes to the international trade in stolen antiquities, the scholars, museum directors, dealers, and private collectors who traffic in such things are insulated by top-notch lawyers, layers of money, and powerful friends. But as Euripides noted long ago, "There is advantage in the wisdom won from pain." In the DA's Office, I have subpoena power and the ability to make deals to get the midlevel fish to "flip" on the bigger ones. I already have good ties with investigators in Scotland Yard, the carabinieri, and others—courtesy of years of working together and hoisting back more than a few cold ones. NYPD has plenty of seasoned investigators ready to help. Not art experts (I've got plenty of those from New York, Chicago, and London), but savvy, experienced cops who know how to squeeze rich people. And when it comes to the trial, a few warriors in robes still remain to do battle.

The rest of the story is in my head, and, I hope, in my future. It won't be easy, but there is little virtue in taking on a battle you know you can easily win. The best fight is one you take on when you know the odds are stacked against you. And stacked they are in the murky, sometimes sinister world out there. As we learned again and again in a country that has witnessed ten thousand years of human history, things are never what they seem, and some questions never get answered.

In summing up our investigation, however, I can offer some—albeit tentative—answers to the most basic questions:

Of the forty objects stolen from the public galleries and restoration rooms, fifteen have been recovered, including five of the finest pieces the museum possessed: the Sacred Vase of Warka, the Mask of Warka, the Bassetki Statue, one of the two Ninhursag Bulls, and a ninth-century B.C. Assyrian ivory headboard from Nimrud. The amnesty program netted two pieces (the bull was returned as a walk-in, and the vase after John Durkin's skilled negotiation), while seizures accounted for the other three—two inside Iraq (the Warka mask and the Bassetki Statue) and one outside Iraq by Jordanian customs (the ivory headboard). Because the recovery of any major item stolen from the public galleries is, by the very nature of these pieces, easier to track, these numbers are accurate as of early 2005, when Donny George, Dr. Hameed, and I last reviewed the status of the items that had been in the public galleries.

We know that at least 3,138 pieces were stolen from the aboveground storage rooms—though this number is likely to go up by as much as one to two thousand as excavation catalogues are checked and inventories completed. Of these, 3,037 have been recovered. Roughly 1,924 of the recoveries were via the amnesty program, and 1,113 through seizures. Since I compiled these numbers in December 2003, there have been other recoveries (through both amnesty and seizures) of excavation-site objects, but I have not personally confirmed those more recent recoveries and do not list them here.

Our efforts to recover antiquities stolen from the basement have not proven so successful. Slightly more than ten thousand cylinder seals remained safe in the museum, but of the 10,686 objects stolen from underground—5,144 of which are those highly prized seals—only 2,307 have been recovered. Part of the problem, as noted earlier, is that the entire haul from the basement could fit in one backpack. Looking at the recoveries of items stolen from the basement another way, 911 were recovered inside Iraq, and 1,396 internationally.

Altogether, then, approximately 5,400 objects have been recovered—roughly 1950 via amnesty and 3450 via seizures. Moreover, another 62,000 pieces were "found" in other locations in Baghdad. These include the display-case items found in the secret place (8,366), the manuscripts in the bomb shelter (39,453), the collection of Iraq's royal family in the Central Bank's old building (6,744), and the burial goods from the royal tombs of Ur and Nimrud in the Central Bank's new building (the last two totaling approximately 7,360 pieces altogether).

Sadly, though, at least 8,500 pieces—many of them truly priceless— are still missing. These include nine Sumerian, Akkadian, and Babylonian cuneiform bricks, a Babylonian boundary stone, and five heads from Hatra: a copper head of winged victory, a stone head of a female deity, and marble heads of Apollo, Poseidon, and Eros. One of the most prominent pieces still missing is the headless inscribed limestone statue from Lagash, from approximately 2450 B.C.

But perhaps the most significant single piece still missing is the eighth-century B.C. ivory from Nimrud, traditionally referred to as the *Lioness Attacking a Nubian*. Archaeologist Zainab Bahrani once pointed out to me the quaint absurdity of this reference. It is the ivory in plate 25—the boy's head is raised offering his neck, his tensed arms hold his body up, his chest is arched forward and the lioness's paw cradles him. Now rotate the picture ninety degrees counterclockwise and look again at the expression on his face. It may be many things, but it is not fear. This is not a man being "attacked." This is a man being nuzzled, or perhaps "ravaged," but not "attacked."

Things are, once again, rarely as they seem at first glance. We have to keep looking, we have to keep digging, and as we dig we will have to integrate the knowledge and insightfulness of scholars like Zainab, Selma al-Radi, Lamia al-Gailani, McGuire Gibson, and John Russell with the investigative skills of law enforcement.

We live in a complex moral universe, but there's nothing new in that. Despite the virtues we associate with the ancient Greeks, their culture also embodied a fair amount of hypocrisy, xenophobia, and other failings. The Athenians condemned Socrates, and it was their imperial hubris that led self-destructively to the Peloponnesian Wars. From the Sumerians on down, the world has been and will always be awash in conflicting messages. That is one reason why, at the core of any effort to make the world a better place, we need the internal guidance system of a code of honor.

When the military informed me that my museum mission was over, Congress ordered the State Department to explore the possibility of overseeing a continuing investigation. I was in D.C. around the time that State got the new assignment, and I was ecstatic. I even offered to draft a charter for the investigation—exactly as I had earlier for Interpol. State, however, never comfortable in dealing with law enforcement matters and having only two staff assigned to monitoring illegal antiquities trafficking for the entire world, demurred.

Other international organizations, such as UNESCO, as well as many private foundations, are equally uncomfortable actively cooperating with law enforcement. Many such organizations and several countries—the United States and Japan, to name two—have admirably pledged millions of dollars to upgrade the Iraq Museum, improve conservation capabilities, and enhance training of the museum staff. But to date, not a single country, international organization, or private foundation anywhere in the world has provided any additional funding whatsoever for purely investigative purposes. They all seem oblivious to the self-evident fact that a stolen item cannot be *restored* until it has been *recovered*. As a result, law enforcement resources to defeat the global criminal enterprise of antiquities trafficking are not what they should be.

Scotland Yard's art and antiquities squad has four personnel covering the entire world, and the FBI's Rapid Deployment National Art Crime Team has eight. London's Detective Sergeant Vernon Rapley and the FBI's Special Agent Robert K. Wittman are probably the best in the business, but there is only so much these men can do. Interpol barely has the funding to assign two officers to the Iraqi Antiquities Tracking Task Force—and they are responsible for other countries as well. Interpol in the United States has the funding for a single officer, and she covers all stolen art and antiquities from every country anywhere in the world.

That the individuals within these organizations have accomplished what they have with such meager resources speaks volumes for their dedication and talent. But they cannot be expected to continue to operate effectively at such staffing and funding levels. Every country should be pressured to increase its budget for specialized and expanded art and antiquities task forces. Interpol's member nations should fund a robust staff dedicated to Iraqi antiquities, and private foundations wanting to help should provide for vehicles, computers, communications assets, and quarterly international conferences, seminars, and training for specialized art and antiquities squads.

In 2004, Dr. Hameed began his own, independent investigation on behalf of the Iraqi government. He scheduled a public hearing in

Baghdad for May 2–3, 2005, at which time his report was to be released. I offered to attend the hearing to provide my findings and answer any additional questions that might be posed. I also offered to assist the Iraqi government in any future prosecutions. But on the day of the hearing, it was canceled without explanation. Dr. Hameed has declined to provide copies of his report, even in draft form, to anyone until after the hearing—and it has yet to be rescheduled.

Meanwhile, many countries don't want to do what it takes to stop the illegal smuggling in antiquities. Although the United States, the UK, Italy, and Jordan have made significant law enforcement commitments, other countries generate sizable revenue by levying import and excise fees on international transactions. Increased inspections would threaten these revenues. Switzerland (think Zurich and Geneva) and the UAE (think Dubai) don't even send representatives to the Interpol conferences on stolen Iraqi antiquities. Some countries decline to assist on the basis of historical animosities toward Iraq. Iran and Turkey have never acknowledged recovering a single Iraqi antiquity. Others are concerned that the emphasis on currently looted antiquities might shine a light on past practices, heating up the repatriation debate.

Still others do not even want to admit there is a smuggling problem. In late 2003, Donny George said he learned through various sources that French border officials had seized five hundred stolen Iraqi antiquities. Donny then mentioned this seizure to the press. Six months later, France sent a delegate to an Interpol conference to "den[y] the reports repeatedly published in the media of the seizure in France of some 500 Iraqi antiquities." Because no Swiss delegate attended the conference, Switzerland—which has never reported a single seizure—could neither confirm nor deny Donny's additional claim that Swiss authorities had seized approximately 250 objects as well.

Ultimately, what we need to combat the illicit antiquities trade is a global strategy that joins together all the elements of international power. For maximum effectiveness, it would have four components. The first part of the strategy would involve an aggressive campaign to increase public awareness of the importance of cultural property, to improve recognition of the magnitude of the current crisis, and to create a climate of universal condemnation of trafficking in unprovenanced antiquities. The second part would be to establish a single code of conduct embracing a single set of standards acceptable to, and binding on, archaeologists, museums, collectors, and dealers to include, among other things, the level of provenance required for a piece to change hands legally. The third part would be to foster greater cooperation among different law enforcement agencies, with Interpol taking a more active role in ensuring seamless and immediate information-sharing among those countries' agencies.

The final part of the strategy would be to increase cooperation between law enforcement and the art and archaeological communities, with the latter acting as law enforcement's eyes and ears, as on-call experts for authenticating and identifying intercepted shipments, and as needed for in-court expert testimony. This cooperation should also include robust mutual training programs. As a model for what can be done, Dr. C. Brian Rose, First Vice President of the Archaeological Institute of America, has developed a program to conduct cultural-awareness training for military personnel scheduled to deploy to Iraq or Afghanistan. A similar program should be offered to the FBI and the Department of Homeland Security on a regular basis in every major city in the United States, with, ideally, other countries following suit. An additional step would be for the archaeological community to request the appropriate law enforcement personnel to provide briefings at every conference in the future that purports to address antiquities smuggling. The call for up-to-date investigative facts should become as standard as the call for papers.

All of this requires enthusiasm and a willingness to get involved. Let me add, however, one caution against the exuberance of enthusiast virtue. In the aftermath of the looting of the museum, archaeologists around the world conducted scores of televised, radio, magazine, and newspaper interviews to galvanize public opinion. As any media-savvy third-grader knows, the more sensational the quote, the more likely it is to make the headlines. In a world of finite resources, more publicity usually translates—as it did in Baghdad—into more resources. The more sensational the quote, however, the less likely that particular expert can ever be used to assist in the actual recovery of a stolen antiquity or in the conviction of a smuggler. Any seasoned defense attorney would take that expert's memorable phrasing and hang him or her with it. In the eyes of judges and juries, nothing is more damaging to an expert's credibility than a highly judgmental paper trail that can be made to look like bias. For the trial of Joseph Braude, many otherwise eminently qualified experts could not serve as prosecution witnesses because Ben Brafman would have had a field day discrediting them with their past statements. This is not to suggest that archaeologists should not forcefully express their concerns or their criticisms. Rather, it is to suggest that they voice their opinions judiciously and with full knowledge of the consequences of hyperbole.

When Zainab Bahrani explained to me her interpretation of the *Lioness Attacking a Nubian,* the revelation started a chain reaction that sent me back to the BBC footage yet again, back to reviewing all my files, and back to reassembling the evidence in different ways, still trying to find new patterns. With the Nubian, once she pulled back the veil, I've never been able to see the piece any other way. And yet, until she dispelled the "assumption" of an attack, I had been content to go along with the conventional, "PG" interpretation.

In similar fashion, I realized that I had accepted certain evidence about the looting at face value. After Zainab's comment, the facts began to gnaw at me. Most powerful among these was the "coincidence" of seven of the most valuable objects in the museum not just being stolen from the restoration room, but having been *moved to* the restoration room *and left there unprotected* shortly before Baghdad fell. The accounts that put each object in the room were scattered and piecemeal. No one person gave me a complete tally. But these seven pieces weren't just any old chunks of rock: the Mask of Warka, the Lioness and the Nubian, the Golden Harp, the gaming plates from the royal tombs of Ur, the ninth-century ivory Assyrian headboard, and the only Assyrian wheeled firebox left in the world. As I reviewed for the umpteenth time this supposedly random assortment, it came into focus as the shopping list of an astute collector.

I've described the sometimes overlapping, sometimes exclusionary rings of security in the museum, with no one person having keys to everything. By moving these items from different rooms and floors in the galleries into the restoration room, someone had taken them outside the central ring, but did not take the additional step of moving them into the secret place, or into one of the several safes in the restoration room itself, located just feet away. All but two of the pieces would have fit in those safes, and the remaining two could have been brought to the secret place, located a few hundred yards away.

A cross section of Mesopotamian art, all signature pieces, pre-staged outside the central core of security. Near an exit. Not only an exit, but an exit near the back. Was the truth now as obvious as the Nubian's posture? It glared at me, pulsing in bright colors. It was as if someone had said, "Back the truck up, boys. I'll have it all waiting for you." But who? Who moved the seven items into the restoration room and who—not necessarily the same person(s)—left them there totally unprotected? Certainly, the mover(s) could have done so innocently, being told that someone else would put them in a secure location. Or not.

The next set of questions concerns who actually stole those seven items. It wasn't necessarily the same person(s) who left them in the room unprotected—but it could have been. Had this person(s) miscalculated like Qusay with the Nimrud treasure, staging everything for a later pickup, only to be preempted by some amateur off the street? After all, someone made off with the bull's head from the Golden Harp, even though some of the staff knew it to be a replica. Or had the professionals calculated right and left the bull's head—knowing it was a copy—to be stolen by a looter and thus helping to cover their tracks? Maybe the restoration room was cleaned out by the men in the two trucks from the Iraqi army, the ones "seen" carrying boxes out a back door? Although everyone in the neighborhood seemed to have heard that rumor, no one we spoke to ever admitted to having seen the event itself.

There were already enough possibilities from within the museum to warm the heart of any detective from the finest drawing room mystery. Nawala's AK-47 boys. Those men in Jaber's office when I'd first dropped by on my initial recon—men I never saw again after that first meeting. Jassim Muhamed, the museum's chief of security, gone for the first two years after the war and the looting. And Hana Abdul Khaliq, the senior Ba'athist whose brother was #41 on the Coalition Provisional Authority's most wanted list.

Professionally, I inhabit a binary universe of guilty or not guilty. To make a choice between the two is to make a factual determination, not a moral judgment. To say that something is red or not red does not mean that I attach a moral judgment to redness. In this sense, it is irrelevant whether the person who is guilty or not guilty is good or bad. Who put the stuff in the restoration room is a question of fact. You answer the question of who did it, then move on to the question of why. Was he or she, for instance, coerced? Was moving the goods a lifeboat staged on deck? An insurance policy? A ticket out?

We run into trouble anytime we conflate separate levels of analysis. That's why I went to such pains to work out a chronology for the battle at the museum, for the timetable of the looting, and for how people entered each area. We should only address one question at a time. Thoughtful people do the same kind of analysis in other areas as well. What is the nature of the good? Socrates does not come out at the beginning of the dialogue and say, "Here's the good." Plato has him spend 450 lines laboriously teasing it out, forcing you to discover it along with him.

Although some questions seem too much like a mystery wrapped in an enigma to even try to answer, others seem as if they ought to be answerable. A case in point is the question of keys that still torments me. Whoever ordered the stuff moved into the restoration room had the appropriate keys. Keys were also used to access the second-floor storage room in which we found the sniper position. Another storage room, just a few feet away, was untouched, its insubstantial green door unopened. The pieces in both rooms are of identical value—excavation pieces. The only difference between the rooms is that one offered a clear field of fire. Thus, it's pretty clear that the door that the looters used to enter the aboveground storage rooms was the door used by the sniper. But how did the sniper get the keys in the first place?

In the basement, the cinder-block wall that was breached was inside a thick metal door that was open when we found it and showed no signs of forced entry. The most logical explanation for how the door came to be open is that the basement intruders had the right keys to the hidden door in the basement—but not the keys to the basement storage rooms' front door. But how did they get them? Why did they have only one set of keys? And how did they get their hands on the hidden keys to the storage cabinets that contained the seals and coins?

Nawala told Selma al-Radi that she thought she "forgot [the keys] on her desk." Elizabeth Stone conducted her assessment and concluded that the thieves got the keys because "all of the safes in the offices were opened (quite professionally in some cases)." Nawala also told Selma that "the keys of the museum were . . . taken from her safe." In writing an article for the *Atlantic Monthly*, Lauren Sandler claimed Nawala "could not explain" how the thieves got the keys. Almira Poudrier finally concluded that the thieves had bribed guards to get the keys. Donny George says that he found four sets of keys on the museum grounds, but we do not know whether they are duplicates of the same set, four different sets, or something in between.

And Nawala's was by no means the only set of keys. There were keys to the exterior doors, keys to the administrative offices, keys to the galleries, keys to the corridors to the galleries, keys to the corridor to the restoration room, keys to the restoration room, keys to the above-ground storage rooms, keys to the basement storage rooms, and, ultimately, keys to the lockers in the basement. No one had them all—except, collectively speaking, the thieves. So where does this leave us?

One possible explanation has been proposed by Sandler's *Atlantic* article, in which she concludes that "most of the museum's holdings had been stolen and sold years before" the war, quoting sources who claimed that Nawala had been in cahoots with Arshad Yassin—Saddam Hussein's brother-in-law and a major figure in looting archaeological sites all over Iraq—from the beginning of her time at the museum. In Nawala's defense, Sandler claims that Donny said, "She's stupid, and she can't do her job in a good way, [but] she would never be with the looters." I had interviewed the same sources that Sandler did and was never able to corroborate their stories. It also made no sense to me for Nawala to team up with Saddam's brother-in-law, who was already in Saddam's doghouse for outrageous abuses going back years. Then again, being off the president's Christmas card list didn't mean the guy didn't still have juice.

So where *does* this leave us?

While the break-in of the basement could have been the work of one stock girl and her nitwit boyfriend, the movement of objects into the restoration room, two of which were quite large, would have been widely observed. It could not have been done by one or two individuals in secret.

Sophocles warned us, "Do nothing secretly; for time sees and hears all things, and discloses all." I certainly hope so, because I will take any help I can get, including the assistance of Detective Time.

At the museum, one potential scenario is just as likely as another. This is reality, not a drawing room mystery. In the final scene, I don't assemble all the potential suspects and stun them by having all the answers. Maybe some questions don't have answers, not just in the theological world but—as hard as this is for me to say—in the prosecutor's binary world as well. Who is to say that the many different scenarios for the different actions are mutually exclusive? Remember that the dozen buildings covered more than eleven acres. It could have been a very "busy night" at the museum, with dozens of actors sneaking through the corridors, each with his or her own agenda, purpose, and motive. More than likely, there is no single person who will ever have all of the answers.

One of the unpleasant truths to emerge from Baghdad is that, in assessing blame for the looting there, and for the confusion that followed, nobody gets off scot-free—not the military, not the press, not law enforcement, not the archaeologists, not the former regime, and not the staff. And in the sale of these stolen items, we find the same widespread distribution of guilt among scholars, museum directors, dealers, and private collectors. "When everyone's culpable, is anyone guilty?"

Ultimately, what I can say about what happened is that it was more civil war than cabal, more self-preservation than concerted action, and more irresistible temptation than evil intent. So what *do* you do when everyone's guilty? Maybe, like Selma al-Radi, you dry your eyes, you roll up your sleeves, and you say, "Okay, Colonel, let's get to work."

But still, in the quiet after the kids have gone to sleep, as I sit in the half-light of my memories, there are lingering questions that haunt me, always bringing me back.

Back to the Nubian's posture. Back to Nawala's wink.

What else did I miss?

It's Baghdad, Matthew.

AFTERWORD

On November 10, 2005—the Marine Corps' birthday, of all days—I was invited to the Oval Office to receive a National Humanities Medal for my team's work in recovering thousands of antiquities stolen from the Iraq Museum during the invasion of Baghdad in April 2003. I was thrilled to see the recovery effort being given such visibility. I was also humbled to accept the award, knowing I had done little more than facilitate the actions of countless talented and dedicated individuals around the world who had borne the same hardships, yet rarely received their share of recognition. But as the president shook my hand and congratulated me on a job well done, I also knew that the work was anything but done. Until every last piece stolen from the Iraq Museum has been recovered and returned to the Iraqi people, I will continue to be haunted by what is still missing.

In the months since this book was published in hardcover, much has happened to reinforce the core lesson we learned in the back alleys of Baghdad: that the genteel patina covering the world of antiquities rests atop a solid base of criminal activity. In New York, the Metropolitan Museum accepted what amounted to a plea bargain with Italian authorities—agreeing to return twenty-one separate antiquities the Italian government says were stolen, including one of the Met's most prized items: the Euphronios krater, a sixth-century B.C. Greek vase. In Missouri, the St. Louis Art Museum has been in negotiations with Egypt over its possession of a thirteenth-century B.C. pharaonic mask, which Egyptian authorities claim was stolen and smuggled illegally out of their country. In California, the director of the J. Paul Getty Museum has agreed to recommend to its trustees that the Getty return antiquities the Greek government says were stolen—while the Getty's longtime curator for ancient art has resigned and is currently on trial in Rome on charges of conspiracy to receive a completely different set of stolen artifacts. More trials will follow.

I am delighted that these nations are moving so aggressively to reclaim their patrimony. I am also delighted to see media attention beginning to illuminate certain well-appointed shadows where money changes hands and legitimate—but inconvenient—questions of the provenance (origin) of the object are too frequently considered outré.

But shadows remain. In March 2006, for example, private collector Shelby White donated $200 million to New York University to establish an ancient studies institute, prompting one of the university's professors to resign in protest over what he considered the questionable acquisition practices of the donor. Ms. White and her late husband Leon Levy have generated considerable debate since at least 1990, when the Met (of which Ms. White is a trustee) presented a major exhibition of two hundred of their artifacts from the Near East, Greece, and Rome—despite the fact that a study later published in the *American Journal of Archaeology* determined that more than 90 percent of those artifacts had no known provenance whatsoever. Italian authorities believe they can prove many of the Roman antiquities in that exhibition were illegally excavated (a.k.a., stolen) and smuggled out of their country and into the United States.

Not only did the Met proudly display that collection, dubious provenance notwithstanding, but it also anxiously awaits its new Leon Levy and Shelby White Court for Hellenistic and Roman antiquities, scheduled to open in 2007. Other institutions continue to hold out one hand while covering their eyes with the other. In 2000, Cornell University accepted a gift from well-known collector Jonathan Rosen of 1,679 cuneiform tablets from Ur. They said, "Thank you very much," despite reports of widespread looting at Ur after the first Gulf War, and despite the fact that the provenance of 10 percent of the tablets consisted of the phrase "uncertain sites." Harvard University has done equally well in neglecting to ask awkward questions—witness its Shelby White–Leon Levy Program for Archaeological Publications.

In 1994, a decade before its current imbroglio, the Getty displayed a major exhibition of classical antiquities owned by Lawrence and Barbara Fleischman—despite the fact that, according to the same *American Journal of Archaeology* study cited earlier, 92 percent of the objects had no provenance whatsoever, and the remaining 8 percent had questionable provenance at best. Of 295 catalogued entries, not a single object had a declared archeological find spot and only three (1 percent) were even described as coming from a specific location.

Sometimes the questionable practices extend beyond merely willful ignorance. The Getty has a stated policy of not purchasing objects unless they have been previously displayed in published collections. The first catalogue for the Fleischman exhibit was very conveniently published by the Getty—of which Ms. Fleischman was a trustee. Fewer than two years later, the Getty purchased part of the collection for $20 million, justifying the acquisition on the grounds that the collection had been published, as well it was—by themselves. Further sweetening the deal, while the collection had been purchased originally at a much lower price, it was valued at $80 million at the time of the sale to the museum. Tax laws use the fair market value at the time of the sale rather than the original purchase price in determining the value of a bequest. As a result, the difference between the 1996 valuation of $80 million and the $20 million sale price to the Getty would be deemed a gift of $60 million—affording a $60 million tax deduction for the Fleischmans. Enron's accounting team could not have done a better job.

In many respects, then, we have advanced very little since the imperial nineteenth century, when Lord Elgin could haul away the Parthenon Marbles (now in the British Museum and commonly referred to as the Elgin Marbles) and Henry Layard could haul away the Nineveh reliefs (now in the Met). Despite the hue and cry of the last several years, the Met's current policy is to require documentation covering only the last ten years of an object's history. This, even though most institutions view 1970—the year of the landmark United Nations Educational, Scientific and Cultural Organization (UNESCO) Convention to regulate the transfer of antiquities—as the cutoff date for requiring impeccable proof that an antiquity was not illegally looted. As if to flaunt the Met's policy of "see no evil," Philippe de Montebello, the museum's director, told the *New York Times* in February 2006 that the context in which an artifact is found is virtually meaningless, in his opinion, accounting for less than 2 percent of what we can learn from antiquity. His position is as absurd as the equally unreasonable view of some purists that context is everything.

But far from this world of museum receptions and limos waiting at the curb, there has been an even more troubling development. As discussed in the first edition, U.S. Marines in northwest Iraq in June 2005 arrested five insurgents holed up in underground bunkers filled with automatic weapons, ammunition stockpiles, black uniforms, ski masks, and night-vision goggles. Along with these tools of their trade were thirty vases, cylinder seals, and statuettes that had been stolen from the Iraq Museum. Since then, the scenario has been repeated many times. It does not take a counterterrorism expert to detect the sinister adjustment that has taken place. In 2003, while pursuing leads to find antiquities, we usually came across weapons and, sometimes, links to violent, radical groups. Now, as our troops pursue leads specific to the trail of weapons and insurgents, we find antiquities. In short, the relationship between the dog and the wagging tail has been reversed. As the 9/11 commission noted, international law enforcement has effectively squeezed radical groups by freezing assets, neutralizing charities that served as fronts for jihadists, and by otherwise cutting off traditional means of financing. But terrorists are nothing if not adaptive.

In late 2005, the German newspaper *Der Speigel* reported that 9/11 conspirator Mohammed Atta had approached a professor at the University of Gottingen trying to sell Afghan antiquities to raise money to buy an airplane. While it appears that nothing came of that particular inquiry, the market is now well established. Like the Taliban leaders in Afghanistan who have learned to finance their activities through the opium trade, insurgents in Iraq have discovered a new source of income in Iraq's cash crop: antiquities.

We do not have hard numbers—this traffic in art for arms is still too recent a phenomenon, and some of the investigations remain classified because of the connection to terrorists. But this illicit trade has become a growing source of revenue for the insurgents; in my view, ranking just below kidnappings for ransom and "protection" money from local residents and merchants. Iraq is a war zone, but it is also the cradle of civilization, with ten thousand poorly guarded archaeological sites. Given this almost limitless supply of antiquities, the insurgency appears to have found an income stream sufficiently secure to make any chief financial officer sleep well at night.

Based on my experience in both counterterrorism and law enforcement, I submit that the first order of business in cutting off this source of terrorist funding must be to protect the archaeological sites. Some of these, such as Babylon and Nimrud, require at least one hundred guards and support staff for protection around the clock. Although the math is daunting—country-wide we are talking about more than fifty thousand personnel with the concomitant vehicles, radios, weapons, and logistical requirements—there is an immediate solution.

In other contexts and in other countries, the United Nations (UN) and the North Atlantic Treaty Organization (NATO) have relied on individual countries to provide contingents of armed and trained forces for specific missions. In Bosnia, Cyprus, and Afghanistan, international troops have been deployed under UN or NATO auspices for specific purposes and—significant for Iraq—with specific restrictions. The first step, then, must be for the UN or NATO to galvanize international support and to mobilize international resources to establish such a mission. Because most archaeological digs in Iraq have had foreign sponsorship—the Germans at Babylon and Uruk (modern Warka); the British at Ur, Nineveh, and Nimrud; the French at Kish and Lagash (modern Tello); the Italians at Hatra and Nimrud; the Americans at Nippur and Ur—many countries have long-standing connections to particular sites. Even those countries that do not have such historical connections can be persuaded to see the protection of our shared cultural heritage as worthy of their time and effort.

To protect the sites, then, I propose to solicit from these countries the necessary guards and resources until a fully functional Iraqi security force can be recruited, equipped, and trained. With the permission of the Iraqi government and under the legal authority of either the UN or NATO, each country would be allowed to pick the site(s) it chooses to protect. That country would then send an assessment team to the site(s) to determine the precise numbers of personnel and type of equipment required. Once such a mission analysis was completed, the nations involved would draft and sign "status of forces" agreements with Iraq, outlining the rules of engagement (specifying, for example, when and under what circumstances deadly force may be used), billeting, funding, and other logistical issues. After which, each country would deploy its security forces (military, police, private contractors, or a combination of all three) to the agreed-upon archaeological site(s).

Each country's contingent would also be assigned a group of Iraqi recruits who would live and work with them. Once those Iraqi security forces were fully trained and mission-capable, each assisting nation would recall its forces on a site-by-site basis. In six months, virtually every single archaeological site of consequence in Iraq could be completely protected from the looters. And the terrorists? They would have to find another source of income.

The logic is so inescapable that—one would think—either NATO or UNESCO, the UN's cultural arm, would already have such plans in the works. One would, unfortunately, be wrong. Although NATO opened a training center in Iraq in September 2005 and its one hundred personnel in Iraq have trained approximately 1,250 Iraqis in the Iraqi Security Forces (with a modest goal of another 1,500 this year), none of these trainees have been assigned to archaeological sites. Not one. Even if they were, at this rate all of the sites will be guarded by the year 2039. NATO claims it cannot do more because of the current security situation. UNESCO has not even bothered to begin training guards for the sites, claiming they do not have a mandate from their member nations to initiate such action. My response to UNESCO's Director-General Koichiro Matsuura? Convince your member nations to do so. Step into the vacuum of international leadership. Seize the bully pulpit. Become relevant.

Individual countries are also slow to respond. Despite repeated requests for wider assistance, to my knowledge, only the Italians, Danish, Dutch, and Poles have joined the Americans and British in protecting these sites—and the Dutch have already left, with the Italians shortly to follow. Other countries have argued that the level of violence does not permit deployment of their forces. The circular nature of this rationalization, of course, is underscored by the fact that it is the failure to protect these sites that is funding those who are creating the unstable and unsafe environment. Of course there is risk. I know this firsthand. But the risks of the failure to act are far worse: more money for the bad guys and the loss of these extraordinary testaments to our common beginnings. Equally risky are the politics of Iraq—a country the involvement in which most leaders throughout the world view as political suicide.

But such an internationally coordinated contribution of personnel by each country would not be a referendum on the war, the current administration, or its policies in Iraq. Saving history has nothing to do with waging war. It would be a purely humanitarian effort to help protect the world's cultural heritage. Any leader worth his or her salt should have no difficulty convincing voters of the distinction between politics and culture. All it takes is honest conversation. It is the very definition of leadership: educating, informing, and motivating into action those who might otherwise be inclined to do nothing.

In more than one hundred speeches delivered in forty-nine cities in nine countries—in venues ranging from universities, museums, and private clubs to governmental organizations, law-enforcement agencies, and both houses of the British Parliament—I have urged a more active role for international organizations, private foundations, governments, and the art community. My goal in speaking out has been to correct the almost universal misconceptions about what happened at the museum in those fateful days in April 2003, to increase awareness of the continuing cultural catastrophe that is represented by the illegal trade in stolen antiquities, and to highlight the need for the concerted and cooperative efforts of the international community to preserve, protect, and recover the shared cultural heritage of all humanity.

The incomparable works of art unearthed in the land between the rivers predate the split between Sunni and Shi'ite. They predate the three competing traditions that have brought so much bloodshed to the Middle East—Islam, Christianity, and Judaism. Attending to this cultural heritage from the very dawn of civilization is one of the best ways to overcome the reductive dualism that is shattering our world. These ancient artifacts remind us of our common humanity, our common aspiration to make sense of life on this planet and in the cosmos that surrounds it. I have seen these pieces of alabaster and limestone with funny writing on them work their cathartic spell. I have seen how they speak a language that is both immediate and universal, visceral and transcendent.

While protecting the archaeological sites in Iraq is a vital beginning, much more needs to be done. I have also outlined a five-step plan of action to combat the global traffic in antiquities—a refinement of the plan set out in the book proper (pages 273–74). First, we must develop and communicate a message that resonates with *mainstream* society— not just with academics. This call to arms needs to avoid the sky-is-falling quotes so beloved by the media, while steering clear of the debilitating rhetoric of red state vs. blue state politics. It also has to keep the discussion of the *illegal* trade separate from broader issues such as repatriation of objects acquired prior to 1970 and whether there should be any trade in antiquities at all. The Parthenon Marbles *are* in the British Museum, but their return is a diplomatic or public relations issue, not a matter for the criminal courts. Similarly, there *is* a legal trade in antiquities that is completely fair, regulated, and aboveboard. And it is simply unproven (and unfair) to argue that the legal trade somehow encourages an illegal trade. Most dealers and museums scrupulously *do* avoid trading in antiquities with a murky origin. Repatriation for pre-1970 transfers and the question of whether all trade in antiquities should be banned are legitimate issues, but they are not my issues. Indeed, every time the discussion about stopping the *illegal* trade in antiquities veers off into these broader realms we lose focus, we lose the attention of mainstream society, and it makes the job of recovering stolen antiquities that much harder.

Second, all countries—but most especially the countries of origin, transit, and destination—must establish robust, specialized art and antiquities task forces, with particular attention paid to the borders and the ports of entry. Where such forces already exist, we must increase their size and scope, with cultural foundations providing art-theft squads with vehicles, computers, communications equipment, and training.

Third, the United Nations, through UNESCO, should establish a commission to continue the Iraq Museum investigation, expanding it to include other countries as well. Interpol, the International Criminal Police Organization, must also become more active, entering into agreements with its 184 member nations stipulating that each country forward to them immediately, along a secure network (that already exists), a digital photograph and the particulars (who, what, when, and where) of all antiquities encountered by law enforcement or military forces anywhere in the world—including those items that were seized as well as those that were inspected and not seized because there was not sufficient evidence of criminality. The global criminal enterprise that is antiquities smuggling must be defeated globally through international cooperation (promoted by UNESCO) and real-time dissemination of information (enabled by Interpol). The consequent ability to monitor the deliveries of illegal shipments to their destinations will enable legal authorities to incriminate and thereafter prosecute each culpable party along the trail. Monitoring deliveries will also serve as a deterrent to those collectors or curators who could never be sure that the next shipment was not being monitored by law-enforcement officials.

Fourth, museums, archaeologists, and dealers should establish a strict and uniform code of conduct. Similar to ethics rules for lawyers and doctors, this code of conduct would clarify the documentation and diligence required for an artifact to change hands legally. If they refuse such self-regulation, then Congress should impose regulation. Until then, I continue to urge academics, curators, and dealers to abandon their self-serving complacency about—if not complicity in—irregularities of documentation. The willfully blind eye of some reminds me of the piety of the New England ship captains and owners who sang hymns and offered prayers while getting rich off human misery through the triangle trade of "molasses to rum to slaves."

Finally, the art and archaeological communities must actively assist investigators by providing indispensable firsthand information on the ongoing trade, while law enforcement must expand its limited universe and begin considering archaeologists as partners in a fight we cannot afford to lose.

These five steps are achievable now, but they require the will to act. Iraq has made the first move. In January 2006, the government of Iraq sent a formal request to Secretary of Defense Donald Rumsfeld asking that I return to Iraq to continue the investigation I began in 2003, and that I assist in establishing a nationwide Iraqi task force. I have told the Department of Defense that, given the requisite authority, resources, and personnel, I am prepared to do so.

And when I do get the call, you can be sure that a few old friends will be getting a call from me. Steve Mocsary, in Tampa, and Bud Rogers, in Key West, are both back at Immigration and Customs Enforcement. John Durkin is back at the New York City Police Department, and Roberto Pineiro has retired from United Airlines. Zainab Bahrani has moved to Oxford University, but Vernon Rapley is still with Scotland Yard and Bob Whitman is still with the FBI. Nawala al-Mutwali has been "reassigned" to the University of Baghdad, but I know where to find her, and Donny George—still Brother Donny to me—is in charge of the museum that is sealed shut, awaiting a more favorable security environment and looking forward to a bright future.

And me? I'm back in New York now, fighting bad guys in court and my buddies in the ring. I still get a knot in the pit of my stomach whenever I pass in front of an open window at night—an ideal target for snipers—and I still have to remind myself it is okay to turn on a light on my way down the hall to the bathroom. But more important,

Claudia is no longer a single parent: I'm coaching Michael's Little League team, catching Diana when she jumps off the monkey bars, playing the Joker to Jason's Batman, and changing Nicole's diapers.

Antiquities trafficking has never been a victimless crime, and it certainly is not now when it helps to fund the roadside bombs that kill our troops. While it will never merit the same attention or resources as terrorism, drugs, human trafficking, or violent street crime, at the very least it deserves to be on the same list. From the faculty lounges, precinct headquarters, and museum boardrooms to the newsrooms, Madison Avenue galleries, and Bond Street dealers, this cultural catastrophe must be confronted and debated.

When my unit was first sent to Iraq, our mission was to track down illegal arms and terrorist financing. My decision to investigate the looting of the Iraq Museum and to track down the stolen artifacts was characterized by many as a deviation. Even some of our staunchest supporters saw it as a distraction. The sad irony is that, given the burgeoning integration of insurgency and antiquities, I seem to have remained on the appropriate and assigned mission all along.

New York
July 2006

NOTES

For a more exhaustive treatment, see M. Bogdanos, "The Casualties of War: The Truth About the Iraq Museum," in the *American Journal of Archaeology* 109 (2005), pp. 477–526 (also available from ajaonline.org). This article includes full Web addresses for the sources cited in the following pages.

CHAPTER 1

2 "The list of missing objects . . ." The Sacred Vase of Warka, dating from ca. 3200 B.C., depicts Sumerians offering gifts to Inanna, the patron goddess of Uruk (modern Warka, the biblical Erech). The 1.06-m alabaster vase was discovered by a German archaeological team in 1940 at Warka, near al-Samawa, in southern Iraq, and was justifiably the pride of the Iraq Museum. The Mask of Warka, sometimes mistakenly called the "Mona Lisa of Mesopotamia" (the consensus claimant for that title is an ivory head from Nimrud), is an exquisite life-size limestone head from ca. 3100 B.C. Unearthed by a German expedition in 1938, it possibly represents the goddess Inanna. The gold bull's head that adorned Queen Puabi's (Shub-Ad) Golden Harp of Ur, from the Early Dynastic III period (ca. 2600–2500 B.C.), was discovered in 1929 by a joint British-American archaeological team led by the archaeologist Sir Leonard Woolley. The Bassetki Statue, so called because it was discovered by a road construction crew in the 1960s near the town of Bassetki, in northern Iraq, dates to the Akkadian period (ca. 2250 B.C.). Cast in pure copper and weighing about 150 kg, it has three columns of text inscribed on the base that record the building of a temple and suggest that the statue once stood in the palace of Sargon's grandson, Naram-Sin, king of Akkad (ca. 2254 B.C.). Although the site of the capital city of Agade has never been identified, it is now believed to have been on a branch of the Tigris in the Diyala area of central Iraq, not far from Baghdad. Just how the statue got to the north is a mystery. The "Lioness Attacking a Nubian" is an extraordinary eighth century B.C. chryselephantine ivory plaque inlaid with lapis and carnelian and overlaid with gold. Dr. Joan Oates, a fellow at the McDonald Institute for Archaeological Research, recalled for me Sir Max Mallowan's 1951 discovery of the 10.4-by-9.8-cm plaque at the bottom of a well at Nimrud. Two such plaques are known to exist; the other is in the British Museum. The museum housed twin bulls from the façade of a temple in Tell al-Ubaid, in southern Iraq, built by Mesannipadda, king of Ur (ca. 2475 B.C.), and dedicated to the mother goddess Ninhursag. Among the oldest known bulls in relief, they were ripped from the wall in the Sumerian room on the second floor of the museum.

2 "Much later, watching the BBC footage . . ." An AK-47, or Automat Kalashnikova Model 1947, is an assault rifle capable of firing up to six hundred rounds per minute at the cyclic rate in its automatic fire mode. Its 7.62-by-39-mm bullet can penetrate U.S. body armor and is lethal to 300 m.

3 "In these same brown and beat-up lockers . . ." The museum possessed two types of seals: cylinder and stamp. The latter were developed as early as the sixth millennium B.C. Cylinder seals, the earliest of which date from the Uruk period (ca. 3500 B.C.) were abundantly used by public officials and private individuals as jewelry and magical amulets and for administrative purposes (notarizing contracts and receipts) until around 300 B.C. During the Ur III period (ca. 2200–2000 B.C.), cylinder seals were considered so important that a lost seal had to be publicly announced (Crawford 2004).

3 "These were the people who'd invented writing . . ." The museum's collection of cuneiform tablets and bricks was, not surprisingly, the finest in the world and, accordingly, highly coveted. Invented by the Sumerians during the Uruk period of the mid-fourth millennium B.C., cuneiform was originally based on a system of pictographs but gradually developed into an ideographic system. Cuneiform was later adopted by the Akkadians (a Semitic people who began adding phonetic symbols) and was ultimately used for both the northern (Assyrian) and southern (Babylonian) dialects. The technique was widely used in Mesopotamia for more than three thousand years. The last known cuneiform inscription is from an astronomical text written in A.D. 75.

3 "Those are the ruins of an ancient commercial . . ." Hatra was a fortified city ("hatra" in Aramaic means "enclosure") between the Tigris and Euphrates Rivers about 110 km southwest of Mosul, in northern Iraq. Beginning as a watering hole near Wadi Thartar in the fifth century B.C., Hatra flourished from about 400 B.C. to A.D. 300 and was at its height during the first century A.D. An entire hall in the galleries was dedicated to the Roman, Hellenistic, and pre-Islamic artifacts from this single city.

10 "Two ICE agents hand-delivered . . ." All U.S. military personnel have their fingerprints on file with the FBI. There were no matches with any known U.S. database, but the fingerprints remain on file for future use. We also fingerprinted all twenty-three of the staff members who returned to the museum after the thefts and who were known to have had access to that basement storage room. Recognizing that whoever was involved was not likely to return to work, we did this more to exonerate those returning staff members than to incriminate them. Many employees did not return, the most prominent among them being Jassim Muhamed, the former head of security at the museum. We did not interview him because he never returned to the museum while we were there and was not present at the only address we had been given for him.

11 "Probably many dozens of people in the museum . . ." We interviewed every single person who returned to the museum who had access to, or knew anything about, this room: all of the senior staff and those most familiar with the room, including Drs. Nawala and George, as well as the eight employees who cared for these storage rooms and another fifteen who knew of the room's existence.

11 "Later, we would determine just how many . . ." After Iraq's invasion of Kuwait in 1990, the museum moved its entire collection of cylinder seals (in 103 plastic boxes that had previously been used for an exhibition in Turin in 1985) to a secret place known only to five senior staff members. Any seals received by the museum after that date were placed into the brown storage cabinets in the basement. The plastic boxes containing the pre-1990 seals were then retrieved from the secret hiding place and returned to the basement for the museum's opening in 2000. Some of the seals were placed in the display cases, but the remainder were kept in the plastic boxes and placed on top of a dozen new safes next to the cabinets in the basement, with the intention of eventually putting all of the seals (from the boxes, cabinets, and display cases) into those safes. That transfer never took place. Thus, in April 2003, the locked storage cabinets contained those cylinder seals received by the museum after 1990, the unlocked plastic boxes contained those cylinder seals received by the museum during and before 1990, and the safes remained unused. Any seals that had been in the display cases were moved back to the secret place.

<h2 align="center">CHAPTER 2</h2>

13 "When we'd arrived two weeks earlier . . ." Countless Web sites and articles featured a picture showing the front of the Children's Museum with the hole created by the tank round without indicating that the tank had actually fired in self-defense. The most outrageous caption, "Shoot first, ask questions later," can be found at http://www.zyworld.com/Assyrian/Baghdad_National_Museum_Iraq.htm.

An RPG, or Raketniy Protivotankoviy Granatomet, is an extremely effective shoulder-fired weapon, using an 85-mm armor-piercing shaped warhead that is capable of penetrating up to 35 cm of armor. The ubiquitous Soviet-introduced RPG-7 weighs 8.5 kg with its warhead and is devastatingly effective up to 500 m against a stationary target and 300 m against a moving target. An RPG-7 can penetrate a Bradley armored personnel carrier, and although it cannot penetrate the heavily armored portions of the U.S. Army's main battle tank, the M1A1 Abrams, there are areas of the tank that are vulnerable as well.

14 "It was the resident diplomats . . ." The Introduction to Polk 2005 claims that some of the thieves were "acting in concert with international dealers and even

with resident diplomats," without citing any basis for such a sensational allegation. We have never uncovered the slightest evidence of the involvement of resident diplomats in the looting. For additional claims and accusations, see the notes to chapter 8.

15 "Launching reporters off into the ozone . . ." For the reporting of the number 170,000, see notes to chapter 10.

16 "At least one museum official in . . ." The official is Muayad Damerji, who was director of Iraq's Antiquities Department from 1977 to 1998. He was also "sure that the Americans, like they were in the Gulf War, are intent on occupying Iraq for religious purposes" ("Treasured Past Once Again at Risk," *San Francisco Chronicle*, March 19, 2003).

17 "I was in Iraq as the Deputy Director . . ." For unclassified details about the formation and operation of the Joint Interagency Coordination Group in Afghanistan and Iraq, see M. Bogdanos, "Joint Interagency Coordination Groups: The First Step," *Joint Force Quarterly*, March 2005.

17 "There are eight storage rooms . . ." Basmachi 1975–76.

21 "The Independent ran a story . . ." "U.S. blamed for failure to stop sacking of museum," *Independent* (UK), April 14, 2003.

21 "In the *Guardian*, Eleanor Robson . . ." "The Collection Lies in Ruins, Objects from a Long, Rich Past in Smithereens," *Guardian* (London), April 14, 2003. See her additional claim that "you'd have to go back centuries, to the Mongol invasion of Baghdad in 1258, to find looting on this scale" in "Experts' Pleas to Pentagon Didn't Save Museum" (*New York Times*, April 16, 2003), repeating Saddam Hussein's earlier comparison of "the United States under President Bush to the Mongol Hordes," in "Treasured Past Once Again at Risk," *San Francisco Chronicle*, March 19, 2003.

22 "Elsewhere, she brought it closer to home . . ." "U.S. blamed for failure to stop sacking of museum," *Independent* (UK), April 14, 2003.

22 "But she was subdued . . ." "The Ransacking of the Baghdad Museum Is a Disgrace," History News Network, April 14, 2003.

22 "Ten thousand years of human history . . ." *NewsHour with Jim Lehrer*, April 18, 2003, in "Pieces of History." For more on the race for hyperbole, see notes to chapter 8.

22 "But the story became more pointed . . ." "Museum's Treasures Left to the Mercy of Looters," *Guardian* (London), April 14, 2003: "U.S. generals reject[ed] plea to protect priceless artefacts from vandals." See also "An Army for Art," *New York Times*, April 17, 2003: "American and British forces are clearly to blame for the destruction and displacement of [Iraq's] cultural Treasures." For more on the reaction against the U.S. for the looting, see notes to chapter 8.

CHAPTER 7

100 "As Journalist Matt Labash pointed out . . ." "Down and Out in Umm Qasr," *Weekly Standard*, April 21, 2003.

102 "There's no beer, no prostitutes . . ." Sky News, March 28, 2003.

CHAPTER 8

110 "Then he showed me the headlines." See also "The Looting of Iraq's Past," *USA Today*, April 14, 2003: "Scores of Iraqi civilians broke into the museum Friday and made off with an estimated 170,000 ancient and priceless artifacts."

110 "UN Secretary General Kofi Annan . . ." "Annan Deplores Loss of Iraqi Cultural Heritage," *Daily Times* (Pakistan), April 15, 2003, http://www.dailytimes.com .pk/default.asp?page=story_16–4–2003_pg7_35.

110 "(UNESCO) immediately convened an . . ." "First Experts' Meeting on the Iraqi Cultural Heritage," *Final Report 1st Experts' Meeting*, UNESCO 2003. See also "Experts Count Iraq Cultural Losses," CNN, April 15, 2003. In addition to UNESCO, several countries also complained. See, e.g., "Museum Treasures Now War Booty," CBS News, April 12, 2003, listing Russia, Jordan, and Greece. Additional countries are listed in "First Experts' Meeting on the Iraqi Cultural Heritage" (*Final Report 1st Experts' Meeting*, UNESCO 2003; fourteen countries) and on the International Criminal Police Organization (Interpol) Web site. In addition, Interpol organized an extraordinary session consisting of eighteen countries and nine international organizations and resolved to establish an "Interpol Task Force for the Tracking of Iraqi Stolen Cultural Property." This conference was held on May 5–6, 2003. Although more than seventy-five experts and government officials, including U.S. Attorney General John Ashcroft, attended the conference, no one directly involved in the investigation was invited.

111 "John Hopkins University Assyriologist . . ." "Looters May Have Destroyed Priceless Cuneiform Archive," *Washington Post*, April 18, 2003.

111 "The *New York Times* wrote . . ." "An Army for Art," *New York Times*, April 17, 2003.

111 "Michael Petzel, the president . . ." "Worldwide Move to Stop Sale of Loot," Inter Press Service News Agency, April 15, 2003.

111 "*Counterpunch* took an especially . . ." "Are Americans the New Mongols of the Mideast?" April 14, 2003.

CHAPTER 9

129 "Then in 1957, the government began construction . . ." The Children's Museum was hastily built before the main U-shaped buildings in a successful effort to reserve the entire plot for future construction in an area that was rapidly filling up with governmental buildings.

134 "We would meet with local Imams . . ." Sheikh Ali al-Satani, one of the most influential members of the Shi'ite population surrounding the museum, and Imam Said Kamal al-Mosul were particularly helpful in exhorting and persuading their followers to return stolen antiquities to the museum.

135 "Weeks later, when we got to room 28 . . ." The 28 galleries are on two floors. The Sumerian and Old Babylonian galleries are on the second floor, while the Assyrian, New Babylonian, and Hatran galleries are on the first floor. There are Islamic galleries on both floors.

136 "But altogether, fewer than a dozen pieces . . ." All of the display cases, except the two that held the Bassetki Statue and the skeletal remains of a Neanderthal man, had been emptied by the staff before the looting. But this fact alone cannot fully explain the remarkable difference in the levels of violence seen in the offices and the galleries.

137 "After the BBC arrived, they . . ." For a verbatim transcript of this and other conversations, see the provocative but factually accurate (at least to the extent that I can attest from personal experience) account in Cruickshank and Vincent 2003, pp. 142–43.

140 "Because many of the oldest archaeological sites . . ." Before the antiquities laws in Iraq were revised in approximately 1968, Iraq permitted foreign expeditions to keep half the finds from a site—though the Iraq Museum reserved the right to take possession of any unique objects and also had first choice of which half of the remainder to keep.

143 "When I asked whether there were any other . . ." There is a photograph of the display case showing the skeleton in Polk and Schuster 2005. The caption reads that "jewelry and artifacts were taken from this skeleton." That is inaccurate.

145 "Donny had overseen . . ." Donny was the field director of Babylon when Saddam Hussein came to visit the ruins, demanding that the palace be rebuilt in time for the first Babylon arts festival in September 1987. As Donny put it when he was criticized for obeying, Hussein was the president. Exactly what would critics have had Donny do? On the digging of the positions, see Cruickshank and Vincent 2003, p. 125, for the same account he told me. On Hussein reading his reports, see Joffe 2004.

148 "Even the BBC joined in . . ." Cruickshank and Vincent 2003, p 142.

CHAPTER 10

149 "Members of the Museum staff were fond . . ." Archaeologists digging at Khorsabad found the bull and, with the onset of the winter rainy season, decided to bury the statue and return later, when the ground was firmer and moving it to the museum would be easier. Before they could return, the men from Mosul cut off the bull's head.

155 "The number 170,000 first appeared in Reuters . . ." "Plunder of past in new Iraq," Reuters, April 12, 2003; "Looters Ransack Baghdad Museum," BBC News, April 12, 2003; "Baghdad Looting Continues," Voice of America News, April 12, 2003; and "Looters Strip Iraqi National Museum of Its Antiquities," *Daily Telegraph* (London), April 13, 2003.

156 "Perhaps the first reporters on the scene . . ." "We're Still Missing the Looting Picture," *Washington Post*, June 15, 2003.

156 "But that does not account for the fact that Amin made her statement . . ." "Iraq's Heritage Lost to Looters," *Washington Post*, April 14, 2003.

156–157 "The media certainly uncritically accepted . . ." Also blaming the media were Lawler 2003: "The 170,000 figure actually refers to the number of items in a museum inventory"; and Deblauwe 2003: "The 170,000 number initially cited by the media turned out to be the number of inventory entries in the museum." These two authors went on to explain that although the museum had more than 500,000 total pieces in its collection, it had only 170,000 pieces registered with "IM" (Iraq

Museum), and that was the source of the original number. This explanation is inaccurate. IM numbers are not the number of items in the inventory but one of five possible designations, specifically "code letters prefixed to numbers of the Iraq Museum general register" (Basmachi 1975–76, 9–10). Also blamed were the difficulties of operating under a brutal regime: "A lifetime's enforced caution about who [*sic*] you tell about what does not suddenly melt away" ("The Dust Hasn't Settled in the Baghdad Museum," *Guardian* [London], June 12, 2003); "The many years of working in a police state and not trusting anyone has left its mark" (Deblauwe 2003). On the other hand, some commentators were just as rash in condemning the museum staff and others for not correcting the 170,000 number as soon as it was reported, arguing that the staff had to know it was false because they had moved most of the items for safekeeping before the war. See, e.g., "Chasing After Saddam's Weapons," *Washington Post*, June 13, 2003: "You'd have to go back centuries, say, to the Mongol invasion of Baghdad in 1258, to find mendacity on this scale."

157 "Some media began reporting as early as April 16 . . ." "Museum Theft Looks Organized," Knight Ridder News Service, April 16, 2003. Other media outlets quickly followed suit; see, e.g., "Museum Pillage Described as Devastating but Not Total," *New York Times*, April 16, 2003; and "Iraqis Say Museum Looting Wasn't as Bad as Feared," *Wall Street Journal*, April 17, 2003.

157 "But then four days later, the Manchester *Guardian* . . ." "U.S. Army Was Told to Protect Looted Museum" (*Guardian* [London], April 20, 2003). Writers "Paul Martin in Kuwait, Ed Vulliamy in Washington and Gaby Hinsliff " claimed that the museum "was ransacked, with more than 270,000 objects taken." Four days later, the *New York Times* attempted to sound the death knell for the 170,000 number in a front-page story, "Loss Estimates Are Cut on Iraqi Artifacts, but Questions Remain," May 1, 2003. Nonetheless, the inflated numbers persisted. Nordhausen 2003 claimed 100,000 pieces missing, as did "Irakisches Nationalmuseum verlor Hälfte des Gesamtbestandes: 'Diese Leute wussten, was echt war oder nicht,' meint ein Experte," *Der Standard* (Austria), May 3, 2003. Such wildly fluctuating numbers, of course, should completely shatter the excuse that all of the originally inflated numbers came from the total number of IM-registered objects.

163 "I never saw the museum director again . . ." "Treasures of Iraq," on Australia's *Dateline* May 21, 2005. *Science Magazine* reported that "George himself took U.S. officers there [to the bomb shelter] shortly after the museum was secure" (Lawler 2003). He did, but it was *after* we had been brought there by the informant. Highlighting one of the dangers of moral judgment, however, the Library of Congress and U.S. Department of State mission to Baghdad later determined that the House of Manuscripts had a "well trained professional staff that knows how to preserve and conserve manuscripts" ("Report on the National Library and the House of Manuscripts October 27–November 3, 2003," April 21, 2005). I was not the only person to whom the people at the local bomb shelter remarked that the director was a notorious Ba'ath Party member. After returning to the museum, I mentioned what had happened to a BBC film crew. They went to the bomb shelter on their own and interviewed the residents themselves: "The store was well prepared and protected and its guardians said they did not want to return the

contents [40,000 precious books and manuscripts] to the museum while the existing Ba'ath party hierarchy remained in charge" ("Return to Baghdad: The Cost of
War at the Iraq Museum," BBC, September 6, 2003.

168 "As for the petition, it turned out . . ." Missing the point of the riot was "Treasures of Iraq," a televised special that aired on July 9, 2003 on Australia's *Dateline*. Arriving after the riot had already begun, the camerawoman filmed and then aired a
scene in which I told the angry crowd to tell me if they had "any information about
where any of the other items are . . . We are looking, we are searching, we are trying
to find everything to try to return them to the Iraqi people." The voice-over com-
mented that "the employees are frustrated with the slow progress of the investigation." That was inaccurate. In fact, I was directly responding to their leader's
statement (not aired) that the "Ba'athist museum staff stole all of the antiquities before the war and we all know it." Some believed it; others were frustrated that we did
not remove the entire senior staff so they could take their places. None of the rioters
ever led us to a single missing antiquity, and none of them ever provided firsthand information about any of the senior staff, despite what they had said that they "knew."

CHAPTER 11

185 "In the annals of great archaeological discoveries . . ." According to John Cur-
tis, Keeper of the British Museum's Department of Ancient Near East, "This is a
discovery which rivals that of [the 1922 discovery of the tomb of] Tutankhamen"
(quoted in N. Reynolds, "An Ancient Golden Age Reveals Its Burial Rituals," *The
Age*, March 14, 2002), and "The Nimrud Treasure ranks alongside that of Tutankhamen" (quoted in "The Nimrud Gold on Display in Baghdad . . . for a Few
Hours," *Art Newspaper*, July 4, 2003). See also M. Gayford, "Gold Fever," *The Age*,
January 14, 2004.

185 "Then, shortly before the first Gulf War . . ." It may be argued that moving
the treasure to the Central Bank in 1990 was a reasonable precaution given the
likelihood of an international armed response to Hussein's invasion of a sovereign
country—particularly after he promised to turn Kuwait City into "a graveyard"
("Iraq tightens its control over Kuwait," *Boston Globe*, August 3, 1990.) But the fact
that the treasure had not been returned to the museum or publicly seen again in
the intervening thirteen years strongly suggests additional motives as well. We also
learned that no one on the museum staff knew with certainty whether the treasure
was still in the bank. The staff knew what we knew: that Saddam Hussein's sons,
Uday and Qusay, had emptied much of the contents of the bank vaults and fled
shortly before the battle for Baghdad began. No member of the staff had seen the
treasure for years. They may have hoped it was there, but since they did not have
the "right" under that regime to inspect the vaults to verify its presence, they
could not be certain.

186 "Referred to in the Bible as Calah . . ." Oates and Oates 2001.

186 "Not until 1988 did anyone notice . . ." Queen Yaba was the wife of
Tiglath-Pileser III, who ruled from 744 to 727 B.C., and Queen Atalia was the
wife of Sargon II, who ruled from 721 to 705 B.C. Damerji Muayad 1999; Hussein and Suleiman 1999–2000; Oates and Oates 2001.

187 "The treasures from Ur came to light . . ." For more on the discovery of Ur, see Woolley and Moorey 1982.

188 "These dated from the Early Dynastic III period . . ." There were several cities named Ur in Mesopotamia at the time, and Abraham's Ur is thought by many Bible scholars actually to have been in the north, near Haran.

188 "Yet another problem was that an exact count . . ." As Dr. Muayad Said Damerji, Iraq's former director general of Antiquities and Heritage, told me, it was difficult to document all the finds given the sheer size of the discovery, the conditions under which he was working, and the treasure's removal to the Central Bank of Iraq. Dr. Muayad was able, however, to provide the following list. Tomb 1 contained at least 31 separate gold and silver necklaces, bowls, rings, and other jewelry. In tomb 2, the sarcophagus alone contained more than 700 tiny gold rosettes, more than 90 necklaces, an uncounted number of gold and carnelian beads, and 157 gold objects (a crown, a diadem, 79 earrings, 6 necklaces, 4 chains, 14 bracelets, 30 rings, 15 vessels, 3 bowls, and 4 anklets—one of which weighed more than 1 kg). There were also additional gold objects on the floor of the tomb. For tomb 3, the numbers are known with precision: 449 separate pieces of gold and jewelry (see Damerji Muayad 1999). The seminal, though incomplete, book is Hussein and Suleiman 1999–2000.

189 "According to Selma, though, the two treasures . . ." Lecture delivered on September 26, 2003, at the Stedelijk Museum Prinsenhof in Delft, Netherlands. See also al-Radi 2003b.

195 "The *Daily Telegraph* reported . . ." "Thieves of Baghdad Rob Museums of Priceless Treasure," April 14, 2003: "Twenty-six statues of Assyrian kings, all 2,000 years old, had been decapitated. Their intricately carved locks of hair, the masterful handiwork of unknown craftsmen, lay jumbled together in a dark corner of the vaults." Almost two years later, the *St. Petersburg Times* ("Raiders of the Lost Artifacts," February 6, 2005) again bemoaned the "methodical decapitation of 26 statues."

195 "Later, the director-general of UNESCO held . . ." On July 10, 2003, UNESCO Director-General Koichiro Matsuura held a press conference in New Delhi in which he is reported to have claimed that among the stolen objects was the Iraq Museum's entire "collection of 80,000 cuneiform tablets that contain examples of some of the world's earliest writing," in "Interpol Joins Hunt for Treasure Thieves," *Independent Online* (South Africa), July 10, 2003. According to Dr. Nawala, the museum's entire collection of approximately 80,000 cuneiform tablets was secure and undamaged.

CHAPTER 12

200 "The 'Why didn't you prevent the looting?' . . ." His full quote was more colorful: "And the only problem with [reports that the museum was 'looted under the very noses of the Yanks, or by the Yanks themselves'] is that it's nonsense. It isn't true. It's made up. It's bollocks" (D. Aaronovitch, "Lost from the Baghdad Museum: Truth," *Guardian* [London], June 10, 2003).

200 "I thought about the Swedish paper . . ." "US Forces Deliberately Encouraged the Looting," *Dagens Nyheter*, April 11, 2003. The author used a single source who just "happened to be there just as U.S. forces told people to commence looting." It was translated from Swedish and posted on the Web on April 15, 2003. This sole source also claimed to have seen U.S. soldiers murder two guards who were trying to stop the looting.

200 "CNN's Jim Clancy reported . . ." "Museum 'Shattered' by Looters," April 16, 2003.

200 "The most outrageous account came from a German . . ." W. Sommerfeld, "Die systematische Verwüstung der Kultur des Irak," *Altorientalistik Marburg*, May 6, 2003. Sommerfeld, allegedly quoting a witness, wrote: "Who looted it? The ones who entered first—the Americans . . . They broke into the museum, officially to look for guerrillas. Then they told the looters: come on in . . . The Americans drove up and removed objects from the museum. Kuwaitis were there with the American troops . . . They took archaeological artefacts out of the museum and loaded them onto seven trucks of the U.S. military. The whole convoy drove away accompanied by armored cars . . . [and] showed up later with five Americans. They claimed that Saddam's Fedayin [*sic*] had hidden themselves in the museum. They broke open the side-door and stayed inside for a while. Then they shouted to the people gathering outside, 'Come in!' That's how the looting began." All of these allegations were carefully investigated, and, as the investigation showed, all of them proved completely false.

200 "The academics had weighed in too . . ." "Iraq's Museums: What Really Happened," *Guardian* (London), June 18, 2003. One of the most inaccurate accounts of how the looters entered is to be found in Elich 2004; in which the author claims that there were several guards left behind at the museum by Dr. George on April 8, 2003: "Far outnumbered, the guards had no recourse other than to unlock the door, permitting the mob to push their way inside while still others smashed and entered through a glass window." First, according to Drs. George and Jaber, they were the last to leave the museum, and there were no guards left in the museum at that time. Second, according to every member of the museum and state board staff I ever interviewed, no guards to the compound had the keys; only the senior staff ever had the keys. Third, according to the guards themselves, they were not in the museum after the directors left nor did they return before April 12, 2003. The same article also claims that "professional thieves forced their way into the basement rooms by prying open the thick doors of the storerooms with crowbars." This is completely inaccurate. In fact, the door to the basement storerooms was first pried open (because those keys were gone) by me in the presence, and at the request, of the museum staff. Frankly, this particular account is so inaccurate that it is impossible to determine the author's source(s). Significant inaccuracies also mar the otherwise superb collection of articles in *The Looting of the Iraq Museum, Baghdad* (Polk and Schuster 2005). Despite its title, fewer than ten pages in the entire book cover the actual looting of the museum—and what little there is on the thefts is often wrong, especially in the introduction. The very first factual statement about the thefts, that the basement's "massive steel doors gave way or were blasted apart," as has already been indicated, is completely wrong (Polk 2005). The author continues with the claim that other thieves took "chain saws to giant statues and wall carvings or simply grabbed what they could from the shattered glass cases." There is no evidence whatsoever that the thieves used any chain saws (if they had, surely they would have severed more than the one head they did). Moreover, only one item (the Bassetki Statue) was stolen from the museum's glass cases. Nonetheless, this collection contains several important contributions, especially Dr. George's foreword, Dr. Diane McDonald's nine sidebars about major artifacts housed in the museum, and the articles "A Museum is Born" (al-Gailani Werr 2005), "Dawn of Civilization" (Crawford 2005), "From Village to Empire: The Rise of Sumer and Akkad" (Collins 2005), and "The Ravages of War and the Challenge of Reconstruction" (al-Radi 2005).

200–201 "When asked about the looting . . ." "US Archaeologist Calls for Armed Clampdown on Iraq Looters," *Guardian* (London), July 8, 2003; and "Professor Calls for Looters to Be Shot," *Daily Telegraph* (London), July 9, 2003.

201 "All it would have taken was a tank . . ." USA Today, April 14, 2003.

201 "We wanted to make sure this didn't . . ." "Pentagon Was Told of Risk to Museum," *Washington Post,* April 14, 2003.

202 "Donny George had told the *Wall Street Journal* . . . " "Iraqis Say Museum Looting Wasn't as Bad as Feared," *Wall Street Journal,* April 17, 2003. Dr. Ahmed Kamel, the museum's deputy director, shared his surprise, remarking that "[w]e didn't think anybody would come here and steal things because it has never happened before" ("Iraq Museum Still Counting the Cost of Invasion," *Peninsula* [Qatar], July 1, 2004).

202 "Some critics made a big deal about . . ." See, e.g., "U.S. Protected Oil Ministry While Looters Destroyed Museum," *Independent* (UK), April 14, 2003.

202 "The law of armed conflict holds that . . ." See the Protocol Additional to the Geneva Conventions of August 12, 1949 (Protocol I), June 8, 1977; Protocol Additional to the Geneva Conventions of August 12, 1949 (Protocol II), June 8, 1977; Convention for the Protection of Cultural Property in the Event of Armed Conflict, The Hague, May 14, 1954; Protocol for the Protection of Cultural Property in the Event of Armed Conflict (Protocol I), The Hague, May 14, 1954; Second Protocol to the Hague Convention of 1954 for the Protection of Cultural Property in the Event of Armed Conflict (Protocol II), The Hague, March 26, 1999.

203 "Individual staff members say that he told them to use the weapons to shoot Americans . . ." See "Staff Revolt at Baghdad Museum," *Guardian* (London), June 17, 2003, for the same account, in which staff "described how Mr. George gathered employees in the museum in the early days of the war at which he ordered them to fight US troops or face the sack."

203–204 "They had planned to stay . . ." See "Return to Baghdad: The Cost of War at the Iraq Museum," BBC, September 6, 2003, for which both Drs. Jaber and George provided the same account. See also "World Robbed of Iraq's Museums, Antiquities," *Executive Intelligence Review,* July 25, 2003, with a transcript of a June 3, 2003 interview of Donny George.

204 "The violence in question was, in fact, part of a brilliant campaign . . ." For a thorough account of the campaign, see Franks 2004.

204 "On April 9, a tank company from Task Force 1–64 . . ." For a thorough account of the battle from the tank company commander's perspective, see Conroy 2005.

205 "Later, many neighborhood residents told Roger Atwood . . ." "Inside Iraq's National Museum," *Wall Street Journal*, July 17, 2003. For this well-researched account, Roger Atwood interviewed approximately thirty neighborhood residents in addition to the museum staff.

205 "According to several accounts from nearby residents . . ." See al-Radi 2003a, which states that she also received information that on April 9 two Iraqi army vehicles drove up to the back of the museum.

206 "Instead of conducting such an assault . . ." See also Lieutenant Colonel Schwartz's interview in "Iraqis Say Museum Looting Wasn't as Bad as Feared," *Wall Street Journal*, April 17, 2003.

208 "The legend began in the . . ." "Pillagers Strip Iraqi Museum of Its Treasure," *New York Times*, April 13, 2003; the same report erroneously reported "at least 170,000 artifacts [were] carried away by looters" in "only 48 hours."

209 "but the *Guardian* soon shifted it to April 11 . . ." "Museum's Treasures Left to the Mercy of the Looters," *Guardian* (London), April 14, 2003.

209 "Then it became April 12 . . ." Poudrier 2003.

209 "Then he became 'Muhsin, the guard . . .'" Al-Radi 2003a.

209 "Eventually, he became 'museum staff . . .'" Elich 2004.

209 "In other accounts, the tank crew . . ." See, e.g., F. Gibbons, "Experts Mourn the Lion of Nimrud, Looted as Troops Stand By," *Guardian* (London), April 30, 2003.

210 "Shooting unarmed looters in civilian clothes . . ." Although the use of nonlethal measures such as tear gas might have satisfied legal standards, several factors would have argued against their employment. First, even "nonlethal" measures sometimes result in death, particularly among the elderly and children. Second, there is the question of effectiveness. Nonlethal measures would have dispersed the looters (and have caused them to drop larger items). But most of the looted items were the smaller excavation-site pieces, and the use of tear gas, for example, would not necessarily have caused the looters to empty their pockets or drop their bags as they ran away. Finally, while it is easy to judge these events with the benefit of hindsight, any argument that U.S. military should have used force, nonlethal or otherwise, to disperse a crowd at the museum, must first consider the extraordinarily negative reaction it would have been expected to cause among a people that in April 2003 believed that such governmental sponsored violence had ended with the fall of the Hussein regime.

211 "Eventually, they come back to earth and hit something . . ." Both of the standard-issue rifles for U.S. forces, the full-size M16A2 as well as the smaller M4 carbine, fire a NATO bullet that measures 5.56 mm in diameter and 45 mm in length, weighs 3.95 g, and leaves the muzzle at a velocity of 905.5 (M4) or 974.1 (M16A2) m per second squared. The bullets return to the ground at lethal terminal velocity.

211 "If I'd raced up from south Baghdad . . ." Cruickshank and Vincent 2003.

213 "There was one exhibit in particular . . ." On one of the second-floor landings was a group of twenty-seven bricks with royal inscriptions placed in chronological order from the cuneiform tablets of Eannatum I (ruler of Lagash, ca. 2470 B.C.), Naram-Sin (king of Akkad, ca. 2250 B.C.), and Hammurabi (king of Babylonia, 1792–1750 B.C.) to Assurnasirpal (ruler of Assyria, 885–858 B.C.), Nebuchadnezzar (king of Babylon, 605–562 B.C.), and—the most recent—a Latin-inscribed brick from a Roman barracks of the first century B.C. The nine that were stolen were carefully selected.

213 "Others used the discovery of a pair of glass-cutters . . ." "Glass cutters left behind at the scene are viewed as another indication of professionals at work alongside the mob" (Rose 2003). Another popular claim is that these professionals "even brought equipment to lift some of the heavier pieces" (F. Deblauwe, quoted in Elich 2003). No one brought any such equipment to the museum. At least, no one used any such equipment. In the case of the Bassetki Statue, we followed the cracks in the floor made by thieves who dropped it several times, and who certainly had no equipment at hand to assist them.

215 "From the two aboveground storage rooms . . ." In the absence of any master inventory, the numbers of missing items are based on the museum's staff's hand counting, shelf by shelf, aisle by aisle, room by room, those items still present and comparing those objects with the excavation catalog for the particular site represented by that shelf and then writing out in longhand a list of the missing items by designation. Thus, the numbers will change as each shelf and box in each aisle in each room is inventoried. I am informed by Zainab Bahrani that the process of conducting a complete inventory of what is missing from those storage rooms is likely to take many years.

220 "A frequent visitor during this period . . ." He held the position until October 2003. A man whose sense of duty was exceeded only by his old-world charm, he died back home in Italy on July 30, 2004.

223 "Weighing more than one kilogram . . ." Basmachi 1975–76, 136.

223 "They go to the very core . . ." Eric Rich, "A Treasure Beneath the Rubble," *Hartford Courant*, June 3, 2003. In April 2005, the Iraqi Ministry of Culture announced the first exhibition of the Nimrud gold and ivories, entitled "The Gold of Nimrud: Treasures of Ancient Iraq." Scheduled to open on October 23, 2005, in Europe, the treasure will thereafter be exhibited in eleven other cities in Europe, North America, and the Far East during a five-year tour. Expected to raise more than $10 million for the Iraq Museum, the tour is being organized by the Iraq Cultural Project Organization, a joint venture of the Iraqi Ministry of Culture and the United Exhibits Group (a Copenhagen-based Danish company). "Iraq's Greatest Treasure Starts World Tour in October," *Art Newspaper*, April 28, 2005. The opening was later changed to the Arthur M. Sackler Gallery at the Smithsonian Institution in Washington, D.C., for February 2007. *Art Newspaper*, April 6, 2006.

CHAPTER 13

226 "Reuters described how the vase . . ." "Iraqis Return Priceless Vase to Baghdad Museum," Reuters, June 12, 2003.

226 "On its Web site, the University of Chicago's Oriental Institute published . . ." The vase was immediately examined by Dr. Ahmed Kamel, the museum's acting director in Dr. Nawala's temporary absence, who knew that the vase had been "broken in ancient times but was mended again with copper wire" (Basmachi 1975–76, 124). He determined that all of the breaks were along ancient fractures, that all of the pieces were recovered, and that the vase was in exactly the same condition as when it was excavated. His assessment was at first reported accurately by the media: "The vase is in no worse shape than when it was discovered by German archaeologists in 1940" (*USA Today*, June 17, 2003). Indeed, the title of the Associated Press story reporting the recovery was "Vase of Warka, Key Piece of Iraqi Museum Collection, Returned Undamaged" (June 12, 2003). The delegation from the British Museum also added that the "Warka vase . . . has been restored in the past and in particular the foot and the base of the bowl are heavily restored" (*Report: Conservation Needs in Iraq Museum, Baghdad*, British Museum, 2003). A portion of the report was published shortly thereafter in M. Bailey, "Picking up the Pieces in Baghdad," *Art Newspaper*, http://www.theartnewspaper.com.

227 "Although most of the major press got it right . . ." *Boston Globe*, September 24, 2003. Of course, this was not just misleading; it was false: the vase had not "survived intact for five millennia." Even respected authorities failed to mention that only the restored parts had been damaged: "Stolen objects . . . included the now famous Warka vase, which had been cemented in place. Last week it was returned in pieces" (Eleanor Robson, "Iraq's Museums: What Really Happened," *Guardian* [London], June 18, 2003). Although virtually every news organization that reported the recovery also reported that there were no new breaks, some did not. The ordinarily reliable *Science Magazine* reported that "the famous Warka vase, a triumph of Sumerian art, was returned in pieces," without explaining that there were no new breaks (Lawler 2003); and the highly respected *Archaeology* initially reported that the vase "was badly damaged" (M. Rose, "Taking Stock in Baghdad," *Archaeology*, April 15–July 11, 2003, http://www.archaeology.org/online/news/iraq3.html [28 January 2005]).

227 "Time to reflect and check the facts . . ." "Archaeologists Review Loss of Valuable Artifacts One Year After Looting," *University of Chicago Chronicle* 23[4]. Unfortunately, as recently as May 2005, it was still being reported that the vase was returned "in damaged condition" without mentioning that only the results of prior restorations had been damaged and not the vase itself (see Biggs 2005b). Such inaccurate or misleading reporting—and the unhelpful dialogue it engenders—is not without cost: It diverts attention from the many historically significant pieces that were damaged, such as the terracotta lion from Tell Harmal and several Hatrene statues, and directly results in creating a general level of skepticism in response to any claims about what was and was not damaged in the museum.

228 "The *Independent* quoted Elizabeth Stone . . ." Cockburn, "Americans Restore

Ancient Treasures to Museum—for Two Hours Only," *Independent* (UK), July 3, 2003. Similarly unfounded was the claim in the same article that the museum was forced to participate in the opening: "No curator in the world would allow this sort of exhibition unless ordered to do so." No one who was in the room when Cordone made the suggestion was ordered to participate in the opening. While the suggestion was as surprising to me as it was to the museum staff, it was a suggestion. I am, of course, familiar with the concept of "orders" phrased as suggestions. I have witnessed them, I have received them, and I have given them. This was not one.

232 "Later that same day, using information . . ." In two other raids, the same unit also recovered fifteen cylinder seals that had been stolen from the museum's basement and, at another location approximately 10 km from the Turkish border, fifty-one excavation-site objects that had been stolen from the aboveground storage rooms, including a 45-cm statue of Ea, the water god (the Akkadian equivalent of the Sumerian Enki).

233 "He invited me to attend the first meeting . . ." The first meeting of the Interpol Tracking Task Force to Fight Illicit Trafficking in Cultural Property Stolen in Iraq (ITTF) was held in Lyons, France, on November 12–13, 2003, with Iraq, Jordan, the United Kingdom, the United States, Italy, and France attending. The ITTF's second meeting was held on May 30–31, 2004, in Amman, Jordan, and was immediately followed by Interpol's Regional Meeting to Fight the Illicit Trafficking of Cultural Property Stolen from Iraq, held on June 1–2, 2004. The minutes, program, list of participants, and recommendations of the ITTF's meetings are available on the Interpol Web site (http://www.interpol.int/Public/WorkOfArt).

CHAPTER 14

243 "In Iraq, he was a "consultant" to businesses . . ." Quoted from "Scholar to go on trial in Iraq relic smuggling," *New York Times*, August 2, 2004.

248 "Braude changed his plea to guilty . . ." Braude was convicted of one count of illegally smuggling three stolen cylinder seals into the United States and two counts of making a false statement.

248 "In 1997, McGuire Gibson noted . . ." Gibson 1997.

250 "He also noted that when he last saw these pieces . . ." Russell 1997a, p 10.

250 "But, as with the earlier claims about glass . . ." McGuire Gibson is as good, brave, and honest a man as you could hope to meet. But he is an archaeologist, not a cop. Noting that the basement "thieves did not find the cuneiform tablet collection . . . [that] had been in this basement storage area, but had been moved some years before," he concludes that this failure to "find" the tablets "argues against allegations in the media that the [current] museum staff were involved in the looting" (Gibson 2003). This conclusion may be accurate or it may be false. But it is clearly premature. As investigators, all we can say for sure is that the thieves did not "steal" the cuneiform tablet collection. Although the thieves may not have known that the tablets had been moved, because the "insider" was not a current employee, it is equally possible that they knew where the tablets were but intended to steal them on a second trip that never materialized. Or they may have chosen to take only the smaller (and more easily transportable) seals and not the tablets. Or they may have only been commissioned to steal the seals. The point is that no hard conclusions can be drawn about their failure to steal the tablets—whether they knew where to find them or not.

250 "Moussaieff told *New York Times* . . ." M. Gottlieb and B. Meier, "Of 2,000 Treasures Stolen in the Gulf War of 1991, Only 12 Have Been Recovered," *New York Times*, April 30, 2003. On the illegal trade in antiquities, see also a superbly thorough series of articles and editorials by Eric Gibson in the *Wall Street Journal* and Martin Gottlieb and Barry Meier, "Loot: Along the Antiquities Trail," *New York Times*, February 23, 2004. Also noteworthy are Atwood 2004, Renfrew 2000, Brodie, Doole, and Renfrew 2001, Watson 1997, and Watson 2006.

257 "According to Human Rights Watch . . ." Human Rights Watch, *The Mass Graves of al-Mahawil: The Truth Uncovered*, May 2003.

257 "His 1989 plan for filling in the . . ." S.N. Kazmi and S.M. Leiderman, "Twilight People: Iraq's Marsh Inhabitants," *Human Rights Dialogue: "Environmental Rights,"* Spring 2004.

257 "In 2004, the Journal of the American Medical . . ." Amowitz 2004.

257 "Between 1987 and 1989 . . ." Human Rights Watch, *Genocide in Iraq*, July 1993.

257 "Access meant success . . ." Joffe (2004): "Western scholars of Ancient Iraq . . . had a long record of silence about the crimes of Hussein and the Ba'ath Party . . . and no [foreign archaeologist] was so bold or foolish as to speak unpleasant truths publicly about Hussein's Iraq."

257 "Having for years . . ." "The Modern Sack of Nineveh and Nimrud," *Culture Without Context*, Autumn 1997.

258 "In March 2001, several U.S. and British . . ." "Birth of Writing Explored in Baghdad Conference," *Chicago Tribune*, March 26, 2001.

258 "Then, in January 2003, seventy-five . . ." *SAA Archaeological Record* 3. Some of the most respected and renowned archaeologists (John Russell, McGuire Gibson, Selma al-Radi, and Lamia al-Gailani, to name a few) did not attach their names to the letter.

261 "McGuire Gibson has described visiting shops . . ." Gibson 1997.

261 "In February 2002, he was found guilty . . ." According to court documents, Frederick Schultz—owner and president of Frederick Schultz Ancient Art Gallery on East Fifty-seventh Street in Manhattan—was convicted by a federal jury on February 12, 2002, of conspiring to receive stolen Egyptian antiquities in violation of the 1934 U.S. Stolen Property Act. In June 2002, he was sentenced to thirty-three months in prison and fined $50,000. Court documents also indicated that Jonathan Tokeley-Parry was convicted in the UK and served three years as Schultz's co-conspirator.

262 "According to Lord Renfrew, although . . ." See Renfrew 2000.

263 "The Illicit Antiquities Research Center . . ." See Renfrew 2000 and Brodie, Doole, and Renfrew, eds. 2001.

263 "The enforcing mechanism for its protections . . ." 19 U.S. Code 2601 et seq.;

Public Law 97-446 [H.R. 4566], 96 Stat. 2329, approved January 12, 1983; as
amended by Public Law 100-204 [H.R. 1777], 101 Stat. 1331, approved 22 December 1987.

263 "Under this crisis provision, the U.S. Congress . . ." The Emergency Protection for Iraqi Cultural Antiquities Act of 2004 allows the president to impose import restrictions under the CPIA without need for a formal request from Iraq or review by the president's Cultural Property Advisory Committee. The Cultural Property Advisory Committee consists of eleven presidential appointees with legally prescribed qualifications who serve three-year terms: three experts in archaeology or related fields, three experts in the international sale of cultural property; two members representing museums; and three members representing the "general public." Convening when any country requests U.S. assistance under Article 9 of the 1970 UNESCO Convention, the committee is responsible for advising the president on an appropriate response through the U.S. State Department's Bureau of Educational and Cultural Affairs. The act continues a restriction on the importation of Iraqi artifacts that has been in effect since August 1990. It also permits the seizure of all undocumented cultural material being imported into the United States and expands the list of materials that may be protected.

CHAPTER 15

270 "Slightly more than ten thousand cylinder . . ." As soon as we discovered the loss, Dr. Nawala's staff conducted an inventory of what was missing from the plastic boxes and the nearby shelves and concluded that 4,795 cylinder seals and 5,542 pins, glass bottles, beads, amulets, and other pieces of jewelry were stolen from the basement. Over a year later, Dr. Lamia al-Gailani supervised another inventory, concluding that actually 5,144 cylinder seals had been stolen. I was not present for this later inventory (as I had been for the first), but I know Dr. Lamia and her careful attention to detail, and we discussed her methodology. Accordingly, I accept her new total. In April 2003, the museum's collection of cylinder seals had grown to well over 15,000. Thus, approximately one-third of the museum's cylinder seals were stolen in a single moment. The more than 10,000 cylinder seals that remain were in four locations. In addition to the cylinder seals in the cabinets (received post-1990) and those few hundred that remained in the boxes on the floor (received pre-1990), there were, according to Dr. Lamia, two other groups of pre-1990 seals that were not stolen: the collection that had been placed in the display cases in 2000 and moved to the secret place before the war, and a second group that another archaeologist had been studying and had stored in an undisturbed cabinet. The thieves did not completely empty the boxes. We observed and photographed hundreds of cylinder seals (as well as pins, beads, and amulets) that had been either left in the plastic boxes or scattered throughout the room. Thus, reports that "the Iraq Museum's entire collection of seals accessioned before 1990 has been looted" (Biggs 2005a) are completely wrong.

270 "Looking at the recoveries of items . . ." Of the 911 items stolen from the basement that were recovered inside Iraq, 820 were returned by the Iraqi Italian Institute of Archaeological Sciences in November 2003. One was handed to me in New York and the remaining 1,395 recoveries of items stolen from the basement all occurred

Check Out Receipt

Main Library - Everett Public Library
425-257-8010

Friday, Sep 12 2014 1:53PM

Title: Thieves of Baghdad : one marine's passion
 to recover the world's greatest stolen treasure
s
Due: 10/03/2014

Title: Voyage to Atlantis : the discovery of a l
egendary land
Due: 10/03/2014

Title: The heir apparent : a life of Edward VII,
 the playboy prince
Due: 10/03/2014

Title: Alexander's tomb : the two thousand year
obsession to find the lost conqueror
Due: 10/03/2014

Total items: 4

*** N E W H O U R S ***
As of September 2nd Library hours will be
changing. Please check www.epls.org or call
425-257-8010 for new hours.

outside Iraq. Of those, approximately 695 have been seized in the United States and the United Kingdom—though it appears from additional information received in 2006 that some of the items seized in the United States may have come from archaeological sites as well as from the museum. And approximately 700 have been seized in Iraq's border nations of Jordan, Syria, Kuwait, and Saudi Arabia. These neighboring countries report having recovered a total of approximately 1,866 Iraqi antiquities altogether (Jordan 1,450 items; Syria 360; Kuwait 38; and Saudi Arabia 18). Donny George believes that approximately 700 came from the museum and the rest from archaeological sites. No antiquities have been seized (or, to be more precise, acknowledged to have been seized) by the other two border nations, Turkey and Iran.

270 "Altogether, then, approximately 5,400 objects have been recovered . . ." Although Italian authorities have seized another 300 artifacts that they believe came from the museum, they are not included this number because neither Donny nor I have yet verified that the items are from the museum.

271 "These include nine Sumerian, Akkadian, and Babylonian . . ." The female deity was the only statue whose head the thieves cut off. Discovered in a Hatrene temple dedicated to the worship of Hercules, it may, therefore, represent his wife (Basmachi 1975–76, 309). The three heads of Poseidon, Apollo, and Eros were exquisite Roman copies of ca. A.D. 160 after Greek originals of the fourth century B.C., possibly imported from a Roman workshop in Antioch, Syria (Valtz Fino 2005).

272 "Other international organizations, such as UNESCO . . ." Interpol and UNESCO have begun to bridge the historically wide divide between the law enforcement and art communities by signing a cooperation agreement on July 8, 2003, wherein UNESCO is to gather information on missing artifacts from assessment missions and partner institutions and Interpol is to disseminate that information to all of its member states through its stolen works of art database. The full agreement is available at http://www.interpol.int.

272 "Scotland Yard's art and antiquities squad . . ." FBI created an eight-member Rapid Deployment National Art Crime Team (FBI, Philadelphia Field Division, "Return of Eight Iraqi Cylinder Seals to Iraq," press release, February 14, 2005). Modeled after similar units in Italy and Spain, and headed by renowned FBI Special Agent Robert K. Wittman, it is the first national-level art-theft unit in the United States specifically designed "to investigate and bring to successful prosecutions those who steal and deal in stolen art and antiquities and to recover those art objects" (J. E. Kaufman, "FBI Sets Up First National Art Theft Squad in US," *Art Newspaper,* February 26, 2005). Long involved with art theft in general, the FBI is a much-welcomed and invaluable asset in the cause of recovering Iraqi antiquities. Although the director of the FBI had previously issued a statement that there were "more than two dozen FBI agents in Iraq" to assist in the investigation into the looting at the Iraq Museum ("FBI to Help Recover Iraq's Treasures," wire reports, April 17, 2003), in fact, involvement in other missions prevented the FBI from sending any agents to work on the investigation at the museum or diverting any agents already in Iraq to the investigation. Similarly, a press release that claimed the FBI would "soon send a team of agents" to Baghdad to collect documentation on the museum's missing items ("FBI: Looted Iraqi Antiquities Surfacing," Associated

Press, April 21, 2003,) also proved inaccurate—again solely due to unavoidable shortages in personnel.

273 "Dr. Hameed has declined to provide copies . . ." Although I have not seen the report, I have spoken to both Donny George and Dr. Hameed about their findings and their numbers are consistent with mine. See, for example, "Once Looted and Forlorn, an Iraqi Symbol Survives," *New York Times*, March 31, 2004, in which Donny said that based on inventories completed as of that time, that he believed that approximately "14,000 artifacts were looted from the museum's collection" and that "7,000 objects remain missing." His higher number of recoveries represents those recoveries made since I left Iraq.

273 "Donny then mentioned this seizure to the press." See "Not All Iraqi News Is Bad," *Jordan Times,* January 15, 2004; and Harms 2004.

273 "Six months later, France sent a delegate . . ." "Regional Meeting to Fight the Illicit Trafficking of Cultural Property Stolen from Iraq," Amman, Jordan, June 1–2, 2004, at http://www.interpol.int.

277 "Nawala told Selma al-Radi . . ." Al-Radi 2003a.

277 "Elizabeth Stone conducted her assessment . . ." Stone 2003.

277 "Nawala also told Selma . . ." Al-Radi 2003b.

277 "In writing an article for the *Atlantic Monthly* . . ." Sandler 2004.

277 "Almira Poudrier finally concluded . . ." Poudrier 2003.

281 "Ms. White and her late husband . . ." Chippindale and Gill 2000. In this groundbreaking study, the authors analyzed seven celebrated collections and exhibitions in terms of their provenance (as defined in terms of an object's origins, or find spot, and its history since unearthing) and concluded that the overwhelming majority had no declared or credible find spots and simply surfaced as orphans without history.

282 "Here again, 91 percent of the collection . . ." Chippindale and Gill 2000. Two thirds of the collection had been shown at the Getty and at the Cleveland Museum of Art. Of 295 catalogued entries, not a single object had a declared find spot and only three (1 percent) were described as coming from a specific location.

p tk "In 1994, a decade before . . ." Chippindale and Gill 2000. Two-thirds of the collection had been shown at the Getty and at the Cleveland Museum of Art.

WORKS CITED

Al-Gailani Werr, L. 2005. "A Museum Is Born." In *The Looting of the Iraq Museum, Baghdad,* edited by M. Polk and A. Schuster, 27–33. New York: Abrams.

Al-Radi, S. 2003a, October. "War and Cultural Heritage: Lessons from Lebanon, Kuwait, and Iraq." *The Power of Culture.*

———. 2003b. "The Destruction of the Iraq National Museum." *Museum International* 55(3–4).

———. 2005. "The Ravages of War and the Challenge of Reconstruction." In *The Looting of the Iraq Museum, Baghdad*, edited by M. Polk and A. Schuster, 207–11. New York: Abrams.

Amowitz, L. L. 2004. "Human Rights Abuses and Concerns About Women's Health and Human Rights in Southern Iraq." *Journal of the American Medical Association* 291:1471–9.

Atwood, R. 2004. *Stealing History: Tomb Raiders, Smugglers, and the Looting of the Ancient World.* New York: St. Martin's.

Bahrani, Z. 2003–04. "Cultural Heritage in Post-war Iraq." *International Foundation for Art Research* 6(4).

Basmachi, F. 1975–76. *Treasures of Iraq Museum.* Baghdad: al-Jamahiriya Press.

Biggs, R. 2005a, February 23. "Cuneiform Inscriptions in the Looted Iraq Museum." *International Foundation for Art Research.*

Biggs, R. 2005b. "The Birth of Writing, the Dawn of Literature." In *The Looting of the Iraq Museum, Baghdad*, edited by M. Polk and A. Schuster, 105–21. New York: Abrams.

Brodie, N., J. Doole, and C. Renfrew, eds. 2001. *Trade in Illicit Antiquities*. Cambridge, UK: McDonald Institute.

Chippindale, C., and David W. J. Gill. 2000, July. "In Material Consequences of Contemporary Classical Collecting." *American Journal of Archaeology* 104 (3).

Collins, P. 2005. "From Village to Empire: The Rise of Sumer and Akkad." In *The Looting of the Iraq Museum, Baghdad*, edited by M. Polk and A. Schuster, 82–99. New York: Abrams.

Conroy, J., and Ron Martz. 2005. *Heavy Metal: A Tank Company's Battle to Baghdad*. Dulles, VA: Potomac Books.

Crawford, H. 2004. *Sumer and the Sumerians*. 2nd ed. Cambridge, UK: Cambridge University Press.

———. 2005. "Dawn of Civilization." In *The Looting of the Iraq Museum, Baghdad*, edited by M. Polk and A. Schuster, 50–66. New York: Abrams.

Cruickshank, D., and D. Vincent. 2003. *People, Places, and Treasures Under Fire in Afghanistan, Iraq and Israel*. London: BBC Books.

Damerji, Muayad S.B. 1999. *Graber Assyrischer Koniginnen aus Nimrud*. Mainz: Verlag des Romisch-Germanischen Zentralmuseums.

Deblauwe, F. 2003, October 17. "Melee at the Museum." *National Catholic Reporter*.

Elich, G. 2004, January 3. "Spoils of War: The Antiquities Trade and the Looting of Iraq." *Center for Research on Globalisation*. http://globalresearch.ca/articles/ELI401A.html (12 March 2005).

Franks, T., with Malcolm McConnell 2004. *American Soldier*. New York: HarperCollins.

Gibson, M. 1997, Autumn. "The Loss of Archaeological Context and the Illegal Trade in Mesopotamian Antiquities." *Culture Without Context: The Newsletter of the Illicit Antiquities Research Centre* 1.

———. 2003. "Cultural Tragedy in Iraq: A Report on the Looting of Museums, Archives and Sites." *International Foundation for Art Research*.

Harms, W. 2004, April 15. "Archaeologists Review Loss of Valuable Artifacts One Year after Looting." *University of Chicago Chronicle*.

Hussein, M., and A. Suleiman. 1999–2000. *Nimrud: A City of Golden Treasures*. Baghdad: Republic of Iraq, Ministry of Culture and Information, Directorate of Antiquities and Heritage; al-Huriyah Printing House.

Joffe, A. H. 2004. "Museum Madness in Baghdad." *Middle East Quarterly* 11(2).

Lawler, A. 2003, August. "Mayhem in Mesopotamia." *Science Magazine*.

Nordhausen, F. 2003, May 3. "Jede Nacht gibt es Raubgrabungen: Der Marburger Orientalist Walter Sommerfeld untersucht derzeit die Plünderungen im Irak." *Berliner Zeitung*.

Oates, J., and D. Dates. 2001. *Nimrud: An Assyrian Imperial City Revealed*. London: British School of Archaeology in Iraq.

Polk, W. 2005. "Introduction." In *The Looting of the Iraq Museum, Baghdad*, edited by M. Polk and A. Schuster, 5–9. New York: Abrams.

Polk, M., and A. Schuster, eds. 2005. *The Looting of the Iraq Museum, Baghdad*. New York: Abrams.

Poudrier, A. 2003, July–August. "Alas, Babylon! How the Bush Administration Allowed the Sack of Iraq's Antiquities." *Humanist*.

Renfrew, C. 2000. *Loot, Legitimacy, and Ownership*. London: Duckworth.

Rose, M. 2003, April 15–July 11. "Taking Stock in Baghdad." *Archaeology*.

Russell, J. 1997a, Autumn. "The Modern Sack of Nineveh and Nimrud." *Culture Without Context: The Newsletter of the Illicit Antiquities Research Centre* 1.

——— 1997b. *From Nineveh to New York*. New Haven: Yale University Press.

Sander, L. 2004, November. "The Thieves of Baghdad." *Atlantic Monthly*.

Stone, E. 2003, May. "Cultural Assessment of Iraq: The State of Sites and Museums in Iraq." *National Geographic*.

Valtz Fino, E. 2005. "In the Wake of Alexander the Great." In *The Looting of the Iraq Museum, Baghdad*, edited by M. Polk and A. Schuster, 147–71. New York: Abrams.

Watson, P. 1997. *Sotheby's: The Inside Story*. New York: Random House.

Watson, P., and C. Todeschini. 2006. *The Medici Conspiracy*. New York: Public Affairs.

Woolley, L., and P. R. S. Moorey. 1982. *Ur of the Chaldees: A Revised and Updated Edition of Sir Leonard Woolley's Excavations at Ur*. Ithaca, NY: Cornell University Press.

ACKNOWLEDGMENTS

In some respects, the production of this book was as challenging as the events it describes. With fact-checking, legal-vetting, copyediting, proofreading, cover design, and photo selection, it is an experience I recommend to none but the hardiest souls. The only wise decision I made—the same one I made in conducting the investigation in the first place—was to surround myself with talented people and let them do all the heavy lifting.

Topping that list is William Patrick. I can say of Bill what Robert E. Lee once said of Stonewall Jackson, his most trusted lieutenant, "I have but to show him my design . . . and straight as the needle to the pole he advances to the execution of my purpose." I would gladly go through a door with Bill Patrick.

There have been others. At Bloomsbury, Karen Rinaldi's insistence on digging deeper, even if—as was usually the case—it meant hitting bone; Colin Dickerman's gentle prodding to expose structural flaws; and Panio Gianopoulos' stoic willingness to review every word for nuance, tone, and accuracy have made this a more honest and revealing work.

Initially, it was the thought-provoking editing of Naomi Norman, editor in chief of the *American Journal of Archaeology*, that prompted this book. But it was Jill Kneerim who ultimately persuaded me to write it and Elisabeth Weed who, like Beatrice, patiently guided me through the rocks and shoals of publishing.

Into their hands I placed my memories. From their talents arose this story.

GLOSSARY

Abaya	Floor-length robe for women
ADA	Assistant District Attorney
AK-47	Automat Kalashnikova Model 1947, Soviet-designed assault rifle
ALICE	All-purpose, lightweight, carrying-equipment pack
AOR	Area of Responsibility—geographic boundaries
ASD	Assistant Secretary of Defense
BBC	British Broadcasting Company
Bhurka	Loose garment (usually with veiled holes for the eyes) covering the entire body
BMP	Bronevaya Maschina Piekhota—Soviet-built armored fighting vehicle
C-130	Turboprop military transport plane nicknamed Hercules
CAT	Crisis Action Team
CBP	Customs and Border Protection
CENTCOM	United States Central Command
CIA	Central Intelligence Agency
CO	Commanding Officer
Corniche	Promenade
CPA	Coalition Provisional Authority
DA	District Attorney
DEA	Drug Enforcement Administration
Dishdasha	Floor-length robe for men
DTRA	Defense Threat Reduction Agency

EMT	Emergency Medical Technician
FBI	Federal Bureau of Investigation
GS	Government Service
Hajj	Obligatory pilgrimage to Mecca
Hijab	The Arabic term for "dressing modestly," mistakenly used for headscarf
ICE	Immigration and Customs Enforcement
IFF	Identification—friend or foe
IMA	Individual Mobilization Augmentee
Interpol	International Criminal Police Organization
ITTF	Interpol Tracking Task Force to Fight Illicit Trafficking in Cultural Property Stolen in Iraq
J1	Joint Manpower and Personnel Directorate
J2	Joint Intelligence Directorate
J3	Joint Operations Directorate
J4	Joint Logistics Directorate
J5	Joint Strategic Plans and Policy Directorate
J6	Joint Command, Control, Communications, and Computer Systems Directorate
JAG	Judge Advocate General
JIACG	Joint Interagency Coordination Group
JOC	Joint Operations Center
Khimar	Cloth used to cover a woman's head
LZ	Landing Zone
MI	Military Intelligence
MI-5	British Security Service
MI-6	British Intelligence Service
MRE	Meals Ready to Eat—prepackaged military rations
NBC	Nuclear, Biological, and Chemical
NSA	National Security Agency
NYPD	New York City Police Department
OPCON	Operational Control—tasking authority
ORHA	Office of Reconstruction and Humanitarian Assistance
OSD	Office of the Secretary of Defense
PR	Public Relations
R&R	Rest and Relaxation
RPG	Raketniy Protivotankoviy Granatomet, Soviet-designed shoulder-fired antitank rocket launcher

SAM	Surface-to-Air Missile
SAS	Special Air Service—British Special Forces
SCIF	Secure, Compartmented Information Facility
SCUD	Soviet-designed tactical ballistic missile
SEAL	Sea, Air, and Land—the U.S. Navy's premier special forces
SOP	Standing Operating Procedure
Souq	Marketplace
SWAT	Special Weapons and Tactics (originally Special Weapons Assault Team)
TACON	Tactical Control—authority to control movements
TF	Task Force
UDT	Underwater Demolition Team
WMD	Weapons of Mass Destruction

INDEX

A NOTE ON THE AUTHORS

Matthew Bogdanos has been an assistant district attorney in Manhattan since 1988. A colonel in the Marine Reserves, middleweight boxer, and native New Yorker, he was raised waiting tables in his family's Greek restaurant in lower Manhattan. He holds a degree in classics from Bucknell University, a law degree and a master's degree in Classical Studies from Columbia University, and a master's degree in Strategic Studies from the Army War College. Commissioned a second lieutenant in the U.S. Marine Corps in 1980, he served as a judge advocate until his release from active duty in 1988, when he joined the New York County District Attorney's Office. Rising to senior trial counsel in 1996, he is called "pit bull" by New York tabloids for his relentless prosecution of hundreds of cases, such as the fifteen-year-old "Baby-Faced Butchers" Daphne Abdela and Christopher Vazquez for their 1997 grisly Central Park murder and rappers Sean "P. Diddy" Combs and Jamal "Shyne" Barrows for their 1999 shootout. Remaining in the reserves, he served in South Korea, Lithuania, Guyana, Kazakhstan, Uzbekistan, and Kosovo.

Recalled to active duty after evacuating his apartment near the World Trade Center on September 11, 2001, he joined a multiagency task force in Afghanistan, received a Bronze Star for counterterrorist operations, and was promoted to colonel. He then served in the Horn of Africa and Iraq (twice) as the head of that task force, receiving a 2005 National Humanities Medal from President George W. Bush for his work recovering Iraq's treasures. Released back into the reserves in October 2005, he still fights for the New York City Police Department Widows & Orphans Charity, has been published in several legal, military, and classical journals, and was recently included in a book covering the two dozen "great opening and closing arguments of the last 100 years." He has returned to the DA's Office and continues the hunt for stolen antiquities.

William Patrick is the author of *Blood Winter*, which the *Wall Street Journal* likened to "the fresh early best of Graham Greene and John le Carré."